A HISTORY
OF THE
ANGLO-SAXONS

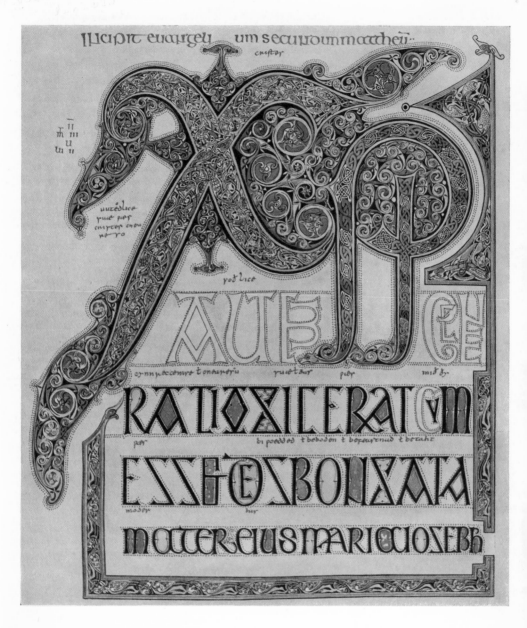

III. LINDISFARNE GOSPELS (Folio 29)

CHRISTI [XPI] AUTEM GENERATIO SIC ERAT CUM
ESSET DESPONSATA MATER EIUS MARIA JOSEPH

(*St. Matthew*, i. 18). $\frac{3}{5}$

A HISTORY

OF THE

ANGLO-SAXONS

By

R. H. HODGKIN

FELLOW AND TUTOR OF QUEEN'S COLLEGE, OXFORD

VOL. II

OXFORD

AT THE CLARENDON PRESS

1935

OXFORD UNIVERSITY PRESS
AMEN HOUSE, E.C. 4
LONDON EDINBURGH GLASGOW NEW YORK
TORONTO MELBOURNE CAPETOWN BOMBAY
CALCUTTA MADRAS SHANGHAI
HUMPHREY MILFORD
PUBLISHER TO THE UNIVERSITY

PRINTED IN GREAT BRITAIN

CONTENTS

VOLUME II

vi *Contents*

LIST OF PLATES

VOL. II

COLOURED PLATES

VOL. II

LIST OF MAPS

VOL. II

LIST OF TEXT FIGURES

(† = Headpiece or Tailpiece)

VOL. II

X

THE STRUGGLE FOR SUPREMACY

MERCIAN SUPREMACY CULMINATING WITH OFFA

IN following the story of the Saints and studying the buildings
and the art of the Golden Age of Christian England, we have
penetrated some way into the eighth century. We have thus
reached a period when Christianity loses some of its first impulse.
The cooling of the ideals—some would say more definitely, the
decline and demoralization—of those later generations is a subject with which we must deal later on. But before we ask how
far Christianity failed when the ardour of the Conversion departed, we must construct our framework of the political facts,
and we must try to understand how it was that in the eighth
century political supremacy was well established by Mercia, but
afterwards in the ninth century passed to Wessex.

The period with which we shall be chiefly concerned in the
present chapter, that from the close of Bede's *History* in 731
down to the decisive victory of Egbert* over Mercia in 829, is
the darkest and most barren century in the history of Christian
England. The interminable strife between the kingdoms and the

HEADPIECE.—Cross-slab from Lindisfarne monastery. ? 8th or 10th century.
  * OE. Ecgberht.

feuds between rival claimants within the kingdoms seem, on a first impression, to be as futile as they are wearisome. On second thoughts, however, it may be admitted that these conflicts are essentially much the same as the more spectacular wars which have moulded and are moulding Europe. Kingdoms rose and fell, they coalesced and dissolved; and through it all an *imperium* of Anglo-Saxon Britain was emerging, an *imperium* which was one stage in the formation of a united England.

The position in the year 731, when Bede finished his *History*, is described in his last chapter. He admits that all the kingdoms south of the Humber were then dependent on Mercia. Wessex had submitted within five years of Ine's death (726), and Northumbria, owing partly to its feuds and partly to its false monasticism, was in a bad way. Under these circumstances the story of the eighth century becomes, in effect, the story of the kings of Mercia; and of these there are two, Ethelbald (716–57) and Offa (757–96), whose long reigns cover eighty years of the century. On these reigns it is most worth while to fix our attention.

Ethelbald, like the great Northumbrian Kings before him and like Egbert of Wessex after him, had his schooling in exile.* It was as a fugitive that he used to find his way to the cell of St. Guthlac, who on one occasion foretold his rise to power. In 716, when the prophecy was fulfilled, Ethelbald showed that his curiosity about the ways of saints did not lead him to emulate them. He was one of the first kings after the Conversion to be branded by churchmen as an immoral man. As late as 745–6, when Ethelbald must have been a middle-aged, perhaps an oldish man, Boniface writing from Germany thought it necessary formally to rebuke him for his licentiousness and 'the two-fold sin' which he committed in the houses of consecrated women.[1] But Boniface could mingle with his admonitions no small praise. He could praise the king for his generosity to the needy, for his suppression of theft and rapine, and for the good peace he made

* See above, p. 332, for references to a theory that Ethelbald was once a pupil and correspondent of Aldhelm.

in the land. Of the actual achievements of Ethelbald we have only the barest mention. We hear that in 733 he conquered Somerton (no doubt the township which gave its name to Somerset), and that in 740 he devastated part of Northumbria while its king was fighting against the Picts. This war has some importance in that it ended the sixty years' peace between Mercia and Northumbria which had been one of the early boons conferred on the island by the influence of Archbishop Theodore.* It appears, however, that Ethelbald derived more lasting results from his campaigns in the south than from those in Northumbria. A charter of the year 736[2] not only calls the king of the Hwicce 'the under-king and ealdorman (*comes*) of his most glorious prince Ethelbald', but it also describes Ethelbald as 'king of the Southern English' (*rex Suutanglorum*) and as 'king of Britain' (*rex Britanniae*), and we see some reflection of this power in the election of three Mercians to the archbishopric of Canterbury, and also in the assistance rendered by the under-kings in campaigns against the Welsh.

The only battle of Ethelbald for which importance has been claimed is that fought at Beorgfeord[3] in 750, in which the West Saxons put the Mercians to flight. It has sometimes been assumed that the result of this 'Battle of Burford' was to make an end for ever of the Mercian supremacy over Wessex. But the charters from which, in the absence of any satisfactory chronicle of the period, we have to piece together our ideas, do not indicate any break in the Mercian hegemony.[4] It seems that the style assumed by Ethelbald, 'king of the Southern English' (that is, of the English south of the Humber), remained a correct description of his position.

The end of Ethelbald was inglorious: he was murdered at night by his own guards. But his long reign had laid foundations for the greatness of Offa, the cousin who, after a short interval of disorder, succeeded him on the Mercian throne. There can be no question that Offa was the most eminent ⟩

* See above, p. 286.

English king before Alfred. In whichever direction we look we
see the impress left by a ruler who was active, many-sided,
ambitious, one who could form grandiose schemes and carry
them into effect. We have the sense of his long shadow falling
over England, but we can-
not discern the man him-
self. Minute investigation
of the scanty sources can
only reveal a few traces
left by this great ruler in his
course through the world.
The traces are these.

SUPREMACY OF
OFFA
BEFORE HIS DEATH
A·D 796

▬▬ Kingdom of Offa.
▬ ▬ Overlordship of Offa.
<u>Northumbriæ</u>- allied to Offa.

English Miles
0   50   100   150

Charters, written in the
year 774, make it clear
that Offa somehow or other
had by then won a position
which encouraged him to
style himself either 'king of
the English' (*rex Anglorum*)
or 'king of the whole land
of the English' (*rex totius
Anglorum patriae*).[5] The appearance of this style *rex
Anglorum* is a milestone on
the road to English unity. Its meaning might be uncertain or
vague, but here the title is charged with an ambitious claim. It
marks the appearance of a new idea.

And what were the facts which underlay the claim? What
was the policy of this first 'king of the English'? To begin
with, there was a consolidation of Mercian authority in the
Midlands. The under-kings of the Hwicce came to an end, and
thus the lower valley of the Severn was welded to Mercia more
securely than in the past. In 779 a victory over the West Saxons
at Bensington in Oxfordshire finally restricted Wessex to a
sphere south of the Thames, and perhaps brought Berkshire

under the power of the Mercians. In 794 Ethelbert, king of the
East Angles, was beheaded at Offa's command, and since there
is no mention of any successor to him, East Anglia may for a
time have been administered from Mercia. These events were
notable steps in the advance of Mercia. The kingdom which in
the sixth century had been a small region round the upper
Trent, which in the seventh century had coalesced with neighbouring peoples between the Humber and the Thames, was
now, at the end of the eighth century, trying to establish
direct rule over its under-kingdoms. Offa was converting
imperium into *regnum*. It is conceivable (though here we must
beware of anachronisms) that he was half-consciously feeling for
natural frontiers.

Let us turn next to Offa's relations with Essex, Kent, and
Sussex. They indicate what we may perhaps consider a deliberate 'English Channel policy'. Mercia was to be no longer merely
a midland power. Just as the absorption of the territory of the
Hwicce had given it control over the Severn mouth, so the
domination of the south-eastern kingdoms was to secure its hold
over traffic with the Continent. A few landmarks in the increase
of this domination are known to us. London, the bridge-head
for the south-east, had long been a Mercian city. As early as 748
it had been the meeting-place of the Mercian council. In 771
Offa reduced the Hæstingas, the folk on the borders of Kent and
Sussex, by his arms. His authority was recognized by the king
of the South Saxons. The kingdom of Kent was treated in a
high-handed way. For a time it was divided between two or
more kings. In 775 a revolt of the Kentishmen was defeated at
the battle of Otford, and the monarchy of Hengist was perhaps
discontinued. Offa disposed of land in Kent without reference
to any local kings; he used the Canterbury mint as his own; and
his name was inscribed on coins issued by the Archbishop of
Canterbury.

About the end of Offa's reign Egbert, a prince of one of the
Kentish sub-kingdoms, was driven out of England by Offa and

by his son-in-law, Beorhtric, the king of Wessex. In the year of Offa's death the Kentishmen again rebelled and, as we shall see later on, the rising was suppressed with great cruelty. Thus were the smaller heptarchic kingdoms ground down in the Mercian mill.

Offa's relations with his larger and less squeezable neighbours, Wessex and Northumbria, are obscure. With them he clearly trusted less to force and more to policy. Some ten years after defeating the West Saxons at the battle of Bensington, he married one of his daughters to their king, and later he bound Ethelred, king of Northumbria, to him by a similar marriage alliance. He ingratiated himself with the West Saxons by building a very beautiful church at Glastonbury, and with the Northumbrians by embellishing with silver and jewels and gold the tomb of St. Oswald at York. It has been asserted[6] that Offa established an ascendancy over Northumbria since Northumbria was part of the *patria Anglorum*. If this ascendancy ever existed, it was of the slightest and most ephemeral kind. It is scarcely borne out by the letters of Alcuin of York. Offa wisely left the Northumbrians to go to destruction their own way. When he claimed to be *rex Anglorum*, he like other imperialist kings before him may well have been content to let his 'All-England' end at the Humber.

Offa's relations with the Continent cannot be ignored. Their prominence is in itself a noteworthy fact. The reign of Offa witnessed the birth of English foreign policy, and there is a certain fitness in the fact that the first 'king of the English' should be the first king to have a quarrel with a continental ruler. The quarrel in itself was childish enough. Charlemagne wished one of his sons to marry a daughter of the English king. Offa was agreeable, but asked that a daughter of Charlemagne should also marry his own son. Charlemagne took offence at the suggestion, and for a time 'dissension, fomented by the devil' led on either side to an embargo on trading intercourse. The cloud soon passed away. Offa was again the Emperor's 'dearest brother', and Charlemagne was interceding on behalf of his

PLATE 52

Offa's Dyke crossing a hill top, in Denbighshire

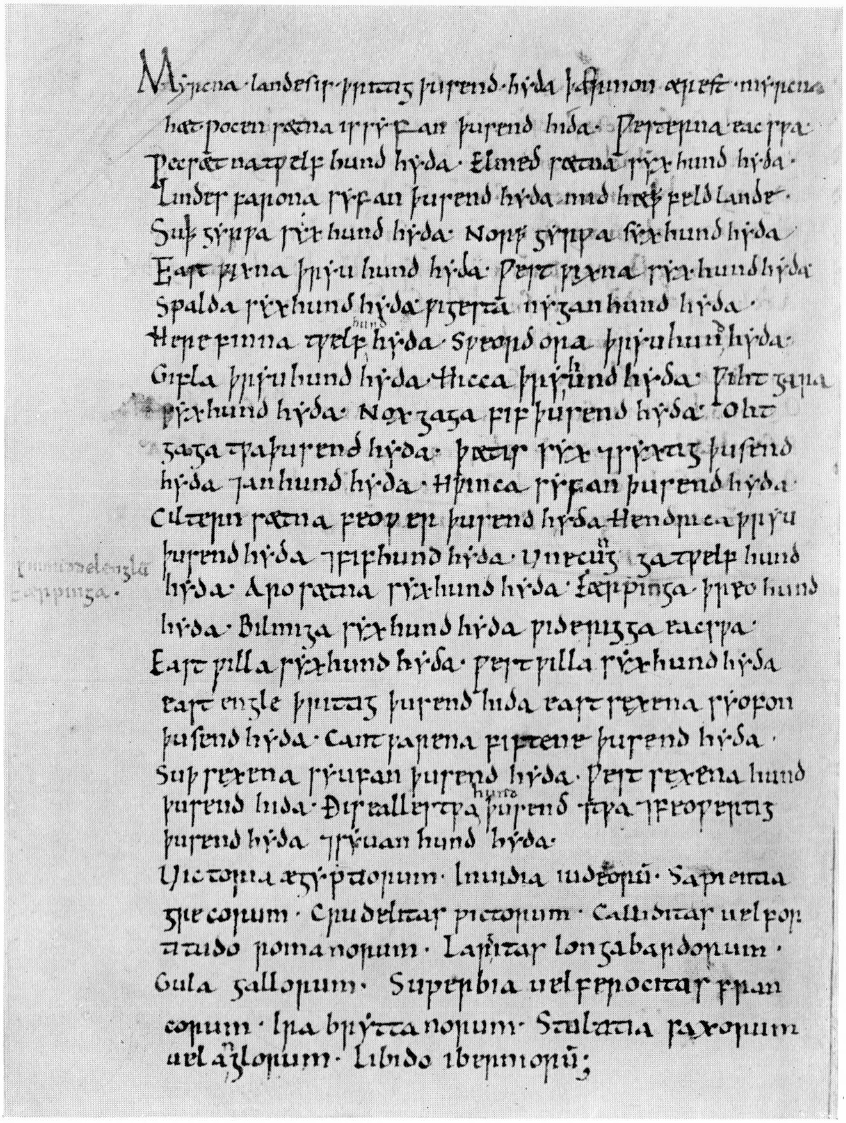

PLATE 53

The Tribal Hidage, ? seventh century

(Harleian MS. 3271, fol. 6ᵛ. Early eleventh century)

[The last six lines are a list of the Characteristics of the Nations.
Note in the last two lines: IRA BRYTTANORUM. STULTITIA
SAXONUM VEL ANGLORUM. LIBIDO IBERNIORUM]

subjects. He was asking Offa to co-operate in repatriating a Scot who ate meat in Lent. He was sending as presents an Avar sword and silken mantles. He was, in the most friendly spirit, arranging that in either kingdom the genuine merchant should have the king's protection 'according to the ancient custom of trading'. He was promising Offa the 'black stones' desired by the Englishman; and, in return, asking for English cloaks such as used to reach the Franks in old days.[7]

The good order which Charlemagne enforced throughout the Frankish empire, and that enforced by Offa in the Midlands and the south of Britain, helped commerce. The Renewal of the Roman Empire brought with it a revival of trade such as the western world had not known since the fourth century.

The only other relations between Offa and the outside world of which anything is known are those with the Pope and with the Welsh. The Pope recognized the enhanced power of the Mercian king by addressing him as *rex Anglorum*. When the *missi* of the Pope visited England in 787, they found their way 'to the hall of

---

TRANSCRIPTION OF THE TRIBAL HIDAGE

Myrcna . landes is . þrittig þusend . hyda þær mon ærest . myrcna hæt . Þocen sætna is syfan þusend hída . Þesterna . eacsþa . Pecsætna tþelf hund hyda . Elmed sætna syx hund hyda . Lindes farona syfan þusend hyda mid haeþ feld lande . Suþ gyrþa syx hund hyda . Norþ gyrþa syx hund hyda . East þixna þryu hund hyda . Þest þixna syx hund hyda . Spalda syx hund hyda . Þigesta nygan hund hyda . Herefinna tþelf 'hund' hyda . Sþeord ora þryu hund hyda . Gifla þryu hund hyda . Hicca þry 'hund' hyda . Þiht gara syx hund hyda . Nox gaga fif þusend hyda . Oht gaga tþa þusend hyda . þæt is syx ꝉ syxtig þusend hyda ꝉ an hund hyda . Hþinca syfan þusend hyda . Ciltern sætna feoþer þusend hyda . Hendrica þryu þusend hyda ꝉ fif hund hyda . Unecu'n'g ga tþelf hund hyda . Aro sætna syx hund hyda . Færpinga þreo hund hyda . . . . . . 'is' in middelenglū Færpinga . Bilmiga syx hund hyda . Þiderigga eacsþa . East þilla syx hund hyda . Þest þilla syx hund hyda . East engle þrittig þusend hida . East sexena syofon þusend hyda . Cantþarena fiftene þusend hyda . Suþ sexena syufan þusend hyda . Þest sexena hund þusend hida .
Ðis ealles tþa 'hund' þusend ꝉ tþa ꝉ feoþertig þusend hyda ꝉ syuan hund hyda.

Offa'[8] and were joyfully received by him, owing to his reverence for St. Peter. A Church Council was held at Celchythe*, of which we shall hear more in the next chapter; and in return for the creation of a Mercian archbishopric at Lichfield, Offa undertook to pay 365 mancuses yearly to the Papacy: one mancus for every day of the year.

In the Dark Ages an alliance with the Papacy was the surest way to success, and Offa, in thus beginning the payment of tribute to Rome, showed wisdom as well as piety.

As for his relations with the Welsh, their annals tell of one 'devastation' by Offa after another. Then came the making of the great dyke from sea to sea. This earthwork was certainly more of a boundary than a fortification. It does not appear to have changed materially what had long been the line separating the two peoples, but marked it beyond dispute, and set a limit to the westward migration of the English.

Sir Cyril Fox's recent survey of the Dyke[9] has produced some interesting conclusions. He shows that small disconnected attempts had been made before Offa to protect English settlers from Welsh raiders at exposed spots. But Offa's Dyke itself was 'the product of one mind'. It was 'designed by a man of military genius and exceptional engineering skill'; and was carried out with such precision that it 'reminds one forcibly of Roman genius and Roman energy'. Fox infers also that the gaps in the line were deliberately left where the forests were dense, and that, since the Dyke was sometimes allowed to take a line more favourable to the Welsh than to the English, it was probably defined by agreement between the two peoples.

With regard to Offa's cultivation of the arts of peace, it is obvious that he was, as was only natural, powerfully influenced by the great renewal of civilization then occurring on the Continent. Since his laws have not survived it is impossible to tell whether the Mercian borrowed directly from the Frank. But Offa's coins have come down to us, and they show that the

* ? Chelsea.

Mercian king made good use of the mint of conquered Kent. He introduced new types, copying the silver denarii of the Franks, and the golden dinars of the Arabs.[10] The silver pennies of Offa were superior to the former sceat coins, in every way: in weight, design, lettering, and in the more life-like representation of the king's head itself. The new type of currency introduced by Offa was to be followed by his successors, English, Danish, and Norman, down to the twelfth century. The gold dinar, on the other hand, was no more than a significant experiment. Only one example of this coin is extant. Like the gold pieces of Charlemagne, it represents a wholly exceptional issue. Apart from the name 'Offa Rex' stamped on it, it is a clever copy of a coin struck by an Abbassid Caliph in 774, and the Arabic superscription, reproduced unintelligently by the Englishman, probably declared that 'There is no God but God, and Muhammad is his Prophet'.[11] This, it seems, was the coin which Offa proudly minted, and perhaps sent as part of his promised tribute to the successor of St. Peter.   (Pl. 81, 1, 2 and 3.)

Such are the traces of Offa; not enough to enable us to speak with any confidence of his character and policy, but enough to leave no doubt of his greatness. We can understand why Alcuin in writing to him should say, 'You are the glory of Britain; . . . a sword against its enemies'.[12]

Offa is accordingly in many ways the Mercian king who most nearly anticipates the work of the West-Saxon Alfred; or, to put the same thing more exactly, it may be said that Alfred, like his grandfather Egbert, built up the supremacy of Wessex on the ground which had been prepared by Offa. If the local dynasties in Sussex, Kent, Essex, and the Hwicce territory had not been ended or tamed by Offa, the West Saxons would have found much greater difficulties in raising their new state. Offa oppressed the south-eastern kingdoms and East Anglia, and set in motion the forces which finally brought them into the arms of Wessex. Thus, to take a long view, his work furthered the ultimate unity of England. He is the *rex Anglorum*, Alfred is the *rex Anglo-*

Saxonum. Alfred uses Offa's laws; he follows Offa in maintaining
relations with the Continent, and like Offa he sends his yearly
tribute to Rome.

But if we emphasize the greatness of Offa by comparing him
with Alfred, the success of Alfred's dynasty throws into relief the
immediate failure of Offa's. Within five months of Offa's death
his only son Ecgferth had followed him to the grave. A distant
kinsman, Coenwulf (796–821), continued to guide Mercia with
fair success through the next twenty-five years. He defeated the
Kentish rebellion of 796. He gave the rebels a lesson which they
were not likely to forget, and put out the eyes of their leader.
He succeeded in withdrawing with dignity from Offa's experiment of a Mercian archbishopric; he inaugurated the new policy
of planting a Mercian dynasty in Kent, by handing over that
province to his brother. He taught the Northumbrians and
the Welsh that the arms of Mercia were still formidable; but in
spite of these successes the reign registered a downward curve
in the chart of Supremacy. Mercian influence was shrinking.
Coenwulf never claimed like Offa to be 'king of the English'.
Some of the south-eastern kingdoms might still be at his mercy,
but Kent, in spite of concessions, was restive, and Coenwulf
drifted into a long quarrel with the archbishopric of Canterbury
now restored to its primacy.

The story of Mercia's decline suggests that the failure of Offa's
plans was due to bad policy as well as to bad luck. Offa was
himself to blame. While there was much to be gained by turning his back on Wales and facing to the south-east and the Continent, the Welsh remained a constant source of annoyance and
weakness. The West Saxons, who drew no dyke across Devon
and Cornwall, and the Normans, who ignored Offa's dyke and
penetrated boldly among the Welsh, did better than Offa,
though it must be admitted that their opportunities were also
better. And then, judging as we are compelled to do by the incomplete facts before us, we may also charge Offa with a certain
want of statesmanship in setting up his Mercian archbishopric,

since this cut across his policy of south-eastern expansion. The new archbishopric came to an end in 802, but it had lasted long enough to do positive harm: it had helped to alienate the Kentishmen and drive them into rebellion. Lastly, he had trusted too much to mere force. This is the line of criticism taken by Alcuin in 796 in a letter to a former thegn of Offa. Moralizing on the death of the son following so closely the death of the father, he says:[13] 'You know how much blood his father shed in order to establish the kingdom for his son, and this has been the destruction and not the establishment of the kingdom.' Offa was a man of blood, and it was not by Englishmen killing Englishmen that unity was to be won.

A few events from the dark period which intervenes between the death of Offa (796) and the victory of Wessex over Mercia at the battle of Ellendun (825)—the period mostly covered by the reign of Coenwulf of Mercia—will emerge later when we deal with the state of the Church and the first raids of the Vikings; but so far as concerns the changes in the balance of power, it must suffice to remember that this is the age of transition from Mercian to West Saxon hegemony.

WESSEX—RISE OF EGBERT—THE BRETWALDAS

Leaving on one side for the moment the monotonous annals of murders, usurpations, depositions, and feuds, which are the only kind of history of Northumbria preserved for us between the age of Bede and that of Alfred, we must give our attention to Wessex. Before this dark horse gets the lead under Egbert, we have only one memorable episode. It centres round Cynewulf, king of Wessex (757–86), a contemporary of Offa; and it gives us a story worth more than all the other annals of the period put together, in so far as it takes us below the surface and shows us how the fighting men of the military caste behaved and thought. It is a good specimen of the commotions of this age—a disputed succession such as too often followed the good work done by a strong king. The story is the only long entry in the early Alfredian Chronicle. Probably it gives us a tale which had been orally handed down in vivid and colloquial prose after the manner of the Icelandic sagas. It is told roughly and with simplicity, for it is about the earliest attempt to narrate a story in English prose. First we have mention of an ordinary contest for the crown between two chiefs belonging to different branches of the House of Cerdic. A certain Sigebryht obtains the kingdom and holds it for a year. Then, in 757:[14]

'Cynewulf and the witan of the West Saxons deprived Sigebryht of his kingdom for his unrighteous deeds, all save Hampshire; and that he held till he slew the ealdorman who continued with him longest; and then Cynewulf drove him into Andred [the great forest], and there he dwelt till a herdsman stabbed him at the stream at Privet; the herdsman did this to avenge the ealdorman Cumbra.'

This is the beginning of the feud. Then it slumbers for twenty-nine years, while Cynewulf reigns and, like a good West Saxon, continues the struggle with 'the Welsh', presumably the Britons of Devon. At the end of that time (786) 'he wished to drive out the ætheling who was named Cyneheard, and this Cyneheard was the brother of Sigebryht'—and so after a long suspension, presumably owing to rivalry between the two branches of the royal house rather than to a mere vendetta, the feud was revived.

'Then Cyneheard learnt that the king was at Merantun* on a private visit to a lady, with but a small retinue. And there he surrounded him, and beset the bower round about, before the king's retinue knew of it.'

The remainder of the story shows in three scenes how brave men should meet their death. To follow it, we must picture the burh of Merantun as a large fenced farmstead, with its women's room and the hall as separate buildings within the stockade. Cyneheard rode through the unprotected gates of this stockade, the outer defence, and surrounded the women's building without the king's thegns in the hall being aware of his approach. The first of three fights then took place at the door of the lady's bower.

* ? Merton in Surrey.

Scene I. 'Then the king perceived that [i.e. his enemies' approach to the women's building] and he went to the door, and defended himself valiantly, till he saw the ætheling; then he rushed out upon him and wounded him sorely. And they were all fighting against the king till they had slain him.'

Scene II. [The thegns of the king's party were roused and rushed up from the hall.]—'Then the outcry of the woman aroused the king's retinue; and thither they ran, each as soon as he could; and to each of them the ætheling offered life and wealth; and not one of them would take it. But they fought until they all lay dead, save one British hostage; and he was sorely wounded.'

Scene III. [The next morning, vengeance]. 'Then in the morning the main body of the king's thegns, who had been left behind, heard that the king was slain; then they rode thither, and his ealdorman Osric, and Wiferth his thegn. And they found the ætheling in the burh: the king was lying dead inside. And they went to the gates, which the ætheling had closed against them. And the ætheling offered them wealth and land, as much as they chose, if they would grant him the kingdom; and his men said that their kinsmen were with him, who would not desert him. But the king's men replied that no kinsman was dearer to them than their lord, and that they would never follow their lord's slayer; but they made an offer to their kinsmen that *they* might depart safe and sound. The ætheling's men made answer that an offer like that had been made to the retinue who had been with the king, and that they for their part recked no more of it "than did your comrades, who were slain with the king". And they fought at the gate, till they forced their way in, and slew the ætheling, and his men, all save one.'

The whole episode no doubt became a favourite story in the mead-halls of the great. It upheld so well the ideals of the war-band. For us it serves as a good introduction to the career of Egbert, in that there can be no better illustration of how it came about that kingship as the prize of such minor forays was quickly lost and quickly won by different branches of the royal house, and the ease with which supremacy passed from one kingdom to another.

In the rise and fall of the kingdoms the personality of the

individual leader was all-important—more so a hundred times than in our modern mechanized world where the machinery of government can work almost unattended. The decisive factor in all these political struggles was the magnetic influence of the chief of a victorious war-band. What Bede says of Oswin, king of Deira (644–51), was true generally:[15] it was a king's handsomeness, his courtesy, and his generosity which attracted thegns to his service, 'from almost all provinces'; above all, it was a king's capacity for leadership on the field.

This must be the chief explanation of the sudden rise of Wessex under Egbert in the years 825–9. Egbert's origin and earlier career, though obscure, are important. The one certain fact about his youth is contained in a sentence of the Saxon Chronicle which says: 'Before he was king, Offa king of the Mercians and Beorhtric king of the West Saxons drove him out of England into Frankland for three years, and Beorhtric assisted Offa because he had his daughter for his queen.'

The events leading up to this incident can only be guessed. All we know is that Egbert's father, whose name was Ealhmund, was for a short time (784–6) king of Kent. If, as seems probable, Egbert was a representative both of the dynasty of Hengist and of that of Cerdic, it is easy to understand why he should be feared by the Mercian conquerors of Kent as well as by an upstart king of Wessex.

The three years' banishment of Egbert no doubt did him as much good as the exiles of Edwin, Oswald, Oswy, Cædwalla, and Ethelbald had done those earlier builders of 'imperial' power. When he succeeded to the kingdom of the West Saxons in 802,* these found a king who had a good first-hand knowledge of continental methods, and had enjoyed the incalculable advantage of studying them under the greatest of all medieval empire-builders, Charlemagne. Even after Egbert's accession to the throne of Wessex, mystery continues to surround his career,

---

* In the Chronicle 800. Here and in the following dates we give the corrected dates instead of those found in the manuscript. Cf. Plummer, *A.S.C.* ii, cii and 44.

owing to the fact that nothing more is reported of him until 825 except the one statement that in 814 he ravaged the West Welsh of Cornwall. We can only guess that during this period he was quietly building up his power in Wessex, securing his position in the Cornish peninsula, and training the army which was to strike so effectively in the years 825–9.

The steps by which Egbert in these four years won the supremacy are best studied in the words of the Chronicle.

825. 'This year there was a fight between the Welsh [of Cornwall] and the men of Devon at Gafulford,* and the same year king Egbert fought with king Beornwulf of Mercia at Ellendun,† and Egbert got the victory, and there was a great slaughter. Then he sent from his army Ethelwulf his son and Ealhstan his bishop and Wulfheard his ealdorman, with a large force into Kent,

and they drove king Baldred [the under-king set up by the Mercians] northward over the Thames: and the men of Kent submitted to him, and those of Surrey and of Sussex and of Essex, for formerly they had been wrongly forced away from his kin.

'In the same year the king of the East Angles and his people sought the peace and protection of King Egbert from fear of the Mercians and the same year the East Angles slew Beornwulf, king of the Mercians.'

Four years later, 829, Egbert and his forces were again on the

---

* Galford, Devon.

† Now Nether Wroughton near the escarpment of the Marlborough Downs just south of Swindon. Cf. G. B. Grundy in *Arch. Journ.* (1918), 181–7.

war-path. 'Egbert conquered the kingdom of the Mercians and all south of the Humber'; and then, after the Chronicle has boasted about his being the eighth 'Bretwalda', it adds, 'and this Egbert led the army to Dore* against the Northumbrians and there they offered him obedience and peace and with that they separated'.

Then, in the following year (830), came the last campaign of his victorious advance.

830. 'In this year King Egbert led the army against the North Welsh; and he reduced them to obedient submission.'

Charlemagne had to wage eighteen campaigns against the Saxons before he secured their submission: Egbert, on the other hand, reduced the Cornishmen and the Mercians in two campaigns each; and for the other kingdoms, even for the North Welsh, a single campaign sufficed.

Were the conquests too easy to be thorough and lasting? We are often told nowadays that too much has been made of Egbert's victories. It is true enough that some nonsense has been written about the reign of Egbert marking the unification of England, but this does not justify the other extreme of denying its significance. The absorption of Cornwall and the south-eastern kingdoms were lasting conquests, and this consolidation of southern England was a real turning-point in English history; it outlined if it did not complete, the expansion of Wessex into a kingdom stretching from the Land's End to Dover.

But how about the superiority which Egbert asserted over the other kingdoms and the Welsh? Was the boast of the Chronicle about Egbert being the eighth Bretwalda well founded, or was it a piece of rather empty antiquarianism? There can be no question that men of learning in this age indulged in speculations about the past much as did their descendants a thousand years later. Alcuin the Englishman played a great part in manufacturing that antiquarian masterpiece, Charlemagne's restored

* In Derbyshire.

'Roman Empire'. In Wales the antiquarian interests of the age were embodied in the History of Nennius. In England they appeared, later in the ninth century, in the Chronicle's version of Bede's passage about the imperial kings, the Bretwaldas. Bede in the first instance classed together conquerors whose positions had little in common: Ælle, the founder of the kingdom of Sussex, who outside that kingdom can have been little more than a commander-in-chief of war-bands; Ceawlin, who was apparently both a commander-in-chief and the organizer of a confederation; Ethelbert of Kent, who built up an overlordship south of the Humber, which then passed easily from kingdom to kingdom, giving its holder an authority greatly coveted but still largely nebulous. The position of no two of the seventh-century over-kings had been quite the same. Their powers were obviously limited. Ethelbert of Kent might secure a safe conduct for Augustine to the borders of the Hwicce to confer with the Welsh, but he could not persuade his under-kings to follow him in abandoning the old gods. Edwin, according to Bede, had even wider dominion—'all except Kent'—but there is no proof that his effective powers were any greater. Oswald we find coming as far as the Thames to be present at the baptism of his under-king, the king of Wessex.

Bede's enumeration of the imperial seven who had exercised the overlordship (*ducatus*) was in his own time sufficiently unsatisfactory, in that it ignored the great Mercian kings, Penda, Wulfhere, and Ethelbald. But when the Saxon Chronicler re-hashed Bede, adding Egbert as an eighth over-king, and calling them all Bretwalda, the continued omission of the Mercians (particularly of Ethelbald and Offa) became ridiculous. In either list provincial sentiment was crossed with antiquarianism.

What lay behind? Did a Bretwalda enjoy any defined position or powers? Here is a question about which the historians of the nineteenth century fought heated battles.[16] It is significant that the only other place where the term in one of its varied forms is used[17] shows that it corresponded to the style *Rector totius*

Britanniae. But apart from this the word does not appear in formal documents. The Saxon had to be in an exalted mood before he began to talk or write about a Bretwalda, 'a Ruler of Britain'.

More important than the word itself is the question of the powers actually enjoyed by the over-kings—a question about which it is easy to collect scattered evidence, but unsafe to generalize.

SUPREMACY OF
OSWY
A·D 655 - 658

—— Probable boundaries of Oswy's Kingdom.
--- Probable boundaries of Oswy's Overlordship.

A.D. 655-6. The South Mercians & Middle Angles were a kingdom under Penda's son Peada

If we go back to a period like the reign of Oswy of Northumbria (642–71), for which Bede and Eddius supply fairly full information, we find that the position of the over-king varied from time to time as well as from kingdom to kingdom. For the three years (655–8) following the battle of Winwæd, Oswy had apparently exercised direct rule through Northumbrian officials at least over the Mercians, since, when the leaders of that people rose under Wulfhere (in 658), they had to expel the *principes* of Oswy.

In a more distant kingdom like Essex we know that Oswy exercised a strong personal influence over the subordinate ruler. We are told that the king of the East Saxons came to Oswy's court at a royal vill near the Roman Wall and was there persuaded by him to be baptized—in much the same way as Cynegils, the king of the West Saxons, had been baptized in the presence of Oswy's predecessor.

But who can say whether these remote kings were liable for the more onerous incidents of political subjection such as contributions of men and money? Tribute was indeed a frequently exacted obligation. Both Bede and Eddius speak of it as if it was a natural consequence of defeat. Oswy made many Picts and Scots 'tributaries'. He himself offered tribute to Penda, when Penda for a time successfully overran Northumbria. Wulfhere also, when he roused all the southern nations against Northumbria, intended to force the Northumbrians 'to pay tribute slavishly'.[18]

The assessments which are found in Bede's *History* and in the fragment of statistics known as the 'Tribal Hidage'* equally imply that from quite early times, certainly from the reign of Edwin, the numbers of hides were well known, the hide being a unit called in Bede *terra unius familiae*, the land of a family. This must mean that conquerors had produced their schemes for taxing the conquered. The Tribal Hidage gives minute information about some parts of the Midlands,† but is satisfied with general summaries about the kingdoms. It presents a picture of Greater Mercia in one stage of its evolution. The Kentish and Northumbrian over-kings had no doubt drawn up similar lists in their days. The figures are often wild. They show the scale on which the kings would have liked to levy contributions and contingents. They are not statistics carefully compiled, but rough computations made at the centre of government. Since the puzzle presented by the Tribal Hidage is in its way an interesting as well as an important one, a facsimile of the document, a transcription, and references, will be found above (p. 389) to guide those who care to look further into the problem.[19]

The impression conveyed by the period of Oswy is no doubt

---

* Pl. 53. Cf. above, p. 193.

† e.g. the folk called Sweord Ora, Gifla, and Hicca (identified as dwellers in the districts (1) near Sword Point, on the edge of Whittlesey Mere in Huntingdonshire, (2) of the Ivel valley in Bedfordshire (*E.P.N.S.* III. xviii. 8, 190), (3) of Hitchin, have only 300 hides apiece. (See map at end of Vol. I: The forms of these names there given are the presumed nominative plurals. Sweorordware is an emendation suggested by C. L. Wrenn.) Many folks, such as those of Elmet, of Wight, of the North and South Gyrwe in the Fens, have only 600 hides. These small units in the list seem to be in part driblets of the original settlement, and in part secondary colonies made in later stages of the advance.

true of the seventh and eighth centuries in general. The rights of the over-kings varied as constantly as did the extents of their empires. Power ebbed and flowed from kingdom to kingdom, its phases changed from decade to decade. In the eighth century, during the eighty years covered by the two reigns of Ethelbald and Offa, there is more appearance of uniformity about the Mercian supremacy, but it is a uniformity produced by dearth of information.

In all this period after Bede, the only rights enjoyed by the over-kings for which we have satisfactory evidence are the rights mentioned in landbooks. These show two things: that considerable estates in the subject kingdoms came in one way or another into the hands of the over-king; and that the over-kings commonly exercised control over the grants of their inferiors. No doubt it was the grantees who had the strongest incentive to appeal to the highest power. A wise abbot or bishop saw to it that a gift of lands was confirmed by the head-king. It was common sense to get his consent. A head-king, however indefinite his legal rights, had behind him forces which might cause trouble

This question of the Bretwalda's rights must end with Egbert since it was raised by the Chronicle's statement about him. The conclusion is that to which we become accustomed in following the ways of the Anglo-Saxons: Egbert's ascendancy varied from kingdom to kingdom and from time to time. The authority of Wessex became relatively complete over Kent and the south-eastern kingdoms, though the annexation was partly disguised by the selection of the king's son as under-king. Over Northumbria the supremacy was barely nominal. 'Obedience and peace' could be safely offered by a state so distant. For about a year after 829 Egbert seems to have exercised some direct rule north of the Thames, minting coins as King of Mercia. Then he restored Wiglaf, and there is no evidence from the middle decades of the ninth century to suggest that Egbert had established any effective lordship over Mercia.

The position of East Anglia and of Essex is doubtful. The Athelstan who issued pennies as King of the East Angles seems to have been a son of Egbert;[19a] but so long as London remained Mercian, East Anglia and Essex could not be closely joined to Greater Wessex. In the event they shared the fate of Mercia rather than that of Kent.

WHY WESSEX BEAT NORTHUMBRIA AND MERCIA

Discussion about the meaning of the term Bretwalda and the powers of the over-kings, can easily end in a desert of arid facts and fancies. The last subject of this chapter has a more living interest. No one can read the history of England between the coming of Christianity and the coming of the Danes without forming some conclusion about the question how it was that Northumbria and Mercia, after some early successes, both failed in the end to make good their claim to supremacy. The question has interest for this reason: that in seeking an answer to it we are, in fact, trying to discover why the north-countrymen and mid-landers failed to keep the lead, while the people of the south succeeded in asserting a lasting superiority in the island. Was it a matter of luck, or of the personality of a few rulers, or was the success of Wessex fore-ordained, being determined by its situation?

Now we must begin by admitting that in the main the rise and decline, first of one power and then of another, were due simply to the chances of this human life, which rendered it improbable that there would be in any one dynasty a long succession of kings who were grown men of outstanding capacity. This must be granted. None the less, there were general causes. Those which determined the fate of Northumbria are the most obvious, and may be taken first.

The wonder is, not that Northumbria failed to keep, but that it ever held the supremacy. Its geographical situation might in itself be deemed enough to handicap the kingdom hopelessly in the race for power. The communications with the south by land were almost confined to the one good Roman road, roughly corresponding to the Great North Road by way of Doncaster. To the east of it were the swamps of the rivers which flow into the Humber, to the west were the forest of Elmet and the wastes of the Peak. The southern advance of Northumbria was thus easily barred, and if the usual identifications of the battle-fields are correct, it was near this narrow gap between the hills and the rivers that many of the decisive battles were fought—those of Heathfield, of the Idle, and of the Winwæd.

Further, we see that there can be little unity between the plain of York and the ribbons of arable land in Bernicia, which stretched up the rivers and along the sea-coast as far as the Forth. The central chain of barren hill-country which modern text-books call the backbone of England, and which men in the Middle Ages sometimes called 'The Waste', was a real barrier. A few Northumbrian settlers might trickle over the desolate water-shed, but those western lands remained as a whole in the occupation of the Britons.

It had only been exceptional circumstances which, in the middle of the century, enabled Northumbria to dominate for a time the Anglo-Saxon kingdoms to the south of the Humber. At first the disunion of the Midland settlements had rendered them defenceless before Bernicia and Deira, united under Ethelfrith and under Edwin. Then, when the Midlands had been forced by Penda and his son to coalesce, the lead of Northumbria had for a while been prolonged by another extraordinary situation. For the first and only time in history, Ireland, thanks to its past immunity from barbarian invasions, excelled the rest of western Europe in learning, culture, and vigorous Christianity. Thus in the middle of the seventh century foreign stimulus came for once in a way from the north, by way of Iona. The Northumbrians, as neighbours of the Scots, had an advantage which in other periods has been enjoyed by those who live in the south of the island, and superiority in culture had its influence on political power. In a sense, therefore, the decision of King Oswy in 664 to adhere to the Roman instead of the Scottish Church was suicidal. So long as St. Peter was acknowledged to hold the keys of heaven, Canterbury and Kent were likely to be the master-keys to predominance in England. Northumbria, unable to control Canterbury, was doomed to become sooner or later a backward territory, scarcely irrigated by the cultural stream flowing from the south. It was bound to revert to type. North-umbrian supremacy had been a result of the abnormal situation which made Ireland for a generation or two a chief source of civilization. Even without any Synod of Whitby, the south was sure to recover its former advantages.

These generalizations help us to understand how it was that in the two centuries after Oswy Northumbria sank from being the most advanced to the most backward part of England. As so often happens, its political failure preceded its cultural decline. We may mark the following stages in the process. First, after the Mercian revolt of 658 came the loss of *imperium* south of the Humber. Then, with the defeat of Ecgfrith at Nectansmere (685), Northumbria lost its empire beyond the Forth (and for a time also that over Strathclyde). It is harder to fix with exactness the third stage, which brought the end of supremacy south of the Clyde. But it seems that the final break-away of the Britons of Strathclyde and the Picts of Galloway came about 800. The third stage, in fact, sees more than the loss of empire. It brings the disintegration of Bernicia itself. The weakness first caused by internecine feuds is now aggravated by external attacks from the north. Viking raids on the coast from Lindisfarne to Wear-mouth are symptomatic of the decline of Anglian sea-power on the east. In the west also Scandinavians appear in the Irish seas, and the disappearance of the Anglian bishopric of Whitern tells its tale.[19b] Thus, at the close of this third stage, somewhere about 800, the destruction of the famous northern monasteries proclaimed to the world that Bernicia was crumbling. The centre was clearly shifting to Deira. The feuds between the rival families struggling for the crown were at their worst. In the fourth and last period of Northumbrian decline, that of the two generations before the conquest of York by the Northmen (866), darkness descends. There were no longer any northern annals. There was no correspondence like that of Alcuin. We only know that in 844 Kenneth MacAlpin united the crowns of the Picts and the Scots; and that the new Scotto-Pictish monarchy took the place formerly held by Northumbria as the aggressive, the imperial power of the North. One chronicle, the Chronicle of the Picts and Scots, has an entry which speaks of Kenneth invading Saxonia (Lothian) six times, and of his burning Dunbar and Melrose.[20] Though not well authenticated it may be a true story. At any rate, the bishopric of Hexham disappeared about 821. The church built by Wilfrid began to fall into ruins. In Deira itself the descent from former greatness was less in evidence. Eanred, the king who is stated to have recognized the ascendancy of Egbert of Wessex, actually reigned for thirty-two years. Though the feuds broke out again soon after Eanred's death, it does not follow that the civilization of Deira or the prosperity of the school at York had notably declined before the invasion of 866. On the whole, we carry away the general impression that, while it was the internal feuds which destroyed Northumbria's political hegemony, it was the Scandinavian attacks from without which cut short its traditions of education and of art.

Feuds of one kind or another are the dominant theme of Northumbrian history from the beginning to the end of the story. At the beginning we had the feud between the House of Ælle and the House of Ida. This we may regard as the consequence of the fatal dualism of Northumbria. The union of Deira and Bernicia had not been a happy marriage. It had produced a disastrous alternation between two policies. Deiran interests had pointed, as under Edwin, to southern ambitions— to the struggle with Mercians and Welsh, and expansion beyond the Humber. Bernician interests had led as naturally to expan-

sion northwards, and to attempts like those of Oswy and Ecgfrith
to conquer the Picts and the Scots. For a poor country like
Northumbria to combine both ambitions, as was done by Oswy,
was folly. But though the dualism of Northumbria contributed
to the early feuds—those between the dynasties of Ælle and of
Ida—and though incompatibilities of temperament between
Deirans, touched by southern influences, and Bernicians, more
under the Celtic spell, may have embittered the quarrels
which raged first round Bishop Wilfrid and then round Bishop
Acca, the feuds of Northumbria were so continuous and so varied,
one succeeding another right down to the Norman Conquest,
that we must look deeper if we are to understand them.

The statistics of the Northumbrian kings[21] summarize
most of our positive information about this period. We know
that in the years 705–806 five times a king was murdered or
slain in a civil fight, five times a king was deposed (sometimes
also 'tonsured', that is, incarcerated in a monastery as a sequel
to deposition): four times a king abdicated, once a king wore the
crown for only two months, once for only twenty-seven days.
There were, it is true, gleams of sunshine between the storms.
One king, Eadberht, managed to reign for twenty-one years, and
in alliance with the Picts he stormed Alclyde (756) and recovered the overlordship of Strathclyde. Occasionally a king was
recalled from a monastery (as for instance, Ceolwulf, to whom
Bede dedicated his History); occasionally a king died a natural
death and in possession of his crown. But these were the rare
exceptions; it was the rule to climb to power by violence and
and to be thrust from it by the same means.

Is it possible now to discover how it came about that a people
who were producing learning such as that of Bede and Alcuin, and
beauty like that of the Lindisfarne Gospels and the stone crosses,
could allow themselves to be dragged down in a welter of un-
restrained passion and disorder? Some of the bare facts help us
to understand the causes of the evil. We can see for instance how
the trouble arose in 716. Osred, the first king to be murdered,

was notorious for his immoralities—a ruler who used his position to seduce consecrated women in the monasteries. No doubt, therefore, his murderers regarded their deed as an act of divine justice, and with that view St. Boniface was in agreement.[22] But in those days of family vengeance one murder begot another. When once the succession had been unsettled, and a successful murderer had established the claim of another branch of the royal house, stability was lost. At other times, the election to the crown was complicated by the necessity of having as king a grown man, capable of being his own commander-in-chief and prime minister. For these and other reasons the succession in Northumbria became hopelessly confused. It was diverted first from the family of one son of Oswy, then from that of another. Later on nobles who traced descent from Ida's bastards, and others who had nothing but the swords of their friends and retainers to commend them, asserted their claims. When once the crown had become the prize of violence there was no end to the chaos. The kings who competed for the Northumbrian crown in the eighth century came from seven different families. Their ambitions brought them to crimes which left deep passions of revenge behind them. The climax was reached towards the end of the eighth century, when the son-in-law of Offa of Mercia, a certain Ethelred, who reigned at intervals between 774 and 796, not only drowned the young sons of a rival in Wonwaldremere,* but also slew treacherously three high reeves.

Now though we read often enough of wars and murders in the kingdoms south of the Humber, we do not hear of vendettas so persistent and so inflamed as those which rendered Northumbria a byword. We can but guess at the underlying causes which disposed the Northumbrian aristocracy to this internecine strife: perhaps the backwardness of the land, where large numbers of men leading the life of herdsmen and hunters were always ready for the war-trail; perhaps social conditions, which gave the high reeves and ealdormen a greater control over their dependants

---

* ? Windermere. But cf. W. G. Collingwood, *Lake District History*, 41.

than in the south; perhaps the fact that the region was, in this
period as later, a borderland where great men thought it wise to
maintain large numbers of rowdy retainers; perhaps some in-
fection from the Celts, since in this kingdom men of Celtic and
Saxon origin were intermingled throughout its whole length.
Whatever the precise reason, the fact remains that the strength
of Northumbria was undermined by its feuds.

If it be agreed that Northumbria was hardly ever in the running for the first place among the kingdoms, and was definitely
left behind from the time when the ealdormen of Mercia banded
together in 658 and ejected the officials introduced by Oswy, it
follows that before the Danish conquests there were two centuries when the headship lay between Mercia and Wessex.
During most of this period Wessex, submitting to the ascendancy
of Mercia, did not appear to be a competitor. Except during the
reign of Ine, Wessex played an inconspicuous part. Then suddenly we read in the Saxon Chronicle of the brief, unheralded,
meteoric campaigns of conquest by Egbert. The subject which
must now be discussed, therefore, is the question why Wessex at
last drew ahead, and why it succeeded in keeping the lead.

The classical passage where this question is investigated will
be found in J. R. Green's *Conquest of England*. Among the reasons
there suggested we may notice the following. (1) It is said that
'the varied composition of Egbert's kingdom . . . was a source of
strength', and it is true enough that there was probably a larger
proportion of alien blood among the West Saxons than among
the Mercians or Deirans. Northumbria had, indeed, two
different brands of Angles, and Greater Mercia was a federation
of different peoples, some of which like the Hwicce were, it
seems, compounded both of Angles and Saxons. But what distinguishes Wessex was the success with which it absorbed its
aliens. The Jutes of the Isle of Wight and of the opposite main-
land were gradually merged with the other folk of Hampshire.
The Britons of the West, even though they continued to speak
Celtic, did in fact throw in their lot unreservedly with the West

Saxons. Green justly says that the newer Wessex (that is, the region west of Selwood) 'was even more West Saxon in temper' than the older Wessex, and that this may be attributed to the more gradual settlement of the west.

Perhaps better reasons for the reconciliation of the Britons may be extracted from the laws of Ine. In them we saw that the Britons were given a definite and substantial place in society. Though protected with a wergild amounting to only about half that of the English—for the ordinary freeman 120 shillings, against 200 shillings; for the owner of 5 hides of land, 600 shillings against 1,200 shillings—Welshmen were employed in the king's service and could even be admitted to the select circle of the king's body-guard.[23]

(2) A chief reason given by Green for the success of the West Saxons is the superiority of their administration, and in particular their division of the kingdom into shires, ruled and led by their ealdormen. This raises a problem of constitutional history. But it will be enough to observe that even if we could decide exactly when and how the West Saxon shires came into existence —whether as stages in the original settlement or as kingdoms when Wessex was divided between sub-reguli—we should still be unable to say whether Wessex here possessed any superiority, since we know even less about the local organization of Mercia.[23a] The annals of the West Saxon Chronicle, in which one ealdorman after another is said to lead the forces of his shire against the enemy, may be supposed to point to the efficiency of the West Saxon shire system. But who can say that if we possessed a Mercian Chronicle we should not read therein of similar campaigns by the ealdormen of Mercian provinces?

(3) In the next place much may be said about the geographical advantages of Wessex. Mercia in comparison with Wessex was clearly wanting in good natural boundaries, and within its ill-defined borders there was little geographical unity. The Midlands could never become a well-developed organism till their marshes were drained and their forests were felled. The

obstacles presented by the marshes are obvious. The fens of
the Wash penetrated for over thirty miles into the interior.
Those of the Trent were enough to prevent Mercia from assimilating Lindsey. The separatist effects of the forests are harder to
estimate. Our maps generally show little more than the so-
called 'forests' which were only hunting-districts of the Norman
and Angevin periods—Sherwood, Charnwood, Arden, Wyre,
Wychwood, and many others. We have to use these names, but
they may easily hide from us the vast extent of the tree-covered
areas of early Saxon times. The maps of this volume follow
some recent Ordnance Survey maps in marking thick and open
woodland according to surface soils; but even these maps show
as open places many tracts which were probably covered with
trees and scrub, and fail to differentiate others which were mere
barren wastes.[24]

Whatever may be the real reason, it is true enough that
Mercia, even more than its rivals, lacked a natural centre of
government. Offa had a palace at Tamworth;[25] some other
kings seem to have regarded Repton as their head-quarters.
Those places and Lichfield, the first ecclesiastical centre of
Mercia, were all within twenty miles of one another, near the
upper Trent, but they never became much more than villages,
and there is no trace that the sentiment of the Midlands gathered
round them.

Wessex, on the other hand, was blessed with well-marked
frontiers, except for some fifty miles between the upper Thames
and the Avon. Wessex could at leisure nibble the West Welsh
until it secured all the south-western peninsula. In the seventh
century it had exhibited powers of recuperation when, after
defeat by the Mercians it moved its bishop's see from Dorchester
on Thames to Winchester. And Winchester did in time collect
or manufacture traditions which gave it special prestige as a
royal city.

There is some truth also in Green's idea that Wessex enjoyed
a certain physical compactness, thanks to the ramparts of chalk

which encircled the Winchester-Salisbury country. These, rising
on the east in the Andredsweald, continued to the north in the
Berkshire and Marlborough Downs, and, bending south-west-
wards through Salisbury Plain to the Dorset hills, formed a chain
of uplands which, though by no means the 'natural fortress' of
Green's imagination, were none the less of real importance in
that they provided admirable pathways for internal traffic. Thus,
while the hills of Northumbria and the fens and forests of Mercia
made those kingdoms poor and kept them divided, the chalk
downs of Wessex held the different parts of the land in touch with
one another, connecting east and west by good turf tracks along
the ridges.

It is easy to produce such general explanations (are they not now
manufactured by mass production in our modern examination
system?), explanations which it is as impossible to prove false as
true; imponderable, but not on that account without value. If
we like we may add to Green's list a more recent suggestion[26]
and say that Egbert owed his opportunity to the fact that he
'alone among the English rulers of his day could claim direct
descent from the kings of the migration time'.

Let us, however, pick out those reasons for the ultimate success
of Wessex which appear to be of primary importance. They are
three: control of the south-east; the personality of Egbert; and
the effects of the Danish invasions. The first of these is the only
one which needs to be re-emphasized. We have already seen that
Offa tried to force the south-eastern kingdoms into dependence
on Mercia, and that in doing so he pursued various methods.
He defeated them in the field, he sometimes divided the old
kingdoms, and to all appearance he suppressed as far as possible
the old dynasties. It is obvious to us, and we may suppose that
it was also obvious to a statesman of the time, that Kent and
the lower Thames valley were the key to supremacy. Mercia,
occupying the middle of the island, had clearly some advantage
in its geographical position. It was within easy striking distance
of all the other kingdoms. It had the interior lines. But it was

not the true centre of the island. That was to be found in the south-east. Traffic with the Continent passed through the Kentish ports and the Thames. London was still as in the time of Bede 'the emporium of many nations resorting to it by sea and land'.[27] Accordingly the importance of the south-east in general, and of Canterbury and London in particular, was such that the prize of ultimate supremacy was likely to go to the kingdom which could secure a firm grip on Kent and the lower Thames.

Now Mercia was quite as well placed as Wessex for dominating the south-east, and it was first in the field. We have seen, however, that a crisis in the relations between Kent and its neighbours came in the years immediately before and immediately after 800. The Kentish revolt of 796 (headed by a certain Eadbert Præn*) seems to have been the turning-point. The motives of the rebels may be guessed—resentment at Offa's strong rule and his tampering with their old monarchy; perhaps friction caused by dues on shipping levied by Mercian kings at London;[28] and lastly, indignation at the erection of the Lichfield archbishopric in 786 to the injury of Canterbury. Offa's record was bad enough, but the barbarism with which the revolt of 796 was suppressed by Coenwulf, his successor, was worse. Coenwulf is said (only indeed in a late version of the Chronicle) to have 'ravaged Kent as far as the marshes,† and captured Præn their king and led him bound to Mercia and put out his eyes and cut off his hands'.[29] If the transfer of the supremacy from Mercia to Wessex is to be attributed to any one event, it may well be traced to this brutal deed, which seems to have alienated the Kentishmen for ever.

The Lichfield archbishopric and the barbarities of 796 did not complete the tale of Mercian blunders. Even after Coenwulf had tried to conciliate the Kentishmen by restoring their archbishop to all his former rights, he still continued to quarrel with the see of Canterbury. The dispute began in 817 when the

---

* See Pl. 81, 4, a coin of Eadberht Præn. † Romney Marsh.

Mercian king seized lands belonging to the monasteries of Thanet and Reculver, lands which had strategic importance, since they bordered on the Wantsum waterway, leading from the Thames estuary to the Continent. Into the rights and wrongs of Coenwulf's high-handed act we cannot enter. But it seems to show that Mercia was still pursuing a deliberate policy of establishing its power by one means or another in that decisive region, eastern Kent. The quarrel was for a time so acute that 'the whole English nation was deprived of its primordial authority and of the ministry of Holy Baptism for the space of almost six years',[30] and it dragged on wearisomely after the death of Coenwulf (822) down to the eve of Egbert's humiliation of the Mercians.

So we come back to Egbert himself, whom we mentioned second among the three decisive factors contributing to the victory of Wessex over Mercia. There were reasons which gave lasting significance to his career, in spite of the evanescence of his authority north of the Thames.

To begin with, Egbert succeeded somehow or other in permanently reconciling Kent and Wessex. If the supposition is correct that he was the son of a king of Kent, and united in his own person the blood of the dynasties both of Kent and Wessex, it follows that the union of the two kingdoms came about in the same way as the union of Scotland and England, that is, in the surest way of all, by the smaller kingdom through inter-marriage supplying a dynasty to the greater. Perhaps, also, Kent and the other small states received better treatment from the house of Egbert than from the Mercians. Home rule for a time under princes of Egbert's blood made it easier for the states of the south-east to sink with dignity from kingdoms into shires.

For the rest, the greatness of Egbert is to be calculated from the achievements of his successors. In this way we may infer that he must have brought with him from his three years' residence among the Franks under Charlemagne a knowledge of the methods practised by the greatest administrator and statesman of the Dark Ages. If for instance Egbert reorganized the West-Saxon *fyrd* with something like the care for military details displayed by Charlemagne, the sudden success of Wessex over the other kingdoms would be fully explicable. Our second inference is that the personal piety which long made the dynasty illustrious, and the sense of family solidarity which saved it from suicidal feuds like those of the Northumbrians and of the Carolingians, are virtues for which the founder of the dynasty should be given some credit. Egbert and Offa are the two all-important unknown quantities in the formation of a united England. But if nowadays we assign an increased significance to Offa, we need not therefore belittle Egbert. This, at any rate, can be claimed—that from the time of Egbert onwards there were good traditions in the ruling house of Wessex, those of strenuous fighting against Dane and devil, and that these traditions may reasonably be supposed to have been implanted by Egbert himself.

In the reign of Egbert the political weather-vane first wavered, and then pointed definitely, if only for a short spell, from Mercia to Wessex. It showed that a change was coming; but no one can question the fact that the change did not arrive till the time of Alfred, and that then it was the result of the Danish wars. Egbert made a beginning by reconciling the south-eastern kingdoms to Wessex; the Danish wars completed what he had begun— by eliminating rival dynasties, by bisecting the rival kingdoms, and by demonstrating, not only to the south-east but to all Britain, the superior leadership of Egbert's grandson.

TAILPIECE.—Details, adapted, from frieze in wall of Chancel of Breedon Church, Leicestershire.   ? 8th century.

...sunt innumera stilo stultissimo ut novimus omnes. in monasteriorum asscripta vocabulum; sed nichil prorsus monasticae conversationis habentia. e quibz aliqua velim de luxuria ad castitatem. de vanitate ad veritatem. de intemperantia ventris et gulae. ad continentiam et pietatem cordis synodica auctoritate transferantem.

XI

THE CHURCH IN THE CENTURY AFTER BEDE

CRITICISMS OF BEDE, BONIFACE, AND ALCUIN

THE century after Bede is generally regarded as an age of increasing degeneration in the English Church. In the following chapter we shall inquire what justification there is for this view. The question has significance, for it bears on the general character of our pre-Norman ancestors. There are those who maintain that the Anglo-Saxons were a nation never able to realize their early promise; that they were capable of heroic efforts for a time, but incapable of sustaining those efforts, so as to win through to ultimate success. What we have to consider, therefore, is whether the decline of the Church, and in particular of the monasteries, in the eighth century, was so marked as to indicate any special weakness or depravity in the English people. Was it internal rottenness or the external blows of the Vikings which reduced the Church to the state of ignorance and ineffectiveness described by Alfred?

Let us see what exactly were the evils denounced by those who in the eighth century had the welfare of the nation most at heart.

HEADPIECE.—[. . . sunt [loca] innumera, stilo stultissimo ut novimus omnes, in monasteriorum asscripta vocabulum, sed nichil prorsus monasticae conversationis habentia; e quibus aliqua velim de luxuria ad castitatem, de vanitate ad veritatem, de intemperantia ventris et gulae ad continentiam et pietatem cordis synodica auctoritate transferantur . . . Extract from Bede's Letter to Egbert, Bishop of York.] [Harleian MS. 4688 f. 92 verso. 11th century.]

In the first place, Bede, shortly before his death, wrote, as x
we have seen, a letter[1] to Egbert, bishop and later archbishop
of York, complaining that certain sham monasteries had been
founded by men who, without any true religious motive, wished
to free their lands from military service and other secular burdens.
These monasteries were ruled by laymen, they were filled with
renegade monks from real monasteries, or with the tonsured
retainers* of the lay abbot. Such monasteries, being 'of no use
either for God or man', should be suppressed, and their endowments should be diverted to increase the number of bishoprics,
so as to enable every bishop to visit all his diocese every year.

Thirteen years later, in 747, an archbishop of Canterbury held x
a Synod at 'Clovesho' (probably near London) in order to pro-
mulgate canons for the guidance of the Church in Britain. Some
of the impulse for the suggested reforms no doubt came from the
Pope, some of it from Boniface, the West Saxon, who had for the
last five years been stirring the Church of the Franks to new life
in a series of synods.† But the English assembly was no mere
shadow. It showed vigour of its own. The archbishop was supported by eleven of his twelve prelates, and by a number of the
lesser clergy. The synod provided[2] that bishops should make a
visitation of their dioceses once a year, and that they should see
that there was no monastery without a priest to care for the souls
of the inmates. Other clauses insisted that both monks and nuns
should lead 'a quiet *regular* life', and observe the seven canonical
hours. They were not to wear showy clothing like laymen; they
were specially to be on their guard against drunkenness. Monasteries were to be kept as places of silence, and not to be the
homes of poets, musicians, and comedians; laymen were not to
be tonsured, nor were they to be admitted to monasteries until
their fitness had been proved. Once admitted, they were not to
be sent away or allowed to wander.

* *satellites.*

† It is uncertain how far the reforms of 747 were directly inspired by Boniface. See
G. F. Browne, *Boniface*, 246–53; H. Hahn, *Bonifaz und Lul* (1883), 219; Hefele-Leclercq,
iii. 903.

Then, forty years after the Synod of Clovesho, we again encounter somewhat similar criticism of English clergy, repeated in the decrees of certain legatine synods. In the years 786–7 papal legates visited England and were welcomed by Offa for their help in furthering his plan of a Mercian archbishopric. They made it their main business to attend provincial assemblies (one held in Northumbria and the other at Celcythe*) and support measures of reform. These provided, *inter alia*, for half-yearly synods and yearly visitations by bishops, for the supervision of bishops over the elections of abbots, for tithes, and for the uprooting of pagan superstitions. But more novel and significant was the decree[3] that, while monks and nuns should live 'regularly, that is, according to their Rule', the secular clergy of collegiate churches (called here for the first time 'canons') should live 'canonically', that is, according to the canons of the Church. In this we see a back-wash of the reform movement which had first been set flowing by Boniface. For it was a disciple of Boniface, Chrodegang of Metz, who about this time had made fashionable the idea that the secular clergy should as far as possible be assimilated to the regulars, and live a communal life with a professed discipline.

Here, then, we have three notable attempts to reform the Church. In each case there is a strong suggestion that all was not well, and it is not surprising that these proposals and decrees should have been commonly quoted to prove that the eighth century was a period of decline, and of 'evil influences'.[4] Such a view, moreover, is strengthened by the correspondence of Boniface and that of Alcuin, our best sources for the thoughts of leading Englishmen in the period after Bede.

During the thirty-eight years (716–54) in which Boniface devoted himself to the conversion of the Germanic peoples beyond the Rhine, the tone of his letters to friends in England changed. In his earlier years he wrote for advice; in his later years he often was moved to criticize the doings—or what were

* ? Chelsea.

rumoured to be the doings—of his fellow countrymen. For instance, a letter which he with five German fellow bishops addressed to Ethelbald of Mercia contrasted the licentiousness of the English king, who carried his excesses even into the convents (an offence which, he says, first began early in the eighth century), with the severe morality of the continental Saxons, whose respect for the marriage tie was enforced by laudable customs. Among these Germans an adulteress was sometimes made to hang herself. Sometimes the virtuous 'matrons lead the guilty woman bound through the village, beating her with sticks and cutting away her garments to the girdle; they cut and prick her whole body with their knives . . .; new tormentors are always joining the band out of zeal for modesty, and leave her dead or scarcely alive'.[5] It is noised abroad, Boniface continued, both in Germany and France and Italy, and even among the heathen, that the English 'spurn lawful wedlock . . . and from such intercourse with harlots a people degenerate, unworthy, mad with lust, will be born, and in the end the whole nation . . . will cease to be strong in war or steadfast in faith . . . just as has happened to the peoples of Spain and Provence and Burgundy' who for their sins have been punished by God through the Saracens. And besides this 'it is said that the *prefecti* (? reeves) and *comites* (ealdormen, or possibly thegns) use greater violence and oppression towards monks and priests than other Christian kings have ever done before'.

In 747 Boniface sent a long letter to the archbishop of Canterbury about the measures of reform which were being mooted both in Germany and England.[6] 'Let us seek to instruct one another,' he wrote, 'you taking the larger and better part.' For his part, Boniface was prompt; and he at once proceeded to criticize the English for four evils. First, for the immorality which too often resulted from the pilgrimage of women to Rome. 'There are few cities in Lombardy or Francia or Gaul in which there is not a harlot of English race: which is a scandal and a disgrace to your whole Church.' Secondly, for the confiscation of monasteries by English kings; thirdly, for luxury in dress; fourthly, for drunkenness. 'In your dioceses, it is said, the evil of drunkenness has greatly increased, so that some bishops, so far from checking it, themselves become intoxicated through excess of drink, and by offering cups unduly large, force others to drunkenness. . . . This evil indeed is peculiar to the heathen and to our race. . . . Let us crush out this sin, if we can, by decrees of our synods.'

At the end of the eighth century the prophet's mantle was taken up by Alcuin. His position was not unlike that of Boniface. Like Boniface, he was an Englishman, occupying a high position on the Continent, and doing work of the first importance. Like Boniface, he knew one part of England well, and had a traveller's acquaintance with some other parts. Alcuin was a Northumbrian and had been head of the school of York (776–82) before he was invited to the court of Charlemagne and made master of his Palace School. Alcuin could thus criticize his fellow countrymen with authority and without fear of consequences. His letters ranged over the whole field of national life, and in the manner of a righteous man he was free with his reproofs. Sins of sex and avarice were denounced, and the feuds which were the ruination of Northumbria. But the vices of English ecclesiastics which were the most constant theme of Alcuin's moralizings were over-drinking, over-eating, and over-dressing. He did not reveal any great scandals, but complained of worldliness in general, love of sport, of hunting, of useless games, and such-like 'futilities'. In letter after letter he has to rebuke his English friends for the pagan way in which they cut their hair and beard, for making their tonsure scarcely perceptible, for their pomp and vanity in dress and their excess in feasting.[7]

To Alcuin, the England which he had left for the court of Charlemagne seemed decadent, and in the strain of Hebrew prophecy he announced that the spirit of faction, the worldliness and luxury of the people, were tempting Providence, and tempting also the pirates of the north, the scourge of Providence.[8]

'The greatest danger is hanging over this island and the people who live in it. You see now a thing which has never been heard of: a pagan people is making a habit of plundering our shores like pirates. Yet the peoples of England, its kingdoms and its kings, are at variance one with another. And now there is hardly one king left of an ancient stock—I cannot say it without tears; and the more obscure the birth of the up-starts, the less is their courage. In like manner, throughout the churches of Christ the teachers of Truth have perished. Nearly all men follow secular vanities, and hate regular discipline. Even their warrior class think more about getting rich than about doing justice. Study Gildas, the wisest of the Britons, and you can see what were the causes which made the ancestors of the Britons lose their kingdom and country. Then contemplate yourselves, and you will find almost the same things existing among you.' [See facsimile Fig. 55 on p. 422.]

Here the case against the Church of the eighth century ends. The witnesses have been heard; how are we to interpret them?

To begin with, we may without special pleading discount many of the general accusations. It was the business both of the synods and of the Fathers of the Church to detect evils and to condemn them. The more they denounced, the better they did their work. Christianity had not transformed human nature in the ordinary run of men. Evils in abundance could always be found—some of them might almost be written down as matters of course. But not all. Our interpretation of the more specific charges must depend mainly on the view we take of these pro-posals for reform. We may seize on them and enlarge on the faults which called for such legislation, or we may argue that anxiety for reform is in itself good evidence that a mood of healthy self-criticism was making itself felt, and that the spirit which had moved Englishmen in the age of the Conversion was not exhausted, but was being directed into new channels.

And then we may remark that the earlier criticisms—those of Bede, of Boniface, and of the Council of 747—were the most damaging; and this may be taken to enforce the argument that for a Church, as for an individual, to be conscious of its own deficiencies is half the battle. Thus the evidence which was once used to convict the age may with better reason be put forward in its defence. This line of argument has its obvious limitations. But if we give weight to the abuses denounced and compare

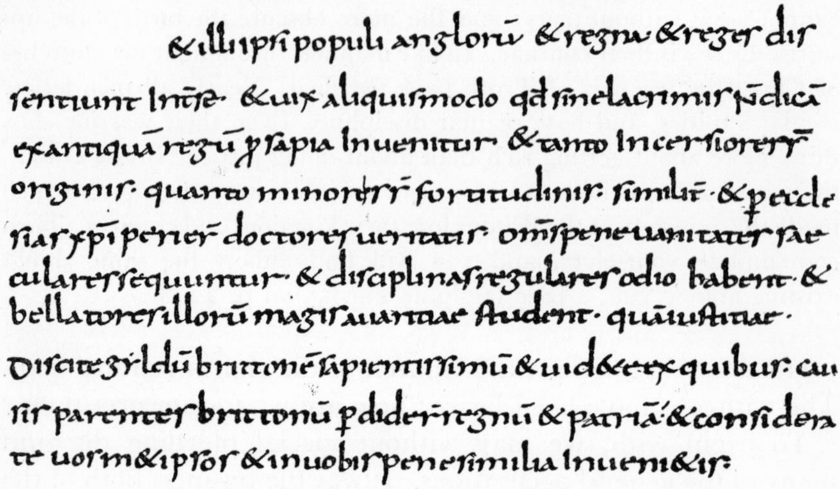

FIG. 55. Letter of Alcuin to the people of Kent (A.D. 797).*

them, we find that the sham monasteries in the time of Bede were an evil more barefaced than those which troubled the later reformers. Since Alcuin directs his main attack against such things as carelessness in dress and manner of life, it may be inferred that the deliberate frauds of the earlier period had been checked.

At the worst, we can always excuse our own deficiencies by showing that our neighbours are greater sinners. It is not an admirable line of defence, but it has its force. This then may be

* [. . . et illi ipsi populi Anglorum, et regna et reges dissentiunt inter se; et vix aliquis modo, quod sine lacrimis non dicam, ex antiqua regum prosapia invenitur, et tanto incertiores sunt originis, quanto minores sunt fortitudinis. Similiter et per ecclesias Christi perierunt doctores veritatis; omnes pene vanitates saeculares sequuntur, et disciplinas regulares odio habent: et bellatores illorum magis avaritiae student quam iustitiae. Discite Gyldum Brittonem sapientissimum, et videte ex quibus causis parentes Brittonum perdiderunt regnum et patriam: et considerate vosmetipsos, et in vobis pene similia invenietis.] [MS. Harl. 208 f. 67. 10th century.]

asserted, that the vague complaints uttered by Bede, Boniface, and Alcuin about the slackness, avarice, and worldliness of bishops, are negligible in comparison with the circumstantial stories about the Frankish dignitaries which enliven the pages of Gregory of Tours. In England synods never deemed it necessary to insist, as was done in Gaul in the sixth century, that a bishop should be constantly attended both day and night by two of his clergy, who were to watch over his morality. There were no scandals like that of the bishop of Bordeaux, who was said to keep a harem in his palace. Clearly bad appointments were sometimes made in England, but there is no trace of persistent simony, such as was a curse in the Gallic Church. The evils were for long incomparably greater among the Franks; their Church was older and richer; its long-accumulated wealth attracted the aristocrats and courtiers, and thus it was that evil-livers bribed their way into bishoprics. Even pious rulers like Charles Martel (Mayor of the Palace, 717–41) treated the wealth of the Church as fair spoil for a patriotic ruler, and used it for the support of his victorious armies. Thus in Gaul there were many calling themselves bishops and abbots who in fact remained soldiers, wearing the soldier's cloak, and girt with a sword.

The corresponding evils in England seem to have been venial. Boniface, it is true, writes[9] to King Ethelbald about the Mercian 'reeves and ealdormen' using 'greater violence and oppression towards monks and priests than other Christian kings have ever done before'. But he was more concerned about the king's licentiousness. Elsewhere[10] he becomes unnecessarily indignant about 'the violent enslavement of monks for royal works and buildings, which in the whole Christian world had never been heard of save only among the race of the English'. But what is this 'abuse unheard of in past ages'? It seems to be no more than the insistence that land granted to the Church should not be entirely relieved of obligations to the State, but should be liable for at least three duties: *fyrdfare, bricgbot,* and *burhbot.* That is to say, the monks should send fighting-men from their lands to the king's army; they should repair the bridges, and the king's fortified places. On these questions Boniface's views seem to have been warped by his experience of Carolingian interference with Church property. Bede, though he also took it for granted that Church lands should be exempted from obligations to the State, showed himself the better patriot in realizing the importance of keeping enough lands in secular hands for the maintenance of the national army. On the whole, the Anglo-Saxon kings exhibited unusual respect for the defenceless property of the Church, and the Anglo-Saxon clergy on their part showed plenty of fight if ever their rights were infringed. When for instance Coenwulf, king of Mercia (796–821), appropriated the monasteries of Minster and Reculver, Archbishop Wulfred withstood his 'violence and rapacity' with persistence and success.*

Thus, looking at the evidence against the English Church as a whole, the prima facie case for its condemnation is not very serious. There is a loss of position when comparison is made between England and the Continent, because the Frankish Church at this time made a rapid advance—thanks largely to the work of Boniface and of the hundreds of other Englishmen who followed him to the Continent, thanks also to Alcuin, and still more to the fortunate series of great rulers who succeeded one another in the Carolingian family. There is in England an apparent dearth of saints and of kings pre-eminent in piety such as the seventh century had produced. There are no spiritual conquests of the few to set against the dead level of the many. But where our knowledge is almost blank, it is idle to lay stress on deficiencies.

POSITIVE ACHIEVEMENTS—PARISHES, REFORMS, PENITENTIALS

Our best chance of estimating fairly the extent of the decay of religion in these generations before the cataclysm of the Danish conquests, is to dwell less on the frailties common to

* See below, p. 457.

human nature, and more on the problems of the age, as we seek out what was accomplished positively for the building up of English Christianity.

Perhaps the most important development which went on unobtrusively within the Church in the eighth century—as also in earlier and later times—was the gradual formation of the parish system. The process by which these divisions came into existence was twofold. There was, first, a missionary expansion from the centre of the diocese outwards, and later there was a spontaneous local formation of parishes, as one big landowner after another built himself his own church. Thus, in the first age of the Conversion, the only 'parish' had been what we now call the diocese of the bishop, and round the bishop's cathedral church were gathered the clergy who were to assist him in converting and administering his whole flock. They were his 'family'.* In the next stage of this evolution, subsidiary baptismal churches had been built further afield, in districts roughly corresponding to modern rural deaneries. These subsidiary centres of work in outlying parts of the diocese had also been served by groups or colleges of clergy. Being collegiate churches, they could be called minsters.† (At the present day they can sometimes be recognized by the survival of the name 'minster'—as at Beverley—or by the existence of stalls for a number of clergy in the choir.) Then in the last stage the local process, going on unobtrusively through many centuries, added to these earlier 'mother churches' or 'old minsters' a ring of private churches, commonly built by local thegns, as chapels attached to their halls.

It is from these private churches that most of our modern parish churches are descended. Their early history is obscure, but since some interesting light has been shed on the subject in recent years[11] it is one which deserves attention. The reasons for the obscurity which surrounds the early history of private churches in England are clear enough. Many of them were endowed on so small a scale that the founders established them

---

* *familia.*   † *monasteria.*

without going to the expense of obtaining formal charters from the king. The local thegn built his own timbered church; he put in a poor cleric to do the duty, giving him as glebe perhaps two virgates of strips in the open fields, as against the one virgate which was the reputed holding of the typical ceorl, and allowed him to pick up what he could from his parishioners in fees for baptisms and marriages, for supervising ordeals and for supplying the holy water for cures. The English incumbent was no serf as was sometimes the parish priest on the Continent; he was a ceorl, and had to spend much of his time working his land, like his fellow peasants. Private churches of this kind became the normal appurtenances of big estates. When we come to the tenth century we shall find that the thegn will be expected to have his church, like his bell-house and other marks of thegnly gentility. But there is no trace to show when the earliest 'parish' churches came into existence: no charter; no buildings. We only infer that where our country church now stands there in Saxon times often stood the timbered church of a Saxon thegn.

But the private churches were not all of this type—they were not all chapels attached to the halls of great laymen. Many of them were 'monasteries', and outwardly resembled in essentials the 'old minsters' with which the king had endowed the bishopric. It was these private monasteries against which Bede had fulminated in his letter to Bishop Egbert; minsters or collegiate churches in name, but not houses of true religion.

Yet another element of confusion is caused by the fact that not a few of the private churches were founded by the bishops and retained by them as their own possessions, 'peculiars', withdrawn from the ordinary rule of the diocese.

The rights retained by a founder were great. He could sell his church, bequeath it, and even abolish it at his will. It was handed down as a piece of property, like a mill. If there was not a cleric in the family it might come into the hands of a lay abbot. Here, as Bede realized, was the great danger to the English Church as it existed in the eighth century.

There has been a discussion about the origin of these practices. Alfred in one of his Laws speaks as if there was a lord for every church;[12] and from other clues it is reasonable to infer that private churches and the law about their rights go back to the early days of the Conversion. Now since this law was not a product of Roman jurisprudence, a further inference follows—that the private chapel of the Christian thegn succeeded to the private temple of his heathen predecessor. Sometimes, indeed, the actual temple building may have been transformed, as sanctioned by Pope Gregory, from temple into church. Since, however, nothing is known about private heathen temples in England and their existence is chiefly inferred from the fact that landowners in Norway and Iceland had private temples on their estates, this theory which connects our parish churches with earlier local temples of Woden or Thunor must remain mere speculation.

The prevalence of the system of private churches and minsters in the eighth century, and the difficulty of regulating such institutions in view of the fact that the rights of the lord were firmly based on secular law, must be duly weighed in any attempt to judge the record of the Church in these early centuries.

We are now in a better position to appreciate the problem which faced the reforming churchmen. They pursued two main ideas.

First, there was an attempt to enforce in the monasteries a stricter observance of their Rules. The application of these Rules in the early days of monasticism had been most diverse. They varied from one generation to another as well as from one House to another, according to the predilections of the founder or his successors. The line between regular and secular, between monk and canon, was uncertain. There has even been discussion about the character of Christ Church, Canterbury, the archbishop's own *familia*. One writer[13] believes that the inmates lapsed early from a strict communal Rule to a less exacting mode of life. Another[14] thinks that monks and secular clergy were probably mingled at Christ Church from the first.

In the eighth century the decrees of the reforming synods tried to clear up the confusion by practical measures. When the Legatine Synod of 787 decreed* that those who were not monks living according to Rule, must live as canons according to the canons of the Church, it was left to the bishops to see that the decree was observed. The only known example of an attempt to enforce the decree brings us back to the community of Christ Church, Canterbury, of which we have just spoken. It is interesting in so far as it illustrates the capacity of the post-Bedan church to grapple with its evils and initiate reforms. The reformer here was Archbishop Wulfred, who held the see of Canterbury for twenty-seven years (805–32) during the critical period in which Kent ceased to be a dependency of Mercia and transferred its allegiance to Wessex. His energies were at times diverted to carrying on the quarrel with the Mercian monarchy. But Wulfred was able to devote himself also to the spiritual needs of his Church. Among the formal documents which remain to tell of his pontificate, we have an agreement of the year 813[15] made between him and his *familia* of Christ Church, Canterbury. The archbishop obtains a promise from the clergy that they will 'frequent together the refectory and dormitory and observe the Rule of the discipline of life in a monastery'. They agree that if any of the community should sleep in his own cell or house, the house should be forfeited, and should be at the disposal of the archbishop. In return for their acceptance of this reform the archbishop on his part concedes that the clergy should be allowed to keep their houses and leave them to any one 'not outside the congregation' who may have been trained in the *familia*. In other words, houses within the monastery must not be left to kinsmen who were not members of the community. The compact appears then to be an attempt to implement the chief proposal of the Synod of 787. It requires the secular clergy of the cathedral to observe a life of discipline, not so strict as Benedictine 'regular' discipline (e.g. private property is allowed),

* As mentioned above, p. 418.

but none the less a life lived partly in common and according to the canons. Some success seems to have resulted from this attempt to revive the quasi-communal life, and when lands are granted to the *familia* of Christ Church in 832, the donor speaks of its clergy as 'monachi'.

Wulfred's action entirely accords with the continental reform movement begun by Boniface and carried further by his pupil, Chrodegang of Metz; and it precedes by three years the Council of Aix-la-Chapelle which made a similar rule of life incumbent on all collegiate churches of the Frankish Empire. It may be objected that Wulfred and the reformers were outrunning the conscience of their generation. That is no doubt true; and the standpoint of the average Englishman can be better seen in a charter drawn up about 800 by a certain Abbot Headda, the head of some small monastery in the Worcester diocese.[16] It says: 'I, Headda, presbyter and abbot, with the testimony of all the venerable *familia* at Worcester, bequeath my own proper inheritance; making this condition, that my heirs in the line of my family of the male sex and in holy orders shall receive it, so long as in my kindred there can be found a wise and prudent man who can exercise ecclesiastical rule in due and monastic fashion; and that never shall it be subjected to the authority of laymen. . . .' Small family minsters of this kind, content as long as they did not fall into the hands of laymen, were no doubt impervious to the reforming spirit of the greater churchmen.

The other main line of advance planned by the reformers in England was to bring all monasteries as well as all churches under the control of the bishops. They did not propose to abolish monasteries in the hands of laymen. Private property had to be respected. But at least a minimum of religion was to be enforced. Accordingly the Synod of 747, besides ordering that there should be a priest in each lay monastery, insisted that there should be no scandals, such as those produced when a woman inherited the headship of a community of men, or a man became the hereditary abbot of a community of women. In the

Synod of 787 the monks were told to take counsel with their bishop before the election of an abbot. Then in 803 a bolder line was taken, and a provincial council decreed that thenceforth no laymen should be elected as lords of monasteries. Finally in 816 it was provided that the bishop himself should have the power to choose the abbots and abbesses within his diocese, but that this must be done with the consent and advice of the *familia*, that is, of the community.[17]*

It must be admitted, then, that whatever the reason may be, whether the coming of the Danes or the ebbing of English enthusiasm, the ultimate results of the eighth-century reform movement were slight. It was indeed something that the bishops' authority over the monasteries should be recognized as a principle. The synods, in committing to them the control of the monasteries with a leading part in the selection of the abbots, were giving the bishops rights which were to be challenged in later times. But since the only increase in the number of dioceses after the creation of Sherborne in 705 and of Selsey in 709 was the short-lived see of Whitern (730–*c.* 805[17a]), it is clear that in many cases a bishop with the best will in the world could not make his control a reality.†

Bede's aims were not attained, but the powers of the diocesan bishops were increased. They escaped gradually both from the effective control of the metropolitans and, to a less degree, from that of the kings. As the heptarchic dynasties came to an end, the bishops ceased to be royal chaplains. They were left by the side of the ealdormen as the potentates of the countryside.

There are many other aspects of the history of the Church in the post-Bedan age which must be omitted to save this chapter from inordinate length. There was discussion and hard thinking about the problems caused by the intrusion of Christian clergy into a primitive society[18]—problems which since they raised fundamental issues about the relations between Church and State were to produce great storms in later times. The English

* See facsimile, p. 446.   † See map, p. 307.

ecclesiastics who in the eighth century faced these matters squarely were doing something less spectacular but not less needful than the achievements of the saints in earlier generations. There were also in the diocese of Canterbury minor experiments in the organization of the Church. Thus archdeacons made their first appearance in the island—but only for a time.[19]

More worth attention are changes where the English Church took a creative part, namely, the development of penitential discipline and of taxation for the support of the Church (tithe for the clergy and Peter's Pence for the Papacy).

Of penance, something has been already said.* We have seen that Archbishop Theodore had been here, as in so much else, a pioneer of Anglican Christianity. It was Theodore who had perceived that the Celtic system of private penance was more tolerable for proud barbarians like the Anglo-Saxons than the public penance which had been the practice of the earlier Church. In the old system, those who had committed grievous sins had been required to expiate them openly, in the face of all the congregation, before they could be readmitted to communion. The private penance instituted by the Irish and British was more efficacious as well as less humiliating, in so far as it dealt with the small lapses of everyday life and the sins of the mind.

The work of the eighth century was to supplement as well as to carry on what had been inaugurated by Theodore. The most notable of the new Penitentials is attributed to Archbishop Egbert of York. To understand what was being attempted, let us see how it revised the article of Archbishop Theodore about drunkenness. Theodore had prescribed the following scale of 'penitence' for this sin: thirty days for the monk who is so drunk that he vomits, forty days for the priest or deacon, and five days for the layman; deposition for a bishop or other ordained person who makes a habit of drunkenness. Vomiting, however, is no adequate test of drunkenness. Egbert's *Penitential* therefore adds

* Above, pp. 308–9.

a milder scale for a less gross form of the vice. If a man stammers and is giddy:* seven days for a cleric (in minor orders), fourteen for a monk, four weeks for a priest, five weeks for a bishop, three days for a layman—without wine and meat.

The Penitentials, though in fixing penances for every sin they stirred the muddy depths of human nature, yet represent one of the greatest schemes for the regeneration of man. The makers of this system were determined not to allow Christianity to remain a religion of faith without works. The code of Christian morality was to be enforced both on clergy and laity. The devil was to be driven out of humanity. The brute in man was to be tamed. Christians were to be cured of minor dirty habits as well as of the grosser sins. Archbishop Egbert follows Archbishop Theodore in legislating against the eating of animals which had died, or of food fouled by cat or dog. Half-cooked food must be avoided, also drink in which dead animals are found.

To enforce this code of morality and decency the authorities insisted that all men should go with their wives and families and confess their sins to the clergy before Christmas—this, it is said, was the established custom of the English. Then after confession the sinner was to make his peace with God by dieting himself on bread and water for the prescribed period; or by suffering more serious penalties. The flesh was to atone for the sins of the flesh. This was the system of private penance following private confession, as evolved in the British Isles, and transplanted in the eighth century to the Continent.

What was the success of the system? The records of Latin Christianity from that day to this supply many and diverse answers. Here we need only observe that already in the eighth century a clause of Egbert's *Penitential*[20] contemplates commutations. The following are equivalents for one day's penance: the saying of fifty psalms with genuflexions, of seventy psalms without genuflexions, of two hundred genuflexions without

* 'quando statum mentes mutantur et lingua balbuttit et oculi turbentur et vestigo [*sic*] erit et ventris distentio ac dolor sequitur . . .' (c. xi. 10, in H. and S. iii. 427).

psalms, or the payment of one dinar and three donations of alms
to the poor. The door had been opened for evasion. Penance
might be obtained without the personal mortification required
by the earlier codes. The original scheme had made impossible
demands on human nature.

Another direction in which the English of the eighth century
perhaps displayed some originality was the development of
clerical tithes. The idea that tithes should be paid for religious
purposes was as old as the Jewish Pentateuch. The first trace of
it in England is in the *Penitential* of Archbishop Theodore. The
payment there required was for the support of the poor as well as
of the clergy. It was to be the voluntary act of every good
Christian. But that was not enough. The clergy wished to make
it an order. Among the Franks they had their way in a decree of
765, and in England in a similar decree of 787. It is generally
assumed that the English were here copying the Franks, but it
has been recently suggested[21] 'that such a law would not have
been promulgated unless it gave voice to a general sense of duty
and made universal (at any rate in theory) a practice that was
commonly followed. For such a feeling to grow up must have
taken time, and it is not unlikely that in England the practice
first established itself, and that it was from England that it passed
into the Frankish Empire as a charge on land.'

We have now reached a point at which it will be well to pick
up the threads of our arguments. In investigating the condition
of the English Church in and after the time of Bede, we have
come across three outstanding features which partially justify
the talk about the 'evil influences' of the period. One of these is
the encroachment of the secular world on the Church. We have
found laymen treating monasteries and churches as their property, for the reason that they or their ancestors had endowed
them; and it has been clear that kings in much the same way
and for the same reason were regarding the Churches in their
respective kingdoms as subject to them, and their bishops as

servants. The only part of this practice which was considered a definite abuse by the reformers of the age was the existence of lay abbots, and we have seen creditable efforts to remedy that evil. But the subject of the relations of Church and State can be considered from a wider point of view and we shall return to it in the next chapter.

Ⓐ   The second evil—one of which the reformers were fully conscious—was the worldliness of the English monks and clergy. This is a characteristic which will be constantly denounced until the coming of the Normans. The complaints are so circumstantial that they cannot altogether be dismissed as a commonplace of moralists. The reason for placing fresh emphasis on them at this point is that they supply a needed corrective for the gloom which we shall find pervading the poetry of the English clergy. The worldliness in question had developed early in the history of the English Church, and took many forms. The most inveterate was the love of dress. Here the *locus classicus* is Aldhelm's description of the attire of a fashionable lady who clung to her finery even in a religious house.[22] She wore a violet under-dress and a scarlet tunic with wide sleeves and hood, both striped or faced with silk. She was covered with necklaces, bracelets, and rings. Her shoes were of red leather. Her hair was curled over the forehead. Her nails were pared to a point. Her face was painted with stibium.

The canons drawn up by the Council of 747[23] complain of monks who cross-garter their legs and wear showy clothes like laymen; they admonish nuns* not to go back to their former secular clothing and wear bright things like ordinary girls; nor to waste their time in making many-coloured garments. It is thus evident that the wearing of gay clothes inside the monasteries was more than a passing fashion. Indeed, the letters of Alcuin make it clear that some laxity in these matters was a normal feature of the English Church, since in addition to his reproofs of the Northumbrian clergy† he has even to warn an

* *sanctimoniales.*   † Above, p. 420.

archbishop of Canterbury that the clergy who accompany him
on the journey to Rome should not appear in silks and finery.

Excessive conviviality was another besetting sin of the English.
The canons of 747 insist that there is to be no drinking in monasteries before 'the third hour', that is, nine o'clock, when the
chief meal of the day was taken. Another says that monasteries
must not be the home of poets, musicians, and comedians.[24]
What would we not give to know more about these uncanonical
but genial entertainments?

One of the ways by which worldly delights found an entrance
into the cloister was the use of monasteries as retreats for
kings and for powerful nobles. Sometimes, especially in Northumbria, these withdrawals from the world were forced on public
men by their enemies. Even when they were voluntary, the fire
of devotion might burn feebly. The great man still wanted his
amusements, he found it hard to live for long without his luxuries;
and it was no wonder that other folk copied the example of their
betters. Thus, when King Ceolwulf retired to Lindisfarne in
854, the brethren of this community, who had previously drunk
only milk and water according to the tradition of St. Aidan, were
now allowed to have their wine and beer.[25]

The happy mean between the extremes of asceticism and
luxury was not easily maintained. On the whole, the reformers
did not lose their sense of proportion. Boniface himself did not
drink wine, but he sent two small casks of it to Archbishop
Egbert of York so that he might 'make a joyful day of it with his
brethren';[26] and Alcuin could complain with much indignation
when the monastery's supply of wine failed.

The third feature of the post-Bedan Church which should be remembered is its pursuit of wealth. The denunciations of this vice,
the sin of Ananias and Sapphira, was the main theme of Bede's
letter to Egbert of York. The fact that the subject becomes less
prominent in the canons and letters of the next period betokens
the blunting of men's sensibility rather than the disappearance of the evil. The spirit of Cuthbert, with its indifference to

the things of this world, faded. The spirit of Wilfrid gained ground. The acquisition of new endowments for a church or monastery came to be regarded as a *summum bonum*. Circumstances were favourable. Good men gave their gifts with the intention of forwarding religion. Bad men bequeathed them in the hope of avoiding eternal punishment in the fires of hell.

LEARNING—THE ARTS—POETRY

To correct any over-emphasis on the endowment-hunting of the monasteries let us turn to their encouragement of learning, literature, and the arts—directions in which the monks had produced their best work in the days of Theodore and Bede.

First, with regard to learning: did the schools attached to the cathedral churches and monasteries fail to pass on from one generation to another the knowledge of letters which had been introduced from abroad by the pioneers? The answer to this question follows on similar lines to those of answers already given in this chapter. We find the synod of 747 lamenting the evils of the time. It exhorts bishops and abbots to encourage the love of reading in their *familiae*.[27] 'It is sad that very few are to be found in these days who have a real love of sacred knowledge. Instead of learning, they are from childhood taken up with all kinds of vanities.' The remedy proposed was that boys should be compelled to go to school and should there be kept at work so that the Church should have a supply of learned men. The fact that the bishops assembled in Council were so much concerned with the problem of maintaining a supply of educated clergy is more remarkable than the complaint about the decay of knowledge. After all, the England of 747 was to all intents the England of Bede. We know enough about the period to say that the traditions of learning were still maintained. Criticism was, here as elsewhere, a sign of health as well as of disease: in part, also, it was a habit. It was easy for venerable ecclesiastics to lament the follies of the young.

And so again at the end of the century it was easy for Alcuin, the old man writing amid the enthusiasm of the Carolingian renaissance, to take up the cry and find much to criticize in the English Church which he had forsaken. He naturally complained that scholarship was disappearing, and that almost all men were following secular vanities.[28] The students must be kept at their books, he wrote; they must not spend their time in fox-hunting, nor wear ostentatious clothes. But because Alcuin had his moods of depression, it must not be assumed that there was on the average less learning at the end of the eighth century than at the beginning. His earlier Latin poem,[29] celebrating the merits of the bishops of York, is excellent evidence of the varied education carried on by a cathedral school in those times. He makes it clear that the students were led through the subjects of the *trivium* (grammar, rhetoric, and logic) to those of the *quadrivium* (arithmetic, geometry, music, and astronomy). Works of Aristotle, Cicero, Virgil, and Pliny, as well as those of the Christian Fathers were in the library at York. The boys not only read Virgil, but they were encouraged to write Latin verses themselves.

So far as York is concerned, there is thus evidence of growth rather than of decay after the time of Bede. We owe this evidence to the fact that Alcuin, in migrating from York to the court of Charlemagne, took with him his poems. Save for this happy chance we should have known no more about the school of York than about the other cathedral schools which disappeared without leaving any record behind them. There are, however, sufficient traces of learning at Worcester from the seventh to the ninth century to indicate that the school of York was not without its rivals. The Abbess Cuthswitha (690–700) owned a manuscript of Jerome and Ecclesiastes. In the later eighth century Milret, bishop of Worcester (743–75), was a correspondent of Bishop Lull. The subsequent survival of letters has to be inferred from the help given to Alfred by Werferth, bishop of Worcester (873–915), and from the fact that very many of the surviving manuscripts of Old English, besides one in Latin, seem to have been copied in the Worcestershire area. It is quite possible that learning at York continued to thrive for two generations after Alcuin, that is, until the city was taken by the Danes in 866. The destruction which followed in the period of Danish ascendancy was sufficiently complete to put an end to culture in the north of England and obliterate the evidences of its former existence. In short, the destroying blight of the Vikings is a certainty; the internal decay which is said to have preceded it is largely, though not wholly, an assumption.

When we come to the art of the period after Bede, it is harder to construct clear schemes of development. What cannot be gainsaid is that everywhere, and especially among the Northumbrians, the upright stone cross remained the form of art on which people's ingenuity was specially expended.* On many estates it was still the custom to have a cross beneath which the itinerant clergy would preach, in default of a church. Other crosses were set up to commemorate events; but most of them were no doubt memorials to the dead. The Anglo-Saxons, having originally taken the idea from the Celts, now led the way. If their crosses rarely reach the high standard of those at Ruthwell and Bewcastle, they display an extraordinary fertility of invention, and at times a power of representing men and animals which distinguishes them from the Celtic crosses both of Britain and of Ireland. Some idea of their variety may be obtained from the following illustrations.[30]

Experts are never likely to agree about the dates at which particular crosses were produced. The nearest approach to a well-authenticated date is given by 'Acca's Cross' (Fig. 56) at Durham. Since there are good reasons for thinking that it was originally placed at the head of the grave of Acca, bishop of Hexham and patron of Bede, it may be assigned to about the year 740. If its harmonious design is, as some maintain, too good to be native work, one may suppose[31] that there was a fresh

* See above, pp. 362–4.

FIG. 56. Acca's Cross from Hexham. About 740.
(Now at Durham.)

introduction of foreign craftsmen long after the first foreigners, brought by Wilfrid and others, had initiated this art.

In the fragments from Abercorn and from Easby (Pl. 54) we have examples of what was produced while the Anglian stone sculptors were still in their prime. In the cross at Ilkley (Fig. 57) we see the beauty of the original vine-pattern marred by heavy double or triple coils, or barbarously broken. The sculptors are ceasing to study nature. The animals which feed on the vine (now known as 'Anglian Beasts') are becoming increasingly strange. Their limbs and tails are being prolonged and twisted uncomfortably, so that the animals themselves become little more than part of an interlace. There is an increasing love of whatever is monstrous. A new prominence is given to the emblems of the Evangelists. There is a growing failure to portray the human figure.

In other directions also decline is perceptible in Northumbrian culture. The Lindisfarne tradition of illumination became feeble in the middle of the eighth century. Then, too, the art of glass-making introduced by Wilfrid and Biscop was lost. A pupil of Bede had to beg that a German craftsman should be sent to Wearmouth–Jarrow for its revival.

When we turn to the south of the Humber, though we find nothing approaching the mastery and inspiration of Northumbria in its best days, some works appear which have a place in the history of art. Many interesting stone carvings in Mercia, produced it seems in or about the age of Offa, have only been recognized as of that date in the last few years. It is possible now to say with some confidence that the so-called Hedda's Stone in Peterborough Cathedral, once assigned to the twelfth century, and friezes and carved stones in the churches of Breedon (Leicestershire) (Pl. 55), of Fletton (Hunts.), and of Castor (Northants), are productions of the period before the invasion of the Danes. These show that here in Mercia there was advance rather than decline, and that there were sculptors who could catch some faint reflection of classic grace, and combine with it

PLATE 54

Easby Abbey, cross-shaft
About the beginning of the eighth century

Abercorn, cross-shaft
Late seventh century

ANGLIAN SCULPTURE

PLATE 55

Sections of frieze; men picking grapes; cocks and falcons

Panel, angel giving blessing in the Greek manner

MERCIAN SCULPTURE OF LATE EIGHTH CENTURY
FROM THE CHURCH OF BREEDON, LEICESTERSHIRE

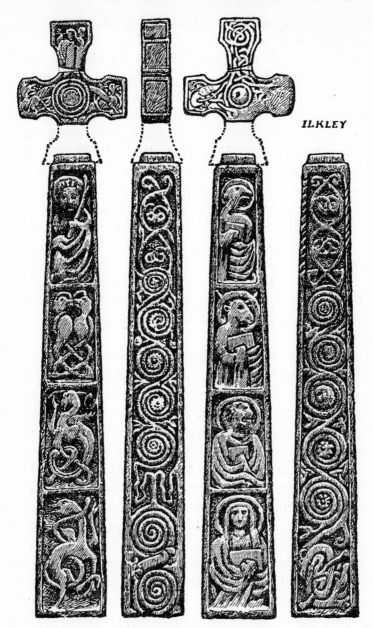

ILKLEY

FIG. 57. Ilkley Cross. Late 8th or 9th century.

studies of everyday objects, such as the Mercian troopers figured on page 415.[32]

Kent, however, is the part of England which may claim to have again taken the lead in art. Kentishmen had proved their unsurpassed skill as jewellers and goldsmiths in the last days of heathenism, when the dead were buried with all their finery. Now, a century and a half later, we find Kentish art re-emerging in a new form. The 'Vespasian Psalter' (Pl. 56) borrows many of its tricks of style from Frankish illuminators, but the artist is not a mere copyist. He has an idea. He says to himself: let us have a really cheerful scene. The Psalmist shall be enthroned with scribes on either hand, ready to write down his poems as the inspiration comes; and in front we must have men making a joyful noise unto the Lord. At Canterbury we know how to enjoy life. 'Too much so,' says Archbishop Wulfred some years later in his compact with his *familia*;* 'you must promise that in future there shall be less conviviality and more communal austerity.'

Art experts are chiefly concerned with pointing out how composite was the style of the Canterbury illuminators. On the whole the borrowings from the Northumbrians and the Irish are less than those from the Franks. We have here another reminder that Kent was in closer contact with the Continent than with the distant lands beyond the Humber. Between the northerners and the Kentishmen lay some two hundred miles of Mercian forest and fen. The art of Canterbury, though it never either early or late reached the heights of Northumbrian achievement, was to be more enduring. We shall find it reappearing in the art of Dunstan's age.

Wessex, even the Wessex of Egbert's dynasty, fails to display any remarkable superiority in the realm of art. None the less, a definite 'southern English' style is recognized in the few objects of the ninth century which have chanced to survive—such as the royal finger-rings† and the ornaments from Trewhiddle.

* Above 428. Cf. note, p. 711.   † See Coloured Plate IV.

PLATE 56

David, with a halo, playing the harp, and attendants

(From the Vespasian Psalter, Cotton MS. Vespasian A. I). ¾
End of the eighth century

PLATE 57

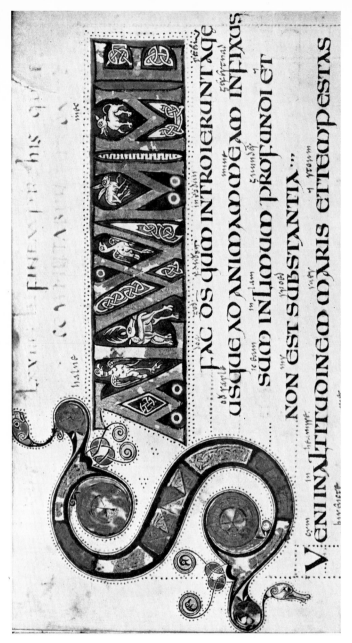

Salvum Me from the Vespasian Psalter. $\frac{1}{1}$

The chief feature of this style is that the design is broken up into panels, each panel containing its own *motif*, such as a *patinette*, an animal, or some knot-work. The style is not a strong one. It may perhaps be taken to symbolize the England which emerged from the reign of Egbert, an England broken up into separate kingdoms, not altogether lacking a sense of har-

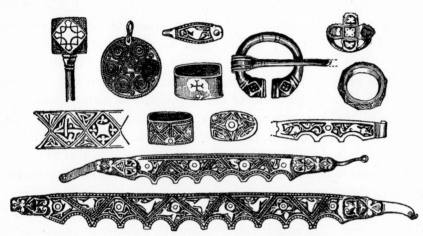

FIG. 58. Ornaments from Trewhiddle. (⅓.)

mony, but badly needing the spirit of a great master to put new vigour and unity into the design.

Thus, looking back on the art of the period, if the latest theories stand the test of time we have found evidence for three conclusions: first, that while there was growing barbarism in Northumbria, the degradation was local rather than universal, only becoming marked towards the middle of the ninth century; secondly, that Mercia and Kent in the eighth century, thanks no doubt to the strong rule of Ethelbald and Offa, blossomed out handsomely, each in its own way; and finally, that the ninth-century Wessex which gave birth to Alfred inherited artistic traditions of some merit.

The theory of eighth-century degeneracy can probably be rebutted better from the poetry than from the art of the period.

But though no subject has been studied more deeply than Old English poetry, on no subject is there more uncertainty. The one well-attested fact is Bede's well-known story about the herdsman Cædmon. This story, with its account of the custom according to which the harp was passed round from hand to hand after dinner, 'when it was agreed to make merry by singing in turn', shows how general was the making and singing of verses. Cædmon's sudden 'gift of song' was thus only the beginning of *Christian* poetry in England. In a sense it was the end rather than the beginning of popular poetry, for the new model of versified Bible and Saints' stories dammed rather than set flowing the inspiration of the people. The songs about the heroes of the heathen age, those for instance enumerated in *Widsith*, were to cease. Didactic poetry with little originality was to take their place. Henceforth the poets' aim was like that of Cædmon 'to draw men away from the love of sin and to excite in them devotion to well-doing'.

Of Cædmon's own composition we probably have no more than the few lines which came to him by angelic inspiration on the night when he discovered his gift—the lines given by Bede beginning:

> Now should we praise the Guardian of the realm of heaven,
> The Creator's might and his mind's wisdom,
> (And the) works of the glorious Father. . . .*

In the fifty years or so which elapsed between this incident and Bede's writing of his History, none of the Englishmen who attempted to compose religious poems were able (in Bede's opinion) to equal the herdsman of Streanæshalch. But Bede's opinion was here biased by the fact that Cædmon had learnt the art of poetry, not of man, but of God. It may well be that

---

 * This in the oldest (early eighth century) Northumbrian version runs:
> Nu scylun hergan hefænricæs uard
> metudæs mæcti end his modgidanc
> uerc uuldurfadur . . . .

much of the best Old English poetry which has come down to us was also composed in that Golden Age of Christian England.

The only other Anglo-Saxon poet who can be distinguished is Cynewulf, and of him we know little more than his name—the name which he has 'buried', introducing it in runes into four of his poems. These poems are all strongly religious. One, entitled *The Christ*, deals in the part authenticated by his signature, that is with the Ascension. Another is about the *Fates of the Apostles*, the other two about heroines of the Church, the martyr *Juliana*, and *Elene* (the Empress Helena, mother of Constantine, who discovered the True Cross in the Holy Land). The internal evidence of his writings does not throw much light on Cynewulf the man: it only shows that he was a well-educated ecclesiastic. The poems chance to be preserved in the West-Saxon dialect; but probably they were first written in Anglian and the poet himself was either a Northumbrian or a Mercian. There is now almost a consensus of opinion that he flourished in the latter half of the eighth or early in the ninth century.[33]

The controversies which have raged round Cynewulf need not detain us. Here we have only to recognize the fact that this literature in the native tongue grew to its greatest abundance about the eighth century. It is not to the taste of the modern age. But even those who find its moralizings stale and unpalatable will admit that for its century it was a great achievement—one which cannot be paralleled in any continental country. To all appearances the stream of this poetry continued to flow right down to the coming of the great armies of the Danes. Some passages will be quoted in the next chapter which even in translation may convey an idea of this most characteristic product of Anglo-Saxon Christianity.

It is obvious, therefore, that the century which followed Bede was far from being a period of unrelieved gloom. Decline indeed there was in certain respects; decline was inevitable. It was natural that there should be reaction after elation. The ardour of the first age could not be retained permanently at white heat. In that first age religion had burnt fiercely, being concentrated in a chosen few. The mass of men had accepted Christianity to please the king or to do what others were doing. In the eighth century saints gave place to reformers. The reformers were, like the saints, a select few. Their work was less spectacular. They lacked a Bede to tell their story. They themselves were not free from blame. Their zeal was not enough to be infectious, as it was in the tenth century. They formed no party. Their results were not impressive. At the end of the period the Church was as much as, perhaps more than, ever weakened by its three ailments—the influence of the laity, the worldly ways of individual clergy, and the general pursuit of wealth. None the less, the age had not been one of mere decay. The Church was still perfecting its machinery. Good men were drawing up their Penitentials. The clergy were drilling the ranks of the laity.

TAILPIECE.—['Kap. quarto. consideravimus decreta; Ut habeat unusquisque Episcoporum potestatem in sua propria diocesi abbatem vel abbatissam eligere, et hoc cum consensu et consultu familiae . . .'] Part of an Act of the Council of Bishops held at 'Celichyth', 816. [Cotton MS. Vespasian A. xiv, f. 150, 11th century.]

XII

THE RESULTS OF CHRISTIANITY

RELATIONS WITH ROME

IN this chapter we change our point of view. We shall now make a wider survey of Christian England and compare the new society with that which went before.

What we now want to see is, how far the Conversion had undone or qualified the results of the Saxon Conquest. How far had the island been reclaimed for civilization and rescued from barbarism? Had the clergy of the Roman Church really won back for the Roman world the province which had been evacuated by the imperial army in the fifth century? Was Britain effectively re-subjected to Rome? Were Germanic conceptions of life dominated by Latin? In short, how deeply did the changes introduced by Christianity penetrate into English society? Such are the general questions which we are to keep before us in the following chapter. What information can be collected by way of answer will be arranged under three more definite headings: the relations of the Church in England with Rome; the relations of the Church to the State; and the attitude of the people to the new religion, as it appears in early Anglo-Saxon literature.

First, then, in the story of the relations with Rome one clear

HEADPIECE.—*Left*, Coenwulf, King of the Mercians, 796–821. *Right*, Wulfred, Archbishop of Canterbury, 805–32, opponent of Coenwulf.

fact stands out in all periods: from the first almost to the last, the Anglo-Saxons were pre-eminent among the converted barbarians in their affection for the Papacy. The feeling had originated in gratitude to Pope Gregory for planning the mission to Britain. The English realized that the emissaries of Rome had not been moved by motives of conquest. When St. Augustine told Ethelbert that he had come to assure to all everlasting joys in heaven, he was speaking the truth without dissimulation. These missionaries were not an advanced guard, opening the way for commerce and political influence. There was no conscious imperialism.

Thus, during the first generation, the Papacy tended its nurseling as modern missionary societies have controlled their mission fields. In the second generation came the clash between the Roman party and the Celtic. This in the end helped to stimulate the devotion to the Papacy, and encouraged the new fashion, first set by Benedict Biscop and Wilfrid, of pilgrimage to Rome itself. In the third generation the link was strengthened by the arrival of Archbishop Theodore and Abbot Hadrian. The spirit of partisanship, fed by the excessive zeal of Wilfrid, did for a time produce a reaction among his enemies. When Wilfrid proclaimed that he fled to the Roman See as to 'a fortress', 'as to our Mother's bosom', King Aldfrith of Northumbria asserted that as long as he lived he would never change because of orders sent from Rome.[1] At this time Wilfrid's ultramontanism drove even Theodore into a certain insularity.

The eighth century in this as in other directions was an age of adjustment. Bede's attitude to Rome may be taken as typical. His loyalty was unquestioned. It is Bede who tells[2] of the blessedness of King Cædwalla, who died at Rome, and of Ine, who journeyed to the neighbourhood of the holy places that he might 'obtain to be more readily received into the fellowship of the saints in heaven'; and it is Bede who commends the zeal of the 'many other Englishmen, nobles and commons, laity and clergy, men and women', who followed their example.

Bede's reverence for Rome was partly based on a knowledge of the ancient majesty of the imperial city. To him, and to the few Englishmen who like him had been brought up on Virgil and patristic literature, Rome was charged with the traditions of the Empire as well as of the Papacy. But for most men in these ages, Rome was almost synonymous with St. Peter. To be near St. Peter at the Resurrection was to be near the Key-bearer of heaven. It was the best possible position for the Judgement Day. Spiritual things were conceived in material ways. St. Peter lived in his shrine, as the northern dead continued to live in their burial mounds. Rome thus drew men to itself as the gate of heaven.

And it had other attractions. It was a store of precious relics. Many of them could be given away by the popes. Others were bought by pilgrims and imported to Britain. The journey to Rome had its perils: the storms of the English Channel, to be dared in an open boat; the threat of robbers along the interminable road through Gaul and Italy; the snow and frost of the Alpine pass. But men and women were sustained by a sense of adventure, as well as by the prospect of reward in the world to come. Then, arrived at Rome, they found themselves in a real city, a maze of narrow streets, over-topped by the vast buildings; the baths and temples of the pagan Empire, as well as the basilicas of Christian times, with their awe-inspiring mosaics and forests of marble columns—a city of marvels, which never ceased to enthral the Englishmen who crowded as pilgrims into their Saxon quarter between St. Peter's and the Tiber.

In the period after Bede the Papacy—stimulated, it may be, by a Boniface or an Alcuin—from time to time woke up to the fact that there were abuses in the English Church which ought to be remedied. It played an important part in bringing about the reforms of 747 and 787; on the first occasion with a letter of encouragement; on the second through its legates. In this same period the creation of the archbishoprics of York and Lichfield, and then the abolition of the latter, are significant but extraordinary examples of papal authority.[2a]

No one now attempted, as Wilfrid had done in an earlier age, to encourage by appeals the active sovereignty of the Papacy over the Church in England. But the connexion was increased in other ways.

The popes had been used to send a vestment called a *pallium* to the archbishops as a symbol of their authority. Now, about the eighth century, the giving of the pallium was regularized; and it became customary to require the metropolitans to come and receive the gift at Rome. Later—in the ninth century—they were forbidden to consecrate until, in return for a formal profession of faith, they had received the pallium. The new system, though it aroused some resentment, was well devised to secure uniformity of faith in the West, and to strengthen the power of the Papacy.

About the eighth century also the Saxon School at Rome was established. This was a military body, formed from the Saxon population resident in Rome, to co-operate in the defence of the City. It possessed a building which seems to have been the head-quarters of the Saxon colony in their 'burh'* near St. Peter's. The School was not unique. There had been similar companies recruited from Greeks and other peoples at Rome, but the Saxons were at any rate the first of the northern barbarians to offer their swords to the successors of St. Peter, in gratitude for the care of their souls.

And this was not all. There is little doubt that the English were foremost in establishing the custom of sending a yearly gift of money to Rome. We have seen† that Offa in 786 vowed to send 365 mancuses every year to St. Peter; and this promise (in spite of contradictory statements in the later Chronicles) may be accepted as the beginning of the payment which came to be known as Peter's Pence, or Rome-feoh. Hitherto, the contributions of the English to the Papacy had been irregular as well as voluntary. Henceforth, especially after the promise had been renewed in a different form by Ethelwulf, the Papacy claimed payment as more of a right.[3]

* Latin *burgus*; hence Italian *borgo*. † Above, pp. 389–91.

These changes in the relationship were naturally followed by some changes in the attitude of the English. There is a letter addressed to a Pope Leo, apparently about 805.[4] In it 'all the bishops and priests of the whole island of Britain' protest against the *ingens labor* of the journey to Rome: they ask that the pallium should be sent to the archbishop elect, and not fetched by him in person, and that it should be given freely, since 'the gift of God was not bought with money'. They even quote the words of St. Peter to Simon, 'Your money perish with you'. This is an unusual tone. It sounds more like the thirteenth century than the Anglo-Saxon period. There can be no doubt that while the old devotion to the Papacy never wavered, it was mingled, as we see later in Canute's letter from Rome, with a certain resentment at papal exactions. From an Irish source we have verses which give expression to some ninth-century disillusionment. 'To go to Rome, much labour, little profit: the King whom thou seekest there, unless thou bring Him with thee, thou findest Him not. Much folly, much frenzy.'[5] But this, it seems, was an Irishman's half-jesting grumble. It was not the Anglo-Saxon point of view.

There were two other developments of the ninth century which produced some changes in the relation between the Papacy and the English—changes in practice rather than in sentiment. One of these was the Danish invasions, which made communication increasingly difficult; the other, becoming apparent towards the end of the century, was the growing chaos at Rome itself. The Papacy then became the sport of factions. The popes, immersed in their own troubles, came to know less and to think less about the English. They almost left the English Church to fend for itself. After the eighth century no more legates were sent to shepherd the English on to the path of reform till the eve of the Norman Conquest. In the later ninth century, as in the fifth century, there was no revolt from Rome. Rome herself became too much distracted by her own feuds to trouble about her distant province.

CHURCH AND STATE

The constitutional results on the English kingdoms produced by the establishment of Christianity must be briefly indicated. The essential effect of the change is obvious: after the coming of St. Augustine there were always round the king bishops and clergy who were better educated than either the king himself or his lay ministers and war-leaders. They were a group who possessed a share in the legal heritage of Rome, and knew something of Roman methods of government. Having access through their education to the accumulated learning of the Mediterranean world, they occupied a position from which they could dominate the king and his thegns. Having a monopoly of the art of writing they could introduce legal methods adapted from those of Rome or Gaul. The union of their Roman ideas with the traditional usages of the Germanic peoples gave birth to what we now call constitutional history. Let us see how the union became fruitful.

In the first place, the clergy needed protection. All the other subjects of the king had their personal money value, their wergeld, fixed by tradition. But tradition could assign no place to intruders like the clergy. In order to fill this gap Ethelbert was encouraged to draw up his Laws and have them recorded in the Roman manner. The king gave the priests when their property was stolen a ninefold compensation, one that was equal to his own.* To a bishop he gave even more, an elevenfold compensation.

In the next place, the clergy had to be supported as well as defended. The difficulty here was that property was held by folk-right. In this sense it was 'folkland': the kinsmen of a landowner had rights of reversion. Therefore a new form of landownership had to be invented, and here the clergy's monopoly of the art of writing again came in useful. 'Landbooks', that is, charters written on parchment, were in time introduced. By

* Above, p. 270.

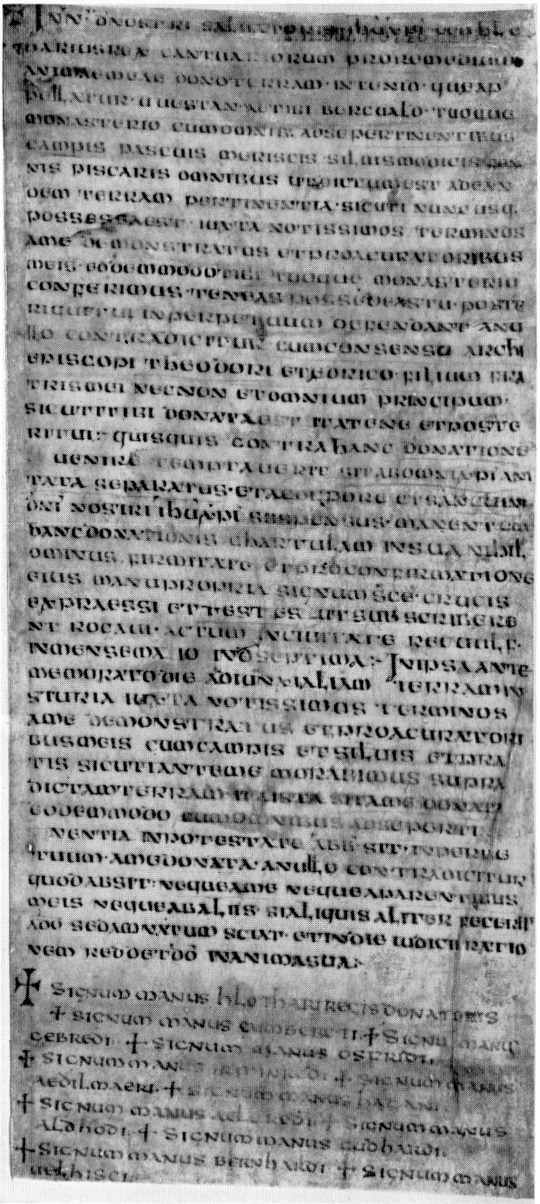

PLATE 58

Charter of Hlothere, King of Kent

A.D. 679. In mixed uncial and capital characters. About ½
(This charter was probably bound up with the Utrecht
Psalter. Why and when this was done is disputed)

The landbook, or charter, reproduced on Pl. 58 (a grant by Hlothere, or Hlothar, king of Kent, to Abbot Bercuald of land in Thanet and Sturry), is probably the oldest original English charter extant. It may be analysed as follows:

In nomine domini nostri salvatoris Jhesu Christi. [This is the Invocation.] Ego HLOTHARIUS rex Cantuariorum pro remedium animae meae ['The saving of his soul' gives the motive of the grant. It is the Proem.] dono terram · in Tenid [Thanet] · quae appellatur UUESTAN · AE tibi Bercuald · tuoque monasterio cum omnibus ad se pertinentibus campis pascuis meriscis · silvis modicis · fonnis piscaris omnibus ut dictum est ad eandem terram pertinentia · sicuti nunc usque possessa est · juxta notissimos terminos a me demonstratus et proacuratoribus meis · eodem modo tibi tuoque monasterio conferimus · teneas possedeas tu posterique tui in perpetuum defendant a nullo contradicitur · cum consensu archiepiscopi Theodori et Edrico · filium fratris mei necnon et omnium principum · sicuti tibi donata est ita tene et posteri tui: [All this long rambling and ungrammatical sentence is the Grant, the important part of the Charter.] quisquis contra hanc donationem venire temptaverit sit ab omni Christianitata separatus · et a corpore et sanguini domini nostri Jhesu Christi suspensus · [This section is the Sanction. In A.S. charters the threat of ecclesiastical punishments in this world and hell-fire in the next is considered sufficient.] manentem hanc donationis chartulam in sua nihilominus firmitate et pro confirmatione ejus manu propria signum sanctæ crucis expraessi et testes ut subscriberent rogavi · actum in civitate Recuulf [Reculver] · in mense maio indictione septima: [This last clause containing the Date is unsatisfactory because the practice of dating from the Christian Era was not introduced till the time of Bede.]

[The Charter then describes in six lines another grant of lands in Sturry, and ends with twelve crosses of the king and his witnesses.]

✠ signum manus Hlothari regis donatoris
✠ signum manus Gumbercti:

. . . .

[It should be noticed that the document says nothing about any immunity from secular burdens, since clauses of this kind were only introduced towards the end of the eighth century. In this case, the monks on their own account made good the defect by adding in a later century the words which had then become the customary limitation on general immunity, *exceptis his tribus, expeditione, pontis et arcis constructione*. (See W. H. Stevenson, in *E.H.R.* xxix (1914), 689–703.) Another interesting point about the charter is that, though now in a Cottonian volume of charters (Augustus ii. 2), it was at one time bound up with the Utrecht Psalter.]

them with the formal consent of the king and of the witan, that is, by an act of State, the old folk-rights could be overridden (except for the rights of a son, which were sometimes upheld when his consent to the grant had not been obtained).[6] The clergy, who copied continental models, introduced these charters in the days of Archbishop Theodore, if not earlier. They stiffened them with their anathemas, and intimidated any who might attempt to violate the donation with threats of the Day of Judgement.

The introduction of the landbook was a turning-point in the history of English society, and in a later chapter we shall see how it led to the formation of big estates and to various further consequences.

It was not only from motives of self-preservation that the clergy were anxious to introduce written laws and written landbooks. From every point of view they were interested in helping the secular rulers to maintain peace and justice and develop the authority of the monarchy which alone could save a primitive people from anarchy.

And so the close partnership between the monarchy and the Church which had been formed in the first days of the Conversion was never dissolved. The king obviously had as much to gain from this partnership as the clergy. He secured in them well-educated advisers and trained ministers. Their influence inevitably raised the monarchy to a new dignity. Hitherto, in the old rough and tumble of Teutonic heathenism, the power of the king had rested partly on custom, partly on a claim to descend from Woden, and above all on force. Now after the Conversion the Church crowned the king with a diadem, consecrated him with solemn rites, anointed him with holy oil, and in its coronation service prayed that God 'who prepared the Roman empire' would give the King the heavenly armour of justice so that the peace of the Church might not be broken by any times of trouble.

It was inevitable that the clergy, inheriting both in their literature and in the organization of the papal Church the tradi-

tions of Roman imperialism, should transfer some of these traditions to the barbarian monarchies. It was the kings who had
taken the lead in the Conversion: it was the kings who continued
to be the most generous patrons of the clergy. In return, the
clergy taught them how to organize their governments, and how
to assess and levy tribute in an imperial way.

While the framework of the State remained Germanic, every
institution, like the monarchy itself, began to appear in a new
light. The councillors whom the king gathered round him, his
witan, now tended to be dominated by the great ecclesiastics.
The king's permanent household also had its mass-priests as well
as its secular thegns. They were needed to draft laws and
charters, they were needed to supervise the king's finance, and
even from early times they seem to have been entrusted with the
education of young nobles attached to the court. Similarly in
less exalted spheres, when the shires emerge as the co-ordinated
centres of local government, we find the bishops taking their
places by the side of the ealdormen, and the lower clergy also
playing a part in the maintenance of justice. It is they who
operate the Judgement of God by ordeal. They lead the accused
to church, they adjure the Deity to perform his part in dis-
tinguishing the guilty from the innocent, they sprinkle holy
water to assist the process; it is in their church that the fire for
the ordeal is lighted and it is across the floor of the church for
nine feet that the hot iron must be carried.

So we see that the clergy were all-pervasive in the State.
Their influence on the growing kingdoms was indirect as well as
direct. The kings learned from Archbishop Theodore ideals of
union more profitable than those suggested by the short-lived
conquests of Edwin or Oswy. Theodore's Church councils
gathered from all the English kingdoms, and Theodore's laws,
passed in those councils for the whole English Church, prepared
men for the conception of a united England.

In few countries, if in any, has the co-operation between State
and Church been more harmonious, more prolonged, and on the

whole more fruitful than in England during the four and a half
centuries between the coming of Augustine and the Norman
Conquest. The long series of laws from Ethelbert to Canute are
the best evidence to the success of the partnership. The kings in
these laws consistently protect the clergy and their privileges,
their rights of sanctuary and the dues of the Church; and they
do more than this—they enforce with positive commands the
Christian ideal. Breaches of the moral code, work on Sunday,
neglect of fasting, failure to baptize a child within thirty days of
its birth—such things are punished as offences against the State.

One last question: how was it that kings and bishops supported
one another so long and so harmoniously? Was it due to an
enlightened recognition of the fact that their interests were inter-
dependent? Was it due to what those who decry the Anglo-
Saxons call sluggishness but what, with more charity, we may
call their spirit of forbearance? Did it mean that the Church
had to compromise with the world and sacrifice some of its
proper independence? There is no doubt some truth in each
of these explanations. Thus, the Church cannot be altogether
acquitted of accommodating its ideals with respect to slavery.
Individual churchmen like Wilfrid sometimes set free their slaves,
but the Church as a whole did not condemn slavery or the slave
trade; it contented itself with trying to mitigate some of its hardships. A lord who whipped a slave to death was to be excom-
municated; if he made a slave work on a Sunday he was to have
some minor punishment.

But there was compromise on the side of the State as well as
on that of the Church. Especially in the earlier periods kings
allowed land passing to the Church to be wholly exempt from
the performance of secular duties which, as Bede complained,
were essential to the prosperity of the State. Later—certainly
from the eighth century—the burdens, to which every one was
liable, the famous *trimoda* * *necessitas*, were enforced more rigor-
ously. But none the less the State suffered, as Bede said; and

---

* Stevenson, op. cit., has shown that this is the right reading, not *trinoda*.

the wide alienation of land to the churchmen may reasonably
be numbered among the causes of England's failure when confronted by the Danes.

As usual, however, generalizations are deceitful. 'Harmony
between Church and State' is a phrase which covers diverse
phenomena in different epochs. Early missionary bishops like
Augustine and Paulinus owed their sway to their holiness, their
personality, their acquaintance with a higher civilization, above
all, to the backing they received from the Papacy. The harmony
between an Aidan and an Oswald was born of the spirit. Later,
as in the cases of Aldhelm and of Egbert of York (732–66), the
bishops were sometimes connected by blood with the monarchy.
In general the harmony was the consequence of the influence
exercised by the kings. The bishops were to all intents appointed
by the kings, and at times removed by them. They were court
chaplains. It is significant that when the Kentishmen in 805
secured the election of Wulfred, a wealthy Kentish landowner,
as archbishop, a long quarrel between him and the Mercian
king, Coenwulf, ensued. This, however, and the earlier imbro-
glio over Wilfrid of York, were almost the only occasions in
Anglo-Saxon history when there was anything like open strife
between Church and State, and the quarrel of the early ninth
century was rather a sequel to Kentish separatism than an
ecclesiastical quarrel of the Norman-Angevin kind. From the
ninth century the danger of a breach was avoided by the supremacy of the House of Egbert, whose kings were often better
churchmen than the bishops themselves.

THE CONVERSION AND OLD ENGLISH LITERATURE

The Christian poetry written in Old English best enables us
to judge how the new religion presented itself to the minds of
ordinary men. Most of the poetry was didactic. Its aim was to
present Christian teaching in such a mode that it might appeal
to the ordinary man, the man on the mead-bench. We have

spoken above of Cædmon, who flourished in the latter half of the seventh century, and of Cynewulf, who is generally placed in the time of Offa or in that of Egbert. Though modern critics as a rule reject many of the works which formerly used to be assigned to these two authors, it is none the less usual to divide the bulk of the Christian poetry between a Cædmonic and a Cynewulfian school. These labels may lead to misconceptions, but they are none the less inevitable, since Cædmon and Cynewulf are the only Anglo-Saxon poets known to us by name. If we use the labels, we must not be misled by them into thinking that all the poems in the style of Cynewulf were later than those in that of Cædmon, or were in fact written under the influence of Cynewulf.

The Cædmonic poems are more appropriately so called, since they do carry out part of the programme ascribed to Cædmon by Bede. They render into English verse certain books of the Old Testament. The task is fulfilled with vigour. The authors only stray from the original narrative in order to make the story more vivid, and to drive it home to their English audiences. Thus in *Genesis* God appears as 'a chief of thegns'. Satan also has his 'strong retainers',* and he can boast that they will not fail him in the fight.⁷ All men have their part in this everlasting war. The whole creation is involved.

This is one way in which the Cædmonic poets attempted to gain the interest of their countrymen. Another is the simple method of stressing and working up the passages in the Old Testament which introduced scenes of battle and conflict. In the *Exodus* poem the heroic stuff of the Cædmonic school can be seen at its best. We have spirited battle narratives, such as the following, which tells of the Egyptian advance against the Israel-ites.⁸ 'The hearts of men lost hope when they saw Pharaoh's fyrd come sweeping on from the south, bearing their shields, the troops gleaming—spears were strong, battle drew nigh, shields shone, trumpets sang—banners reaching aloft, the host treading the road. Birds of prey, greedy for battle, screamed in wheeling

* *geneatas.*

flight over the corpses. The wolves sang their dread evensong in hope of the feasting'—and so forth.

Here then we see the form in which popular Christianity was conveyed to the ordinary Englishman. His attention was turned to the Old Testament rather than the New. He was fed on the spirit of the Old Testament as well as its stories. The new religion was coloured as a new form of warfare, to attract a pugnacious people.

When we turn to the so-called 'school of Cynewulf' we are taken from the Old Testament to the stories of Christ, of His disciples, and of the saints. Many of the characteristics of the Cædmonic school recur. The Anglo-Saxon verse is often no more than a dull paraphrase of some work in Latin prose. There is, for instance, very little that is original in Cynewulf's poem about St. Juliana, the virgin martyr. But while in the Cyne-wulfian poetry the interest is still largely obtained by the old device of spiritual militarism, something more is added. At times a deeper, a more personal note, is heard. It appears, for instance, in the account of himself which Cynewulf inserts at the end of his poem the *Elene*, before he buries his name in runes in the text.[9]

'Thus I, old and near my death through the body's frailty, have woven with skill in words and gathered wondrously, often pondering and arranging my thoughts with travail in the night. I knew not fully the truth about the Cross. . . . I was sullied by my deeds, fettered in sins, afflicted by sorrows, bound in bitterness, oppressed by cares, until in glorious wise the radiant King of Might gave me knowledge, a per-fect gift, as a comfort to my age. . . . He unfettered my heart, unlocked the power of song, which I have gladly and joyously used in the world. Not once but often I had thoughts of the Tree of Glory before I dis-covered the wonder of the bright Cross, as, in the course of things, I found it written in books about the Sign of Victory. Till then the man was buffeted by cares, *Cēn* [A torch, the name of the rune ᚳ=C] was losing his strength, although he received precious gifts of bossed gold in the mead-hall. . . .'

And so he goes on to spell out his name in runes. In this and some similar passages we see that the personal note of which we spoke is one of Conversion. Turbid gloom is turned by the Cross into song and joy. We have here an Anglo-Saxon parallel to the sudden 'conversions' of the modern English, those of the Puritans and the Evangelicals.

Once more as in *Beowulf* the kinship between the latter-day Englishman and his early ancestors is manifest. The spirit of Cynewulf is essentially similar to that of Bunyan. The Christian is conscious of the heavy burden of his sins. He turns his back on the worldliness of his youth, and his face to the Cross or to the Heavenly City. It is in the magic of the Cross, the Sacred Tree, that the difference between the Saxon and the Puritan appears. We may call it an accidental difference, but it is none the less pronounced. Let us recall the *Vision of the Rood*, the later development of the poem carved on the Ruthwell Cross.[10]

'Lo! I will declare the best of visions which came to me in the middle of the night, when human creatures lay at rest. It seemed to me that I saw a wondrous tree rising aloft, encompassed with light, the brightest of crosses. All that sign was overlaid with gold; fair jewels were set at the surface of the earth; there were also five upon the cross-beam.

.   .   .   .

'I was all troubled with sorrows; I was full of fear at the fair sight. I saw the changeful sign alter in garments and colours; at times it was bedewed with moisture, stained with the flowing of blood, at times adorned with treasure.

'Yet I, lying there a long space, beheld in sorrow the Saviour's cross, till I heard it speak. Then the most excellent tree began to utter words:

' "Long ago . . . I was cut down at the edge of the forest. . . . Men bore me on their shoulders there, till they set me on a hill; many foes made me fast there. I saw then the Lord of mankind hasten with great zeal that He might be raised upon me. Then I durst not there bow or break against the Lord's behest, when I saw the surface of the earth shake; I could have felled all the foes, yet I stood firm. . . ." '

The magic of this Tree is something other than that of the battle Cross of St. Oswald, with its wonder-working qualities.

The Tree of *The Vision* is animated. It feels, it suffers. In this heroic poetry the Cross as well as the Crucified is the hero. The Anglo-Saxon's devotion to the Sacred Tree was admittedly in part primitive and animistic, but it was much more than that. It was Teutonic, redolent of the vast forests which had been the home and defence of the ancient Germans. It was English, clouded with sombre thought. But it was also Christian; it was orthodox and Catholic—the fruit of an age when controversy between iconoclasts and iconodules raised the Cross to new reverence as the one undisputed emblem of the Christian world.

We may bring this survey to a point by comparing the attitude of the Cynewulfian poems with that of the *Beowulf* epic. Though the last is half-way to Christianity there is, as we have seen, enough of the heathen atmosphere in it for a contrast to be yielded between the ideas of the heathen and those of the converted Anglo-Saxons. In Beowulf's world, stress is laid on the material rewards of heroic action, on the winning of gold and choice weapons, on wide dominions and plenty.[11] In the *Christ* Cynewulf emphasizes the spiritual rewards of men: eloquence, wisdom, knowledge of the law of God, the skill of the harpist, of the writer, of the seaman, of the smith—these are the gifts which 'God's spiritual son' bestows on his followers.[12]

The contrast which has become so commonplace in the course of centuries came home to the contemporaries of Cædmon and Cynewulf with the force of novelty and paradox. Perhaps the way in which we can best appreciate its novelty is to see once more how much of the old view of life—conceptions of worldly success and physical heroism—still clung even to the poetry of the Cynewulfian school. Let us therefore glance for a few minutes at the *Andreas*, a poem near enough in style to the signed poems of Cynewulf to have been in the past attributed to that author.[13] The poem well illustrates the resemblance between a typical Christian legend, as prepared for popular consumption, and the Beowulf story, compounded from the traditions of heathen society. The legend of the *Andreas* is derived ultimately

from a Greek romance (and immediately from a Latin translation which survives only in parts). The parallelism between the
Anglo-Saxon poem and the Beowulf story may well be deliberate.
The enemy is now man-eating Myrmidonians, not a man-eating
monster. They have seized and imprisoned St. Matthew. But
the apostles were 'twelve glorious heroes, thegns of the Lord. . . .
Their majesty failed not in fight when banners clashed together,
after they had disbanded. They were men renowned on earth,
eager leaders and active in *fyrd*, bold warriors.' And so God
directs Andrew to go and rescue Matthew, and, like a good thegn
in the spirit of the *comitatus*, he obeys. God Himself (apparently
the Second rather than the First Person of the Trinity) comes
down from Heaven, like an Odin or a Hermes, to help His
followers. He comes disguised as a steersman of the ship which
is to carry Andrew with his two thegns to the land of the Myrmidonians. The poet dwells on the bargaining which takes place
before the ship is chartered, and he works up the incidents and
storms of the voyage. The touches added by the Anglo-Saxon
are most characteristic. As in *Beowulf*, we see that the love, or at
any rate the feeling, for the sea, is still strong. 'No skulker in
battle was Andrew, but hard and high-hearted, and eager for
war. Wherefore at opening of day he went over the sand-links
and to the sea-stead, his thegns with him, trampling over the
shingle. The ocean thundered, the billows beat the shore.'[14]
Then, later during the voyage: 'The grey gull wheeled about,
greedy for slaughter; the candle of the sky grew dark, the winds
rose, the waves dashed, floods were fierce, the cordage creaked,
the sails were soaked. The terror of the tempest rose up with the
might of hosts; the thegns were afraid.'[15]

The interest of the story is not so well sustained as in *Beowulf*,
because there is no place for feats of physical strength. The
thegns of Christ are able to overcome their enemy and the other
difficulties which they encounter by the comparatively simple
expedients of prayer and miracle. Andrew and his companions
do not swim like Beowulf for days in the sea. They escape from

the storm by being carried asleep through the air. When it comes to a fight in the land of Myrmidonia, God makes the weapons of the enemy 'melt all away in the battle like wax, so that . . . the horrible foes could do no hurt by the strength of swords'.[16] Thus were the older conceptions of the heathen world diluted with Christian legend—diluted, but not entirely thrown away.

The spiritual distress and exaltation of Cynewulf and of the *Vision of the Rood* were only for the elect. The multitude went on their way clearly little changed. Normal men, with their minds running on sport and the game of war or immersed in the interminable round of the year's work, wanted stories containing as much as possible of the old apparatus about fighting and the sea. They wanted poems of action, whether Christian or pagan. The Christian intelligentzia did their best to supply the demand.

If we wish to find Christianity reduced to its minimum, we must look at the books of the Anglo-Saxon medicine-men. In them it becomes no more than a new form of magic, to be mixed in with the old. The sacraments are welcomed as new spells against the evil spirits. This was inevitable. Woden and Thunor had been overcome by Augustine and Aidan, without much of a fight. But these were the older, the more primitive imaginings, stored deep in the grey matter of men's brains, so deep that they could not be expelled. They might be denounced by the clergy as relics of paganism, but they held their ground, half accepted as 'popular superstitions'. The elves and giants and such-like lived on, sinking perhaps in the social scale of supernatural beings, but still powerful enough to raise all kinds of fears in the minds of rich and poor.

In previous chapters we have dealt so fully with the saints' lives and with many of the finer manifestations of English Christianity, that we shall be justified in touching on this shadier side of the new Christian England. Let us then see how pagan elements were combined with Christian throughout the subsequent Anglo-Saxon period. Many of them need only a passing reference. 'Easter', of course, retained some slight trace of pre-Christian origin, in its name and its eggs. May Day continued to be celebrated with scarcely disguised heathen rites. The 'fertility' spirit was re-captured in each village with the ancient, the primitive, usage. As in heathen times, the country-folk covered themselves with the spring's new greenery, they danced round the green tree, they processed with clamour round the fields—not indeed with the image of a god, but bearing a garland of flowers which could, by confusion with the new religion be called 'Our Lady'; they stormed into the church-yard or the church with their pagan riot, and in the night as in the day there was a resurgence of the primitive instincts of man. The other festivals of the year bear about them much the same patent heathenism. The Rogation-tide of the Church was still known as the 'Gang-days'—the days in which the folk per-ambulated the bounds of their fields in order to call for a blessing upon the fruits of the earth. The Midsummer Fires, the 'Harvest Homes', and the midwinter festivals might be rechristened, but their heathen traditions were again unmistak-able.

Such were the regrettable signs of affection for their old ways displayed by the Anglo-Saxon peasantry. The authorities of the Church protested, but at times they also connived at the survival of heathen customs. Pope Gregory himself had told Augustine, 'It is impossible to cut off everything at once from rude natures'; he had therefore allowed the English to continue for a time their old practice of slaughtering cattle at their feasts. His own *Dialogues* were nothing less than a blend of Christian and pagan traditions. In them he told the faithful how the devil held his court at midnight and reviewed his demons, how the demons had traffic with wizards and witches, and in what manner they gained admission to men's bodies.

The Irish Church also passed on to English Christianity stories and beliefs of pagan origin ascribing to its saints much of the magic which had been the great weapon of their enemies, the Druids. Even the Druids seem to have survived till the seventh century and the poets of the Irish, the *fili*, retained till much later their heathen lore.

When Rome and Ireland, the two great schools to which the English resorted for instruction in their new religion, were thus flooded with pre-Christian thought, it is not to be wondered that the English themselves followed with a good conscience the examples of their masters. Even Bede, the most enlightened of the Anglo-Saxons, accepted without question the notions of the Christian magic which he found all round him. It seemed to him in keeping with the ways of Divinity that those should be healed who dosed themselves with water containing the dust from the ground where the body of St. Oswald had fallen in battle, or containing chips from his cross. Theodore too, the great archbishop, educated though he had been in the school of Athens, was not much better. Englishmen used to quote his opinion that it was dangerous for medical men to bleed patients when the moon is waxing and the tide of the ocean is waning. When ideas such as this were sound learning, it was no wonder that the authorities had difficulty in suppressing the superstitions of the vulgar. But they made the attempt. Theodore in his *Penitential*[17] set his face against spells, soothsayings, and charms in general, and in particular against the custom of placing a daughter upon the roof or over a hearth-fire as a cure for fever.

The attack on the grosser forms of heathenism gathered force throughout the eighth century. The archbishops and the provincial councils legislated against such diabolical customs as soothsayings, spells, the use of amulets, divinations, the eating of horseflesh, the slitting of horses' noses, and the docking of their tails. All such abominations were to be suppressed.[18]

The influence of heathen Scandinavians in the ninth century interrupted these efforts; and the Saxon *Leechbooks* prove that the use of charms and magic continued with little or no abatement.

These books[19] are full of prescriptions which show the uses to which the Christian religion was put in everyday life. The following example is taken from the *Book of Bald* (a work probably composed in the tenth century):[20]

'A drink for a fiend-sick man [i.e a man possessed or lunatic]—When a devil possesses a man or affects him from within with disease . . . a drink to be drunk out of a church bell. Take githrife, yarrow, betony, [and many other herbs, &c.]. Work up the drink with clear ale, sing

seven masses over the worts, add garlic and holy water, and drip the drink into every drink that he shall afterwards drink; and then let him drink it out of a church bell; and let the mass-priest sing this over him after he has drunk it. "Domine, Domine, sancte Pater omnipotens . . ." '—and more of the like.

FIG. 59. A diseased man, molested by the shot of (?) elves.

The *Leechbooks* enable us to see into the minds of the medical experts, and to understand after a fashion what was thought to happen when their Saxon patients fell ill. A man had a fever: it was caused, not by a germ, but by an elf of some kind or other. His eyes became tearful and downcast, and his nails turned livid: it was the 'water-elf disease'. He had a hiccup: the elves were again to blame. A horse, too, if it took ill, was said to be elf-shot. Then, if there was a monster birth or if a man's son became lunatic or got the mumps, these things were the work of the dwarfs. It was not much use asking how these enemies of mankind operated. Dwarfs had their own ways of making themselves invisible, and everybody knew that elves could shoot their minute shafts at a man. And there were little wormlike things which wriggled somehow into a man's skin. There was also the noxious elf-breath, which, being simply wafted into the air, was enough to bring disease with it. There were specific venoms which might attack a man—there were nine of them, nine 'on-flying things', 'the loathed things which run through the land'. These latter ideas have been recognized[21] as characteristics of Germanic thought on these recondite subjects.

The leeches, as the servants of humanity, were ready, for a fee, to assist the suffering with every kind of remedy. The charm for a sudden stabbing pain (probably lumbago) tells us how the wicked women (the witches) were in league with the elves; and how the spears of disease shot into a man by their witchcraft could be outed. It begins as follows:[22]

'For a sudden stabbing pain; take feverfew and the red nettle . . .; boil in butter—(and say):

'Loud were they, lo! loud, when they rode over the hill,
Resolute were they when they came riding over the land,
Fend thyself now, that thou mayest survive this violence!
Out, little spear, if herein thou be!
I stood under my shield, under a bright buckler
Where the mighty women arrayed their power and sent whizzing
    spears;
I will send them back another
Flying arrow in their faces,
Out, little spear, if herein it be! . . .
If it were the shot of gods, or if it were the shot of elves,
Or if it were shot of witch, now I will help thee.
This to relieve thee from shot of gods, this to relieve thee from shot of
    elves,
This to relieve thee from shot of witch; I will help thee.'

The cure which best illustrates the method advocated in these later centuries for binding the powers of Christ mediated through the clergy with the powers of the pre-Christian popular magic, is the recipe for making poor land fertile. The farmer is recommended to cut turves from the land. They were to be sprinkled with holy water. Hallowed soap and hallowed salt were to be placed on the farmer's plough, and he was then to say the half-heathen incantation beginning:[23]

'Erce, Erce, Erce! Mother of Earth,
May the Almighty, the Lord Everlasting, grant thee
Fields growing and flourishing,
Fruitful and reviving
Store of gleaming millet-harvests,
And broad barley-crops,
And white wheat-crops,
And all the crops of the earth.

.   .   .   .

'Then let the plough be driven forth and the first furrow made. Then say:

"Hail to thee, Earth, mother of men!
Be fruitful in God's embrace,
Filled with food for the use of men".'

It concludes with the instruction to 'say thrice: *Crescite, in nomine patris, sitis benedicti. Amen* and *Paternoster* thrice.'

Can we argue on the strength of passages like the above that Christianity was for most men little more than a new charm? Can we say that the Christianity of the ordinary man was represented by these magical formulae and not by the ecstasy of the poet who wrote the *Vision of the Rood*? 'The ordinary man'—there is the difficulty! How hopeless is the quest to seek for his thoughts? Is it not certain that such a Saxon would be unable to give adequate expression in words to the confused ideas of his mind? None the less, it is easy to see that there is one part of the Church's teaching which appealed to all and sundry. It hung like a thick cloud over every man. Its thunder rumbled ominously round every topic in Anglo-Saxon poetry. The Last Judgement and the pains of Hell—this was what Christianity meant for the multitude. Doomsday for all and Hell for the majority. The Northumbrian witan had welcomed Christianity because it promised a solution of man's hitherto unanswered questionings about the Whence and the Whither. The answer of Christianity was both detailed and alarming. The missionaries knew what happened to the sparrow when it flew out of life's hall. In the darkness outside the hall there yawned the mouth of the Whale, vast, cavernous, waiting to swallow the sinner—the entrance to Hell.

The idea fascinated the converted barbarians, and above all

Fig. 60. The Mouth of Hell.

the Anglo-Saxons. The preaching of it had been the easiest line of argument for the missionaries, and the converts responded. A poem *De Die Judicii* is probably Bede's, and he followed it up with authentic visions of the spirit world narrated with peculiar zest. He told how St. Fursey on his way to heaven had had a passing glimpse of the four fires, the four besetting sins, which would one day kindle the world. Drythelm, a simple freemen of Tweeddale, had seen more. He, having died and then come to life, could describe from his own experience the terrible valley of hell, with its flaming fire and freezing cold. The memory of that sight so affected him that he made it his custom by way of penance to stand, winter and summer alike, up to his middle in the chilly waters of the Tweed—a good example of the cold water mortification, passed on by the Scots to the Saxons. Boniface also, Apostle of the Germans, had a story of an Englishman, a monk of Wenlock, who, like Drythelm, died and came to life again; and who, in addition to beholding the horrifying spectacle of hell, heard from the lowest pit the awful weeping and wailing; heard too (as he confidently asserted) enraged demons clamouring for the soul of the then reigning king of Mercia.

The poets who composed in the Saxon language improved on the efforts of their countrymen who had written in Latin. Descriptions of hell and, with less emphasis, of heaven were obtruded at every turn. When the subject is a paraphrase of Genesis, the poet sees an opening for a description of Satan with his fallen angels; and his poem (*Genesis 'B'*), based though it is on an 'Old Saxon' original, is remarkable for its anticipation of much in Milton's *Paradise Lost*. When Cynewulf writes about Christ, some one tacks onto his poem another almost equally long about the Doomsday and the horrors of hell. In other poems[24] a northerner's frost and east wind are added to the fire, and the teeth of the damned are made to chatter; or the soul in anguish is allowed to return once a week for three hundred years to upbraid the dust of its body. 'What wilt thou say to the Lord on the Day of Judgement? . . . What shall we twain do when He has made us to be born once again?'

Here plainly we see the changes brought about in the minds of the Anglo-Saxon people by the teaching of the seventh and eighth centuries. A few generations back the ancestors of these poets had been burying with their dead kinsmen the weapons, jewellery, work-boxes, or whatever possessions had been most treasured in life. Now, under Christianity, much of the old heathen mentality survives; the corpse is still thought to retain its individuality, and the result is this notion, more Teutonic than orthodox, that when the trump of Doomsday sounds, the resurrection of the body may bring a curse to its former occupant, the unhappy soul.

Thus for many men the part of the Christian theology which remained vivid and alive was the doctrine of hell.

There is, of course, another side to the picture. The hopes of eternal bliss which came with Christianity, though heavily overlaid by the fears of eternal damnation, were never completely smothered. In Old English poetry, heaven reappears almost as often, though not with the same elaboration, as hell. It is a glorious city, filled with light. At times it is a Teutonic heaven:

FIG. 61.   Agriculture.

a home with spreading fields and roses; or a hall of the Prince of Victory, where his followers may feast. Even for those who could only conceive of heaven in terms of everyday material life, the new religion offered through repentance and penance a hope of bliss.

Lastly, we must not forget the material alleviations which came to the English along with Christianity. The clergy added in manifold ways to the lesser comforts of men. Their wax candles could be used for the illumination of a room as well as of a church altar. The cultivation of fruits and vegetables was improved. Condiments like pepper were imported. In scores of small and unrecorded ways the life of the Anglo-Saxons after the Conversion became more varied.

Yet when all is reckoned up so small were the beginnings of these new departures in civilization that we should not be far from the truth if we argued that the life of most laymen went on almost unchanged. The villages were so scattered, the parish churches were comparatively so few, that masses of the people must have remained to all intents untouched either by the material or the spiritual principles of Christianity. They laboured at the plough, they felled their clearings in the forest, they hunted or fought, just as they had done before the coming of St. Augustine, as oblivious to the new candles and condiments as to the new terrors of hell.

XIII

THE VIKINGS[1]

FIRST RAIDS

'ANNO 793.[2] This year terrible portents came over the land of the Northumbrians and miserably frightened the people. These were exceptional high winds and flashes of lightning; and fiery dragons were seen flying in the air. A great famine soon followed these signs; and a little after that in the same year on the sixth of the Ides of June* the harrying of heathen men miserably destroyed God's church in Lindisfarne through rapine and slaughter.' The above was the later tradition in the north of England about the first coming of the Vikings.† In the south there was a tradition of a raid on Dorsetshire some time in the reign of King Beorhtric of Wessex (786–802):[3]

'When the pious king Byrhtric was reigning over Wessex and the people scattered innocently about the countryside were devoting themselves in all tranquillity to the plough . . . a small fleet of the Danes consisting of three war-ships suddenly arrived; and that was the first arrival. When the king's reeve‡ who was then stationed in the town called Dorchester heard it, he mounted his horse and went forward with a few men to the port, thinking that the new-comers were merchants rather than enemies. He addressed them in a commanding tone and ordered them to be brought to the king's vill. But he was killed there and then, and those that were with him. And the name of the reeve was Beaduheard.'

Such was the story told about two hundred years later by Ethel-

* Emended from *Ianr̃* of the MS.

† The word 'Viking' (OE. Wicing) had been current among the English in the eighth century to describe marauders. The derivation is disputed; but there is probably a connexion either with ON. *vik* (a creek) or with *wic* (*vicus*). See Kendrick, 2.

‡ *exactor*.

weard, a member of the royal family and ealdorman of west Wessex.

These two incidents were remembered by posterity as the beginning of the trouble. Even in 793 there were one or two far-seeing men who half realized the significance of what had happened. Alcuin of York heard the news soon after he had taken up his residence among the Franks, and his agitation at once expressed itself in a number of letters—addressed to the bishop of Lindisfarne and his monks, to the king of Northumbria and his nobles, and to the archbishop of York. 'For almost 350 years', he wrote,[4] 'we and our fathers have dwelt in this fair land, and never have such terrors appeared in Britain like these which we have now endured from a pagan people; and it was not thought possible that such havoc could be made.' Hitherto the sea had always been to the English their friend. They had long ceased to use it for war-ships, but they had used it for coast-wise trade and communication. They had made verses about it, and about the heroes and saints who dared its storms. Cuthbert and the hermits had wandered along its shores at night. They had withdrawn to the solitude of its islands to brood in peace. And now out of the sea there had suddenly appeared these ships filled with violent men, with heathen who destroyed St. Cuthbert's own church, the very home of Northumbrian Christianity. Monks dedicated to God had been made captive. Violent hands had been laid on treasures and holy relics. This was indeed dumbfoundering. 'Where can there be any confidence if St. Cuthbert, with so great a company of saints, does not defend his own?' Alcuin tried to see in the destruction a just punishment for the luxury of the Northumbrians, for their extravagances in dress, and their excesses in drinking and eating. None the less, the thought of it haunted him as 'the beginning of misery and calamity'. In his letter to the people of Kent he told them to read Gildas, and learn from him why the Britons had formerly lost their country. 'Then consider yourselves and you will find that you are almost in the same case.'[5]

A year after the raid on Lindisfarne the heathen reappeared on the Northumbrian coast and sacked the monastery at Jarrow. On this occasion there was some comfort to be found in the fact that St. Cuthbert did not permit them to depart unpunished: some of the raiding ships were destroyed by bad weather, many heathen were drowned, and those that came ashore were slain.

These three isolated raids—two on the Northumbrian coast, one on Dorset—were the first rumbles of the coming storm, a storm which was to overshadow the land for more than two hundred years, and then was only to disappear after the Norman Conquest. The first rumbles were heard, and then the storm seemed to blow over. The Frisians might have it, the Franks, the Irish; but the English were scarcely disturbed. Then, more than a generation later, in the five years 838–42, premonitory raids again occurred. There were descents on the south coast from Cornwall to Kent, and on the east coast in Lindsey and East Anglia. Egbert, however, was still alive in 838, and in that year in the last great battle of his life he defeated at Hinxton Down, west of the Tamar, a coalition of Danes and Cornishmen. The subsequent raids were unpleasant, but they too seemed to be passing incidents, and in the following seven years (843–50) our shores, except for one ominous reminder, escaped molestation. It was not till the middle of the ninth century—not till the first wintering of the raiders in our island (in 850–1)—that the English people as a whole woke up to the fact that the Doomsday of this world was upon them, and that they were fated to undergo the ordeal, an ordeal by fire and by battle.

Let us avail ourselves of this interval of some two generations between the first raids and the real invasion of England to find out more about the intruding Northmen. Whence did they come, and why? What had they been doing in the past, what manner of men were they, and why was it that they waited for so many decades after 793 before they took full advantage of the vulnerability of English monasteries?

About the home of the first raiders there has been much

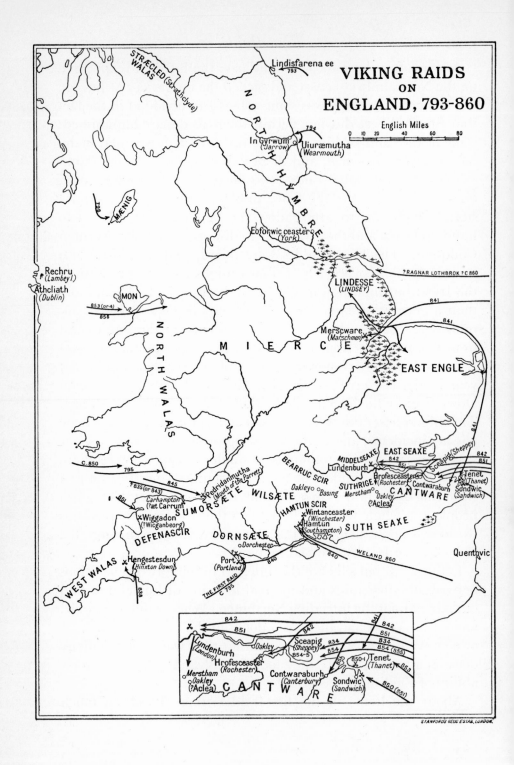

VIKING RAIDS
ON
ENGLAND, 793-860

English Miles

0 10 20   40   60   80

Lindisfarena ee
793

STRÆCLED (Strathclyde) WALAS

NORTHYMBRE

In Gyrwum (Jarrow) 794
Uiuræmutha (Wearmouth)

MÆNIG 793

Eoforwic ceaster (York)

Rechru (Lambey I.)
Athcliath (Dublin)

MON 853 (or 4) 855

LINDESSE (LINDSEY)

? RAGNAR LOTHBROK ? C 860

841
841

Merscware (Marschmen)

NORTH WALAS

M I E R C E

EAST ENGLE

C. 850 795

MIDDELSEAXE EAST SEAXE Sceapig (Sheppey) 842
Lundenburh 851
BEARRUC SCIR Hrofesceaster (Rochester) Contwaraburh Tenet (Thanet)
Pedridanmutha (Mouth of the Parrett) Oakley Basing SUTHRIGE Sandwic (Sandwich)
845 WILSÆTE Merstham Oakley CANTWARE
835 (or 843) Oakley (?Aclea)

Carhampton (?æt Carrum) 851
Wiggadon (?Wicganbeorg) SUMORSÆTE HAMTUN SCIR Wintanceaster (Winchester)
DEFENASCIR DORNSÆTE Hamtun (Southampton) SUTH SEAXE
841

Hengestesdun (Hinxton Down) 838 Dorchester Port (Portland) 840 840 WELAND 860 Quentovic
WEST WALAS THE FIRST RAID C 795

842
851
Lundenburh (London) Oakley Sceapig (Sheppey) 834 834
Hrofesceaster (Rochester) 854-5 854 854 (855) 853
Merstham 850-1 850-1
Oakley (?Aclea) Contwaraburh (Canterbury) Tenet (Thanet)
C A N T W A R E Sondwic (Sandwich) 850 (851)

STANFORDS GEOG ESTAB., LONDON.

dispute. It is not a question of supreme importance, since these
early raids quickly came to an end. We need only note that the
pirate crews may have been the first ripple either of a northern
stream of Vikings, voyaging from Norway to the Shetlands and
Scotland, or of a southern stream which came from the Danish
seas by way of Frisia. Alcuin at the time evidently assumed that
the 'pagans' who had sacked Lindisfarne were not Norse but
Danish, since he held out a hope that Charlemagne might be
induced to 'do something' on behalf of those carried into captivity. In later years the continental chroniclers generally call
the raiders 'Northmen'* without attempting to distinguish between the different peoples of the North. The English chroniclers
normally call them 'Danes', and though this shows whence most ⚬
of them were thought to issue, the word was used in a loose
general sense, and without precision. These facts are a reminder
to us that the Scandinavian nations in the eighth century were
less clearly differentiated from one another or from other Nordic
peoples than in modern times. About the beginning of the
Viking Age, however, great changes in Scandinavian dialects
occurred which tended to sunder the Northmen from their
Germanic kinsmen.

Among the Scandinavians themselves, also, processes were at
work which gradually collected the old small tribes into three
or four great groups. Two of these groups scarcely concern
us, since they faced to the east and played only a small part, ⸰
through individual adventurers, in the attacks on Britain: the
Götar or Geats, famous as the nation of Beowulf; and the Swedes,
the inhabitants of the country round the Mälar Lake, whose
conquest of the Götar in the latter part of the eighth century laid
the foundations of the Greater Sweden of modern times.[6]

It is the two remaining groups, the Danes and the Norwegians,
who were about to deflect the whole course of English history, ⸰
and it is these whom we must learn to understand. They were
the wild progeny of wild lands. Jutland, for instance, had great

* *Nordmanni.*

stretches of heaths, of marshes, and of forests reaching down to the sea. 'A sterile land of a vast solitude', says Adam of Bremen,[7] writing in the eleventh century, ' . . . wilder even than Germany, barren inland and infested by pirates on the coast.' The inhabitants of Norway had an even harder struggle, being isolated by forests more vast than those of the Danes, and forced to scrape together a bare living in the small patches of cleared land which appeared like oases among the interminable trees and the rock-strewn mountains.

The characters of these Northmen were formed to an unusual degree by their surroundings. The sea, penetrating far into the land, was their one highroad. Even in Jutland there were waterways (in particular the Limfiord, now largely silted up) which helped to bring the sea within general reach. It was sea-fishing which eked out the poor supplies of oats and rye. But the struggle for existence in their barren lands made the Northmen not only active and enterprising: it made them also hard and selfish. It rendered their younger sons discontented, and drove them to seek ampler or more fruitful lands oversea.

It is easy to paint a highly coloured picture of these Northmen. In their own literature they appear with many savage traits; they are cruel, blood-thirsty, crafty. Before they broke into Christendom, plundering and destroying, they had been long preying upon one another, burning one another in their homes, sacrificing human life to their gods. In the *Ynglinga Saga*, founded on the ninth-century poem the *Ynglinga-tal*, we see how the ancestors of the kings of Norway, generation after generation, had been fated to come to violent ends. The saga tells that before their migration from Upsala one was burned by his subjects for good luck; one was hanged by his wife; one, 'Aun a wise man', obtained the gift of long life by the sacrifice of nine of his sons to Odin. Time and again brother slew brother; and one of the brood—the 'grimmest of all men'—ended a long career of treachery by burning, in one royal holocaust in his hall, himself, his wives, his daughter, and a crowd of drunken subjects. Some of these kings can be recognized in *Beowulf*. The traditional burial mound of one of them, Ottar Vendel-Crow, grandson of Aun, has been fairly well identified by recent excavation[8] (Pl. 59). But even when the tales are myths, they have significance as evidence of national character.

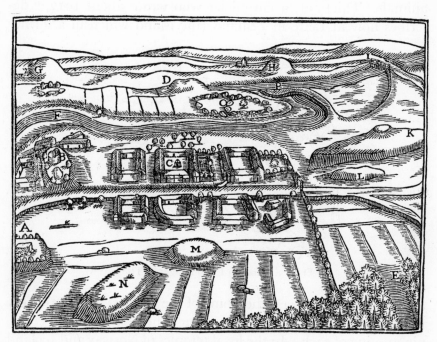

FIG. 62. Leire in the seventeenth century.
Note c, once the site of the King's Court.

Much the same note continues to be struck when we come to the poems and sagas about Northmen more within the bounds of history. The blood-lust is still dominant. Life is held cheap. Hatreds are rancorous. A conqueror cuts a 'spread-eagle' on the back of his slain enemy, shearing apart all the ribs and drawing out the lungs. Another cuts off an enemy's head and has it put on a stake; or he has a skull mounted as a drinking-cup. The fury of the blood-lust reaches its height in the warriors called *berserks*, who, it is said,[9] were Odin's own men, and 'went

without armour, and were mad as dogs or wolves, and bit
their shields and were strong as bears or bulls'.

If we study the religion of the sagas, we find similar ferocity.
The gods of the northerners thirsted for blood as did their worshippers. On occasions men had to be sacrificed as well as
animals. Thietmar, a chronicler who wrote about 1012,[10] describes how at Leire in Zealand (the island which in a former

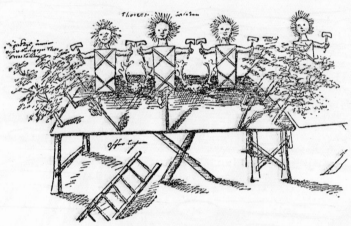

FIG. 63. Modern Lapp images of Thor.

age had probably been the home of the goddess Nerthus) every
nine years a sacrifice was made of men, horses, dogs, and cocks,
ninety-nine of each. In the local temples of Norway and Iceland
we read of animals being offered rather than men. The sites of
some of these temples have been excavated (Fig. 64) and within
the long narrow building, divided somewhat like a church, in
the inner or holier place where stood the images of the gods, the
blood of slaughtered animals flowed freely. Bowls were filled
with the blood of cattle and horses; blood was sprinkled about the
temple and on the worshippers. The religion of the Northmen
clearly had its savage aspects. It seemed to reflect the sombre
primitive surroundings in which this species of mankind lived,
isolated by forests and mountains, remote from civilization, lost
in the night of a sub-Arctic winter.

Now though this picture of the Northmen is highly coloured, it cannot be dismissed as wholly fanciful. Rather it should be considered a caricature. In the rest of the chapter we shall be modifying the picture, sometimes correcting, sometimes adding, sometimes also confirming its ugly features.

At the outset an Englishman can find reason to question the

FIG. 64. Site of Temple at Hofstathir (Iceland).

In the foreground is the Sanctuary. Beyond is the Hall, with stone supports of a double row of wooden pillars. Length about 36 metres; breadth 5 to 8 metres.

talk about the blood-soaked Viking in the fact that the Scandinavians, who took up their abode in England settled down apparently as tolerable neighbours by the side of the older Anglian population. We hear of no extreme racial bitterness. The Anglo-Saxon Chronicle, in telling the story of the invasions, often describes the Danes as 'heathen', but it does not dwell on their atrocities.[11] The English do not recoil in horror from these new intruders as the Britons had recoiled from their Saxon conquerors. There is no refusal to mingle with them in society. We shall see that Alfred, in describing the Scandinavians, gives no hint that their customs were particularly strange or detestable.

There is thus a presumption that our picture of the conventional Viking, the Viking of popular imagination, is grotesque. But where exactly are its mistakes?

Now, to begin with, it is sufficiently obvious that the method of simply putting together the unpleasant features, whether of a people or of a man, is not the way to obtain a true portrait. Even if all the tales of Viking savagery were true, those acts were exceptional. They made good stories. There was a demand for tales about berserks, spread-eagles, and such-like. But there is no more reason to condemn the Norsemen wholesale for such tastes than to write down our own generation as criminal because it enjoys stories about crime.

Our conventional portrait of the Norsemen is therefore wrong because it has stressed what was exceptional and has omitted the normal. To obtain a truer idea of the Scandinavian invaders, we should learn more about their manner of life when they were at home; we should study, not the war-heroes and the berserks, but the peasantry who were to form the mass of the immigrants; and we should distinguish the local communities which were the true units of society. These things, however, are for the most part hidden from us; and we can do little more than note some points of contrast between the Norwegians and the Danes. Even with this limited aim, it is hard to fill in the details.

Take, for instance, the history of the two peoples before the Viking age. At first sight we may think that the traditions of the Scyldings, the Danish family which ruled at Leire in Zealand, were less darkened by tragedy and treachery than was the tale of the Ynglings, who established themselves as lords of Westfold at the head of the Oslo fiord. But the story of Rolf Kraki, the sixth-century king who was the last of the Scyldings, was ended by a crime, and this story, like that of Hamlet,* prince of Jutland, seems to have in it vestiges of genuine tradition.[12] The English, in the epic of *Beowulf*, remembered the Scyldings for the magnificence of their hall Heorot, for the stateliness of their court and

* Amleth.

their lavish generosity; but in the Danish traditions they were handed down as a family doomed by its passions. Brother murders brother; father commits incest with daughter; and Rolf Kraki, the offspring of the incest, though raising Denmark to a short spell of empire over its neighbours, in the end by threefold treason—that of a sworn vassal to his lord, that of kin to kin, and that of the guest to his host—is brought to destruction; for the last scene in the hall of Leire, the hall in which Beowulf had fought with the monster Grendel, is the slaughter of Rolf Kraki and all his men save one in the dead of night by the hands of their guests.

The contrasts in the religious practices of the Danes and Norwegians are less obscure. Here archaeology again comes to our help. Throughout most of Denmark at this time the dead were buried without a heathen display of grave-goods. The influences of southern civilization appear more positively in the use of wooden coffins. It is not till we come to the northern tip of Jutland that we find the dead being cremated, or their graves furnished in the heathen style.[13] The dearth of references to human sacrifice among the Danes, though not conclusive, where all is so little known, perhaps indicates that the wholesale sacrifices of men and of animals at Leire, as described by Thietmar, were peculiar to that island. They could indeed be paralleled in Sweden. At Upsala there was a gilded temple and a sacred wood, and in the wood victims were offered to the gods every ninth year at the coming of spring, nine men and nine of various kinds of animals, whose corpses were nailed to the surrounding trees, and were then left to rot. But in Jutland the Danes were, it seems, new-comers, colonists who had flowed in to fill the places left empty owing to the migrations of the 'folk-wandering' age. We are too much in the dark to dogmatize about these matters; but we may infer that the majority of the Danes were little touched by the mysteries of Odin and Thor, stolid under heathenism as they were to be under Christianity in later days; farmers and fisher-folk of a practical turn of mind, thinking of their fields and of their boats.

Among the Norwegians as among the Danes some variations in heathenism can be discerned. The Ynglings were said to have come to Westfold from Upsala, and to be descended from Yngvi-Frey, a Vanir god, older than Odin and Thor. This connexion was perhaps the reason why heathen practices were most vigorous in the land of the Ynglings, that is, in the south-east corner of Norway. People flocked to the sacrifices at Skiringssal from all the Vik. Ship-burials, a Swedish fashion which spread to parts of Norway, were here unusually magnificent. While in Denmark there were kings ready to be baptized by Christian missionaries, in Westfold the cult of the old gods was maintained and developed throughout the ninth century. It became the home of a 'heathen revival', a deliberate reaction against Christian influence.[14] So also in the north of Norway, where men were influenced by neighbouring Finns, a race full of sorcery and magic, devotion to the old gods, and especially to Thor, long flourished.

Thus, the more we study the Scandinavians who inhabited the coasts and inlets which gave access to the British seas, the more diversities we find among them. From the Arctic circle to the borders of Saxony there were differences of every kind, religious, political, social, and economic—minor differences, it is true, but none the less enough to make us suspicious of generalizations.

Politically, the Danes had clearly advanced a stage farther than the scattered folks of Norway. Unity was more possible among them, because the country was smaller and was less cut up by mountain ranges. It is not easy, however, to say just how far their unity went. The chroniclers of the Franks wrote about the Danish monarchy as if it was normally one and universal. But there is evidence which points to the frequent existence of two or more kings at the same time, and to intermittent internal wars. Even if there were periods when an overking enjoyed some nominal superiority over all Danes, his actual power was conspicuously imperfect. The situation changed from generation to generation; there were kaleidoscopic groupings and regroupings as in Heptarchic England.

The Norwegians, however, had not even reached the stage of theoretical unity. In some parts there were the beginnings of a local consolidation. The eight folks* round the fiord of Trondhjem were coming together for a common worship—the worship of Thor—and for common justice. The small kingdoms within reach of the Oslo fiord were beginning to feel the gravitational pull of an ambitious monarchy. But elsewhere the small folks under their petty kings or chieftains† went their own way, and fought out their own quarrels.

Some light can be thrown on the economic conditions of the north at the beginning of the Viking age. Archaeological finds dating from the sixth to the eighth centuries prove that the Norwegians during the whole of that period were in communication with the peoples of distant lands.[15] They were discovering the want of small articles—weapons, ornaments, &c.—which could be obtained in the south, and at the same time they were developing the art of ship-building, which enabled them to voyage far afield, and import what they needed from Christendom.

It seems that the north already had its trading-ports which had been for some time the resort of Frisian merchants, especially those from Dorestad, and which probably flourished all the more when the Scandinavians themselves replaced the Frisians as the chief traders of the northern seas. Skiringssal, on the Oslo fiord, was not only a religious centre for the people of the Vik, it was also a market where men from the far north could bring their furs and walrus hides and carry away with them beautiful swords, amber from Prussia, or precious oriental things which had been transported by the river route from the Black Sea. The town of Schleswig, called by the Danes Hedeby (Haithaby),[15a] was the most famous of the Danish ports and tapped most of the trade which flowed between the Baltic and the North Sea across the neck of the Danish peninsula. Birka also, on Lake Mälar, was

* *fylki.* † *hersar.*

establishing its position as the emporium of the Swedes, and was perhaps linked up with a chain of other Birkas throughout the northern seas.[16]

What we wish to know most about are the fishing villages, the hamlets, the byes of Denmark, since it is clearly from these that the bulk of the ships' crews were recruited which sailed to harry or to settle in England. But it is just these about which we know least. There are no Danish laws which can be traced back to pre-Viking times. The houses and temples, being built of wood, have left no traces behind them. We may infer that where the earth was rich enough to feed a large population, there were good-sized villages, as in Zealand, and also on the Limfiord, 'which is so full of fish that it seems to yield the natives as much food as the whole soil'.[17] Districts like these made the Danes far more important than the other Scandinavian peoples. It has been guessed that their total population was more than 500,000, while that of Norway was only about 200,000. In the interior of Jutland we may imagine the forests and moors as described by Adam of Bremen dotted with patches of reclaimed land round small thorpes—a wild country indeed, but a land of peasantry enjoying much equality and freedom.

'We infer', 'we guess', 'we imagine'—that is all. The Danes must be left an unknown people.

We shall now turn to the story of the Viking movement, trying first to understand the exodus from Norway by a northern route, and then the attacks which came by way of Frisia and the south, and remembering as we go that the narrative may fill in some of the features of the Scandinavians which have so far escaped us.

THE NORTHERN ROUTE TO THE BRITISH ISLES

Here we have a story which is new, new at any rate in the sense that for the first time it is authenticated by the positive evidence of excavated farmsteads, and by a systematic study of place-names.[18] The story begins in western Norway, where the peninsula bulges outwards towards Scotland and the Orkneys and Shetlands, the stepping-stones across the North Sea. It is the region of the great fiords—Hordaland, round the Hardanger Fiord, and south of it Rogaland, Jaeren, and Agder—a region where even more than elsewhere the cultivable soil is curtailed by mountains, by stony wastes and peat moors.

We see these lands some two centuries before the Viking age settled by 'odel'* families living in farmsteads which commonly would be called by a name ending in *-baer* (corresponding to the *-by* so frequent in the Danish districts of England). The seventh and eighth centuries are here a period of prosperity. The iron axe has found its way to these outposts of civilization. It is enabling men to build houses that are a great advance on the round huts in which men in the past have sheltered from the northern cold; also to fell trees tall enough to roof stone buildings—great long barn-like houses, each of which can hold a patriarchal family and its dependants. The remains of these farmsteads, with their stone foundations, have been excavated in recent years, and are solid witnesses to the congestion of population in this western Norway before the Viking age.

At this point the study of place-names takes up the story. It is claimed that the expansion of the population in the pre-Viking period can be traced by place-names ending in *-setr, -bolstad,*† *-land,* since names like these show that, when the descendants of a patriarchal family became too numerous and had to be provided with new homes, they moved to the outlying sheds or shielings of the old farms. It seems that up to about 700, the expanding population was provided with the land it needed, either by new clearings from the waste, or by a more intensive cultivation of the old estates. Then the pressure of population became too great. A new outlet had to be found. Some of the young people trekked eastwards into the uplands. But some, more adventurous, discovered that there was also an outlet 'west over-sea'. The new iron tools had made it possible to construct ships strong enough

* Ancestral freehold.   † Both *setr* and *bolstad* meant originally a dwelling-place.

to sail the open seas. The low wind-swept islands, first the Shetlands and then the Orkneys, became for these western Norsemen the America of that age. Unoccupied cultivable land was
to be had for the taking. Homesteads with names ending, like
those of the new farms of western Norway, in *-setr, -bolstad, -land,*
&c. were planted in the islands. Many of the farms in the west
of Norway, those which had been established on the worse lands,
were forsaken.

The humble settlers in the Shetlands and Orkneys were, all
unknowingly, Pilgrim Fathers, pioneers of the new movement of
the nations. The stream of Scandinavian emigrants which had
begun to flow towards the British Isles was to change all the
history of Western Christendom.

The migration, which seems to have gathered strength in the
eighth century (though its dates cannot be fixed with precision),
was a peaceable colonization, carried out by farmers. Then the
warrior classes—the landed aristocracy and their retainers—
woke up to the fact that the new colonies offered good bases
for piracy. Their ships explored round the north of Scotland
and down the west coast of the Isles, and so into the Irish seas.
In time the depredations of these adventurers were mentioned
in the Irish annals. The burning of the monastery at Rechra
(? Lambay Island) in 795 aroused the Irish, as the raid on Lindisfarne in 793 had aroused the English, to the new danger. But
while the English raids ceased some decades after the failure of
794, the harryings in the Irish and Scottish seas continued with
little abatement.

Ireland offered a tempting prey to the sea-rovers. Beneath a
nominal head-king and kings of five provinces, the real power
was splintered into fragments in the hands of innumerable petty
kings and chieftains. These kings loved to fight one another, but
not with the savage efficiency of the Northmen. By tradition
war in Ireland was a gentlemanly sport. It had its rules and conventions. The warriors had shields, but no coats of mail. They
took the field in fine clothes—in fringed mantles and gay tunics.

PLATE 59

The King's Mounds at Old Upsala

Ottar's Mound in Vendel

From a sculptured stone, Stenkyrka, Gotland

PLATE 60

Northman's burial mound. Loch of Asta near Tingwall, Shetland

Tortoise brooch from a Northman's grave at Unst, Shetland

They were accompanied by poets, musicians, jugglers, and jesters. Thus it was that Ireland, enjoying a Celtic civilization which had not in the past been ruined either by Roman or by Anglo-Saxon conquest, attracted to its shores the Northmen. Though Irishmen had raided one another, and at times plundered a monastery, before the coming of the Vikings, the accumulated wealth of centuries was still stored in the island. The monasteries were rich and numerous. There were hoards of gold and jewels; and there were valuable supplies of men and beautiful women, who could be carried off and sold as slaves. The details of the story need not detain us—the ominous descent on Iona in 802, the yearly devastations of the Irish coast from 803 onwards, the use of Ireland as a stepping-stone to Brittany and the Continent. It is enough to say that within half a century the Irish learnt the whole scale of Viking fury, culminating about 834 in a continued occupation of the north of Ireland, almost a conquest, by a Norwegian called Turgeis. This chieftain before his death in 845 'usurped the abbacy' of Armagh, and his wife Aud, a fortune-teller, to the horror of Christendom gave prophetic answers from the high altar of Clonmacnois.

Thus was the northern route from Scandinavia to Britain opened up: first by peasants who colonized the Shetlands and Orkneys; then, about the last decade of the eighth century, by well-born adventurers who discovered that the new route enabled them to win a living overseas in ways less laborious than farming and fishing. The immigrant peasants, burying their dead without the costly furnishing of the old-fashioned heathen graves, left behind them no trace for archaeologists: the freebooting gentlemen for a time maintained the old custom, and buried their heroes with the panoply of war. In one famous grave at Colonsay a chief, interred in his ship, had beside him not only his two-handed sword, his axe, and his horse's harness, but also the scales and weights which he had used as he added the profits of trade to the profits of plunder.

In the middle of the ninth century the Viking stream which

came, like this Colonsay warrior, from Norway by the north of
Scotland, was met and opposed by the Danish stream which
flowed round Cornwall into the Irish seas. For a time the 'Black
Strangers', the Danes, had the upper hand; then the 'White
Strangers', the Norwegians, in 853 were reinforced by a fleet
from Norway under a certain Olaf. Olaf obtained the upper
hand. He ruled for nearly twenty years (853–71) at Ath Cliath
(Dublin)—one of the new Viking stations on the east coast of
Ireland—and he founded a dynasty which was in the end to play
a great part at York as well as in Ireland.

THE SOUTHERN ROUTE INTO CHRISTENDOM

Scandinavian attacks by the southern route were developed
about the same time as those which came by way of Scotland.
In other respects this advance into Christendom was different.

In its first important phase it was political in character. There
was a clash between 'the king of the Danes' and the king of the
Franks. The Franks were in a sense the aggressors. For the extension of Frankish influence over the Frisians undermined the
power of the race which had hitherto stood between Scandinavian barbarism and Christendom. Heathen as many Frisians
were till about 800, they were by instinct peace-loving sea-
farers. Having occupied a part of the gap along the German
coast caused by the migration of the Saxons to Britain, their
settlements extended along the whole coast, from the mouth
of the Scheldt up to and even beyond the Weser. They had
become the carriers of the northern seas, the intermediaries between heathen and Christian. The subordination of the Frisians
to the Franks, a process which went on intermittently throughout
the eighth century, was a threat to the Danes. The conquest of
the Saxons by Charlemagne (772–804) was a second threat.
Both the buffer states, that on land as well as that by sea, were
thus removed. Thenceforth the Danes were next neighbours to
the Empire of the Franks and an encounter between the two
peoples was a natural sequel.

Charlemagne had stirred up the wasps' nest. He himself, how-ever, had enough wisdom to see the danger, and enough skill and good luck to elude it after a first warning. The story is told in a well-known passage in the *Life of Charlemagne* by Einhard:

'The last war of Charles was undertaken against those Northmen called Danes, who, beginning with mere piracy, then came and ravaged the coasts of Gaul and Germany with a greater naval force. Their king Godofrid (Godfred) became so swollen with over-confidence that he hoped to make himself master of all Germany. He regarded Frisia and Saxony as his own provinces. Already he had reduced his neighbours, the Abodrites, and had made them pay tribute. He boasted also that he would soon come with a great force to Aix, where was the king's court.'

Though King Godfred did not make good the boast which was put into his mouth, the attacks which had been begun in 800 culminated in 810, shortly before his death, when a fleet of 200 ships ravaged the Frisian coast and exacted tribute from Charle-magne's subjects. Such were the beginnings of the age-long strife. The motives which moved the Dane are inadequately described by Einhard. In his heart there was surely fear rather than lust for conquest. His attack was essentially defensive.

There are points in the above narrative which should be specially noticed. Einhard says that the Danes began the trouble with piracy. As the Frisians' power declined, the seas along their coast had been opened to the Scandinavian freebooters, and the raids on Lindisfarne and Jarrow in 793–4 may well have been private ventures of this kind.

Then the size of Godfred's fleet should be observed. If the number of 200 ships is anywhere near the truth, it is evident that the Danish kingdom already possessed an elaborate naval or-ganization. And it must have been a large kingdom, possibly including for the moment, besides Scania and other districts in what is now the south of Sweden, the kingdom of Westfold in the south of Norway.

Another point, and one of more importance, which we should carry away from the story of Godfred's quarrel with Charlemagne is the fact that the advance of the Vikings by the southern route did not receive its impulse, like the advance by way of the Shetlands, from the outburst of an over-populated country. The Danes were not, as yet, hungering for more land to plough.

The death of Godfred (810) was a piece of good luck for Charlemagne. But Charlemagne had shown the kings of Christendom the right way to meet the Scandinavian danger. He had not only planted forts and garrisons along the threatened shore, but he had also set his subjects to build ships in order to repel the enemy before they could land. These preparations, and the civil war in Denmark after 810, helped to check the advance of the heathen fleets by the southern route for more than twenty years. Then, when the Danes again in large numbers terrified Christendom, their success was largely the fault of Charlemagne's son and grandsons. The main plan of his son Louis the Pious was sound enough. His idea was to convert the Danes to Christianity instead of to tame them by force. Louis did, however, incur fresh trouble for himself and all Western Christendom when in his simplicity he assumed that two Danish princes, Harold and his brother Rorik, who had submitted to baptism in order to win Frankish support against their Danish rivals, the sons of Godfred, could be treated and trusted as good Christians. Louis granted Harold the county of Rüstringen at the mouth of the Weser, and when Harold, presumably owing to his Christianity, was promptly expelled from his Danish kingdom, he and his family were compensated by Louis with further cessions of Frisian territory. The grants were so lavish that these 'Christian' Danes seem ultimately to have had possession of all the seaboard from Walcheren to the Weser.[19] The grant was no doubt based on some idea that the easiest and cheapest way to guard the Empire by sea was to hire the Danish fleet for the purpose. Whatever the motive, it was a disastrous error for which England and all Christendom were to suffer. The second error, following quickly on the first, was more ruinous and less excusable, the fatal family quarrel. This shattered not only the Empire of

Charlemagne but the prestige of Christendom. One year Louis was deposed by his sons, another he had himself publicly scourged for his sins. Then, when he died in 840, his three surviving sons quarrelled over the inheritance; and on the field of Fontenoy (841) the best forces of the Empire slaughtered one another in fratricidal strife. As soon as the civil wars broke out, the Northmen began to discover that Christendom, which they had hitherto respected, was at their mercy. In 834 and the following years they ravaged Frisia. Dorestad, near the mouth of the Rhine, till then the most important commercial centre of western Europe, a town which was said to contain fifteen churches, was raided four times. In these years the plan of setting Danes to defend the Empire against Danes proved a miserable failure. If Harold was not himself an accomplice in the devastation of Frisia, suspicion certainly fell on his brother Rorik. The partition of the Empire in 843 gave Rorik his opportunity. It became possible to play one grandson of Charlemagne off against another. Thus, when Rorik quarrelled with Lothair, king of the Middle Kingdom and nominal Emperor, he could find refuge in the kingdom of Louis the German. Then, with a new warband, he returned to Frisia, and re-established himself in despite of his imperial lord, and it was from this base that he and his allies were able to harass not only the Continent but the opposite shores of England. With good reason he was called the *fel Christianitatis*.[20]

This, then, is the situation which from 834 produced in the second phase of Viking trouble attack by the southern route. We suspect that there was an element of official or semi-official support behind the new onslaughts. The fleets which sail down the Frisian coast are often so large and the operations are conducted with so much method that they seem to have the backing of one or other of the Danish dynasties. Can we then say that these attacks were in any sense political, as in the days of Godfred? The voyages of the Elizabethan sea-dogs show how a ruler and private adventurers can co-operate in profitable enterprises on the high seas. Doubtless the Viking movement of the ninth century was frequently sustained by a similar combination.

But the life of the movement came from the enterprise of younger sons of the well-to-do who went out to seek their fortunes. The collapse of Ireland early in the century had first shown the Norwegians what wealth was to be had from plunder overseas. The collapse of the Frankish Empire in the 'thirties and 'forties advertised to the Danes even more effectively the profits of the Viking business. When the first ships came back packed with gold and silver chalices and crosses, with silk vestments, and with all the miscellaneous spoils of an 'emporium' like Dorestad, when the stories told by the raiders made it clear how defenceless were the towns and monasteries of the Christians, then the minds of the northern peoples were fired. For centuries these northerners had been fighting one another and raiding one another. Now they found that it was easier and more profitable to turn their attention to the Christians. The north which had long simmered boiled over.

If, then, we look at the causes of the Scandinavian invasions, we see that while the origin of the influx from western Norway was land-hunger, and while that of the attacks by way of Frisia was, in part at any rate, political, both in time quickly developed into mere scrambles for plunder. First the dissensions of the Irish, and then the insensate quarrels of the Carolingians, tempted the Northmen into British seas. The English kingdoms suffered because they lay between the two streams of invaders.

INVASIONS OF ENGLAND, 800–51

Now, knowing something of the Vikings, and how they crept round Scotland into the Irish seas and down the Frisian coast into the Channel, we can resume the story of their raids on the English. Having the framework, we can see these raids in their proper setting. What we see is that after the early piracies (at Lindisfarne and Wearmouth–Jarrow in 793–4, and somewhere about the same time in Dorset) the immunity of the next generation was due to the fact that the Vikings who came by the northern route could satisfy themselves in Ireland, while for the time being the southern stream had ceased to flow. It was only when the Franks invited the Northmen into Christendom by their grants of Frisian lands to Harold and Rorik, and by their own suicidal quarrels, that the Danes returned, first trickling and then flooding down the Frisian shore.

Of the attacks which in the following years descended on the English coasts from one direction or another, three are specially memorable. The first of these was the coming of 'a great ship-army to the West Welsh' (the Britons of Cornwall) in 838. They had chosen a vulnerable point. It was only twenty-four years since the Cornishmen had been first reduced by Egbert. A coalition of Northmen and of Britons might have produced chaos in our island. The heathen did in fact manage to bring a force of Cornishmen into the field as their allies. Egbert, however, was still on the throne of Wessex, and succeeded in wiping out the stain of a minor reverse inflicted by Vikings in 836 by giving the allies a sound thrashing at Hinxton Down. It was the last achievement of the founder of Greater Wessex, a Wessex extending from Cornwall to Kent.

The second of these raids which deserves to stand out in our memory is one on London in 842. All that the Chronicle* has to record about it, is that 'there was great slaughter at London and at Quentavic and at Rochester'. What did it mean by 'great slaughter'? Was it a loss incurred outside the walls by a defending force? Or were the Roman walls of London now, like those at York, so ruined that pirate bands could come surging in through the gaps and sack the city as well as commit the 'great slaughter'? Or was the city, like Paris three years later, saved from the worst destruction by the payment of a geld? Some light on the meaning of the Chronicle's phrase is thrown by a Frankish historian,[21] who tells us that in 842 'a fleet of Northmen so ravaged the emporium called Quentavic that they left nothing

* *Sub anno* 839.

in it except the buildings which were ransomed'. It does not of course follow that what happened in the French 'emporium' happened also in the English. London, at any rate, did not like Quentavic pass out of existence. None the less we have here a striking example of the limited interest of the Saxon chronicler. The chief centre of trade in the island was probably sacked, and yet the chronicler simply enters the event as 'a great slaughter'. London at the time was a Mercian city. Its fate did not specially concern the West Saxons.

We, however, need not follow the chronicler in letting this raid pass undistinguished from the other raids up and down the coast. At the risk of explaining *ignotum per ignotius*, the fate of Roman and of Saxon London may be compared. In the fifth century the Britons of Kent, defeated by the Romans, had 'fled like fire' to the shelter of Londinium's walls. Now, in the first half of the ninth century, things are different. The raiders come and go. Englishmen lose their hoards of corn and their valuables, perhaps their liberty, in some cases even their lives. The heathen have to be endured for a few days or weeks, and then they disappear. There is no fleeing before them from one province to another. The attitude of the English about this time is illustrated by the will of a Kentish lady,[22] who, in arranging for a yearly supply of loaves and other food to be given to the brethren of St. Augustine's Abbey at Canterbury, made provision that 'if it should come to pass that any panic should arise through a heathen invasion or any other calamity, so that this cannot be provided that year, then twice the amount must be given in the following year. Then if still it cannot be paid, three times the amount must be given in the third year.'

The raid on London and Rochester was but one of many which peppered the English coasts from the Wash to the Severn in the opening years of the reign of Ethelwulf. This king had succeeded his father Egbert on the throne of Wessex in 839. Though the change for the worse came with his reign, it cannot fairly be ascribed to him. For more than ten years before 839

Ethelwulf as under-king had ruled Kent, Sussex, and Surrey, the region most exposed to the stream of the Danish Vikings. After 839, though he succeeded Egbert as king of all Wessex, the effective rule of the eastern sub-kingdoms was handed over to Athelstan, his brother. Accordingly, the chief blame for the failure at London in 842 must be laid on the king of Mercia, and that for the raid on Rochester on the under-king of Kent.

The third memorable raid is that of 850–1. If it does not make an epoch, it marks one. It was in this year that a large army of the Vikings first wintered in England—in the Isle of Thanet. Hitherto, England had simply lain in the path of the invaders, and had not borne the brunt of their attacks. Now, in 850, though the summer coast-raids of the old type were not to cease for many a decade, an age of deliberate conquest was foreshadowed. The raid had the backing of a dynasty, which at times was able to supplant its rivals of the House of Godfred on the throne of Denmark—a dynasty whose princes had held positions of trust within the Empire, and had an intimate knowledge of affairs in the Northlands, in Germany, and no doubt also in England. Rorik, the Danish prince who had re-established himself in Frisia, was in touch with large forces. Besides the English expedition, another band under his nephew, Godfred, was operating on the Flemish side of the Channel.

The story of the English expedition is told in the Chronicle under the date '851', the year which according to the Anglo-Saxon method of reckoning (introduced by Bede) began on what we should call September 24, 850:

'In this year . . . king Athelstan [the brother of Ethelwulf, and under-king of Kent] and the ealdorman Ealchere slew a great force [of the enemy] at Sandwich in Kent, and took nine ships and put the others to flight, and the heathen men for the first time remained over winter [in Thanet]. [The words 'in Thanet' are found only in MSS. B, C, D, E.] And in the same year came 350 ships to the mouth of the Thames and stormed Canterbury and Lundenburh (London),* and put to flight

* 'sacked them', says Asser.

Beorhtwulf, king of the Mercians, with his army, and then went south over the Thames into Surrey, and there king Ethelwulf and his son Ethelbald, with the army of the West Saxons, fought against them at Aclea,[23] and there made the greatest slaughter among the heathen army that we ever heard tell of up to this present day, and there gained the victory.'

Though our English Chronicle gives no hint of the connexion between this invasion and Rorik, the Danish lord of the Netherlands, its words convey a sense of the greatness of the danger and of the consequent relief of the Saxons when the danger was for the time removed by Ethelwulf's victory at Aclea. The heathen may have numbered some 10,000 men—perhaps a greater force than that which fought under the Norman at Hastings. It was no wonder that such an army should have been able to storm both Canterbury, the centre of English religion, and London, the wealthiest of English towns. Nor is it surprising that it should have defeated the army of Mercia, even though Mercia had till recently been the strongest military kingdom.

The victory of the West Saxons was a great achievement. None the less, it did not bring any lasting relief. Hitherto the Vikings had been for the English little more than a nuisance. Henceforth they became a menace.

THE NORTHMEN AT HOME

Now that we are reaching the middle of the ninth century and the full flood of the Viking movement, it becomes possible to speak with more authority about the Northmen, both those at home and those who became sea-rovers. It is necessary to wander from the immediate history of England in order to understand the character of the attacks made by the Vikings on our shores in this period.

For our present purpose the most illuminating discovery of the twentieth century has been the Oseberg ship, unearthed in 1904 from a mound not far from the west side of the Oslo fiord, in

PLATE 61

The Oseberg ship in its burial mound

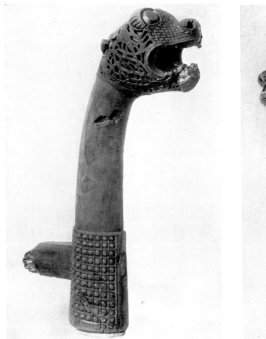

Carved posts from the Oseberg ship

PLATE 62

The Oseberg ship in the mound, showing the carving on stem and railing

the Ynglings' kingdom of Westfold.[24] In the ship was buried a great lady, whom the archaeologists claim to have been Asa, once the wife of Gudröd,[25] a wife who murdered her husband. Let us go back in imagination to the funeral of the queen. The time is the end of summer, and the period is somewhere about the middle of the ninth century. The ship in which the corpse is to be laid is an old one, perhaps built about 800. It is a vessel of great beauty, with a high graceful prow and carved stern-post and gunwale. It is not a ship in which Vikings have been harrying Christendom, because it was never built for the open sea, and its sides are low. It is rather a yacht in which a king or queen could make a stately progress on the quiet waters of a fiord. And now, when it has been dragged on rollers from a neighbouring watercourse and before the earth is heaped over it in a mound, the attendants place in the boat the belongings which the queen most treasured—her best bed, and her second best bed, her chair, her kitchen utensils, her best sledges, and, most magnificent of all, the old-fashioned wagon, used, it seems, only for religious ceremonial. These are almost all beautiful objects (Pls. 61–64). They show that art is very much alive in this part of Norway, and that the wood-workers are skilful in adapting ideas or *motifs* borrowed from the south and from Ireland, the *motifs* which they found on the spoil now pouring into the north.

For us, the contents of the mound at Oseberg deserve study, not because of the technical development of northern art, but simply as an unmistakable proof that there were districts in Scandinavia where the standard of material civilization was high. The Oseberg finds dispel most effectively the old idea that the Vikings were nothing but backward barbarians. Just how high their civilization should be placed is, of course, a debatable matter. Even if we grant that phenomenal progress was made in the north during the ninth century owing to the stimulus which resulted from constant contact with southern countries, the Oseberg ship itself and the carving on its prow show that there were Scandinavians well advanced even at the beginning of the Viking age. The place now claimed by distinguished Scandinavian historians for Viking civilization is perhaps too high. According to one,[26] the Oseberg and other finds 'show that the Norsemen long before the Viking age were as civilized as the Anglo-Saxons and the Franks'. According to another,[27] 'in comparison with western Europe it can safely be said that the Norwegian peasant civilization of about the year 800 possessed a more highly developed standard of boat-building and a richer and more comprehensive production of iron weapons and implements than any other contemporary civilized race in the west and north'.

Their pre-eminence in ship-building is, no doubt, incontestable. But since neither the Franks nor the Anglo-Saxons of the age thought it necessary to provide their dead with a complete outfit of bedsteads, ironmongery, and kitchen utensils, the rest of the comparison is perforce one-sided. Certainly we leave the Oseberg ship with a vivid sense of the barbaric beauty of the dead queen's belongings, of the ingenuity and vigour of her craftsmen, of the colour and gorgeousness of this Norse society, where the chief men and their womenfolk could appear in silks and gold-embroidered clothes imported from the south, or in homespuns brilliant with blue, red, yellow, and dark-green dyes; with massive gold and silver rings round their arms and necks, and with heavy tortoise-shaped brooches holding their mantles on the shoulder. We carry away a sense that the gaudiness and variety of their outward display and the vigour of their art illustrate what has been called[28] the 'buoyancy and unrest in the very soul of the nation'.

One incident in the burial of the Oseberg queen remains to be noticed. When the queen had been laid in her cloth of gold, when her furniture and her household paraphernalia had been carried on board, the provision for her needs in the world of the dead was still incomplete. She must be given her horses and her dogs; and she must have an attendant. Accordingly, the burial

PLATE 63

Wagon from the Oseberg ship

PLATE 64

'The Great Bed' (restored) from the Oseberg ship
Beech wood, 1·65 m. long, 1·80 m. broad

Iron tripod and cooking-pot from the Oseberg ship

ended with a sacrifice: thirteen horses, six dogs, and one woman.
The strain of savage primitive thought had not been eliminated
by the infusion of art and of material civilization.

Let us now pursue another way by which it is possible to
approach the Scandinavians of the Viking age—their literature.
Certain of the so-called Eddic poems, though written down in
Iceland, seem to carry us back into the heathen period and even
into the ninth century or earlier. One of these, the *Havamal*,[29]
a composite poem of traditional lore, illustrates the softer side of
the Scandinavian character. It shows that the hardness en-
gendered by the struggle for existence among the mountains and
forests of the north, the cult of force, was not unchallenged.

The *Havamal* is the Northman's Book of Proverbs, but it lays
no stress on the qualities of the conventional Viking. Only in
one or two verses does it praise valour. For the most part it
teaches manners for men and is full of worldly wisdom. It en-
courages friendship. It upholds moderation. It advises men to
be eloquent and 'constantly talk of the heroic'. Caution and
craft are the qualities needed in this world. 'If you have an
uncertain friend, address him with fair words but crafty heart,
and repay treachery with lies.'

'Look not up in battle lest spells be cast upon you.'

'Be cautious but not too cautious.'

'Praise no day till evening, no wife until she is buried, no
sword until tested, no maid until given in marriage, no ice until
crossed, no ale until it has been drunk.' Odin himself has become the lord of cunning, a master of mighty spells, especially
of runes, 'letters of great power and might'. Giants with their
mere brute force are the beings whom the Northmen despise.
They are the enemies of the gods. Men can win by other means
than mere force, but win they must—win at least fame. 'Cattle
die, kinsfolk die, even to ourselves will death come. One thing
I know will never die, the reputation we all leave behind on our
death.'

Here, then, in the *Havamal* and in the Oseberg ship we see

patches of the background which the men of the North left behind them when they sailed south to gain plunder and, maybe, fame among the Christians.

NEW VIKINGS AND NEW SHIPS

We again follow the Vikings to sea. What manner of men shall we find them in this middle of the ninth century, when all Scandinavia is astir and ships by the hundred are yearly descending on the coasts of Christendom? Plunderers we know they will be, but what else? Will they be land-seekers, like the early emigrants to the Shetlands, or heroes lusting for bloodshed, like the conventional Vikings? Or men of culture, like those who buried the Queen of the Oseberg ship, the courtiers of Queen Asa? Or men who practise the maxims of caution and craft advocated in the *Havamal*?

The time has come to find answers to our general questions by studying the men themselves. We must take typical leaders and incidents. The first of our representative Vikings can be no other than the Danish chief, Ragnar Lothbrok,* Ragnar of the Leather Breeches—if we wish to be more exact we may describe them as shaggy leather breeches, the hide turned outwards like a cowboy's but, unlike a cowboy's, reaching only to the knee.[30] A historian in search of the genuine Viking might find good reason for avoiding this Ragnar, in that later admirers of his, the scalds and saga-men of the north, embellished his achievements with so much myth and fable that the real man cannot well be distinguished. Even the shaggy breeches of his nickname were worn, says Saxo, for a combat he undertook with fire-breathing snakes or dragons. But it is this fact that Ragnar became in every northern country, from Iceland to Denmark, the pre-eminent hero of the early Viking age, which entitles him to some kind of a place in history. Moreover, in the history of England he has this additional claim, that (rightly or wrongly)

* ON. Loðbrók.

tradition remembered his death as the *casus belli* of the great invasion of 865, and said that its leaders, his sons, were vowed to avenge the death of their father.

The origin of Ragnar is a mystery. The most plausible conjecture connects him in some way with Harold and Rorik, the fugitive Danish kings baptized by Louis the Pious. It is possible that he was a bastard brother of theirs, or a nephew. In the cloud of myth and legend surrounding him we touch solid fact in one episode, his expedition up the Seine to Paris in 845. The story told by the Frankish chroniclers with some fullness may here stand for the raid on London three years earlier, about which nothing is known. We are told[31] that Ragnar, with 120 ships, entered the Seine in the March of 845. The expedition rowed up the river to Rouen—no new feat, that: raiders had been there before them in 841. But the crews of Ragnar pressed on and no one resisted them. As they ascended the river their plundering parties spread far afield on either bank. They carried off men and women; they killed; they sacked the monasteries; they burned the churches; they drove off cattle. It seemed to the men of that generation that the like of this had not been heard of since the creation of the world. Charles the Bald, king of the Franks, gathered an army; but that was all. Ragnar discovered that Charles and his army could be disregarded. Within sight of them he sacrificed 111 captives—'an offering to Thor', it is conjectured by some modern historians. Charles the Bald looked on at the sufferings of his people, and he beat his breast. Finally, on Easter Day, Ragnar and his heathen bands entered Paris. The population had fled and the city lay at their mercy. We hear of them cutting beams from the church of St. Germain-des-Prés for the repair of their ships. We hear of them carrying off the iron work of the city gate, for the king of the Danes as a symbol of their triumph. We hear also of certain miraculous events, including the subsequent death of Ragnar, which we may treat with some scepticism. For us the lesson of the raid is the daring of Ragnar and the success which attended his daring.[32] When he withdrew from the Seine, his fleet was not only packed with the loot of the Seine lands, but in addition to this it carried 7,000 pounds of silver—the bribe with which Charles had bought the departure of the heathen, the first of many notorious Danegelds.

Why was it that Ragnar, more than any of his contemporaries, was remembered by later generations of Scandinavians? We may perhaps infer that he owed a part of his fame, both in his lifetime and later, to the fact that he had links with more than one of the Scandinavian peoples: that while he came of a Danish dynasty he had been brought up in Norway; that he had wives in many ports; and that his large family of sons inherited or forged connexions with most of the countries of the north, from Ireland to the Baltic lands. Again, it is probable that he was the first member of a royal House to distinguish himself in the Viking business. His expedition to Paris shows that his campaigns were boldly planned and executed. The traditions in Saxo, though they may transfer to the family some deeds of other men, suggest that Ragnar and his sons were the first to realize the extent to which command of the sea opened up the water-ways of Europe to the Northmen.

Ragnar's expedition to Paris should also remind us that the Viking movement was passing into a new phase. A leader belonging to a royal house could have the title of king, though he did not possess an actual kingdom. If he had that which counted highest, a great following of ships' crews, he could become a new kind of king—a sea-king. And the followers for their part were becoming a new kind of nation—a nation of wandering seamen. The Viking's only home might now be his war-ship.

Ragnar and his sons no doubt did much to form the Viking ideal of which they became the exponents in the eyes of later romanticists—the ideal that men must 'trust in their own skill and strength',[33] and that 'he only might be called a sea-king that never slept under a sooty rafter, and never drank in the chimney corner'. At any rate it seems to have been in the times

of Ragnar and his sons that the Northmen began more deliberately than in the past to disguise the brutality and sordidness of
their calling by decking it out with a certain cult of hardihood.
Norse poets were not slow to reflect this fashion and poured contempt on the young men who sat indoors and loved warm bowers
and pillows stuffed with down.

To complete our picture of the Vikings as they have developed
by the middle of the ninth century, we must examine the ships
which are making them the masters of Western Christendom.

Of the thousand ship-burials noted by archaeologists, that
which best represents the Viking craft of the ninth century is the
famous ship unearthed in the mound at Gokstad and built somewhere about A.D. 900 (Pl. 65). The improvements made by the
Vikings and their ship-builders during the ninth century can be
gauged by comparing the Gokstad ship with vessels assigned to
the seventh or eighth centuries;[34] one of these which may have
been used in the earlier Viking voyages has only ten oars a side.
But it will be best for us to obtain a more general idea of the progress of shipbuilding among the Scandinavians by comparing
the Gokstad ship with the Nydam boat,* used by the Angles five
centuries earlier.

While the Gokstad ship[35] resembles the Nydam boat in its
general design, being clinker-built and undecked, long and
narrow and low, rising in height at stem and stern, it is in every
way a better-made vessel. It has, unlike the Nydam boat, an
external keel and a strong frame, with a block into which a mast
can be fitted. Thus the vessel can carry a square sail. Its total
length is eighty feet, and it has sixteen oars a side, as against
fourteen in the Nydam boat. The oars are longer, and owing to
the improvements in the rowlocks (now holes cut in the main
strake) they can be much more effective than the Nydam oars.
(It will be remembered that in the Nydam boat the oars were
rowed against a single rowlock, rising from a block which was
only tied and not nailed to the gunwale—an unsatisfactory

* Above, vol. i, pp. 22–4.

arrangement, since the bast fastening would clearly get worn out by the oar.) A better method of steering has also been developed by the ninth century. Instead of an oar-like rudder to be held in the hand at the stern, there is now a rudder-blade ingeniously fixed in the starboard (steer-board) side, and manipulated by a tiller. In numberless smaller details also the Viking ship shows the increased skill of the race which won command of the sea. For example, cleverly contrived shutters are fitted to close the oar-holes when the vessel is under sail.

The general seaworthiness of the craft was proved in 1893, when a model of the Gokstad ship crossed the Atlantic in four weeks, making at times ten or eleven knots in spite of its relatively weak sail. When they were rowed, these vessels, having some sixteen oars a side, could move up and down a river so as to outstrip their enemies on the land. They drew so little water that they could be beached on any shore. They were small enough to be hauled by hand for portages. In short, these war-ships were the decisive invention of the eighth and ninth centuries.

The mere appearance of the ship was inspiring to its own men and terrifying to the enemy. Instead of the old-fashioned trading vessel which had been shortish, grey-coloured, and ill-manned, the new Viking ships were a brilliant sight. They had usually at the prow, and sometimes also at the stern, dragon-heads; from the masthead, a streaming pennant; sails striped red and blue and green; sides painted with bright colours; and hung over the gunwale were the gaudy shields of the warriors. Inside, the ship was naturally divided up by the thwarts upon which the rowers sat. The average crews of these boats have been put at very different figures. The best opinion[36] estimates forty men to a ship for the early decades of the ninth century, and fifty to sixty for the later part of the century. This may well be too generous for an average, though no doubt a single ship might here and there contain a formidable company, mustering say sixty, eighty, or a hundred men.[37]

The men were recruited by leaders marked out by birth or wealth or personal prowess. Partnership among the leaders was common. The ventures were largely conducted as joint-stock undertakings, and each member of the crew, even if it was only his skin which he had risked in the enterprise, expected his due share of the plunder.

The commander had his quarters in the space of the ship aft of the rowing benches, and by his side was the steersman. Those next in rank occupied the corresponding space in the fore-part of the vessel. There also was the chest wherein were kept the men's weapons and armour. The plunder of a raid was either stowed in the fore-part or under the planks beneath the oarsmen's feet. Each of the crew had to make his sea-home as best he could in the few feet of room which were to be found between his own rowing-bench and that of his next-door neighbour. Into that space he could contrive to fit a small box for his belongings, and by its side between the benches he had at night to lay himself down to sleep in his skin bag.

When the ship was in harbour, it was sometimes covered over at night by an awning striped in various colours; and then, before the men settled down to sleep beneath the awning, they played by a flickering light at chess or at mill, gambling with their ill-gotten spoil, or they told stories of gods and heroes.

The ships gave the Vikings the command of the sea. The life lived on the ships helped to give their crews a superiority over the Christians on land. From it they derived strength, discipline, comradeship. Their muscles were hardened by rowing and baling. Crews which had faced the storms of the North Sea together could be trusted when campaigning to fight in perfect accord. Their ships gave them a ready-made organization. As the men had their places on board, so also on land. In this common life of the ship, free men and men of humble origin soon gained a sense of equality. As sharers in a common venture the social distinctions of their native lands were largely obliterated.

Whatever their origin, the Vikings became by their regular profession of arms the equals of the warrior classes of Christendom. They were as good as the landed gentry.

In these ways the fighting man-power of the Scandinavian peoples increased of its own accord. Men were recruited, trained, and organized as new expeditions were projected and new ships were commissioned.

There is one aspect of the Viking movement on which we have scarcely touched, its commercial side.

At this period raiding was still more profitable than ordinary trading. None the less the two could be worked together. To illustrate how this was done, let us turn to an account of the first Viking expedition to Spain in the year 844. Its story as told by the matter-of-fact Muslems of Spain is more convincing than that of Ragnar's expedition to the Seine lands in the following year.[38] The general plan of operations was similar. The Vikings in 844 sailed from France in 150 ships; raiding up one Spanish river after another they came in time to the Guadalquiver, and rowed up to Seville among its orange groves. There, while one detachment besieged the castle, three or four plundering expeditions were sent out in different directions. For some weeks there was a general panic and flight of the Moors. Then, however, the Moorish troops managed to ambush one party of raiders, and the others thought it wise to escape while they could. So they sailed down the river. The inhabitants of the country following along the banks poured on them curses and threw stones. When they arrived a league below Seville the Vikings shouted to the Moors: 'Leave us in peace if you wish to buy prisoners of us.' The stone-throwing then ceased, and the Vikings demanded payment in clothes and food, not in gold and silver.

The story brings out well the commercial methods of the Vikings even at this early stage. There is no talk of captives being put to death as in Ragnar's raid to Paris. Though the inhabitants are captured, they are not retained to overburden the ships. What is wanted is a quick re-sale.

Now, having learnt something about the Vikings and their ships as they were in the middle of the ninth century, we can take up once more the thread of English history.

XIV

THE COMING OF THE GREAT ARMY

ETHELWULF AND HIS SONS

WHEN we last touched on the affairs of England, the Viking invasion of 851, though checked by the great victory of Ethelwulf at Aclea, had sounded a warning to the inhabitants of England. The time had come which would show whether the English kingdoms, after two centuries of Christianity, could stand the continued strain of barbarian assault. Would they realize the impending danger in time? Would they prepare to meet it? The Northumbrians for their part gave no signs of anxiety—London and Canterbury were a long way off; their own feuds were urgent. The Mercians also seem to have been oblivious—they were mostly an inland people; in spite of the raid on London, they did not appear to be in much danger from sea-rovers.

Wessex was the kingdom which was most exposed, and the mind of Ethelwulf of Wessex was clearly perturbed.

The ships of his under-king had given a good account of themselves at Sandwich. He himself and his land-army had fought manfully at Aclea. They had won; but the danger remained. The Danes still hovered round Thanet. What then was to be done? The question was more than a military problem. It

PLATE 65

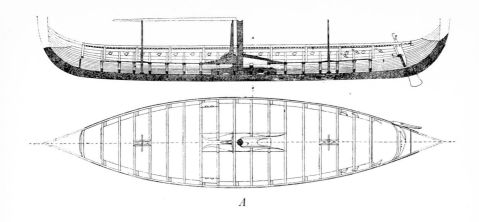

A

B

THE GOKSTAD SHIP

A, Section and plan. *B*, A reconstruction

PLATE 66

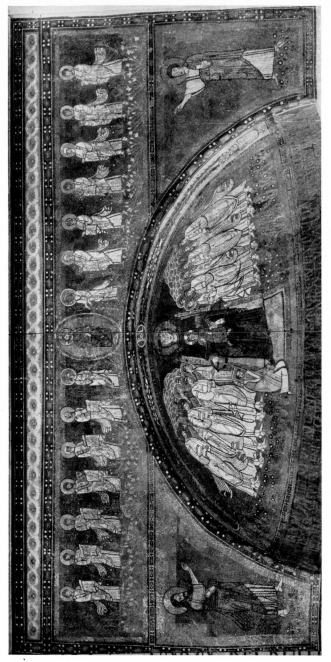

Roman Art of the ninth century. Mosaics in S. Maria in Domnica

Within the tribune, Pope Paschal I (817–24) kneels before the Virgin and Child with angels
ranged on either side. On the walls, the Saviour surrounded by two angels and the twelve
Apostles in a flowery paradise; below, two Prophets

made a man face fundamental beliefs about the events of this world. There was every reason to suppose that these heathen were sent upon Ethelwulf and his people as a punishment for their sins. In that age there could be no doubt about it. It was the teaching of the Church. At the first appearance of the *o* Vikings in 793, Alcuin, the most learned of Englishmen, had recognized that the pirates were sent as the chastisement of the Lord. It was a commonplace of the age, and it appealed with special force to Ethelwulf.

As early as the first year of his reign his mind had been impressed by a vision which had come to one of his clergy—so greatly impressed that he had sent an embassy to the Franks announcing his intention of journeying to Rome for the purpose of prayer.[1] This vision had made it clear to Ethelwulf that 'if Christian men do not speedily repent of various crimes and wickednesses, and do not observe the Lord's Day better and more reverently, great and intolerable danger will speedily come upon them: namely, for three days and nights a very dense cloud will overshadow their land, and straightway the pagans will come upon them with an immense number of ships, and will lay waste with fire and sword most of the land of the Christians, and the people themselves with all that they possess. But nevertheless, if they are willing to show true repentance and study to put away their sins according to God's ordinance by fasting and prayer and almsgiving, then by the intercession of the saints they may succeed in escaping all these perils and punishments.'

For sixteen years Ethelwulf had allowed his good resolution to go unfulfilled. Then the recurrent plague of Vikings and, it may be, the admonitions of St. Swithin,* bishop of Winchester, convinced Ethelwulf that the time had come for heroic, spectacular sacrifices of the Christian sort. He must give the best of his own and of his subjects' belongings to God. First, he sent his youngest son Alfred, his best beloved, to the shrines of St. Peter and St. Paul. In 853 Alfred, a child of four years, made the

* OE. Swiðun.

journey to Rome. He was decorated by the Holy Father with the insignia of the consular rank, and returned to England. But the threat of Danish attacks still hung round the coast. Ethelwulf then resolved that he must himself go and pray at the shrines of the Apostles. The salvation of himself and of his subjects both in this world and in the next seemed to depend on this pilgrimage. Accordingly, in 855, Ethelwulf, like Cædwalla and Ine and un-numbered others, taking with him his son Alfred, 'went to Rome with great pomp, and dwelt there twelve months'.

But in the vision of 839, God had required almsgiving as well as prayer. Ethelwulf was therefore a cheerful giver. Before he left England he 'booked the tenth part of his land throughout all his kingdom to the praise of God and for his own eternal health'. It seems that this famous 'donation' to the Church was made only from the king's own lands, and that the grants were assigned to the king's thanes in the first place, on the understanding that they should afterwards be bequeathed to a church.[2] At Rome too he offered to the Blessed Peter chalices of the purest gold and silver-gilt candelabra of Saxon work; and at the request of the Pope he distributed gold to the clergy of St. Peter's, and scattered silver among the Roman populace. More than this, in his will he 'commanded that every year great store of money should be brought to Rome for the good of his soul'. Clearly his intention was to revive the tribute inaugurated by Offa, the Peter's Pence of the Middle Ages.[3]

So far the conduct of Ethelwulf can be easily understood. The pilgrimages and the almsgiving had been acts of the highest ecclesiastical merit; they were according to the teaching of the clergy calculated to assuage the wrath of God. But what followed was more questionable. Why, on his return from Rome, did the king of Wessex spend many months at the Frankish court, and why did he, a man perhaps fifty years old, to the disgust of the Saxons, end his pilgrimage by marrying Judith, the twelve- or thirteen-year-old daughter of Charles the Bald? She was a girl who, to judge by her later matrimonial escapades, was as little

FIG. 65. Part of Rome. From a plan drawn *c.* 1475

1. St. Paul's. 2, 2, 2. The Tiber. 3. The Aventine Hill. 7. The Janiculum.
8. The Castle of St. Angelo. 9. Church and Hospital of Santo Spirito (formerly the
Saxon School), within the Borgo. 10. St. Peter's.
(1 and 10 received endowments from King Ethelwulf.)

suited in character as in age to be the wife of the religiously minded English widower. Was this the folly of a man senile before his time, or was it an act of policy? Those who study the internal troubles of the Franks in these middle months of 856 will have cause to suspect that such policy as there was in the marriage came from Charles the Bald rather than the English king. But the importance of this marriage lies chiefly in the reaction which it produced in England. The story of what occurred is discreetly omitted in the official Chronicle, but is told by Asser the Welshman.

'While king Ethelwulf was staying across the sea for this short time, an evil deed, and one which was contrary to the wont of all Christians, was done in Wessex west of Selwood. For king Ethelbald and Ealhstan, bishop of the church of Sherborne, together with Eanwulf, ealdorman of the shire of Somerset, are said to have plotted to prevent king Ethelwulf from ever being received in the kingdom on his return from Rome. Now many ascribe this unhappy business with its unheard-of treason to the bishop and to the ealdorman alone, on the ground that it can be traced to their counsels. But there are also many who think it was due solely to the pride of the king [i.e. Ethelbald] because that king was headstrong and did many other perverse acts besides this. I have heard this view brought out by certain persons in their account of these affairs, and it tallies with what was to follow. For on king Ethelwulf's return from Rome, this same son and all his counsellors, or rather conspirators, tried to commit the great crime of preventing the king from entering his own kingdom. But God would not permit this to come to pass, nor would the nobles of all Wessex* consent thereto. For lest, with a war between father and son (or rather a rebellion of the whole people against both), an irreparable evil should be brought upon Wessex—one which like a civil war would grow day by day more fierce and cruel—by the wonderful forbearance of the father and with the consent of all the nobles, the kingdom which had before been united was divided between father and son. The eastern districts were assigned to the father and the western to the son. Thus, where the father should by right have ruled (since the western part of Wessex has ever been of

* Saxonia.

greater account than the eastern) there reigned his wicked and head-strong son.

'Therefore, when king Ethelwulf returned from Rome the whole nation, as was right, so rejoiced at the coming of their lord (*senioris*) that, if he had allowed it, they would have altogether expelled his headstrong son Ethelbald with all his counsellors from the kingdom. But he, as we have said, with great forbearance and with prudent counsel would not have it so, lest it should endanger the realm.'

It was a decisive moment in the history of the Saxons. If the quarrel had been allowed to develop, the House of Egbert would have been ruined, as was the House of Charlemagne at this very time by a similar family quarrel. Ethelwulf and his advisers evidently deserved the praise bestowed upon them for their for-bearance and good sense. That the king should have consented to treat with his rebellious son, to refer the compromise to a meeting of Saxon nobles, to moderate the pugnacity of his own supporters, and to resign the rule over the more important half of his dominions—all this testifies to the fact that Ethelwulf's Christian spirit did not exhaust itself in the giving of lavish charities to the Church, but availed to reconcile him to the sacrifice of prestige and power in the cause of national peace. At the same time, Ealdorman Eanwulf and Bishop Ealhstan were something better than selfish conspirators. In the past they had deserved well of their country, having led the forces of the west and defeated the Danes in 845. Posterity has not unnaturally discovered motives which explain, if they do not justify, the revolt of 856, especially disgust at the king's munificence and at the unpractical piety which had led him to desert his kingdom at a time of great danger. Whether or no the readiness of the two parties to accept the compromise can be held to illustrate a national characteristic, it is a fact which helps to explain the ascendancy of the House of Egbert over the other kingdoms, an ascendancy which had become moral rather than military. Ethelwulf and his three elder sons seem to have wellnigh for-gotten Egbert's short-lived assertion of overlordship over Mercia and Northumbria. Their charters made no high-sounding claims to wide dominion. All that these kings did was to go when called upon to the help of the Mercians. At one time (853) they supported them against the Welsh; at another (867–8) against the Danes. For the rest, they showed their contemporaries that they were prepared to fight like men against the heathen, and that they would not, like Northumbrians and Franks, allow themselves to drift into civil wars. The piety of Ethelwulf was therefore not unrewarded, and a spirit of compromise springing from his 'wonderful forbearance' may be remembered as a chief result of his reign.

In the events which followed Ethelwulf's death in 858 there is little to detain us. While Alfred grew to manhood, his three elder brothers succeeded one another in quick succession on the throne of Wessex—Ethelbald reigning till 860, Ethelbert till 865, and Ethelred till 871. It was in the reign of the last of these, and while Alfred was his right-hand man, that the sons of Ragnar landed on our shores with a 'great army' of the Danes—the beginning of the invasion which was to leave its mark on England for all time. To this and other activities of the Vikings we shall soon return. But in the meantime let us pursue farther the subject of the solidarity of the family of Ethelwulf.

So long as Ethelbald the usurper lived, the danger of friction was not removed. 'Unbridled' is the adjective with which Asser describes his rule. To the horror of the clergy both in England and on the Continent, the young king married his own stepmother, the Frankish Judith. On Ethelbald's death, however, his youngest brothers—Ethelred and Alfred—re-established the family tradition of harmony. They preserved it by placing the interests of the family before the claims of the individual. They in turn refrained from laying claim to the eastern half of the kingdom. This departure from the practice observed since the time of Egbert enabled all the south of England to be for the time united under the direct rule of one king. When Ethelred succeeded to the crown in 865, Alfred was recognized as what

Asser calls the *secundarius*—a word which the Welshman probably took from the vocabulary of the Celts and which probably only meant that Alfred was the accepted successor, the 'tanist', of his brother. The unusual word was fitting for an unusual situation. According to Asser:[4] 'While his brother was alive, Alfred, if he had wished to have it, could most surely have obtained the government with the consent of all men, since he certainly surpassed all his brothers in wisdom and in all good qualities, and also because he was very warlike.'

The will of Alfred tells how harmony was preserved in a similar way by an arrangement about the private property of the royal house. The will states that Ethelred and Alfred had given up their share in trust to Ethelbert. Later on, it continues, when 'it came to pass that we were all harassed with the heathen invasion, then we discussed our children's future—how they would need some maintenance, whatever might happen to us through these troubles. When we were assembled at Swinbeorgas,* we agreed, with the cognizance of the West Saxon witan, that whichever of us survived the other, was to give to the other's children the lands which we had ourselves acquired.'[5] . . . In this way, if in no other, Wessex was prepared for the coming storm.

EVENTS LEADING TO THE GREAT INVASION

In 865, seven years after the death of Ethelwulf, the storm broke upon England with the force of a hurricane. But the gathering of the storm can be observed in the preceding period. In the Saxon Chronicle this period, lying between the battle of Aclea (851) and the great invasion of 865, is punctuated with two short entries about raids. The first says: 'This year [854-5] the heathen men for the first time remained over winter in Sheppey.' To this the Lindisfarne Annals[6] add the information that the army of the pagans comprised Frisians as well as Danes, and that

* Not identified.

the leaders were Halfdene, Inguar, and Ubbe, the last of whom is afterwards described as duke of the Frisians.*

The second entry, about a raid on Winchester, in the year 860, will be quoted later on.

To understand these fifteen years we must again look elsewhere than to our English sources. In the general history of Western Europe, the age is one of intensified confusion. The old order on the Continent is visibly breaking down. Chaos is let loose. The quarrels of the older generation breed fresh conflicts. The whole Carolingian Empire hastens to its perdition. Once more sons of Carolings turn against their fathers; once more brother leads an army against brother; once more the old bonds of fidelity between lord and man are broken. On every side there is rebellion or apostasy. The Bretons join forces with the pirates. Pippin of Aquitaine, great-grandson of Charlemagne, not only unites with them but turns apostate. Here we have something worse than the dissolution of an empire. The State itself, the social structure, seems to be crumbling. Each province, each locality, is to find its own saviour of society, or else lie helpless before the Vikings.

But if Christendom in these years is drifting to chaos, so also are the Vikings. The success of the first generation, i.e. of Ragnar and his contemporaries, has brought all the North into the scramble to get rich quick. The safe monopoly of the 30's and 40's has gone. No longer can the Norwegians regard Ireland as their own sphere, nor can the Danes move yearly undisturbed from one river of the Continent to another. Now, in the 50's and 60's, there is cut-throat competition.

To understand this phase of the Viking movement—the phase from which is to issue the great invasion of England—let us learn what we can about the sons of Ragnar who attacked England once in 854-5 and again in 865, and also about Weland, leader of the raid on Winchester in 860.

We may think of this period before the great invasion as the

* *dux Fresonum.*

age of the sons of Ragnar. These sons are as slippery buccaneers as their father. They elude the modern historian seeking for well-authenticated facts, just as in their own day they eluded the rulers of the states of Christendom. If the historian turns to the Scandinavian traditions, these contradict one another. If he turns to the Christian chronicles of the age, he finds certain Viking chiefs bearing names which correspond to those of the sons of Ragnar, but the paternity of these men is not recorded. Some modern historians are therefore cautious, and refuse to link up the chiefs mentioned in the chronicles with the heroes of tradition.[7] If in the following pages we take a less sceptical, some may call it a less 'scientific', view, it is in the belief that we shall thereby be getting nearer to the actual truth.

The names of Ragnar's Viking sons appear in the annals of the Christians suddenly, about 854. This is perhaps a consequence of a great civil war which was fought out in Denmark in that year. We are told that the pirates were drawn back to Denmark to take their part in the struggle, and that a three days' battle ended in the killing of all the members of the House of King Godfred, except one boy (Horic II), who was thereupon raised to the throne. Whatever is the explanation of their sudden emergence, the sons of Ragnar come on the scene of the Viking raids with grand schemes. The chief river of England, and then the chief river of France, are occupied in turn. The three sons (Halfdene, Inguar, and Ubbe) who planned to establish themselves on the Thames, struck first; but they seem to have withdrawn from England after spending the winter of 854 in Sheppey. In the following summer Berno (presumably the son of Ragnar who appears in Icelandic tradition as Bjorn Ironside) entered the Seine. There he joined forces with a leader called Sidroc. Berno and Sidroc in the Seine valley could advance more boldly than the sons of Ragnar in the estuary of the Thames. They rowed above Rouen up to Pîtres. There they left their ships, and the crews were converted into a land army which plundered far afield in the territory between the Seine and the

Loire. In the winter they installed themselves at Jeufosse, a natural fastness half-way up the river between Rouen and Paris.

Thus we see already elaborated the plan of a plundering campaign which will reappear in England: the well-defended river camp—often, it seems, a stockaded fort—which is used as a collecting-station for the booty as well as a base of operations; and horsed raiding-parties, capable of penetrating quickly and far into the surrounding provinces.

Berno remained near the Seine for another year or so; then, enriched with the spoil of the monastery of St. Denis and with an immense ransom for its abbot, a grandson of Charlemagne, he sailed from the Seine to take part in the most daring of all these Viking expeditions, the Mediterranean cruise of 859–62 —an adventure which stands out in this age like Drake's circum-navigation of the globe in the age of the Elizabethan sea-dogs.

From Berno let us turn to the Viking chief Weland. The information which can be gathered about him and his followers from continental sources will illustrate the changes which were coming over the Vikings in this generation. It will show that the Danes who suddenly swept down on Winchester in 860 and were beaten by Ealdorman Osric as they returned laden with spoil to their ships were more formidable than a horde of barbarians, fresh from the wastes of Jutland.

When we first hear of Weland's bands, in 859, they are plundering in the country of the Somme. By the following spring they have made a compact with Charles the Bald to kill or expel an army of the Seine Vikings who had now been long established on a fortified island at Oscelle. The Somme Danes under Weland* made a businesslike contract with the Frankish king, that they should be paid 3,000 pounds of silver for their services, and that it should be paid by weight and tested. When the payment was not made at the stipulated time, the Danes took hostages to ensure a later fulfilment of their bargain, and decided to occupy themselves in the meantime with the expedition to

* Weland's name is not actually mentioned till 861.

Winchester. But for the Frankish annals, we should never have
guessed that the Danes were in England—either in Hampshire
or elsewhere—for something like a year, and that though for the
moment unemployed, they were still under contract as mer-
cenaries of the Frankish king. Nor without the Frankish sources
would it be apparent that these Vikings who changed their base
of operations from river to river and from country to country
were so moved by considerations of gain and by little else, that
when the pay was high enough they would turn on one another.
These adventurers who negotiated like Christians with Christians, and had the intelligence to avoid, as far as possible, actual
fighting either with rival Vikings or with the Christians, had
evidently shed much of the elemental violence of the primitive
Northmen. The influence of Christendom was beginning to
work. Weland in the end commended himself to Charles the
Bald. He and his family were baptized. But this was going too
fast for his followers. One of them challenged the chief to a duel,
and in the duel Weland was killed.

The Danes at last (in March 862) removed to the sea. More
Danes returned, however, a few years later, and it was not till
July 866 that they really disappeared for a long spell from the
Seine valley. They disappeared from France, but 'turned to
desolate the Church of God elsewhere'.[8] One squadron, it seems,
made for the Rhine mouths; that district could not long feed a
large army, and there can be little doubt that most if not all of
these bands found their way to England to swell 'the great army'
of the sons of Ragnar.

Our digression about the Northmen in France has introduced
some of the characters who will play a part in the invasion of
England. Of the sons of Ragnar and Sidroc we have learnt little;
but of the crowd, the nameless crews which followed them, we
know at least this: that many of them had been long in France,
learning at first hand its civilization, mixing peacefully among
the Franks as well as plundering them. The conversion to Christianity of Weland, the leader, is memorable; but it is significant

that the convert was promptly slain by one of his followers. Influences of Christendom and heathendom were acting and reacting.

THE GREAT ARMY IN ENGLAND, 865–70

The scene now shifts to England, and the stage is set for the entry of the 'great heathen army'. The Saxon Chronicle says that in the year '866' (i.e. a year beginning, according to our reckoning, in September 865)⁹ 'a great heathen army came to the land

FIG. 66.

of the English and took winter quarters among the East Angles and were horsed, and they made peace with them'.

For many years the story of this army will be the main theme of the Chronicle, and we shall have to follow it as it wanders from one kingdom to another, destroying or conquering. The landing in East Anglia in the autumn of 865 thus marks the beginning of the Danish Conquest, almost as distinctly as the landing at Pevensey in 1066 marks the beginning of the Norman Conquest.

Why is it that few Englishmen who know what happened in 1066 could say what happened in 865? The events are comparable, both in the importance of their consequences and probably in the number of the invaders. But the earlier invasion is overshadowed by the later for two reasons. First, the destruction caused by the Danes was more obvious than their work of construction; and secondly, their conquest lacked a historian or a

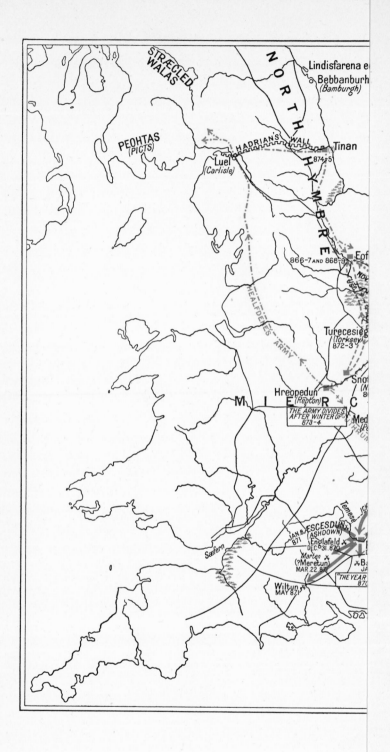

poet. The Danes themselves left nothing which can be accepted as an authentic record, and the meagre narrative of the West-Saxon Chronicle supplies but a feeble thread of information, until it swells to the patriotic story of the salvation of Wessex by Alfred. For the first five years of the invasion, we have no records but the bare outline of the Chronicle and a few later traditions. Once more we must resort to conjectures, if we are to discern the inner meaning of events. We are forced to speculate about the invaders, who they were and whence they came; but to begin with let us follow in its outline the opening of the campaign.

It seems probable that the heathen spent not only the winter of 865–6, but also the greater part of the year 866, concentrating their forces in East Anglia, and organizing themselves into an army which could operate with hope of success against the greater English kingdoms. Little is known with any certainty, either about Edmund, the young king of East Anglia who had begun his reign as a boy in 854, or about the condition of his kingdom since its submission to Egbert in 825.[10] But the reasons which induced the Vikings to choose East Anglia for their concentration are not far to seek. Thanet and East Kent, already often raided in the past, had been again denuded in the summer of 865. East Anglia, therefore, a few miles north across the mouth of the Thames, offered the next coast suitable for their first pounce. It was within easy reach of Frisia, which was no doubt, now as earlier, their advanced base on the Continent. It was the smallest and presumably the weakest of the English kingdoms. It was not, like Kent, under the direct rule of the formidable kings of Wessex. It was in the middle of the east coast, and so was a good centre from which an attack might be launched, either against Northumbria or Mercia. At the same time it was almost as defensible as Thanet itself, being protected by forests and by the fens of the Ouse and the Cam.

In this small, outlying kingdom, covered by its belt of woodlands and marshes, the Danes chose to spend the winter and summer following their arrival. The East Angles made no attempt at resistance—none, at least, worthy of record. Edmund, the young king, was not yet ready for martyrdom. He had to 'make peace', and supply the heathen with the food and tribute and horses demanded. For the Vikings, a peace could be the easiest way of skimming the wealth of a people. A more complete denudation could be left to different methods at a later stage.

In the late autumn of 866 the Danes moved from East Anglia. They rode down the Roman Ermine Street, and then were ferried 'over Humber mouth'. On November 1 they stormed the city of York, pouring through the walls which the Angles had once wrested from the Romano-Britons, walls which by 866 were said to be partly in ruins. Their success had been swift because the Northumbrians were, as usual, weakened by their own feuds. 'At that time', says the Chronicle, 'there was great dissension of the people among themselves; and they had cast out their king Osbert, and received a king Ælle not of royal blood.' King Ælle, the usurper not belonging to the old dynasty, fled before the invaders. What then happened is told in an imaginative strain by Simeon of Durham:[11]

'The army raided here and there and filled every place with blood-shed and sorrow. Far and wide it destroyed the churches and monasteries with fire and sword. When it departed from a place, it left nothing standing but roofless walls. So great was the destruction that at the present day* one can scarcely see anything left of those places, nor any sign of their former greatness. On this occasion the barbarians advanced to the mouth of the Tyne, but did not cross it, and then returned to York.'

It has been suggested with some likelihood that the borderland between Deira and Bernicia was ravaged for strategic reasons, as well as for booty.

Some five months after the fall of York, on the Monday before Palm Sunday, March 21, 867, a Northumbrian army in which the forces of both factions were united came upon the Danish army outside York. The heathen fled to the shelter of the city.

* i.e. about 1104–9.

PLATE 67

Charles the Bald enthroned, from the Vivian Bible

Count Vivian, lay Abbot of Tours (843–51), standing by the throne, points to the Bible
held by three canons; other canons and their Prior in the foreground. Less than ½

PLATE 68

A. An attack on a city

B. The Multangular Tower and walls of York

C. Flight from a city

A and *C* are from the Franks casket. In *B* Roman stonework is surmounted
by medieval

There they rallied, turned on the Christians, and overwhelmed them. There was an immense slaughter of the Northumbrians, some within the walls and some without. Both the kings were slain. The remnant of the Northumbrians which escaped made peace with the enemy. Almost all the fighting stock of the North was wiped out.

So ended Anglian Deira. The Bernician kingdom was allowed to live on with little glory under a king called Egbert, but the north of England never recovered from the shock which it now received. The schools and monasteries dwindled into obscurity or nothingness; and the kingdom which had produced Bede and Alcuin, which had left the great stone crosses as master-pieces of Anglian art, and as evidences of Anglian poetry the poems of Cædmon and the Vision of the Rood, in the generation following the defeat of the year 867 sank back into the old life of obscure barbarism. No other battle in the north of England ever produced so great a cataclysm. At Flodden a king and the flower of a nation were cut off, but in the battle of York a dynasty was broken, a religion was half smothered, and a culture was barbarized. The archbishop of York and some of his clergy survived, but their energies were henceforth concentrated on the mere struggle for existence. The whole character of the north was changed.

Such is the story of the first great victory of the Danish invaders. Now let us try to understand who these invaders were, why they had come, and why they met with such resounding success. First—who were they? The only memorable names of the leaders which emerge in the course of the story are Sidroc (presumably the chief who had harried the Seine valley in 856–7), Inguar or Inwar (supposed to be the same as Ivar the son of Ragnar Lothbrok), Halfdene his brother, and, according to tenth-century tradition, Ubbe, a third brother.[12]

Imperfect as is the evidence for the sons of Ragnar, the few references to them are none the less leading clues to our understanding of the invasion. If, as is almost certain, Ivar son of Ragnar can be equated not only with the Inguar of Asser but also with the Imhar of the Irish annals, we know something of his maraudings in Ireland in the interval between his wintering in Thanet in 854–5 and his landing in East Anglia in 865.[13] It would seem that knowledge of the troubled state of Northumbria drifted to him across the Irish Sea.

Halfdene, on the other hand, seems to have been less of a pirate and more of a Danish statesman. His name did not live in Viking tradition; but in a German chronicle we read of a Halfdan who in 873 negotiated with Louis, king of the Germans, for a firm peace, and was recognized as king of the Danes 'between the Eider and the sea'.[14]

Of Ubbe there is little authentic information. It must suffice that he is described in one chronicle* as *dux Fresonum*.

If we are rash enough to build a theory on such ill-cemented scraps of information and on the legends, we may conjecture that the sons of Ragnar gathered their own bands as well as those of their confederates from east and west—from Denmark itself as well as from France, from Frisia, and from Ireland. They themselves provided an element of family unity in the inner councils of the invaders, something like the nucleus of a general staff for the army.

The traditions, both Icelandic and Danish, insist that the expedition against Ælle of Northumbria was organized by the sons of Ragnar in revenge for the death of their father. Ragnar, it was said, when attacking Ælle of York, was taken and cast into prison, and was there killed by serpents and adders. Many of the embroideries of the story are late and palpable fables— the snake-pit itself and Ragnar's gloryings in the snake-pit ('I have fought fifty battles and won, I never thought that serpents would be my death. . . . The porklings would grunt if they knew of their old boar's need').[15] There are those who would dismiss not only these embellishments but the whole story that the

---

* The Lindisfarne Annals. See above, p. 518.

invasion of 866 was an act of retaliation.[16] On the other hand, the story of the great vengeance must have existed at least as early as 1027, since there is an obvious reference to it in a stave of that date which told of the blood-eagle carved by Inguar (Ivar) on the body of Ælle.[17] There may therefore have well been some root of fact from which the fable grew, and we may think of the sons of Ragnar as they planned their campaign being moved by passion for revenge. In the hearts of these leaders the invasion was, it seems, an act in a blood-feud; but it was also an adventure, and the motives of their comrades and followers were, no doubt, those of ordinary pirate crews. We shall scarcely err if we assume that the movements of the Army, that is the Danish Army,* were mainly determined, like those of smaller bands, by calculations about food and plunder. Thus the chief reason for the coming of the Army in 865 was the necessity to open up a new country, when France and Ireland were, for the time being, exhausted. It was the law of diminishing returns which induced the Vikings time and again to have recourse to lands hitherto untouched.

By 865 the business of raiding was not what it had once been. Ireland, France, Frisia, German Saxony—wherever a Viking leader turned outside England, he found a more strenuous resistance. In Ireland the High King Aed had proved by force of arms that the island could no longer be considered a happy hunting-ground for foreigners. In France the new local leaders such as Duke Robert, even Charles the Bald himself, were arousing an unwonted spirit of resistance. There were good reasons for calling off the pack of freebooters from France and Ireland. There were even better reasons for choosing England for attack. It contained the richest accessible country yet unravaged. Hitherto, little more than fringes of the coast had been raided. The invasion was planned much like other Viking invasions of

---

* Here and in subsequent pages we follow the convenient custom introduced by Victorian historians, and distinguish the Great Army of the Danes by a capital or capitals.

France, England, or Ireland. The Danes presumably did not come with cut and dried schemes of conquest. But when the deaths of the Northumbrian kings in 867 opened the way to conquest, they took their opportunity. At the same time, it is, of course, possible that the Danish leaders were sufficiently far-sighted to see that since England stood between Viking Ireland and Viking Frisia, a conquest of England would consolidate their position as nothing else could. It would give them a northern empire.

Thus, if our conjectures are right, the army which landed in 865 was as miscellaneous a body as has ever invaded our shores. And it was clearly not to mere numbers that the Vikings owed their superiority.[18]

To what, then, was the success of the Great Army due? Was it to the genius of their commanders, to their organization, or to their superiority in the art of war? Or was it rather the consequence of the weakness of their opponents? Inguar was no Napoleon. What little we know about the organization of these predatory armies points to a large measure of equality among the leaders. In the battle of Ashdown, we shall read of two kings and five jarls commanding the Danes, without a suggestion that any one of them was a commander-in-chief. The army which had dominated the Seine lands for so many years before the opening of the English campaign had been a collection of companies, *sodalitates*.[19] Weland's army had been a *societas*, a word meaning, doubtless, much the same as a *sodalitas*. One group could be a collection of smaller groups. The ramifications of a big 'combine' formed to exploit—in the Viking way—a Christian region could be as manifold as an industrial combine or cartel of the present age. Each component company, being a joint-stock association formed for the capture and division of food and valuables, was an independent unit. Hence the ease with which the kaleidoscopic Viking armies were both collected and dispersed. Self-government, whether oligarchical or democratic, was to remain a feature of these immigrants, long after their 'armies' had settled down to cultivate the fields of eastern England. But the independence of the Danes of the Danelaw, so much belauded in later centuries, must in the Danish army of conquest have been a source of weakness as well as of strength. An army not at the disposal of a single commander but ruled by councils of equal chiefs started heavily handicapped.

Difficulties caused by any excess of equality and liberty were compensated by more positive advantages. Their command of the sea and of all the more navigable water-ways leading from the sea had long enabled them to strike where they would. In their land campaigns they still retained the initiative; they got themselves 'horsed' as soon as they could after landing, and thus continued to score by mobility and elusiveness. Then when it came to a fight they trusted to the terror caused by their reputation, to the steadiness and discipline born from their life at sea and nurtured by constant campaigning, to their consequent power of performing manœuvres such as feigned flights, which deceived the less practised levies of their enemies and broke their ranks. But above all they trusted to their own good weapons: their long, tapering, two-edged swords, well protected by a metal guard and well balanced with a heavy pommel; their strong spears; their axes, evolved for battle use from the heavy felling-axes with which they had for so many generations been clearing new lands for settlement in their northern forests. They were now able also to improve their supply of arms and byrnies manufactured by Christians. With the wealth which came to them from plunder and Danegelds, and often also from trade with their victims, they could afford to buy the best equipment in Europe. And finally, in case they should be worsted in open fight, they developed the art of fortification. Their quickly-made river camps, protected by earthworks or stockades, served a double purpose. They were depots for plunder and they were an insurance against complete failure. When the Vikings reached England in 865 these tactics had passed the experimental stage. The Ragnar family and Sidroc and the rest had been for years training their men in warfare. In England they had only to apply with massed armies the lessons which they had learnt on the Continent.

We must now return to the operations of the Great Army after its conquest of York and Northumbria in 867. In the years which then followed, the Danish Army wandered from kingdom to kingdom, impelled restlessly forward by need of food as well as lust of plunder. Each year the Army had to seek a new centre for its winter quarters. In the autumn of 867 they struck south into Mercia, and dug themselves in at Nottingham. This place was doubtless chosen because it was near the Fosse Way and well situated for the transportation of supplies and booty by river. Down to the end of the Saxon period, the Trent remained an important means of communication. Of the condition of Mercia at the time we know next to nothing. We have not even traditions or romances of a later age. All that can be gathered from the Chronicle is that Burhred, who had been king since 853 or 852, had been an ally or dependant of Ethelwulf. In 853 he and his witan had 'begged of Ethelwulf that he would aid him to make the North Welsh obedient to him'. And now, in 867, he made a similar appeal for help. Since 853 the link between Mercia and Wessex had been strengthened by the marriage of Burhred to Ethelwulf's daughter Ethelswith. So when the Danes openly attacked Mercia in 867, and when the brothers Ethelred and Alfred led the forces of Wessex to support Burhred, they were answering the call of their sister's husband, as well as fulfilling an old political obligation. And what is most important of all, they were setting an example of co-operation to all Christian kings and peoples. Asser, in reproducing the Chronicle's account, adds that the army which marched to the aid of Burhred was 'immense', and that it was collected from every part of the kingdom of Wessex.

When the West Saxons joined the Mercians before Nottingham, they found the Danes established behind their earthworks, refusing to be tempted into the open, and the Mercians unwilling to assault the Danish defences. There seems to be a note of dis-. gust in the statement of the Chronicle that 'there was no heavy fight there, and the Mercians made peace with the Army'. A chance was missed which was not to recur. The Danes escaped from the combined forces of the two greatest Christian kingdoms of the island. Ethelred and Alfred had to return home without a victory, but with knowledge at first hand of the heathen and of their ways. The Mercians no doubt had to pay the Danes their price for the peace which they had obtained. The enemy presumably waited in Mercia till their geld had been collected and the crops had been harvested. Then, towards the end of 868, and not till then, they steered their laden ships down the Trent, and the Army swung back to Northumbria.

A year later 'they rode across Mercia to East Anglia', and the monasteries which, since the time of St. Guthlac of Crowland, had sprung up as centres of civilization in the Fens, were wasted by the destroyers. The post-Conquest historians here fill in the scanty record of the contemporary Chronicle by painting the horrors endured at this time by these monasteries of the Fen country. They describe, for instance, how at Medeshamsted (afterwards Peterborough) the heathen came and burnt and broke everything, slaying the abbot and the monks, and all that they found in the place; 'and that which was formerly full rich they reduced to nothing'.[20] Bardeney, Crowland, Ely, all had their later traditions of destruction and martyrdom. But all that can be recorded as authentic history is the great silence which now descends on this region. The Danes sweep across eastern Mercia and the district of the Fens; and for two generations Christianity in these parts seems to be withered and lifeless.

With the autumn of 869 the main army of the heathen was once more in East Anglia. It took up its winter quarters at Thetford. 'And that winter [869–70] King Edmund fought with them and the Danes gained the victory and slew the king and subdued all that land.' More than a hundred years later (about

985) the Frenchman, Abbo of Fleury, wrote the *Passion of St. Edmund*, telling a story which he said he had from the lips of Archbishop Dunstan, who in turn had it from an armour-bearer of Edmund himself. This story, describing how Edmund was tied to a tree, pierced with arrows like St. Sebastian, and then decapitated, does not quite tally with the few words of the Chronicle quoted above. Perhaps the chief value of Abbo's book lies in the evidence it gives of the growth of the traditional view of the Danes among the clergy of the tenth century. This is well illustrated in the following extract:

'Wherefore he [the enemy of mankind] sent one of the limbs of Satan as an adversary to Edmund. . . . This adversary was called by name Inguar, and he with another called Hubba [i.e. Ubbe] as wicked as himself attempted (and nothing but the divine compassion could have prevented it) to bring to destruction the whole land of Britain, and no wonder, seeing that they came hardened with the cold of their own wickedness from that summit of the world whence he had fixed his abode who in his mad ambition desired to make himself equal to the Most High. In fine, it is proverbial that from the North comes all that is evil, as those have had too good cause to know who through the spite of fortune and the fall of the die have experienced the barbarity of the races of the North. These, it is certain, are so cruel by the ferocity of their nature, as to be incapable of feeling for the ills of mankind, as is shown by the fact that some of their tribes use human flesh for food'—

and so forth. Then, after describing the attack on the province of Northumbria, the monk continues to adorn his tale:

'Having raked together their booty, Inguar left on the spot Hubba, his associate in cruelty, and approaching [East Anglia] suddenly with a great fleet landed by stealth at a city in that region, entered it before the citizens were aware of his approach, and set it on fire. Boys and men, old and young, whom he encountered in the streets of the city, were killed; and he paid no respect to the chastity of wife or maid. Husband and wife lay dead or dying together, on their thresholds; the babe, snatched from its mother's breast, was, in order to multiply the cries of grief, slaughtered before her eyes. An impious soldiery scoured the town in fury, athirst for every crime by which pleasure could be given to the tyrant who, from sheer love of cruelty, had given orders for the massacre of the innocent.'[21]

That there was something unusually brutal in the slaying of King Edmund, or unusually heroic in the way he met his death, may be gathered not so much from the rhetoric of Abbo as from the readiness with which he was acknowledged to be a saint both by English and Danes.

The sequel to the martyrdom is less obscure. We see that the Great Army, within five years from its first landing, having put an end to the old kingdoms of Northumbria and East Anglia, and having ravaged much of Mercia, had to seek a new prey. Where next were they to find their supplies of food and plunder? Kent had been already devastated. It was a choice, therefore, between the Midlands and Wessex. Wessex was the richer land and the less likely to receive help from outside. Accordingly, the choice fell on Wessex; and it was clear that, if Wessex went the way of Northumbria and East Anglia, the whole island would lie at the mercy of the heathen.

In this and in the last chapter we have set before ourselves two aims: one to discover the true character of the Northmen, the other to trace the events leading up to the decisive wars in which the kingdom of Wessex, encompassed on every side by the heathen, stood at bay. Now that we have reached the moment in December 870 when the great heathen Army launched its attack on Wessex, we have accomplished our second task. It remains to pick up further clues to the general character of the Northmen which have emerged piecemeal in the course of the story. The savage Viking of the conventional type has chiefly put in an appearance when we have seen these ninth-century raiders through the eyes of men of later centuries—clerics like Abbo of Fleury and Simeon of Durham, or Icelandic poets. True, there have been examples of cold-blooded brutality, such as Ragnar's slaughter of 111 captives on his Seine expedition of

845. There have been stories of ruthless slave-trading, beginning with the first descents of the marauders in 793 and the kidnapping of the boys of Lindisfarne. Though the Saxon Chronicle in its account of the Great Army has said nothing about this side of the Danish operations, we seem to get a side-light on it from an Irish Chronicle,[22] which reports that Imhar (? Inguar) returned to Ath-cliath (i.e. Dublin) with 'a very great prey of men, English, Britons, and Picts in captivity'. Some more matter-of-fact chronicles of the Arabs and Franks give the impression that the captives were generally taken in order to extort a ransom from their friends and kinsmen, but there are plenty of references to Christians who were carried off to Scandinavia.[23] The Christians had indeed good cause to add to the Litany the well-known petition, 'From the fury of the Northmen, good Lord, deliver us'. But the fury for the most part was conducted on commercial lines.

If we say then that the history of the ninth century reveals in the Northmen, as in the rest of us, a mixture of good and bad, we must qualify our statement by recognizing that they lived more intensely than men in most other periods; that they were more their own masters, more vigorous. When we read of their brutality and of their destruction we should not forget that these same Northmen or their contemporaries were also performing the most daring exploits; that a brother of Inguar, the murderer of King Edmund, had according to tradition been a leader in the great Mediterranean expedition which had aspired to put even Rome to ransom; and that other Northmen in the following years would turn the high prows of their undecked ships northward beyond the Orkneys and Shetlands, to find and settle in the Arctic seas lands which had never yet been peopled by mankind.

Who can wonder that the later romantic conception of the Vikings grew out of such exploits? What enterprise! What daring! What successes already achieved—the kingdoms of the English overthrown, Northumbria, East Anglia, Mercia; new colonies founded in the Scottish Isles, in Ireland, in England! Already, it may be, talk about a man's chances in Iceland.

Where in the scale of humanity shall we find a place for these men, with their savage traits combined with their promise of high civilization? They have been compared to the Kaffirs; to the Japanese in the days before 1868; to the English sea-dogs of the Elizabethan age, part pirates, part traders, part statesmen. And the fact that certain resemblances can be found with peoples so widely different as these is an illustration of the contrary currents which were battling in the souls of the Northmen.

One other comparison must be noticed, that of Stubbs.[24] He asserts that the civilization of the Danes 'was probably about equal to that which the Angles had had three centuries before'. What we have seen of them in these chapters shows that the true comparison is by no means so simple as this. The material civilization of the Northmen was not only higher than that of the Anglo-Saxons of the fifth century but in some ways they were ahead of the Anglo-Saxons of the ninth century. They could beat them in ship-building, in wood-carving, and in the ingenuity if not in the beauty of their versification. They had a capacity for self-government and a gift for devising new methods of warfare which placed the greater part of Western Christendom at their mercy. In the end we have to admit that all these comparisons leave us still far from the truth. There can be no cut and dried answer. After all, the Vikings were men drawn from the most various folks, belonging to very different classes of society, and subjected to very diverse influences.

Our confession of ignorance cannot be too often repeated. While we have learnt something about the Norwegians, about their monarchs, their chiefs, and their war-bands, what we sought to discover was the character of the Danes rather than that of the Norwegians, and the ways of the peasantry rather than of the upper strata of society. There has been no answer to the question, what manner of men were the Danish peasants, those who were about to affix their names to the byes and the villages of eastern England—the Grim of Grimsby, the Ketil of Kettleby, the Hacon of Haconby, the Gunnarr of Gunnersby, and all the rest.

Some implements of bone, such as those to be seen in the York Museum, some debased stone crosses of the Danish period, these indeed indicate how comparatively low was the general level of culture of the immigrants. A love of independence, a capacity for co-operation, great vigour—such characteristics may be inferred from their descendants, the freemen and socmen of the Danelaw; but that is all. The story of Alfred's wars will reveal certain other features—intelligence, 'slimness', elusiveness.

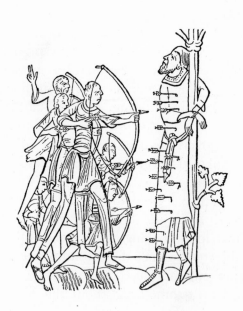

TAILPIECE.—Martyrdom of St. Edmund by the Danes.

THE DANISH WARS, 871–8

ALFRED'S YEAR OF BATTLES, 871

FROM December, 870, when the army of the Danes stole away from East Anglia and began its campaign against Wessex, the decisive factor in the affairs of our island became the personality of Alfred. Somehow or other one of the world's great men had been produced. Here was one who could master adverse circumstances and change defeat into victory, a king whose beneficent influence was to be felt for many generations.

How had this wonder come to pass? Can any account be given of the processes by which this great man had been fashioned?

For the most part when we speak of Alfred we are dependent on what we are told by Asser, the Welsh bishop who came about 885 from St. Davids to help the king in Wessex. This elderly bishop was unfortunately not the man to understand fully the mind of a many-sided layman, born of a hard-fighting stock. The side of Alfred's character with which Asser could best sympathize was the religious. The biographies known to Asser were the Lives of Saints, and he was therefore naturally inclined to magnify, according to the conventions of hagiography, the saint-like characteristics of his hero.

HEADPIECE.—*Left*, Northman's head from a wagon shaft from the Oseberg ship. *Right*, head of Alfred, from a silver penny.

The story which Asser tells of Alfred's struggle with ill health is confused and rhetorical, but in essentials it is not inconsistent. Stripped of exaggeration the story seems to have been this. When Alfred reached the difficult stage of adolescence* a horror of sexual immorality compelled him to seek out churches and relics in order to pray (like the saints whose conduct under temptation he had no doubt heard extolled by the clergy) that God would strengthen him by sending him some physical infirmity. Soon afterwards he began to suffer from some ailment which Asser calls the *ficus*, and which may perhaps have been haemorrhoids. Having endured this for some years he not unnaturally prayed that the hateful complaint might be exchanged for something else. Again his prayer seemed to be answered. He recovered from the *ficus*. Then, however, when he was nineteen years old, during his wedding festivities, he was suddenly attacked by a new and quite different complaint. His contemporaries failed to diagnose it, and it is hopeless for us to attempt to do so: epilepsy, neuritis, stone in the bladder, whatever it was, it continued to trouble him down to the time when the Welshman wrote his Life.

When we read these passages in *Asser*, we may well wonder how the morbid youth and the valetudinarian whom he portrays could be the man to save a kingdom. But elsewhere Asser gives other details and corrects the false stress which he has laid on the ascetic strain in Alfred's character. He tells us that Alfred was an 'ardent hunter', surpassing all others in his skill; that he loved to listen to the recital of Saxon poems—no doubt secular poems like *Beowulf*, as well as the religious products of the Cædmonic and Cynewulfian schools. He tells us the well-known stories of Alfred's love of learning. We can see how this zeal, conceived no doubt during his Roman journeys, was stimulated by the obstacles which he met—Danish entanglements and worldliness among the clergy. Asser's portrait showing a man of the eager, quick-minded, nervous type, can be supplemented

* This is compatible with Asser's use of the word *infantia*.

from Alfred's revelation of himself in his own writings. We have, for example, a glimpse of his youth when he describes[1] how, when men go hunting, they 'place their dogs and nets high up on the hills and in the woods', and how those who wander on the sands by the sea-cliffs know 'at what river mouths to look for fish'. We see that though there had been small opportunity for study, his youth had not been wasted. While he rode with the royal household on progress from one king's vill to another,

FIG. 67. Hunting scene from the Utrecht Psalter.

and while he hunted with hounds and horn, and snared wild game in nets, he had been learning the lie of the land. When the war came upon him, he knew from his own observation the ridgeways of the downs, the paths of Selwood, hiding-places in the fens of Somerset.

It is possible then to understand how Alfred, inheriting in full measure the piety which had distinguished his father, and the military traditions which had enabled his grandfather to raise the power of Wessex above that of any other Anglo-Saxon kingdom, grew up among the anxieties and hardships of the middle of the ninth century into the greatest of the Anglo-Saxon kings. No other Saxon king had been to Rome as a boy. In Alfred, the virility of the northern peoples was quickened by his remembrance, however youthful, of southern culture.

But what chiefly distinguished him from the other able kings and brave war-leaders of the age were the two God-given

qualities which have already been remarked. One of these was
the readiness to subordinate personal claims to the good of his
family and of the community—a readiness exhibited in his
arrangements with his brother Ethelred about their shares in
the family inheritance.* The other characteristic was a power
to see to the heart of things. Just as he used the tales of his sailor
friends, Ohthere and Wulfstan, to understand the genuine
Northmen as they existed behind the mask of Viking ferocity, so
he had penetration to perceive the secrets of success through the
turmoil of the age. Around Alfred were clergy ready to persuade
him, as they had persuaded his father, that the Viking troubles
were a manifestation of Divine wrath, and that they must be
cured by prayer and pilgrimage. Alfred, however, instinctively
grasped the realities of this world. His actions reveal a mind
which was ever at work reasoning out the causes of English
failure in the past, and calculating how such failure could best
be corrected in the future.

If we are right in thinking that he possessed an insight of
this kind, we can understand why the situation of Wessex in
December, 870, could seem by no means desperate. The Danes
might have a superiority in their weapons—their axes and their
long well-balanced swords; they might be better disciplined,
owing to the traditions of the ship's crews and the continuous
campaigning of recent years; they might be skilful in field
engineering, and in the crafty tactics of a feigned flight; above
all, they might intimidate their enemies by their reputation for
ferocity; but there were grounds also for hope. The number of
the Danes was not overwhelming. The army which could be
packed into a camp between the Thames and the Kennet was
not a migrant people like some of the hordes which had flooded
Roman provinces in the fifth century. It was an assemblage of
predatory bands, loosely kept together by the instincts of the
wolf-pack. Time was bound to bring disagreement among the
leaders. The pack was certain to break up.

* Above, pp. 516–17.

Moreover, though the Vikings had swept over one country after another, their successes had been due to the faults of their enemies as much as to their own valour. The Irish and the Franks had collapsed because of their own dissensions. The Frisians had succumbed because they had been first conquered by the Franks, and then deserted and handed over to Danish lords by the descendants of Charlemagne. In England the East Anglians had been too few to resist the Great Army, and the Northumbrians too much weakened by their feuds. Experience had already shown that the Vikings were not so irresistible as they sometimes seemed. They had long ceased to molest the Moors of Spain, because after the raids of 844 upon the Spanish rivers the Emirs had had the sense to build ships to defend their coasts. The 'Old Saxons', since the burning of Hamburg in 845, had suffered little, partly because they were poor, but partly also because they were warlike. These things showed that the Vikings had small love of fighting for the sake of fighting.

And there was every reason to expect that the West Saxons would give a good account of themselves. The military revival, begun by Egbert, was clearly not yet exhausted. It was but twenty years since Ethelwulf had won his smashing victory at Aclea. It was but ten years since Ealdorman Osric of Hampshire and Ealdorman Ethelwulf of Berkshire had claimed a victory over Weland's army—the army of 200 ships which so long terrorized the regions of the Somme and the Seine. The record of these victories in the Saxon Chronicle shows that the West Saxons possessed at least two advantages: a strong sense of patriotism—this seems to be proved by the Chronicle itself— and a national army which was well organized by shires, each led by a shire ealdorman.

Such were some of the circumstances which might have occurred to any who calculated the chances of success or failure at the beginning of the campaign. They were sufficient to justify a courageous policy of resistance.

The campaign[2] which was begun by the rapid march of the Danes from East Anglia to Reading in the darkest days of winter, towards the close of December 870, is the first in English history which can be followed in some detail. The site at Reading chosen for the Danes' base camp was so well guarded by the waters of the Thames and the Kennet (and no doubt also by ditches like the Plummery ditch) that no great length of earth rampart had to be thrown up to complete the defences. There, according to Asser,

'on the third day after the Danes' arrival, two of their jarls, with a great part of their army, rode out to plunder, while the others made a rampart between the two rivers. . . . And Ethelwulf, ealdorman of Berkshire, with his comrades* encountered the pagans at a place called Englefield. Both sides fought bravely. They kept up the fight for a long time. One of the pagan jarls† was killed, and the greater part of the army was destroyed. Then the rest escaped by flight. So the Christians gained the victory and held the battle-field.'

This opening skirmish between the ealdorman of Berkshire and the Danes is significant. It illustrates the nature of the Saxon army: its unit, the shire war-band, under the shire war-leader. Ethelwulf, the ealdorman of Berkshire, is a prototype of the later ealdorman, who replies to the messenger of the Danes before the fight at Maldon (A.D. 993), 'Say . . . here stands an earl with his band, who will defend this fatherland . . . the home of Ethelred my lord, his folk and field'.[3] The success at Englefield within three days of the Danes' arrival in Wessex showed how well the army system left by Egbert and Ethelwulf was working. The striking features in the opening of the campaign are the promptness with which the West Saxon forces were collected, and the spirit with which they at once confronted the Danes.

Four days after the auspicious success of the Berkshire ealdorman, the king and Alfred had a good-sized army‡ round them, and boldly 'advanced to the gate of the fort [at Reading], slay-

---

* *cum suis sodalibus.*

† Jarl Sidroc, or Sihtric, according to the Chronicles B and C. ‡ *micle fierd.*

ing and laying low all the heathen whom they found outside the fort. But the heathen themselves fought with valour, and rushing out of all the gates like wolves, joined battle with all their might. There for a long time both sides fought fiercely, but alas! the Christians at last turned their backs and the heathen gained the victory and held the battle-field. And there among the others fell the said Ethelwulf, the ealdorman.' If this attack by Alfred and his brother had been planned to be a surprise assault

Fig. 68. Warfare in the Dark Ages.
From the Utrecht Psalter. This MS. dates from the ninth century, but does not portray the weapons of that period. See p. 382 *c*.

on the Danish camp, it was daring to the point of rashness, for such an attack on Viking entrenchments had never yet succeeded. But it may have been no more than a reconnaissance in force—one which, meeting with unusual success, was pushed dangerously forward. The West Saxons were at any rate fortunate in somehow evading the pursuit of the Danes. Four days later, that is, about January 8, the Saxon army (no doubt reinforced with fresh levies from the remoter parts of the kingdom), was facing the invaders on the Berkshire Downs—'Ashdown', as the whole range was then called. Since the Danes had sallied from Reading with all their army under their two 'kings' and many jarls, the movement was something more than one of the normal plundering raids such as we have seen Viking armies sending forth from base camps in former years—for instance, the three raiding parties from Seville in 844. One aim of the march along Ashdown may, indeed, have been the collection of stores of grain from the corn-growing villages of the Vale of the White Horse. But the story of the ensuing fight gives colour to the view that the Vikings were, for once in a way, departing from their usual methods of war, and were actually seeking a battle in the open, thinking to follow up the victory which had been begun at Reading. The precise point of the Downs where the two armies met is unknown, but it was probably nearer to the Streatley end than to the prehistoric White Horse on the western hills above Uffington.[4] Asser had himself gone over the battle-field. We must listen to him as he tells the story of the fight:

'The Christians with all their forces went forth in good heart against the aforesaid army, at a place called Ashdown. . . . The heathen formed their host into two divisions and made ready two shield-walls* of equal size. And having two kings and many jarls, they gave one †part of the army to the two kings, and the other to all the jarls. The Christians, perceiving this, divided their army also exactly into two, and without delay formed their shield-walls.

'But Alfred with his men, as I have heard from truthful eye-witnesses, came to the place of battle more quickly and in better time than his brother; for his brother, king Ethelred, was still in his tent, occupied in prayer and hearing Mass, and declaring that he would not depart alive until the priest had finished the Mass, nor leave the Divine service for the service of men. And so he did. And the faith of the Christian king availed much with the Lord, as will be told more fully in what follows.

'Now the Christians had determined [the phrase suggests that there had been a formal or informal council of war] that king Ethelred with his men should undertake the battle against the two heathen kings, and that his brother Alfred, with his forces, should take the chance of battle against all the heathen jarls. And when things were thus disposed on either side, since the king remained very long in prayer, and the heathen had come quickly onto the field and were ready for battle, Alfred, who was then second in command‡ could bear the attacks§ of the enemy no longer, and he had to choose between withdrawing altogether, or beginning the battle without waiting for his brother. At last, like a wild

* *testudines.*

† Adopting the emendation of Stevenson, p. 234, *unam* for *mediam.*

‡ *secundarius.* § *hostiles acies.*

boar, he led the Christian forces boldly against the army of the enemy, as he had before proposed, in spite of the fact that the king had not yet arrived. And so, relying on God's counsel and trusting to His help, he closed the shield-wall in due order, and thereupon moved his standards against the enemy.

'But here I must tell those who are unaware of it that the field of battle was not equally advantageous to either side. For the heathen had seized the higher ground, and the Christians had to advance up-hill. There was in that place a single stunted thorn-tree which we have seen with our own eyes. Round about this tree, then, the opposing ranks met in conflict, with a great shouting from all men—one side bent on evil, the other side fighting for life and their loved ones and their native land.'

There are ambiguities in the story. We may wonder what exactly it was, during the pause when the Saxons were waiting for their king, that determined Alfred to advance. When Asser wrote of the *hostiles acies* which could not be longer endured did he in effect mean that missiles were discharged from the higher ground, or did he only refer (and this surely is the more probable) to the shouts and cries which might affect the morale of the in-experienced Saxon troops? We may wonder too whether Alfred commanded the king's division as well as his own to advance, and what exactly Asser meant by likening him to a wild boar. The advance of the 'shield-wall' cannot have been made in any 'wild rush'.[5] That would have involved a fatal disarray of the shield-covered line.

But at any rate there was no doubt about the victory itself. The fight was a long one, as well as fierce. It was maintained with great courage on both sides—but then at length the heathen gave way and fled back to Reading, with the Saxons pursuing them; fled till night-fall, even till the next day, and 'the whole breadth of Ashdown' was strewn with the bodies of their dead. King Bacsecg was among the killed and five jarls, including Sidroc the elder and Sidroc the younger (the elder being pre-sumably the sometime ally of Berno* in the Seine valley). Asser

* ? Biorn.

says, perhaps with some exaggeration, that 'many thousands' of the Danes, more than half their army, were slain either in the fight or the flight.

No famous victory of English history yielded such insignificant immediate returns as this of Ashdown. Within a fortnight the Danes were again in the ascendant. None the less, it is right that the fame of Ashdown should be preserved. Even if the military advantage quickly vanished, the victory remained a symbol. Its lesson could not be forgotten. Henceforth both invaders and invaded knew that in a pitched battle the massed forces of the Saxons could be stronger than the Great Army of the Vikings.

The victory gave the Saxons a new confidence, confidence in themselves and confidence in Alfred. And for Alfred, the moments in which he had to make his choice precipitated the mental processes of a lifetime. What was he to do? Trust primarily to the prayers of the priest, or act on the assumption that God helps those who help themselves? Ethelwulf his father had tried both courses at different periods of his life. At one time he had fought his battle at Aclea, at another he had deserted his kingdom to visit the shrines of the Apostles. And here one cold January morning on these Berkshire uplands were Ethelwulf's two younger sons, confronted by marshalled lines of heathen, and compelled to make each his great decision.

The battle at Ashdown is for us something more than the outward evidence of the continued valour of the Saxon thegnhood and the practical sense of Alfred. Thanks to the few descriptive sentences of Asser, the battle remains in the memory of the Anglo-Saxon race to represent all the ninth-century fights against the Vikings. Nay more; does it not stand for all the hundreds of encounters which before Alfred through unnumbered centuries had been fought out hand to hand upon these hills, battle storms which broke the silence of the downs for an hour or two, deciding the fate of tribes and peoples, and then passing into the oblivion of that which is forever unrecorded?

To us who live round Oxford the low ridge of Ashdown—of the
Berkshire Downs as we now call it—forms our southern horizon;
we know well the ridgeway which winds along the top of Ashdown following the undulations of the escarpment. It is a grassy
track, little changed since the days when before the coming of
the Saxons the massive ramparts of the forts built along its route
by men of the prehistoric Iron Age were already disused relics
of the past. Then, as in the time of Alfred, its grass was a main
road between the east of Britain and the south-west, a link in
the great highway which led eastwards across the Thames by
the Chilterns to the region of the Wash, and westwards over the
Marlborough Downs, to the Stone Circles, the deserted temple,
at Avebury; and thence on to Salisbury Plain and the Dum-
nonian peninsula. To us the words of Asser come with a full
meaning, and his mention of the solitary thorn-tree round which
raged the fight on the bare down reminds us how little that
countryside has changed, and how in the times of Alfred and of
Halfdene, as now, the chalk uplands were waterless, and therefore sparsely settled, while the villages were crowded near the
Port way, along the base of the escarpment.

Little imagination is needed to recall certain other sights
and sounds of that fateful day. For we have some knowledge
of the gaudily painted shields with which the Vikings formed
their shield-wall (round shields like those hung on the gunwale
of the Gokstad ship), of their mysterious banner with its emblem
of the bird of Odin, the raven which fluttered its wings when the
god promised victory, of the pennons of the lesser chieftains, of
the polished byrnies of the warriors. We know also how their
arms shone with gold or silver bracelets as they were raised to
throw a light spear or to wield sword or axe. They were no
doubt altogether a gayer body of men to look upon than the
English opposed to them, since they carried so much of their
plundered wealth on their persons, and moreover, they outdid
even the English in their love of brightly coloured clothes and
shields. Otherwise there may not have been much to distinguish

the two armies in appearance; the Danes, like the English, presumably had tunics drawn in at the waist with a sword-belt, and
cross-gartered hose (their big cloaks, we suppose, tied back out
of their way or discarded for the fight). These primitive hand-
to-hand encounters were as unlike modern battles in their
sounds as in their sights. The Vikings, knowing what terror a
noise could put into an enemy, heralded their attacks with
shouting and abuse. The Saxons no doubt shouted back their

FIG. 69. The place of slaughter.

cry in the old Germanic way. It was presumably during this
preliminary shouting and din that Ethelred refused to stir until
the Mass was ended, and Alfred decided to lead the attack without delay.

   If we now return to the story of the campaign of 871, it is the
ephemeral results of the victory of Ashdown which will strike
our attention. The Danes apparently continued to retain Reading as their base, and for the next four months they sallied out
time after time to scour the country in different directions. All
that the West Saxons could do was to hold up the heathen raids
whenever possible—at Basing, near Basingstoke (about January
22); then at Meretun, probably Marten, eight miles south-east
of Marlborough (about March 22),[6] and in other minor skir-
mishes; but the Danes usually 'held the place of slaughter'.

   Why was it that the Christians failed to follow up the success
which they had scored at Ashdown? Various explanations

suggest themselves: it may be said that the recent experience of
Ethelred and Alfred before the camp at Reading had taught
them caution. Then, too, the difficulty of blockading a position
such as that occupied by the Danes at the junction of two deep
rivers is obvious. There can be little doubt, however, that the
chief cause of the West Saxon failure, in the later combats of
the campaign, was the difficulty of keeping a national levy in the
field for any length of time. The English leaders could not supply
their own followers, as did the Vikings, by the plunder of the
countryside. The thegns and their men were always anxious to
get home. They were not accustomed to be long away from
their own shires. They wished to be sure that their own homes
were safe. They had their estates which must be attended to.
And after a victory like that of Ashdown every Saxon, feeling
that the worst was passed, wanted to talk at home about his
share in the victory and show the bracelet or the spear which he
had picked up on the battle-field. Leakage of this kind was the
fundamental difficulty which beset every national army. The
Danes at Reading, being professional warriors in an enemy
country, were not only free from such leakage, but they could
receive reinforcements from overseas. Such reinforcements did,
in fact, arrive. In the spring what was called 'a summer army',
composed, presumably, of ships' crews fresh from Denmark,
came and joined itself to Halfdene's force—'a summer army
innumerable . . . eager to fight against the army of the West
Saxons'.[7]

The last weeks of Lent were a dark time for the West Saxons,
since the reverse at Meretun was the most serious blow which
had yet befallen them and opened the way to the south-west.
But misfortune of a different kind followed. About Easter
(April 15), when the 'summer army' arrived and reinforced the
Danes, came the news that King Ethelred, young though he
was, had died, his health undermined, perhaps, by the winter
campaigning.

Though Ethelred left two young sons behind him, the crisis

of 871 was no time in which to put children on a throne, and Asser tells us that Alfred, the *secundarius*, had long been recognized as the heir to his brother. About a month after Alfred's accession occurred the most desperate of the later encounters of this campaign. It was fought at Wilton, on the hill south of the river Wilye, four miles to the west of what is now the city of Salisbury. Its position is enough to show that the Danes were penetrating to the heart of Wessex. Alfred had only 'a small band' left with him, and the reason assigned for its smallness is the fact that the people had all been worn out by the many fights. At Wilton his men fought fiercely and successfully for the greater part of the day, and it was apparently only the favourite Scandinavian ruse of a feigned flight which, in the end, encouraged the Saxons to break their ranks and led to the indecisive victory of the Danes.

Alfred now realized that the time had come when his kingdom must be saved by some other method than mere fighting, and so he came to terms with the invaders. We are told[8] that 'the Saxons made peace with the heathen on the condition that they should depart from them. And this they did.' But this clearly is not the whole story. Unless the Vikings were beaten in the field, they only made peace when they were paid for it with a heavy geld. No doubt this was what Alfred now promised, and the delay of three or four months before the Danes moved down the Thames to London may be regarded as a normal interval for the collection of the tribute—the first Danegeld that had ever been raised in the kingdom of Wessex.

Who had scored the point in this first round of the great fight between Alfred and the Danes? The answer depends on the view of what the Danes were fighting for. If their chief aim had been to conquer the kingdom of Wessex, they had clearly failed. If their aim had been simply to plunder the heart of Wessex, they had no less clearly succeeded; and by the agreement made with Alfred at the end of the campaign, they were free to transport themselves and their plunder.

Alfred had cleared the enemy from Wessex, but as they only moved down the Thames to London, they were still within easy reach of Sussex and Surrey and Kent, districts of which the king of Wessex was the recognized ruler and protector. This was no great victory.

The coins struck by Halfdene at London (Pl. 82, 6) illustrate the completeness of the hold which the Danes for a time retained over the city.[9]

In a sense, then, the campaign of 871 was indecisive. There had been no knock-out blow. In fight after fight the Saxons had come back undiscouraged. Alfred had kept their faces to the enemy. Then, having taught the Danes that the Saxons were a fighting race, Alfred showed statesmanship in making peace, even though an inglorious peace. 'The Saxons as a people were almost utterly worn out,' says Asser; but they had a sense of having won a moral victory, for in the eight battles of the campaign the heathen had lost one king and nine jarls, besides soldiers without number,'and this takes no account of the countless attacks by day and by night which the oft-mentioned Alfred and all the leading men of that people with their followers and very many of the king's thegns also made upon the heathen, with a keenness which never flagged'. The year of battles gave the West Saxons, in spite of some failures, a reinvigorated morale. The inglorious peace gave Alfred five years' respite.

THE DANES IN MERCIA AND NORTHUMBRIA

The five years which intervened between the departure of the Danes to London, towards the end of 871, and their reappearance in Wessex in 876, were Alfred's breathing-space. No doubt he used it to begin the reorganization of his kingdom; but our information does not enable us to distinguish between his earlier and his later work. Accordingly, the thread of the story—a slender thread—must be formed, as in the Chronicle, by the career of the Danish invaders: they move from the Thames to the Midlands; in the Midlands they divide; one part of them turns to Northumbria, while another part turns south, first to East Anglia, and then again to Wessex.

While Halfdene and his army were camped at London during the winter of 871–2, 'the Mercians made peace with the Army'. A sufficient comment on the nature of the peace is contained in a charter[10] in which Bishop Werferth of Worcester explains that his reason for selling a piece of land is the necessity of finding money for 'the immense tribute to the barbarians in the year in which the heathen settled in London'.

The next winter (872–3) was spent by the Danes at Torksey, on the lower Trent, and the winter following that (873–4) at Repton, higher up the same river. At Repton the heathen were in the heart of ancient Mercia, and in a favourite home of the old Mercian kings. The doom so long hanging over the Midland kingdom now descended. The Danes, says the Chronicle, 'drove king Burhred over sea about twenty-two years after he had obtained the kingdom, and they subdued all the land; and he (Burhred) went to Rome and there settled, and his body lies in St. Mary's church, in the School of the English'.

'After his expulsion' [we now quote from Asser] 'the heathen also subjected the whole kingdom of the Mercians to their lordship, and by a wretched agreement they committed it to the custody of an unwise king's thegn, called Ceolwulf, on this condition, that he should peacefully hand it over to them whenever they might wish to have it again. And he gave them hostages as surety, and took an oath that he would not in any way obstruct their wishes, and that he would be obedient in everything.'

There is no need to trace the poor part played by Mercia in this crisis of the heathen invasion. It cannot be only West Saxon bias which prevents the Chronicle from mentioning a single battle fought by the Mercians against the Danes. The contrast between the feebleness of Mercia under Burhred in the ninth century and its vitality under Offa a hundred years earlier is unusually marked; but who can say whether the decline is to be attributed to the extinction of Offa's dynasty, to a loss of morale such as so often accompanies a loss of empire, or simply to the incapacity of Burhred and his advisers? Whatever the cause, there is no denying that the submission of Mercia to the Great Army was more inglorious than either that of Northumbria in 867 or that of East Anglia in 869–70.

All England north of the Thames was now at the feet of the Danes. But the question what was to be their next step evidently puzzled their leaders. For the time being their policy was to extract the wealth of western Mercia through their nominee, 'the unwise king's thegn'. Except for parts of Wessex, there was no wealthy district which still offered an attractive field for the raider. It is no wonder that there was a division of opinion. Halfdene and his followers wished to try their fortune in the north. The rest of the Army—who perhaps had not, like Half-dene, a vivid remembrance of the flight from Ashdown—nursed thoughts of returning to Wessex. And so, after the wintering at Repton, came an all-important turning-point in the history of the heathen Army. It divided, and to this and subsequent divisions can be traced the beginnings of the Scandinavian States of the Danelaw.

Only a few facts are clear. First, one section of the Danes left the camp at Repton towards the end of 874. 'Halfdene went with a part of the Army into Northumbria, and took winter quarters by the river Tyne; and the Army subdued the land and often harried the Picts and the Strathclyde Welsh.'

In this and in the following moves of the Army, the aims of its leaders are more than usually open to question. Hitherto the lure of unravaged territories has seemed a sufficient explanation of the twists and turns of the Danes. Now, however, we are reaching an age of permanent conquest and settlement, and it begins to be reasonable to infer that the motives of the Danes were becoming more complicated by political considerations. Since Halfdene and his army were contemplating a settlement in Deira, the campaign of 875 against Bernicia and against the

Picts and Strathclyde Welsh, once subject to Bernicia, may have served a double purpose. The wasting of the north may have given assurance to those about to settle that there would be nothing to be feared from that quarter,[11] and it may also have provided them with the stock and the implements with which to set up their own farms in Deira.

At any rate, in the following year (876) Halfdene and his division of the Great Army recognized that the inevitable end had come to the policy of mere destruction; and, first of the Danes, they took the step which was, in process of time, to convert them from Danes into Englishmen. 'Halfdene divided the Northumbrians' lands, and [from that time] his men were ploughing and tilling them.' These words of the Chronicle tell us of the beginning of the Danelaw, but not of the establishment of a new dynasty. For the sons of Ragnar were better at destroying than at building. The curse of their old life was upon them, and so far as we know not one of the brood, in spite of their successes in many lands, founded a lasting dynasty. Biorn is said to have died soon after his return from the great voyage into the Mediterranean seas in 859–61. Inguar* vanished from English history after his conquest of East Anglia in 870 and his slaughter of King Edmund. If he is rightly identified with 'Imhar' of the Irish Annals[12] he had, in 869 and 870, co-operated with Olaf, king of the Dublin Vikings, in a siege of Alclyde which ended in the storming and sacking of the old British fortress; then, in 870, Imhar† accompanied Olaf back to Dublin bringing 'a great spoil of captives, English, British, and Pictish',[13] and finally, in 872, this 'king of the Northmen and of all Ireland and Britain' ended his life. And now Halfdene[14] vanished like Inguar before him from the scene of his Northumbrian conquests—vanished, says Simeon of Durham[15] in the conventional strain of the Church, with God's punishment upon him, that is, madness and an intolerable smell which made him hateful to his own men.

What little is reported about Northumbria in the following

* Ivar.   † ? Inguar.

PLATE 69

The Brunswick Casket, probably plundered by the Danes about 866–70 from the Abbey of Ely (founded as a numnery by St. Etheldreda in 673) A runic inscription on the base says 'Holy Virgin, be Thou a light to Thy Ely'. Walrus ivory. Eighth century

PLATE 70

The coffin of St. Cuthbert, restored

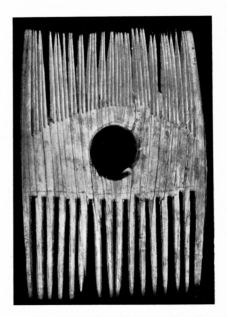

The Stonyhurst MS. of St. John's Gospel, found in the coffin of St. Cuthbert A.D. 1104. Binding of the seventh century

Ivory comb found in the coffin of St. Cuthbert, A.D. 1104

years points to the utmost confusion. The Danes were not strong
enough or united enough to set up a stable dynasty of their own.
The turmoil and the panic of the time is best seen in the story of
the monks' flight from Lindisfarne with the relics of St. Cuthbert.[16]
Hearing of Halfdene's depredations north of the Tyne in 875,
the abbot of Lindisfarne took up the uncorrupted body of St.
Cuthbert in its coffin, one which had been made for it and wonderfully adorned soon after the Saint's death (Pl. 70). He also
placed in the coffin the bones of St. Aidan, the head of St.
Oswald, king and martyr, the bones of other venerable priests,
St. Cuthbert's portable altar, and one at least of their illu-
minated manuscripts, doubtless the beautiful Lindisfarne Gospels. The coffin, engraved with runes and with lozenge-eyed
saints and angels, was then transported, sometimes on the
shoulders of 'seven clerics', young men who had been educated
in the monastery, sometimes in a cart drawn by a bay horse.
The fugitives wandered away into the remote hill-country of
western Northumbria, confident that so long as they preserved
the body of St. Cuthbert they need not fear the loss of their
homes. At first they were accompanied by a number of Christian laymen, with their wives and families. These, when they
came to the barren moorlands, were compelled by want to
abandon the flight. But the remnant wandered on. 'They fled',
says Simeon of Durham, 'like sheep before the wolves.' They
fled by sea, and through upland wastes. They came to Whitern
in Galloway; after a time to Craike, ten miles north of York.
They were indeed fleeing 'like sheep', since after all, in spite of
Halfdene's devastation in 875, the Christian princes who continued to rule at Bamburgh, within a few miles of Lindisfarne,
would have been their natural defenders. Their flight lasted,
according to their own reckoning, seven years. In the end their
faith (or their sheepishness) was justified, and when the clouds
lifted, many years later, we find the fugitive brethren of St.
Cuthbert settled at Chester-le-Street, and claiming—it seems
not without some reason—that Guthred the successor of Half-

dene had endowed them with all the lands between the Wear and the Tyne, to the east of the Roman road. The extent of the donation may be exaggerated, but it was at least the beginning of a new patrimony for St. Cuthbert, which would grow in time to be an endowment fit for a prince.

The extent and nature of the Danish settlement will concern us when we come to the history of the following centuries. For the present we need only think of Halfdene and his chiefs allotting lands to their followers according to some plan which cannot now be known. We may think also of the wooden farmsteads, springing up mainly in the fertile valley of the Ouse— groups of halls and byres, constructed with Scandinavian skill in log-building.[17] A large settlement, a village, was generally called a *thorp*. An isolated farm was a man's –*by*.

The Danes settled in Deira were doubtless still held together by a military organization, but they were clearly not strong enough to establish a well-founded kingdom. They had been able to destroy monasteries, but they could not, perhaps they did not wish to, destroy Christianity as a whole. All was confusion. What had once been the leading kingdom of the island must be left in its obscurity. It is something to know that the Danes who had followed Halfdene from the camp at Repton in the winter of 874 were ploughing the great plain of York, and that their heathenism was sufficiently tolerant to allow them to endow the Christianity which had survived the great upheaval. But that is the extent of our knowledge. We must return to the south of England to obtain an intelligible account of the events of the time.

THE CRISIS—ALFRED'S SECOND WAR, 876–8

We now take up the story of the division of the Great Army which in 875 trekked from Repton to Cambridge. It remained at Cambridge for one year, under the command of three kings— Guthrum, Oskytel, and Amund. Its operations begin to be narrated in more detail in 876, when it, or part of it, 'stole away into Wareham, eluding the West-Saxon fyrd'. This was the end of Alfred's respite, the beginning of his three years' struggle against Guthrum—the crisis of the interminable wars between the Vikings and the English.

The position of Wessex was in some ways worse in 876 than it had been in 871. For the Danes were now masters of Mercia, Ceolwulf, 'the unwise thegn', holding it in readiness for them. Alfred therefore could feel no security along the whole of his northern frontier. On the south coast also he had to meet an attack by sea as well as an attack over land. The Danes had arranged that a sea-army should co-operate with the land-army. Part at any rate of this sea-army had come, if we can trust Ethelweard, 'from the west'—that seems to mean from Ireland or the Irish seas. Wessex was thus encircled more closely than it had ever been in the past. The Viking tides from the east and from the west were synchronized. The kingdom of Alfred, the last independent kingdom in England, was in imminent danger of being submerged.

The attack of the heathen was clearly well conceived, besides being sudden and well timed. Wareham, where the land-army and the ship-army joined forces, was an ideal situation for a Danish camp. It was already a fortified town, a *castellum*;[18] and being placed on the narrow spit of land between the Frome and the Tarrant where their streams run parallel before they debouch into Poole harbour, it was well sheltered from attack by land. At the same time its admirable anchorage gave the Danes a good opportunity to use their sea-power in raids up and down the coast.

Alfred with his fyrd followed after the heathen; perhaps he bottled up the land-army by occupying the spit of land between the rivers to the west of Wareham. As in 871 he showed that he was ready both to fight the Danes and to buy them off. The Danes, either because they had exhausted the plunder of the neighbourhood and wanted to move on, or because they were uncomfortably hemmed in by Alfred, were ready by the summer

for a treaty. They made peace—doubtless on their usual conditions of a money payment. They swore to it 'on the holy ring',
a ring usually placed on the altar of a heathen temple and
reddened in the blood of the sacrificial animals. To take such
an oath was a thing 'which before they would never do to any
nation'. It seemed to be a clever idea of Alfred to bind them in
this way. But it was a failure. The Army, says Asser, 'resorted to
its habitual treachery; and disregarding their hostages and their
oaths and their promises of good faith, they broke the treaty'.
In the autumn they made a dash for Exeter; and Alfred and
his mounted men rode after them, 'but could not overtake them
before they were in the fortress where they could not be come at'.[19]

Then occurred the saving mercy. 'Flavit Deus, et dissipati
sunt.' The ship-army, setting out from Wareham and no
doubt intending to rejoin the land contingent at Exeter, was
caught in a storm off Swanage. A hundred and twenty of their
ships were wrecked. Some five thousand of the heathen may be
reckoned to have perished beneath the cliffs of Dorset—a loss for
them greater than any yet recorded. It was a good lesson for
heathen oath-breakers.

In other respects the Exeter episode had much the same
history as that of Wareham. The Danes in Exeter (though they
had with their usual cleverness chosen the strongest river-fortress
in the west country), being hampered by the destruction of the
'ship-army', found that they were no match for Alfred. Any
hopes they may have cherished of rallying Celtic malcontents
were disappointed. And so the Danes, having perhaps had their
pickings from the district round Exeter, were, by the summer of
877, ready once more to make peace, once more to swear great
oaths and give hostages—'as many as Alfred would have'. This
time 'they kept a good peace', and in August they moved across
the northern frontier into Mercia. The 'good peace' lasted just
about five months.

We now come to the most puzzling part of the whole story.
The Chronicle, after reporting that the Danish Army kept their

peace and went in the autumn to Mercia, then says that the Army 'divided'* part of Mercia 'and gave the rest to Ceolwulf'. Since the army of Guthrum was back again in Wessex by the following midwinter, three or four months' interval was a short period in which to partition a kingdom. It is so insufficient that one can only speculate about what really happened: whether it was the Danish boroughs of the south-east Midlands or some other Danish settlements which now had their beginning. Some think that the main Danish settlement of eastern Mercia really went back to the period of 872–4, when the Army was in these parts. Groups of Danes may then have established themselves in and round certain fortified places, notably in those which came later to be known as 'the Five Boroughs'—Derby, Nottingham, Lincoln, Stamford, and Leicester. Other historians[20] think that these boroughs may have been formed by groups detached from Halfdene's army in Northumbria. The Danish boroughs of the south-east Midlands may have been first organized by sections of the Cambridge army which did not follow Guthrum to Wareham in 876. There is room for these and other guesses since the data are insufficient for the formation of any solid theory on the subject.[21]

The one thing which is certain is that Guthrum renewed the struggle against Alfred in the early January of 878. The story of his quick success and of the collapse of Wessex is soon told in the words of the Chronicle. In 878 after Twelfth Night, the Army under Guthrum 'stole away to Chippenham and overran the West Saxons' land and occupied it and drove many of the people oversea, and of the rest the greater part they conquered and the people submitted to them, save the king Alfred—and he with a little band withdrew to the woods and to the fastnesses of the moors'.

What had happened? The story of the *débâcle* and the subsequent rally, culminating in the victory of Ethandun and the Peace of Wedmore, is so familiar to us from childhood that it

---

* *gedældon*.

may easily be taken as a matter of course. Yet even when we have eliminated the later fabrications about Alfred's burning of the cakes and his harping in the Danish camp, the meaning of the events remains open to question. Why, for instance, did Wessex, after two fairly satisfactory campaigns, in 876 and 877, suddenly collapse? Since Mercia had been 'divided up' in 877, the army of Guthrum may have been smaller than that which had been checked at Wareham and at Exeter. Now there can be no reasonable doubt that Guthrum scored his quick success partly because Alfred was surprised (Twelfth Night was just the time when Christians would be occupied by a great festival), and partly because the Saxon thegn-class was suffering from war-weariness. In the past the thegns had been accustomed to an occasional campaign against the West Welsh and the Mercians— a campaign which yielded a profit and was always short. But by the winter of 877 they had probably been in the field for a large part of two years. These campaigns had brought no glory or spoil. The thegns and their men had been kept away from their farms and families, and they had nothing to show for it. To turn out for yet another campaign in the coldest part of the year was too much for human nature. No doubt they thought they knew what it would mean—nights spent in the open, in the open in January! And what would be the end of it? What but another futile peace, with the Danes taking another geld and giving in return worthless heathen oaths? Besides, the king himself was a fugitive. Was a man to blame for thinking that his first duty under these circumstances was to defend his own home, or at any rate not to forsake his shire?

Guthrum had at last got Alfred off his guard. Whatever was the reason, Alfred failed for the moment to organize any effective defence.

Yet even so it is not self-evident why Alfred withdrew with his bodyguard to the west of Somerset. It cannot have been simply to obtain the protection of the marsh. The depths of the Andreds-weald would have been sufficient shelter for him, as they had been for earlier fugitives. There was clearly some further reason which determined Alfred's choice. Perhaps it was only the opportunity afforded by the Somerset swamps and forests for molesting the enemy as they harried north-western Wessex. But it may be that ideas of a more comprehensive strategy entered into the schemes of the heathen and also into those of Alfred, calculating how best to counter them.

At this point, therefore, it becomes necessary to come to an understanding about the aims of Guthrum. When we study the last map we shall agree that one, possibly the sole, consideration which guided the Danish leader to Chippenham was the fact that the country round it—east Wiltshire, Somerset, and north Devon—was the only rich district of Wessex yet unravaged. But the story of 878 and of the years preceding it yields some clues which suggest that Guthrum and the other leaders of the Viking armies were keeping in touch with each other's movements, and were working according to a concerted plan. For what is the next event in the spring of 878? It is the descent of a brother* of Halfdene on the coast of Devon.

We may safely assume that this invasion was the result of an understanding between the two Viking leaders. The brother of Halfdene had been spending the winter in south-west Wales: Guthrum, until his descent on Chippenham, had been at Gloucester.[22] Communication between the two would have been easy. The wisdom of concerted action was too evident to be overlooked. But if Guthrum was collaborating with the brother of Halfdene in 878, is it not likely that his other movements since he parted company with Halfdene at Repton in 874 had also been according to an agreed general plan? If so, we must recognize the possibility that the Viking armies, instead of simply drifting from province to province in search of food and plunder, had been co-operating in a scheme for a complete conquest of all England. According to this interpretation of the events, while Halfdene had accepted the task of making Deira

* Identified as Ubbe but on the slenderest evidence. Cf. Stevenson, 263–5.

a Danish kingdom and of eliminating the danger of interference from the north, Guthrum and his colleagues had undertaken to reduce Wessex. They had moved to Cambridge, presumably to build up their forces with fresh drafts from Scandinavia or the Continent. Wareham had been chosen as the best position in which to get into touch with the ship-army 'from the west'. The next move to Exeter was also, it may be, a step in the pre-arranged plan. An alliance with the Cornishmen may have seemed the key to success in the south of England. It had failed in 838, but it might succeed at a second attempt. In 877 the plan was frustrated, partly because Alfred followed up the land-army too promptly, partly because of the annihilation of the fleet in the storm off Swanage. But Guthrum showed more consistency of purpose than was usual with the Vikings. The plan for 878 seems to have been a revised edition of that for 877. He had got into touch with a new fleet 'from the west'. Once more co-operation with a son of Ragnar; once more the idea of a Danish base in Dumnonia and of a possible alliance with the Cornish-men—here was a plan which offered the chance of a knock-out blow against Alfred. And the plan was, in fact, all but successful.

If the above interpretation of events is correct, the attacks of 876–8 are seen to be threats of a more dangerous character than the invasion of 871. In Guthrum's mind, behind the immediate purpose of feeding his army and ravaging a virgin country, there was the ulterior purpose of obtaining land for settlement in Wessex and of winning security for all the Danes in the island by a conquest which would eliminate the one powerful Saxon kingdom.

But what was the order of the day when the surprise attack of January 878 met with its quick success and Alfred retired to the marshes of Somerset? The Danes of course wasted the country round their base camp during the winter, covering, as usual, a wide circle. Did they also disperse their bands over Wessex as a whole? Did they maintain anything like a blockade or regular operations against Alfred and his men in the marshes? The

Chronicle says that the Danes 'overran and occupied', that is conquered, more than a mere district, 'the land of the West Saxons',* and this is supported by Asser later in his story, when he speaks of 'such of Hampshire as had not sailed beyond sea for fear of the heathen'—a passage which makes it clear that at least a part of central Wessex was overrun in addition to Wessex west of Selwood. The flight of these Hampshire men must have been across the Channel to France. As a rule the Viking sphere of devastation was a restricted one. In 871, however, they had appeared at Wilton, nearly fifty miles from their base camp at Reading, and it would not be a longer expedition for marauding bands from Chippenham to ride down the Roman road to Winchester. On the other hand, when Alfred took the field in the early summer, he encountered a Danish army which was concentrated apparently within easy reach of Chippenham. Yet because the Danes were concentrated in May it does not of course follow that they had not been dispersed far afield during the winter months.

The view we take of Guthrum's plan necessarily affects our views of Alfred's strategy. If Guthrum was counting on the co-operation of the brother of Halfdene and on disaffection among the West Welsh, it is easy to understand why Alfred after the collapse of January turned to the fens of Somerset instead of to the Andredsweald, where he might have rallied the eastern kingdoms. In Somerset he was near enough to the West Welsh to give them any moral support required to keep them firm to the cause of Wessex and Christianity. In the woods and swamps of Somerset he could find not only security for himself and his few followers, but he could threaten the wandering bands of plunderers in the western shires. Moreover, from his refuge in Somerset he could quickly strike when the opportunity offered at the Danish head-quarters.

It is time to return from these speculations about aims and strategy to the events themselves. Asser's story makes it clear

---

* *geridon Wesseaxna lond ond gesæton.*

that there were two phases in Alfred's withdrawal among the Somerset marshes. Before Easter we hear nothing of Athelney. We only know that at that time Alfred 'with a few of his nobles and with certain thegns and vassals led an unquiet life in great tribulation among the woods and marshes of Somerset. For he had nothing wherewith to supply his wants except what in frequent sallies he could seize either stealthily or openly, both from the heathen and from the Christians who had submitted to their rule.'

The combination of woodland with fenland in west Somerset made it an ideal country for carrying on a guerrilla warfare against the enemy. It was surely for this purpose rather than simply to save himself that Alfred took to the fens. The marshes stretching inland for about twenty miles were what the Chronicle calls 'moor fastnesses'. They changed from swamp to lagoon (Pl. 71) according to the rainfall and the tides, and therefore could hardly be approached either by water or by land. This fenland was enclosed in an irregular horseshoe of hills, and the hills were largely covered by forest, especially the great Selwood near the far eastern horizon. Protected by these swamps and woods, Alfred had the advantage of the interior lines. He could dominate the whole of western Wessex. He could keep in touch with the men of Devon to the south, and the Danes could never know where he would next emerge.

The winter and the early spring before Easter were the darkest period of all. We have already seen what it might mean for a Christian country to lie at the mercy of the Vikings—the systematic desecration and destruction of churches and monasteries, the murderings, the lootings, the slave-raiding and slave-trading. To what extent Wessex suffered these calamities is not clearly stated. Alfred, however, tells[23] 'How before all was utterly ravaged and burnt the churches throughout all England were filled with treasures and books'. Asser mentions that in Dyfed, his own native land, the heathen, under Halfdene's brother, had massacred many Christians, and the fact that so

PLATE 71

Athelney in time of flood

As it may have appeared before its monastery was built

PLATE 72

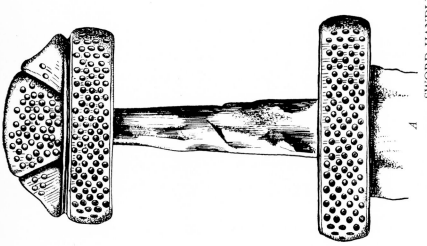

SWORD HANDLES OF THE NINTH CENTURY

A. Norwegian.   *B.* English, from the Thames at Wallingford

The silver inlay on the upper guard of *B* includes symbols of the four Evangelists

many Saxons were driven into exile speaks in itself of the horrors which were to be apprehended for those who remained. The Saxons now fled oversea before the Danes as once the Britons had fled before the Saxons. Doubtless it was no more than the beginning of a migration, but the flight was no mere imaginative fiction of the chronicler. It receives some confirmation from two other sources. In one of these, a charter of Alfred's son, we learn that a certain ealdorman, Wulfhere, accompanied by his wife, forsook his lord the king and his fatherland, so violating the oath which he had sworn to Alfred. For this crime his lands were forfeited.[24] In the other source, a continental biography,[25] we hear of a 'British' fugitive who appeared at Montfaucon, in France, at a time when 'all the inhabitants of that island (Britain) were being killed or driven into flight'.

Shortly before Easter the tide of misfortune began to turn. The defeat of Halfdene's brother by the thegns of Devon was the first sign that the panic was checked. It is an event of which Asser gives some picturesque details.

'In the same year the brother of Inquar and Halfdene came with twenty-three ships from Dyfed* where he had wintered, slaying many Christians, and sailed to Devon.† And there in the midst of his wrong-doing he came to a miserable end, being slain, and 1,200 men with him, by the king's thegns before the fortress of Cynwit.‡ In this fortress many of the king's thegns with their men had taken refuge. Now when the heathen saw that the fortress was ill-prepared and altogether unfortified, except that it had only walls made after our [i.e. the Welsh] fashion, they began to beset it. The reason why they did not exert themselves and storm it was that the place, owing to its situation, is very secure on all sides except the eastern, as we ourselves have seen. In besetting it they thought that these men would soon give way to hunger and thirst and be overcome by the siege, since the fortress has no supply of water. But it did not fall out as they expected. For the Christians, before they endured any such distress, by the inspiration of heaven judged it to be

---

* *Demetica regione*, i.e. South Wales.   † *Domnonia*.

‡ Probably Countisbury, a hill in Exmoor near the sea on the borders of Somerset and Devon. So *E.P.N.S.* viii. 62–3.

better either to suffer death or to gain the victory. Accordingly at day-break they suddenly rushed forth against the heathen, and at the first attack they laid low most of the enemy, including their king. A few only by flight escaped to their ships.'

It is a fine story; and for once in a way we are grateful to the *Annals of St. Neot*, a compilation of the twelfth century, for adding a touch which gives reality to the scene even though it stands out with the vivid colouring of folk-lore.

'There they captured no little spoil. And among it they took the banner which they call the Raven. Men say that the three sisters of Inguar and Ubbe, the daughters of Lothbrok, wove that banner and did the whole of it in a single day. Moreover men say that in every battle in which that banner went before them, the raven in the middle of the design seemed to flutter as though it were alive, if they were going to have the victory. But if they were about to be beaten in the coming fight, it would hang down without moving. And this was often proved to be true.'[26]

The victory of the thegns of Devon was decisive in more ways than one. Not only did it put an end to any possible plan of detaching the Cornishmen from Wessex, but it proved once more that the Northmen, even when led by a son of Ragnar, could be beaten by their own methods. To stand up to them with confidence, if possible to surprise them, was enough. Alfred, then, had good grounds for hope. Yet the reasons for despair had been such as to drive a king like Burhred out of the island. To go to Rome, like Burhred, and win eternal blessings at the shrines of the Apostles—that might tempt a king. Alfred's thegns had almost all deserted him; he had an excuse for following the others oversea.

It is no wonder that Alfred was, as Asser tells us, 'in great tribulation'. No Christian king before him so hard pressed had emerged successfully. Alfred was a pioneer in the work of up-holding an apparently hopeless cause. He could not buoy him-self with thoughts of the successful endurance of a Bruce or a William the Silent; and it was only later in his life when he read in the history of Orosius about the struggle of the Romans against Hannibal that he learnt how the Romans 'would never shrink from the war though they often stood on a small and hopeless foundation, so that at last they had the mastery over all those who before nearly had it over them'.[27]

For some eleven weeks Alfred led the hard life which has been described; sallying out from the woods and swamps of Somerset to carry off what was necessary to feed the small band which still followed him. Then, after Easter (23 March), there came a change. 'Alfred with a little band made a fort* at Athelney, and from that fort warred on the Army with that part of the men of Somerset that was nearest.' Asser's account is slightly different: 'from this fort with the vassals of Somerset he made constant attacks on the heathen, without wearying'. Thus this second phase of the withdrawal saw a much more hopeful activity than the first. Alfred, encouraged by the victory in Devon, was more aggressive than before. He had a larger band of followers; he was making a stronghold against emergencies after the fashion of the Danes (so far as we know it was his first fort); and he was sending out his messengers to arrange for the concentration of the fyrd of the neighbouring shires early in May.

Not much labour can have been necessary to make the island of Athelney in the Parret marshes into a safe refuge. Its twenty-four acres of dry land, rising some thirty or forty feet above the surrounding swamps, now became the nation's ark of salvation.

Then, in the seventh week after Easter, just as spring was at its greenest, came the great deliverance. The concentration of the troops of Somerset and Wiltshire, and of those of Hampshire who had not fled beyond the sea, was effected at 'Egbert's Stone' to the east of Selwood, near the high ground (Penselwood) where three shires meet.[28] 'And when they saw the king they received him like one risen from the dead, after so great tribulations, and they were filled with great joy.' This scene, one of the most memorable in the history of the English kingship, is

* *geweorc.*

described by the Chronicle in three words: *his gefægene wærun*—
'they were fain of him'. The next day the levies moved to Iglea.*
At dawn on the third day Alfred again led them forward. Before
them, it seems, rose the steep chalk hills of what may be called
the north-western promontory of Salisbury Plain. A white track
leading up the hill-side, near the embankments of Battlesbury
Camp (Pl. 73) showed a path which could bring them in about
five miles to Ethandun, a down on the northern ridge which had
given its name to a royal vill below, now the village of Edington.
Since Alfred in his translations[29] displays an ineradicable conviction that battles are fought on 'downs', we are not likely to
be wrong if we assume that this battle of Ethandun, the supreme
contest of the Danish wars, was fought, like Ashdown, on
the chalk uplands, perhaps near Bratton 'Castle', and not in the
valley. At this point by a strange coincidence there is cut in the
turf, as at Ashdown, another White Horse, which, though 'new
modelled', seems to be prehistoric. From the crest across the
Vale of Pewsey the Marlborough Downs are silhouetted in the
morning light, those downs on which the ancestors of Alfred had
fought so many decisive battles. To the north the well-wooded
plain of Wiltshire is seen like a map, almost up to Chippenham,
where, thirteen miles away, there was still, it may be presumed,
the base camp of the Danes with its store of collected plunder.

We know of this decisive battle but a few bare facts: that Alfred
had the whole army of Guthrum against him; that he formed
his *testudo*, or shield-wall, closely; that the fight was long and
fierce, till at last the Christians defeated the heathen with
great slaughter and rode after them as they fled to their fort,
pressing upon them and smiting them down. There was a
sameness in the contests of this primitive hand-to-hand warfare,
which enables imagination easily to fill in some details, from the
first gleam of the forest of spears as the armies catch sight of

---

* So spelt in the Chronicle (Æcglea in Asser), identified with the spot about two
miles south of Warminster in Eastleigh Wood, where there was once an Iley Oak and
near it earthworks forming a camp.

PLATE 73

Battlesbury Camp, looking back over Alfred's probable line of
advance, to the hills east of Selwood

Bratton Castle on the N.W. angle of Salisbury Plain

Edington Hill is seen on the right, beyond the earthworks. The name
Ethandun may have had a wider application

PLATE 74

Escarpment of Salisbury Plain, showing the ramparts of Bratton Castle and the White Horse (as 'new modelled' in 1778)

one another, to the recognition of the banners, *signa horribilia*,[30] as they draw together, and the word-strife when they are within shouting distance. From other Anglo-Saxon descriptions of battles we know that when the warriors had dismounted and left their horses in the rear, a 'shield defence'* was formed with great care. The leaders used to go round their forces, showing the men how they should stand and how the shield should be held right forward with a firm grip. The Old English poets often dwell on the noise of the battle-field, the deliberate clashing of spear on shield, the shouts of the rival armies before they close, the hum of the bows, and then the ring of metal in 'the game of iron'. We may recall one Old English poem in particular, since many scholars refer it to a period but little later than this, and if we substitute Englishmen for Hebrews and Danes for Assyrians we have a fair description of what may have occurred at Ethandun.[31]

'The valiant men and warriors marched out, bore banners of victory; they set straight forward to the fight . . . at break of dawn; the shields rang, resounded loudly. The lean wolf in the wood rejoiced at that, and the dark raven, the bird greedy for slaughter; both knew that the warriors purposed to provide them with a feast of fated men; and behind them flew the dewy-feathered eagle, hungry for food; dark-coated, horny-beaked, it sang a song of war. The men of battle marched on, warriors to the strife, protected by shields, hollow linden targes,—they who erstwhile had borne the flaunting of foreigners, the taunt of the heathen. . . . Then keenly they shot forth showers of arrows, adders of war, from their bows of horn, strong shafts; the raging warriors loudly stormed, cast spears into the press of brave men; wroth were the heroes, the dwellers in the land, against the hateful race; sternly they stepped forward; stout of heart, they harshly aroused their ancient foes. . . . The men with their hands drew from the sheaths the brightly adorned blades with trusty edges; fiercely they smote; . . . they spared no living man of the host, mean or mighty, whom they could overcome. So all morning the noble warriors pursued the foreign people.'

Napoleon is supposed to have said that 'the art of war is to march twelve leagues, fight a battle, and march twelve more

* *scyldburh.*

in pursuit'. The saying sums up well enough the day of Ethandun. Though the fort to which the army fled is not mentioned by name, it is commonly and with good reason assumed to be Chippenham.

For fourteen days the army of Alfred besieged the Danish camp. Then, according to Asser,

'the heathen terrified by hunger and cold and fear, and at the last full of despair, begged for peace on these terms: that the king should have from them as many picked hostages as he liked and that he should give none to them. They had never before made a peace with anyone on such terms. And when he had heard their embassy, the king acting according to his natural disposition had pity on them and received from them the picked hostages, as many as he desired. Thereupon the heathen swore that they would straightway depart from his kingdom. Moreover their king Guthrum promised that he would accept Christianity and would receive baptism at the hand of king Alfred.

'All these things he and his men fulfilled as they had promised. For after [three] weeks Guthrum the king of the heathen came with thirty* men chosen from his army, to Alfred, to a place called Aller, near Athelney. And king Alfred stood godfather to him and raised him from the holy font of baptism. Then, a week later, his "chrism-loosing"† took place in the king's vill called Wedmore. After the baptism he remained with the king for twelve days, and the king with all his men gave them many excellent gifts.'

Why do we recognize these three events—the victory of Ethandun, the treaty of Chippenham, the baptism of Wedmore —as a turning-point in English history? There had been plenty of victories over the Vikings before 878, and there would be need for plenty more before the ninth century came to an end. Whatever Asser may say, the peace was not altogether unlike other peaces, both those which preceded and those which came after it. The Danes had found themselves in a tight place, and they had readily promised anything in order to extricate themselves. No one could be confident that there would not be another

---

* The Chronicle says 'twenty-nine'.

† That is, the ceremony of unbinding the linen fillet round the head of the baptized.

collapse, as sudden and unexpected as that of the previous January. Nor was the forced baptism of the Danish leaders an effectual safeguard. There is a well-known story[32] of a Northman who at a baptismal ceremony complained that he had 'gone through this washing' twenty times and that the garment (the alb) then given him was not up to standard nor fit for a warrior. Are we to think, then, that there were guffaws scarcely smothered when the Danish chiefs, in their white robes, holding their lighted tapers, saw the linen fillet in the form of a cross bound round the head of their king, to keep the holy oil, the chrism, in the place where it had been applied? And Guthrum—is it thinkable that the old warrior, in his alb and his fillet, looked back at his chiefs with something like a wink? Such things as these are possibilities, even though they are unrecorded in history. Across the Channel Charles the Bald, in 873, after besieging a force of Vikings until they yielded, had extracted from them terms not unlike those obtained by Alfred in 878.[33] Yet the kingdom of Charles was to suffer thereafter Viking invasions and settlements worse than anything which had preceded them. In the case of Guthrum, however, it is clear that the combined effect of a military defeat and of the contact with a Christian of heroic type was more lasting. The Danes had been shaken.* And, even if they were not able to comprehend the spiritual teaching of Christianity, they could at least be overawed by the mysteries of the dim church, with its diffused scent of balsam (evidently the odours of Paradise).[34] There was magic in this which even a hardened Viking could hold in dread.

And the magic which did more than anything else to cast a spell over Guthrum and his twenty-nine chiefs was surely the personality of Alfred himself. Alfred had enough of the Northern heroic spirit to know how to appeal to these rough adventurers from Scandinavia. He knew that by killing the Danes when they had sued for peace he might have brought the vengeance

* *perterriti.*

of a blood-feud upon his kingdom, whereas by sparing his enemies, by binding them with solemn oaths to Christianity, by feasting with them, by being a bracelet-giver, by forming bands of foster-brotherhood, he might convert his enemies into friends. In spite of their 'slimness', the Northmen reverenced the heroic ideal. Alfred thus put a double spell upon them, both the heroic and the Christian, and it worked. Those twelve days when Guthrum and Alfred were together at Aller were all-important. Alfred presumably lectured his guests with that mixture of intense conviction and common sense which are found in his later writings.

The two kings had taken the first official step towards a new England, a land in which Englishmen and Danes could co-operate and form a mixed Anglo-Danish race. This is why the events of May 878 were, as has long been recognized, in truth 'a turning-point'.

XVI

WAR AND PEACE, 878–92

ALFRED'S RELATIONS WITH MERCIA, LONDON, AND EAST ANGLIA

THE fourteen years which intervened between the treaty of 878 and the last great invasion of Alfred's reign, in 892, were on the whole a period of peace, when Alfred was mainly engaged in attempts to restore order and civilization. But it was only in the last half of this period that he enjoyed anything like real tranquillity. In the first half there were still alarums and invasions; and it was doubtful whether the fruits of 878 could be lasting. Guthrum during the winter which followed his baptism remained with his army at Cirencester, in dangerous proximity to Wessex. It is possible that both Alfred and Guthrum realized that, for the time being, Guthrum's army was safer in the west of the island than in the east, for within a few months of the ceremony at Wedmore a fleet of Vikings had entered the Thames and disgorged a new host of invaders. The new-comers had presumably steered for the Thames because they had heard the winter's news of Guthrum's victory over Alfred. They had thoughts of co-operating in the work of gleaning in a Wessex open to the Northmen. They did indeed get into touch with

HEADPIECE.—Alfred pennies minted in Mercia. *A*, at Gloucester (ÆT GLEAWA). *B*, at Oxford (OKSNA [?Orsna] FORDA). *C*, at London (with London monogram).

Guthrum's army, and if the latter had moved eastwards, his men might have gone over in mass to the newly arrived leaders, seeing that these were not hampered by a treaty or tainted with an imposed Christianity. As it was, when Guthrum in 879 marched his army from Cirencester to East Anglia, the new-comers, after spending the winter at Fulham, had sailed away. For the time the centre of the Viking storm shifted from England to the Continent.

Guthrum and his men were presumably acting in accordance with Alfred's wishes when they turned to East Anglia and there occupied and divided the land—thus founding the last of the great Danish colonies in the plains of eastern England.

The eight years following the victory of 878 were troubled by minor wars. In 881 there was a naval engagement between a small fleet under Alfred and four ships of the Danes. In 884 there was more fighting at sea. 'The afore-mentioned army'— the Great Army which had been campaigning since 879 on the Continent—returned to try its luck once again in our island. The invaders besieged Rochester and dug themselves in, making a fortified camp or 'fastness'. When, however, Alfred marched up with the fyrd, the Danes fled to their ships. The most serious feature of this attack was that the war-spirit of Guthrum's Danes was again aroused. 'The army in East Anglia broke peace with king Alfred.' These are the only hostilities mentioned in the Chronicle, but there were clearly other disturbances which found no formal record in its pages. Little as we know about these years, we know just enough to see that the period was of the utmost significance in determining the future of England. Three questions were prominent, each of them concerned with the re-ordering of society to the north of the Thames: Mercia, London, East Anglia (i.e. the enlarged East Anglia of Guth-rum)—how were these three wrecks of the war to be salved for civilization, and how related to Alfred's Wessex?

(1) Alfred in his dealings with western Mercia—that is, with what was left by the Danes of the old Midland kingdom—was

facing a problem as fateful as the one which confronted Edward Plantagenet on the death of the Maid of Norway. The old dynasty was no more; the country was prostrate; it was defeated and humiliated. But the memories of its former greatness were fresh; in 878 it was less than a century since Offa of Mercia had treated Charlemagne as his equal, it was under fifty years since a Mercian king had yielded to Egbert. The utmost tact was necessary. Alfred had to steer a middle course. He must not arouse Mercian susceptibilities by trying to absorb their terri-tories too rapidly. He must not re-establish a Mercian monarchy which might fall under Danish influence or impede the work of damming up the Danes into their new-won provinces.

The first step taken by Alfred in his solution of the problem was to get into touch with Ethelred, a Mercian ealdorman whom King Burhred, before his departure for Rome, seems to have accepted as *Dux Merciorum* (let us say, saviour as well as war-leader of the Mercians).[1] Ethelred's chief connexion seems to have been with the old kingdom of the Hwicce, to which the Danes had withdrawn on leaving Wessex.[2] His interests co-incided with those of Alfred. In 879 both rulers wanted Guth-rum's army to be cleared out of Cirencester, and after that it was equally to the interests of both to keep the Danes confined to the eastern parts of the island which were now becoming a country under Danish law—a 'Danelaw'. It was natural that Alfred should resume the role of protector of the Mercians—the role in which he had made his first appearance as a commander in 867. The Mercians might be fully reconciled to Wessex by kindness, and the natural intermediary in the reconciliation was Ealdorman Ethelred. They had to choose between Ceolwulf, the nominee of the Danes, and Ethelred, who stood for the policy of friendship with Wessex and resistance to the heathen. There could be no doubt about the issue. Ceolwulf, 'the unwise king's thegn', vanishes from the scene after 875, and Ethelred is found in charters acting as the acknowledged subordinate of Alfred. In the years which followed, Alfred managed to forge new links

O

with Mercia. He formed a close friendship, literary as well as political, with Bishop Werferth of Worcester, the most influential leader of the Mercian Church. Somewhere about 886 he married his eldest daughter Ethelflæd to Ealdorman Ethelred. The bride was but a girl of some sixteen years at the time; the bridegroom was old enough to be her father. But never in the history of England has a political marriage produced happier results. It set a seal on the Mercian–West-Saxon alliance, and about the same time the first fruits of the alliance were won.

(2) London was recovered from the Danes. All that the Chronicle reports of this event is contained in a sentence about the year 885–6,* 'King Alfred restored London, and all the English— those of them who were free from Danish bondage—turned to him, and he then entrusted the *burh* to the keeping of the ealdorman Ethelred'. The actual ejectment of the Danes from London is only mentioned in an interpolation referring to 882-3. It has been suggested[3] that the words are misplaced, and that they really refer to the operations of 885–6. What this passage says is that Alfred vowed to send alms to India when he and his forces 'took up their position against the Army at London'. Elsewhere in Asser[4] we are told that London was restored and repopulated by Alfred 'after the burning of cities and much loss of life'. From this and an obscure passage in Ethelweard[5] emerges the bare fact that there were in these years important campaigns of which no satisfactory record is preserved.

For centuries London had been the great prize of war. Though Bede speaks of it as the metropolis of the East Saxons, and though the bishop of London was the bishop of that people, it had fallen to Kent under Ethelbert, perhaps to Wessex under Ine. In the eighth century it had become so closely tied to Mercia that even the victories of Egbert had not detached it. Now, about 886, while Alfred recognized the strength of its Mercian traditions by handing it over to the care of Ethelred, the city became that for which, as the nodal point of the Roman road system, it

* M. L. R. Beaven's chronology.

had been predestined—the centre where men from all provinces, meeting and trafficking, could forget ancient rivalries and enmities and learn that Angles, Saxons, Kentishmen and soon Northmen also, had a community of interests.

Alfred's restoration of London meant something more than its re-establishment as the 'emporium' of Christian England. It was now organized as an advanced fort of Anglo-Saxondom.

To the Kentish kings London had been a *wic*, a trading centre. On the coins of Egbert of Wessex it had been termed a *civitas*. With the Danish invasions of the ninth century, especially after this restoration by Alfred, we read of it as a *burh*, that is, a place of defence, fortified and garrisoned.[6] Its leading men are organized as a military force. They are the *burhware* of whose exploits we shall hear in later wars.

The Londoners did not, of course, give up their trading because some of them now took to soldiering. Evidence of this, if evidence is needed, is to be found in a charter of 889 in which 'Alfred, King of the Angles and Saxons, and Ethelred, under-king and patrician of the Mercians',* with the consent of the bishops and ealdormen of either nation (i.e. both of Angles and Saxons), grant to Bishop Werferth of Worcester a court† at an ancient stone building within London, extending from the public road up to the city wall, for the purpose of buying and selling. From this it may be gathered that whether one were a bishop or a layman there was nothing more profitable than to have a shop in London.[7] The Viking interlude had been no calamity comparable with those which, in former ages, in the days of Boudicca and of the Saxon invasions, had overwhelmed the city. The Vikings, who under Halfdene had established their own mint within its walls, had begun to give it a new importance as a centre of northern trade. The restoration of London in 885–6 was the beginning of an era of increasing prosperity in the history of the city.

(3) To appreciate the position of London in the later years

* See below, p. 582.   † *curtem.*

of the ninth century we must turn to the famous treaty of Alfred
and Guthrum, and this brings us to the third political question
which emerged as a result of the war—Alfred's relations with
his new neighbours in East Anglia. The treaty was probably
negotiated in 886, after the Danish outbreak of 885. It is something more than an agreement between the kings; it is a treaty
between the two peoples. On the one hand is 'the English
nation', the new amalgam of Angles and Saxons, hammered into
union by the war. 'The councillors of the English nation'* are
mentioned by the side of Alfred. On the Danish side are 'all
the people† who dwell in East Anglia'. These cannot be represented, like the English, by their witan because Guthrum has not
yet contrived to organize them into a State. Behind Guthrum
is an Army; subordinate to the Army are the former inhabitants.
The new kingdom of East Anglia is still only half-formed, and all
that Alfred can do is to get Guthrum and some of his leading
men to discuss the obstacles to a permanent peace and to swear
to terms when agreed. The points at issue were: what should be
the exact boundary of Guthrum's kingdom, and what the relative
value of Danes and English in the law-courts; in what ways
should charges of border robbery be determined, and (since
the new boundary was not a natural frontier) what could be
done to prevent quarrels between the two peoples?

The solutions of these problems as embodied in the treaty
illustrate well the statesmanship of Alfred. The first clause
settled the boundary: 'up the Thames, and then up the Lea and
along the Lea to its source, then straight to Bedford, and then
up the Ouse to Watling Street'. We are completely in the dark
about the frontier in the years immediately preceding this peace
(i.e. 880–6), and it may be doubted whether there had been any
clear agreement on the subject. The new boundary was unsatisfactory. It was not a natural barrier—that, indeed, was not to
be found with the Danes established in an East Anglia which
overflowed into the Midlands. At its southern end the Lea was

---

* *Ealles Angelcynnes witan.*   † *ðeod.*

unpleasantly near to London. To the north there was no word about the continuation of the line beyond the point at which the Ouse met the Watling Street. It is to be presumed that the English made other agreements, verbal or formal, which have not been preserved, delimiting the frontier through the northern Midlands.

The second clause of Guthrum's treaty is that which has given rise to the greatest controversy: 'If a man is slain, whether an Englishman or a Dane, we shall all place the same value on his life—namely eight half-marks of pure gold—except the ceorls who live on gafol-land, and their [the Danes'] freedmen. These also shall be valued at the same amount in either case—that is, at 200 shillings.'

The passage gives us two equations:

(1) The Danes' freedmen (*liesing*) = the English 'ceorls on gafol-land', with wergelds of 200 shillings.

(2) The Danes who are freemen but not freedmen = the English who are not 'ceorls on gafol-land', with wergelds of eight half-marks, i.e. about 1,200 shillings.

Now the problem which was tackled in this clause bristled dangerously with points of class and racial honour. Northmen in their own lands had been valued in different currencies to that of the English—in marks and ores, a standard of weight.* All manner of complications could be brought in to confuse the issue, the relative value of gold and silver, the manifold varieties of social status in the North, the changes produced in these distinctions by the common life lived by the Vikings on board ship and in camp. How could these sources of dispute be circumvented? What did Alfred in fact agree to do? Did he and Guthrum simply work out with their best mathematics the respective money values of their subjects? Was it simply a plain fact that the English 'ceorl on gafol-land' was, according to the pre-existing wergelds, no better than a Danish freedman? Or were Alfred and the English being generous for the sake of peace?

* Eight ores = one mark.

Famous historians can be found ranged behind each view.[8] Whatever may be thought of Alfred's equation of a Saxon 'ceorl on gafol-land' to the Danes' freedman, there is little doubt that in accepting an equivalence between the simple Danish free- man (the *bonde*) and the English thegn, he was allowing the immigrants what have been called 'fancy wergelds'.[9] If the cal- culations of Chadwick are correct, the *bonde* doubled his wergeld as the result of the Conquest. While in Scandinavia his value was reckoned to be no more than 100 oxen, in England the compensation payable to buy off a blood-feud was now raised to 200 oxen. It was not, however, only Northmen who had their value doubled. The English six-hynd men seem to have been treated with similar generosity.

The agreement could only be defended on the ground that the fundamental class distinction in that age was that between the soldier and the peasant. The man who fought for his king or his community with sword and shield was worth his 200 oxen, his 1,200 shillings. He was a twelf-hynd man. The man who worked on the land, herding cattle or following the plough, was worth but 1/6th of that amount. He was a twy-hynd man, a 200 shillings man.

Alfred's agreement, even if it ceded something to the invader, was at any rate preferable to a crop of blood-feuds. It was better than the law ascribed by tradition to Frodi, a king of the Danes, the law which demanded that the death of a Dane at the hands of a foreigner must be redressed by the death of two foreigners.[10]

The other clauses of the treaty were of less importance. In Clause 3 some disputable points about procedure in trials were settled. Clause 4 aimed at preventing border disputes by insist- ing that when a man bought slaves or horses or oxen, the trans- action must take place before a warrantor or witness. Clause 5 forbade ordinary trading between the two nations. The kings evidently held that the best chance of preserving peace was to keep their peoples as far as possible apart. The new frontier was to be a barrier. When trade was really necessary, it was to be safeguarded as an international act by a formal exchange of hostages.

In every clause the pact tried to remove a possible cause of conflict. The Danes were treated generously in the hope that they might settle down on their side of the boundary as law-abiding citizens.

Unsatisfactory as is all the information about these years of chequered peace, enough has now been patched together to illustrate the care with which Alfred endeavoured to strengthen the northern frontier of Wessex against the evil day when the great Viking armies might swarm back from the Continent to our island. The Danes of Guthrum's kingdom had been firmly pressed back behind the river Lea, but their ordinary fighting men had been placated by a wergeld equivalent to that of a Saxon thegn. By the re-establishment of English authority in London, Alfred had saved the great junction of the Roman roads, which linked up Kent with Mercia and Wessex. London bridge, guarded by the garrison of London burh, may have become an obstacle to Viking ships raiding up the Thames; but this is no more than a possibility, since the bridge is not mentioned in any document till fifty years after Alfred.

The achievement which above all others makes these years memorable in spite of their obscurity is the political union of the western Midlands with Wessex. According to J. R. Green, Alfred had become 'not merely a West-Saxon overlord of Mercia, but a Mercian king'.[11] There is certainly evidence which tends to support this view. Alfred's treaty with Guthrum settles the boundary of Mercia without any mention of Ealdorman Ethelred. Coins are minted with Alfred's name in the Mercian cities of Oxford, Gloucester, and London.* The Mercian charters, so long as Alfred is alive, usually give Ethelred only the title of *Merciorum Dux* or its equivalents;[12] but that which perhaps best

---

* See p. 573, headpiece. It may, however, be argued that the names placed on their coins by moneyers were not necessarily those of their rulers.

sums up the situation is the charter to Bishop Werferth,[13] in which Alfred is described as *Rex Anglorum et Saxonum*, and Ethelred as *Subregulus et Patricius Merciorum*, and they are said to act with the assent of the witan 'of either nation'. Alfred, however, is not in so many words 'king of the Mercians'. If the Mercians had been asked whether Alfred or Ethelred was the successor of King Burhred, their replies would doubtless have been confused. It was the policy of Alfred to be satisfied with a control over English Mercia without troubling about titles or theories.

His new position north of the Thames had come to him as a natural recognition of the fact that the only man who could save the people of the Midlands from the heathen was the king of the West Saxons. In the words of the Chronicle, 'All the English— those of them who were free from Danish bondage—turned to him'.* But that is not the whole story. His position was also the result of policy. It must not be forgotten that the way to reconciliation had been opened as early as 853 with the marriage of Burhred of Mercia to Alfred's sister; that it had been smoothed by Alfred's own marriage, which made his children half Mercian by blood. Thus the marriage of Alfred's daughter, Ethelflæd, to Ealdorman Ethelred was but the last of a series, and Ethelred was a protégé of Alfred's brother-in-law, King Burhred, before he became the son-in-law of Alfred and his viceroy in the Midlands. The Mercian people in the mass turned instinctively to Alfred as the champion of Christianity; while their leaders were further conciliated by well-sustained diplomacy.

MILITARY AND NAVAL MEASURES

The lull in the Viking storm after 878 gave Alfred an opportunity to strengthen his military as well as his political position. Ultimately he gave his kingdom a triple defence: first, a fleet (if this is not too imposing a word for the few ships of which we read); then, a ring of forts, or burhs, round Wessex, each the

* s.a. 886: 'thy ilcan geare gesette Ælfred cyning Lundenburg, & him all Angelcyn to cirde, thæt buton Deniscra monna hæftniede was . . .'.

military centre of a definite district; thirdly, a reorganized army. In each of these ways Alfred was doing something to counteract the advantages hitherto enjoyed by the Vikings. His fleet was to challenge their command of the sea. His burhs were to imitate on permanent and more systematic lines the forts of the Danes. His reorganization of the army was an attempt to remedy the fatal defect of the English levies, their failure to keep the field for a long campaign.

1. *The Fleet.*

We are told of three occasions[14] on which Alfred in the first half of his reign tried to beat the Northmen on their own element. In 875 and again in 882 Alfred himself went to sea with his ships and took part in minor engagements. Seven ships in the first, four in the second, were put to flight. Alfred was gaining experience. Then, in 885, a year when 'the Army in East Anglia broke peace with king Alfred', he took the initiative and, either to punish Guthrum's men for their perfidy or to forestall an attack, carried the war into the enemy's own waters.

'King Alfred sent a ship-army to East Anglia. As soon as they came to the mouth of the Stour, they met sixteen ships of Vikings, and they fought against them, and captured all the ships, and slew the men. When they were returning homeward with the war spoil, they met a great naval force of Vikings and they fought against them on the same day, and the Danish men had the victory.'

So far had Alfred's navy developed when his last war broke upon him. The need for ships which were swifter and more powerful than those of the enemy was brought home to the king not only in the desperate years after 892, when the Danes baffled him by using their sea-power to land troops from the Danelaw in the far west of Wessex, but also in the last years of his reign by the continued plundering of the south coast by flotillas of privateers hailing from Northumbria and East Anglia. It was to meet these in particular that Alfred began to build the new ships described in the famous paragraph of the Chronicle under the year 897:

'Then king Alfred commanded to be built against the Danish war-ships, long ships which were well-nigh twice as long as the others. Some had sixty oars, some more. They were both swifter and steadier, and also higher than the others. They were shaped neither as the Frisian nor as the Danish, but as it seemed to himself that they might be most useful.'

We have anticipated the building of the long ships in the last years of Alfred's life in order to envisage the naval war as a whole. The objections sometimes raised to his claim to be the creator of the English navy are not formidable. It is said that already in the time of his father (i.e. in 851) the Kentish fleet had been able to win a more notable victory than any ascribed to Alfred; it had defeated 'a great force' at Sandwich and had taken nine ships. There are, however, uncertainties in the text and in the meaning of this entry in the Chronicle.[15] And the fact remains that with the reign of Alfred for the first time our information about the king's ships becomes clear and comparatively full. It is also said that Alfred's successes at sea were insignificant and that the fleet which he established was not to have a continuous existence through the centuries. To this it may be replied that Alfred's ship-building was, in fact, a turning-point in more ways than one. It was the beginning of a fleet which, in the following reign, was numbered by the hundred, and which did in fact for most of a century effectively protect the shores of the kingdom.

The inventions of Alfred had, it seems, their reactions on the other side of the North Sea: there was competitive ship-building among the Scandinavian nations. The ships of the Gokstad type (with sixteen and seventeen oars a side) which, in the latter half of the ninth century had given the Vikings command of the sea, soon became obsolescent. Long ships with forty or sixty oars or even more began to take their place. So far as we know, it was Alfred who first showed the Scandinavian nations that they could be beaten in the art of ship-building, in which for some centuries they had had the lead. The statement of the Chronicle that Alfred's ships were shaped 'neither as the Frisian nor as the Danish' is interesting; it suggests that the Frisians had already developed their type of roomier trading ship known later, and perhaps even in Alfred's time, as the cog. Since Frisians were largely used by Alfred to man his ships, it is easy to see how he obtained the ideas and the technical skill required for experiments in ship-building. At the end of the ninth as at the end of the seventeenth century it was the Dutch who helped the English to their power in the narrow seas.

We have to go on to the early Tudors before we find an English king who again conceives the idea of making Englishmen masters of the sea by building king's ships more powerful than any others in western waters. But neither Henry VII nor Henry VIII went himself to sea as Alfred did in the ships he had built, taking command of them against an enemy.

Alfred's enterprise can be gauged better if we compare him with his contemporaries. Apart from Charlemagne and the Emirs of Spain, Alfred was the only ruler throughout the ninth century who saw the truth (so obvious to us) that the one and the only effectual reply to the Vikings must be made on the sea. He realized that since the English could not beat them in the number of their ships, they must beat them in size and speed; and the fact that subsequent kings forgot this truth merely indicates that Alfred's claim to have originated the navy must be shared with others. If not *the* founder of the English navy, he is *a* founder, the first and the greatest of half a dozen sovereigns who can make out pretensions to that title.

2. *The Burhs.*

Alfred's coherent scheme of land defence was more successful than his fleet during his lifetime, and after his death more far-reaching in its results. The nature of the scheme is to be inferred from the list of burhs, which goes by the name of the *Burghal*

Hidage, a list which was compiled either at the end of Alfred's reign or some fifteen years later.[16]

It is necessary to study the map (on p. 598) to appreciate Alfred's plans. We see a string of burhs encircling Wessex. To each burh was ascribed a number of hides (mostly in multiples of a hundred), denoting the size of the district of which it was the military centre. The burhs of Kent are omitted, either by accident or because Kent was still a sub-kingdom with a separate organization of its own.[17] Accordingly the list begins with Sussex. There we have Hastings, Lewes, Chichester, Porchester, and others. Continuing along the south coast we have Southampton, Twyneham (Christchurch), and Wareham. We have also inland a line of forts running through Winchester, Wilton, and Shaftesbury. The coast defences reappear at 'Brydian' (? Bridport)[18] and Exeter; then the line turns inland so as to include Dartmoor but exclude Cornwall; and, turning again northwards, we have many smallish burhs up the Severn Sea and round the marshes of the Parrett. The smallest of all is that at Lyng, close to Athelney, with a district of no more than a hundred hides. Following the northern, that is, the land frontier of Wessex eastwards, the burhs are few and their districts are large. Bath is reputed to have 3,200 hides; then Malmesbury, Cricklade, Oxford, Wallingford, Buckingham (here we see Wessex reclaiming territory long ceded to Mercia), Southwark—these have seemingly all of them more than 1,000 hides and are beginning to look like the county towns which some of them were to remain.

A glance at the *Burghal Hidage* is enough to show that its system was elaborately planned. Its strange want of uniformity may be due to the fact that it had been partly evolved during the stress of war. The small burhs of west Somerset may reflect Alfred's ideas formed during the campaign of 878. They may represent the first steps taken by him before the complete plan had shaped itself in his mind. The big gaps along the Wessex-Mercian frontier are doubtless due to its immunity from the baffling attacks of the Viking fleet, or to the natural defences offered by the forest region. Possibly they are an evidence of that slackness among Alfred's subjects which aroused the indignation of Asser. Writing in the middle of the next war he complains that some of the forts* which Alfred had ordered to be built had not been begun, or had been begun too late to be perfectly complete before the enemy bands once more invaded the kingdom by land and sea. When these negligent Englishmen saw their kinsmen killed by the invaders and carried into captivity, they repented too late and praised the king's wisdom in ordering the forts to be constructed. It is easier to imagine what these defensive places looked like than to guess exactly how the garrisons in them were maintained. Where an old Roman fortification was available Alfred fitted it into his scheme, and doubtless patched up its stone walls.[19] Elsewhere, it seems, the defence consisted of an earthwork circumvallation strengthened by a forward ditch and a palisade, according to the normal Viking and Anglo-Saxon plan.

Traces of these Alfredian works are perhaps visible in the massive ramparts at Wallingford and at Wareham. But we shall obtain a better idea of the plan of a burh when in a later volume we come to the wars of Edward the Elder.

Now let us estimate the originality of Alfred's burh scheme. Whence was it that he derived his ideas? Burhs there had been in England from the earliest times; the word meant no more than a fortified or defensible place, small or great. Some of them, like Canterbury (*Cantwara-burh*), were new growths within the old walls of Roman towns. These might be large and populous, comparable to burhs in the later sense of the word, but most of the burhs before the Danish wars had been less conspicuous. They had been stockaded dwelling-places, belonging either to a king or to a big landowner. The obligation of burh-building[20] had been one of the famous three burdens which charter after charter asserted to be necessary or common for all, and

* *castella.*

from which none (in theory) could be excused; and it was no doubt chiefly the maintenance of the modest defences round the king's vills which was demanded with so much insistence.[21] The well-known law of King Ine[22] which fixes the scale of penalties for breaking into burhs,* begins with a king's burh and goes down to that of the ordinary noble landowner;† and thus points clearly to the fact that early burhs were, for the most part, mere country houses. Their stockades or ramparts were erected to keep out thieves and lawless bands, not to be strongholds in time of war; and in the records of Anglo-Saxon wars there is no mention of such places ever standing a siege. None the less, the existence of these older burhs and the recognition that burh-building was a national duty must have helped Alfred to get his new forts made and maintained. Even so the paternity of Alfred's burhs should be traced not so much to the small private forts of the English as to the larger fortifications of the Danes or of the Franks. The Danes may have set the fashion of constructing large permanent burhs which became in time the county towns of England; but they cannot have had much of a start, and their famous Five Burhs were probably fortified about the time that Alfred set his subjects to work on his own scheme of defence.

The burhs of Alfredian England may also claim kinship with those of the Franks, which in their turn were related to the *burgi* of the later Roman Empire. In this as in other activities of the ninth century the creative mind was Charlemagne's. The forts which he constructed at the river-mouths against the Northmen[22a] and those for holding down conquered Saxony may have been the original models both for heathen and Christian. It is certainly significant that while Alfred was growing to maturity the Franks were busily constructing fortifications in Flanders and other regions near to England.

Alfred's scheme was an advance on anything that had gone before, inasmuch as his burhs were fitted into an elaborate permanent organization. In the *Burghal Hidage* with its thirty

---

* *burgbryce.*　　　　　　　† *gesiðcundes monnes landhæbbendes.*

forts scattered from Sussex to Devon, from Southampton to Buckingham, we see a well-thought-out plan of defence.

But how exactly did the plan work? In the wars which we are approaching (both the last wars of Alfred and those of his son Edward) we shall hear about the doings of the militant burgesses of the burhs, the *burhware*, 'the men who keep the burhs' as they are called in the Chronicle. They will of course be the defenders of their own fort or district; but besides this in great emergencies they will be available to fill the ranks of a field army. They will not refuse to march across the country against the Danes. The question how these garrisons were maintained drew from a great historian[23] the theory that the thegns of the shire were 'bound to keep houses and retainers in the burh of their shire'; that this duty was apportioned among the great estates; and that the retainers in the county burh should 'hoard provisions sent in to meet the evil days when all men should wish to be behind the walls of a burh'.

The evidence for these disputable propositions mostly comes from later periods and need not be discussed here. Two facts should, however, be noticed. The first is that Oxford (a town which can well claim to be one of those built by Alfred 'where none had been before')[24] is the town where something like the above 'garrison system' is best attested in Domesday Book. Secondly, the making of a burh at Worcester in the time of Alfred 'with his cognizance' is mentioned in a contemporary charter.[25] This tells us that 'through the entreaty of Bishop Werferth their friend, Earl Ethelred and Ethelfled have ordered the burh at Worcester to be constructed for the protection of all the folk and also that the worship of God may be celebrated therein [with security]'; and that the earl and his wife have accordingly given to the lord of the church of Worcester (i.e. to the bishop) half of their profitable rights 'both within the burh and without'. Amongst the rights thus in part transferred there seems to have been a *scot*, or rate, for maintaining the burh walls.*

* *burhwealles sceating*—but the meaning is conjectural. Cf. Bosworth-Toller.

This authentic story shows clearly that the fortification of Worcester, the making of it into a burh, was the result of a bargain between the ealdorman and the bishop. We may assume that elsewhere Alfred, like Ethelred, had to adapt his plans to the circumstances of each place. A Saxon king, we know, was far from omnipotent. He might give orders; he could not be sure that they would be obeyed. He might think out a consistent and uniform scheme; but since it was the local officials who alone could put his ideas into effect, the best conceived scheme might in practice be imperfect, lop-sided, marred by local anomalies.

However, the fact on which it is important to insist is the real value of the new organization. Henceforth the 'men who keep the burhs', whether living by their own agriculture or maintained by the landowners of the county, will be trained troops spread over the frontiers of Wessex. They will be local police; and behind their walls and stockades they may even be able to hold up invaders until an ealdorman or the king can collect a fyrd.

3. *The Land Forces.*

The functions of the burh will be better understood if we consider Alfred's armies as a whole. In a previous chapter (above, p. 211) we have referred to the view that the Saxon fyrd was not a national militia of all the freemen, but a small army of select fighting men, personal followers of the king or of his thegns. With the wars of Alfred we have reached a period when it becomes possible to form more definite ideas on this subject. We can faintly distinguish some five or six different elements in the land forces which saved England from the Vikings; if we are to appreciate what we are told about Alfred's division of the forces, it is necessary to avoid confusing these different elements in vague talk about 'the fyrd'.

(i) The fighting men of the king's household must have the first place. But in addition to the King's Thegns who held high

office (such as the Horse Thegn, whose death is specially
recorded in the Chronicle under 897), and in addition to the
thegns (*ministri*) whose names are appended as witnesses to the
king's charters,[26] there were of course others who 'followed'
the king, and were, doubtless, included among the 'followers' to
whom Alfred in his will bequeathed two hundred pounds—many
of them presumably men of humbler rank without the status of
thegns. While we can form no exact estimate of the numbers
of the war-band which attended Alfred, it is apposite to remember that when Cynewulf, king of Wessex, was trapped by
his enemies in 786 on his visit to the lady at Merton, eighty-
four men were slain beside him, although he had left the
main body of his men behind. We may suppose that Alfred, in
the stress of the Danish invasions, would maintain a much larger
bodyguard than Cynewulf.

Asser praises Alfred's arrangement for giving his bodyguard,*
and his thegns who were not fighting men, two months at their
homes for every one month spent at his court; but this puts some
strain on our credulity. When the court itself was on the move
and the difficulties of travel so great the system described by
Asser with eight journeys a year for every warrior and thegn,
to and from court, cannot have been carried out with anything
approaching the calendar-like precision ascribed to it.

On the whole it seems reasonable to suppose that his highest
officials and his unmarried retainers remained constantly at
court, and that this element of continuity made more tolerable
the confusions which must inevitably have arisen from the
system of rotation for the older landowners.

There is a passage in Alfred's *Boethius* from which one may
infer that his bodyguard was never a resplendent company
like the housecarles of Cnut, but preserved to the end much of
the simplicity which it had known in the stress of the Athelney
campaign. He points out[27] that it is over-proud and unwise
kings who 'are surrounded by a great company of their thegns,

* *bellatores* or *satellites*.

4014.2   P

decked out with belts and golden-hilted swords and with war-gear of many kinds'.

(ii) We find ealdormen fighting like kings at the head of retainers.* Thus, when the Danes descended on Reading in December 870, Ethelwulf, the ealdorman of Berkshire, within

FIG. 70.   Retainers (from a Frankish illumination, *c.* A.D. 850).

three days attacked one of their raiding parties with his *sodales*. The core of these was no doubt the ealdorman's 'hearth-band'[28]; others of them may have been thegns of the shire, who were regarded as *sodales* of the ealdorman inasmuch as they had taken the thegnly oath to fight with him to the end.

(iii) What has just been said justifies us in placing the generality of the shire-thegns and their followers under a different head to the hearth-band of the ealdorman, even though they gather round the same standard and there is no outward sign to distinguish them. It was to this, our third category of fighting men,

* *sodales* or *satellites*.

that the most famous of the military reforms of Alfred must have applied—the division of the fyrd. Alfred's plan of rotation for the *bellatores* of his household had been a device to ease the thegns who attended him in time of peace. This other division was introduced to make more efficient the troops who were only embodied in time of war. The Chronicle mentions the plan when speaking of the campaign of 893, saying that 'the king had divided his force into two so that they were constantly half at home, half abroad, besides those men whose duty it was to hold the burhs'. Alfred's greatest sources of trouble in his earlier campaigns, especially in the failures after the battle of Ashdown, had been the tendency of the militia, composed of landowners and their men, to melt away to their homes and their land work. A victory is gained or a few weeks of campaigning pass, and off they go. Alfred's remedy for the evil—his division of the fyrd into two parts—had its own drawbacks, as the campaign of 893 was to show. But his reform was at any rate another proof that he had the capacity to regard deep-rooted customs with a clear-seeing and critical eye.

There were, no doubt, many other ways in which his inventive-ness and mastery of detail helped to bring success. One of these may perhaps be inferred from chapter 37 of his Laws; and though its interpretation is doubtful, the law deserves more attention than it has often received. It begins as follows:

'If a man wishes [to go] from one district and seek a lord (*hlaford*) in another district* he must do it with the cognizance of the ealdorman whom he formerly "followed" in his shire.

'If he does so without his cognizance he who maintains him as a dependant must pay a fine of 120 shillings; but he must divide the pay-ment [paying] half to the king in the shire where he formerly "followed" and half in that to which he has come.'

What does it all mean? Let us pursue the military interpreta-tion[29] indicated by the words in which we have rendered the passage. It seems that Alfred was chiefly concerned to prevent

---

* *Of boldgetale in oðer boldgetael.*

any leakage of his fighting men. Those who were the men of a lord and who, in the retinue of their lord, 'followed' an ealdorman in the fyrd, were not to evade their services by simply passing from one district to another. The whole army must be maintained on business-like lines. There must be method in keeping the lists of fighting men up to date, and there must be no poaching by one ealdorman on the war-bands of another.

We now have the following picture of Alfred's fyrd. The king has his ealdormen, nominally one to a shire. The ealdorman has his *hlafords*, and the *hlafords*, both thegns and higher clergy, have their fighting followers.

It is necessary to insist on the contingents of the clergy, since these become prominent in the ninth century. The leading part taken by Bishop Ealhstan of Sherborne in winning Kent for Wessex (825) and in fighting the Danes (845) was not unique.[30] From the time of Wilfrid onwards there had been bishops who liked to be attended by a large band of thegns or other fighting men. But it seems to have been among the Franks rather than among the English that the custom had grown up of encouraging the upper clergy to take the field in person.

(iv) We pass to the humbler ranks of the army. First after the full thegns come a mysterious class of men who, in the Laws of Alfred, are graded with a wergeld of 600 shillings—six-hynd men.[31] Some of them were no doubt, as in the time of King Ine, Welsh landowners, owners of five hides or more, who were disqualified by their foreign birth from having the full 1,200 shilling wergeld of the Saxon twelf-hynd man, the thegn. Others may have been men belonging to the thegnly class who had no land, or at any rate not enough to enable them to qualify as full thegns. But it is conceivable that the class was recruited from ceorls who rode with their lords when the fyrd took the field, or fought in the bodyguard of a king or an ealdorman. We only know that the six-hynd men died out in the following century. Even in Alfred's day the class may have been small and unimportant. They are ignored by Alfred in his treaty with Guthrum. On the other hand the silence of the laws is not conclusive, and it is possible that they may have borne the brunt of the fighting against the Danes.

(v) The ordinary freemen or ceorls. What part did the free peasants take in the wars—those who were neither twelf-hynd men like the thegns nor six-hynd men, but simply ceorls, with lives reckoned to be worth their 200 shillings? Are we to think of Alfred carrying on his wars with popular levies, or only with thegns backed by their dependants? It is a crucial question; one on which recent writers have differed.[32]

No one can question the fact that there were often large numbers of ceorls to be found with the Saxon forces—ceorls who carried food to the troops, ceorls who might be ordered out to dig a fort, ceorls who might even be used to man a burh, and of course above all ceorls who followed their lords to the wars as retainers (later commonly called *geneatas* or riding-men). What is doubtful is whether there was in any effective sense a fyrd, a nation in arms, distinct from the 'lords' and their followers.

An argument against the theory of a fighting folk may be found in the words of Alfred himself about the contrast between the 'fyrd men' and the 'work men' in the well-known passage[33] about the three orders of society, where he says: 'A king must have men of prayer, men of war (*fyrdmen*), and work men (*weorcmen*). . . Further, he must have . . . means of support for the three classes above spoken of.'

Even though the threefold division of society was a commonplace of the age, the fact remains that in the mind of Alfred the commonplace corresponded with the facts. His words just quoted and chapter 37 of his Laws are enough to indicate that, in so far as the Saxon freemen took part in the wars, they normally came in the following of a 'lord'.

(vi) The *burhware* must be mentioned as the last branch of the Saxon army. While King's Thegns were the chief defenders of the forts, a few ceorls are said by the Chronicle to have been occupying an unfinished fort which was stormed by the Danes in 873. It remains a question whether these country-men were there to fight or only to do the digging.

From these controversial matters we return to the military reforms of Alfred with a conviction that 'the division of the fyrd', for which he rightly received high praise, was a measure of somewhat limited scope. It could not apply to the household retainers of the king, nor to those of the ealdormen, nor to the *burhware*, nor to the mass of the freemen, since these were 'work men' and not 'fyrd men'. It applied only to the ordinary thegns of the shire, and to the few men who by custom accompanied them when the 'shire' took the field.

Some historians who wrote in the last century[34] attributed to Alfred an extension of the thegnhood, 'by subjecting all owners of five hides to thegn service'. The theory never rested on any solid evidence; but this was not its only defect. The notion that any special proclamation or distraint of service was necessary to encourage landowners to be thegns is anachronistic. It mis-represents the prevailing sentiment of Anglo-Saxon society. There was no more need to press the Saxon owners of five hides into the ranks of thegnship than to command the big landowners of the Victorian age to enrol themselves in county 'Society'. Thegnship had its rights and its duties, but, so far as we know, there was no period when the Anglo-Saxon landowners were slow to accept either the one or the other. From time to time there may have been small changes in the idea underlying the position of these followers of the king. When they are called *gesithcundmen* (i.e. gesith-born) in the Laws of Ine, the emphasis may be rather on the qualification of good birth; when the designation 'thegn' gradually creeps in and supersedes the older word, it may for a while imply a revived stress on the qualifica-tion of service to the king; but both early and late the two ideas—the possession of an estate and service to the king—seem to have been closely connected. The follower of the king is rewarded with land. The large landowner in turn is expected to fight for the king even if he is not required to attend him in his household.

From the eighth century onwards, that is, from the period when the land-charters become comparatively numerous, we find a tendency to regard the estate of five hides (or thereabouts) as that of the normal holding of a thegn.[35] There is thus no reason for supposing that Alfred's reign produced a change in the thegnship other than the *a priori* reason that Alfred's wars were unusually prolonged and his own mind unusually inventive.

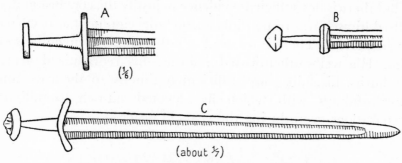

FIG. 71. Three types of swords of the Viking age.

A. Found in Norway. Type I (8th and 9th centuries).
B.   ,,   River Lea at Enfield. Type II (8th and 9th centuries).
C.   ,,   River Thames, near the Temple. Type V (*c.* 875–950).

Before we leave the subject of Alfred's military reforms we may ask whether he did anything to improve the weapons used by his men. On general grounds one might surmise that a king who took the trouble to invent a new lantern for the purpose of reading would apply his inventive faculty to improving the arms of his troops. Though the evidence is too slight to be conclusive, it seems that, since the migration, English smiths had fallen behind those of western and northern Europe in the manufacture of swords.[36] There are, however, in our museums one or two specimens which have been assigned to the Alfredian period (e.g. Pl. 72 B). There can be no doubt that the makers of these swords were taking their ideas in this, as in other things military, from the Vikings. In Fig. 71 the following characteristics should be noted: the tapering of the blade to a point; the well-made iron guards replacing the wooden guards used in the age of the migration; and the solidity of the pommels, made heavy in order to give the sword balance. They are features of the Viking weapons reproduced in English swords like those found in the Thames near the Temple and at Wallingford. This last type was actually an improvement on the Viking swords, in so far as the curved guard and pommel made the handling of the weapon easier.

But there is not sufficient evidence to justify the conclusion that Alfred himself was responsible for such development as occurred in the period. There is no need to father dubious inventions on him. His well-authenticated reforms—his reorganized army, his burhs, his ships—are sufficient testimony to the care and thoughtfulness with which he devoted himself to military preparations even during the years of peace.

WESSEX WELL FORTIFIED, *c.* 890.

XVII

THE RESTORATION OF ORDER AND OF LEARNING

THE NEW MONARCHY

AFTER each of his three great wars with the Danes Alfred enjoyed a few years of comparative peace—from 872 to 876, from 879 (or more completely from 886) to 892, and from 896 till his death (which probably, though not certainly, occurred in the year 899). These periods gave him opportunities for constructive statesmanship. The projects which above all others he kept near his heart were (1) the revival of learning and religion, and (2) the strengthening of the military and naval defences. But his subjects could not be educated nor could they be well organized for war unless internal order was enforced, and the spirit of orderliness revived.

It is true that in the Dark Ages no foreign war was necessary to throw society into confusion. Disorder was normal. But in Alfred's reign the heathen invasions had shaken the State to its foundations. Wave after wave of barbarism had swept over

HEADPIECE.—From Alfred's letter to Bishop Werferth. [Reduced to about ⅔.] Forðy me ðyncð betre gif iow swæ ðyncð ðæt we eac sumæ bec, ða ðe niedbeðearfosta sien eallum monnum to wiotonne, ðæt we ða on ðæt geðiode wenden ðe we ealle gecnawan mægen, & ge don swæ we swiðe eaðe magon mid Godes fultume, gif we ða stilnesse habbað, ðæt[te] eall sio gioguð ðe nu is on Angelcynne friora monna, ðara ðe ða speda hæbben ðæt hie ðæm befeolan mægen, sien to liornunga oðfæste, ða hwile ðe hie to nanre oðer[re note ne mægen . . .]. See p. 618 for translation.

the island. The forceful greed of the heathen had set an example of violence to the natives; it had brought out those savage and criminal instincts which are never far from the surface in humanity. And this was not all. Alfred's kingdom was suffering not only from the recurrent wars of his own reign, but also from the demoralization produced before his accession by chronic raiding, repeated decade after decade. The world had grown accustomed to lawlessness of a peculiarly deliberate and systematic kind.

Reflections of these evils can be perceived in the laws of Alfred. We see bands of marauders emerging from their secret places to steal or to kill. We see men fleeing on horse or foot from enemies who pursue them. If they flee to a church it must give them sanctuary without food for seven days. That is the law; but there are 'gangsters' who are reckless, men who will drag a fugitive from a church in despite of the church's sanctuary and the king's protection. We see the king, allowing men to pursue their own feuds; they may besiege a foe if they can in his house. It is only when a man has not enough power to conduct the siege himself that he may ride to the ealdorman or to the king and ask for help.[1]

Pictures of disorder or crime drawn from the legislation of a strong king are unconvincing. The anarchy of Alfred's reign must not be exaggerated. Though the Vikings had overwhelmed the government for a moment, the king with his ealdormen and reeves had reappeared. Society might for the time be loosened by the slaughter or destruction caused by the Danes, but the king's government remained in command. Wessex was to sink into much worse anarchy a century later during the second Danish invasion. Since the old régime had stood the strain, at any rate in Wessex, there was no evident need to refashion the political machinery of government. Alfred, we know, had the kind of mind which loves to devise new and better ways of doing things. But if we may judge from the preamble to his Laws, in affairs of state where custom was strong and men were suspicious of change, he was ready to be cautious and curb his inventive faculty. 'I have not dared to presume to set down in writing many laws of my own, for I cannot tell what [innovations of mine] will meet with the approval of our successors.'

It will be time enough to say something about his institutions when we come to the great work of Alfred's descendants in the tenth century. Then it will appear that, for all his conservatism, there were radical changes in government which grew out of his reign even if they were not deliberately planned by him; and that the burhs of Alfred with their dependent districts, purely military in origin though they might be, were indeed the nuclei for new growths in the body politic. Some of these new growths, such as the shires of Oxfordshire and of Buckinghamshire round the burhs bearing those names, may well go back to the times of Alfred; and in the end the constitutional reforms of the ensuing generations may leave us wondering whether after all Alfred, with his creative mind, was not the prophet of the new order. The tradition which found its way into the *Gesta Regum* of William of Malmesbury, attributing to Alfred the creation of Hundreds and Tithings, may not be wholly ridiculous. If, however, we confine ourselves to facts and exclude conjectures, there is not much to show for Alfred's constitutional work except his Laws.

Many motives combined to induce Alfred to draw up his Book of Laws.*² He had the examples of his greatest predecessors before him; that of Ethelbert, the first Christian king, of Ine, the first king of Greater Wessex, and of Offa, the most powerful of the Mercians. He knew that Charlemagne with his capitularies had set the fashion of legislation among the Frankish rulers. Since there had been no great lawgiver in Wessex for two hundred years, it was evidently time to revise and supplement the Laws of Ine. And so Alfred, perhaps about 893, set to work. When he studied the subject with the thoroughness which was characteristic of him, he found that there was a conflict of laws,

* *Dômbôc.*

both between the Mosaic Code and the teaching of Christ, (which he sums up in a negative version of the Golden Rule: 'that what ye will that other men should not do to you that do ye not to other men'), and also between the Mosaic and the Saxon penalties. The comparative mildness of these last he attributed to the fact that bishops and witan had followed the teaching of Christ in their legislation. The statement, though weak historically, formed a good transition to the subject of the Saxon Laws.

Alfred's long Biblical introduction to the Laws was characteristic of him. It was no mere display of learning. It had a purpose; and that purpose was, by drawing attention to the conflict of laws and by emphasizing the 'Golden Rule', to remind his people that there should be a place for equity as well as legality. Neither customary law nor the decrees of previous legislators were sufficient in themselves for perfect justice. The good 'judge' —that is, the good president of a folk-moot—must study, and use his wits.

What were the other aims which Alfred kept before him in compiling his Code? The preamble tells us something. 'Now I, king Alfred, have gathered together these laws and I have ordered that many of those which our ancestors held should be written out, those which seemed good to me. But many, those which did not seem good, I have rejected by the advice of my witan, and [in other cases] I have ordered changes to be introduced.' Accordingly, he had collected from the laws of Ine of Wessex, of Offa of Mercia, and of Ethelbert of Kent, those which seemed most just.

Now every clashing of one law with another—that of Kent with that of Wessex or that of Wessex with that of Mercia—every dispute about the amount of a wergeld, was a cause of friction impeding a general pacification and lessening the force with which the English could confront the Danes. One would expect, therefore, that Alfred, who had come to an agreement with the Danes about wergelds in his treaty with Guthrum, would have embodied an agreed tariff as between West Saxons, Mercians, and Kentish men, in his Book of Laws. This, however, does not seem to have been done; and the Book of Laws as it has come down to us only half realizes the programme of Alfred's prologue. The long section of Ethelbert's Code which gives a complete tariff for injuries to different parts of the body is revised, and adjusted from Kentish coinage to West Saxon—30 shillings for an ear, 60 shillings for a nose, 8 shillings for a front tooth, 4 shillings for a back one, and so forth.

This tariff is indeed a step towards consolidating the south of England. But there does not seem to be any corresponding assimilation of the Mercian laws of Offa.[3] Alfred legislated as king of the West Saxons. The witan who assented seem to have been West Saxons. Though in the latter part of his reign he might describe himself as *Angul-Saxonum Rex*, it would have been unwise to experiment with too sudden a mixture of Anglian and Saxon traditions. The Code as planned was a step in the right direction; but that was all.

Certain other ideas in Alfred's mind which he impressed on his laws are interesting. We see that he was determined to do what he could to promote morality by direct state action. He did not, like some later kings, adopt a preaching tone and introduce vague exhortations about keeping the Sabbath and other points of God's law. Alfred's Code was more practical. The laws formed to check violence to women were precise and enforceable. The fines laid down were adjusted according to differences in the degree of violence, and to differences in the social scale of the injured. Above all, the fine was doubled if the woman was a nun. The underlying idea was, of course, as old as Germanic society. Alfred made it peculiarly his own by giving it special emphasis.

The fundamental problem of the age was that of order. What then did Alfred do to cement society, shaken by the long wars? We see in the laws that he laid great stress on two or three principles.

First and foremost, all oaths and 'pledges' must be kept. 'In the first place we enjoin you, as a matter of supreme importance, that every man shall abide carefully by his oath and his pledge.' In days when formal legal documents were few, every kind of contract had to be solemnized by the giving of a visible pledge— a wedding ring, a glove, an arrow, a stick. The observance of contracts must be enforced as a foundation of order.

Then, secondly, the stability of society was to be preserved by upholding the authority of lords* over their men. It is an idea which Alfred stresses time after time. In his preamble he says that for the offence of treason to a lord the bishops and witan of old 'dared not assign any mercy because God Almighty had judged none to them who despised Him . . . and Christ commanded that a lord should be loved as oneself'. He deals with the subject in his first chapter, laying down that if a man has to choose between betraying his lord and breaking a promise it is better to break a promise. He returns to the subject again in his well-known treason law. Here it is not the protection given to the king by awarding a death penalty which seems the important novelty so much as the protection given to lords in general. 'And likewise with regard to all classes both ceorl and eorl, we ordain: he who plots against the life of his lord shall forfeit his life to him and all he possesses.' The ealdormen and the thegns had taken the foremost part in fighting the Danes; they had earned their rights. The authority of the landlords— ecclesiastical as well as lay—was still needed; order and civilization could only be restored through them. Alfred could stamp his own influence on the 'lords' but he had to leave it to them to pass on the impress to their men. Upon them, and more particularly upon those of them who held important offices under the king, depended the lot of Englishmen in general. Personality was what counted most in the tribulations which the coming of the Vikings had brought on Christendom. The Franks also were learning their lesson on the other side of the Channel, but

* *hlafordas.*

their lords, not being under the hand of firm kings, were drifting towards the local independence which led to feudalism. Between the development of lordship in England and France there lay a world of difference. The ealdormen and thegns of the English were and would long remain obedient tools of the monarch.

Monarchy itself was the third principle on which rested the stability of society. It was, of course, upheld in the treason law; but in general its importance was not emphasized in the laws as strongly as the need for keeping pledges and for obedience to lords. Little was said, for the simple reason that under a king like Alfred the powers of the kingship could more than ever be taken for granted. They were circumscribed partly by custom and partly by the limitations imposed by nature upon the actions of one man trying to rule a widely extended country; partly by the fact that it was essential for a king to retain the confidence of his ealdormen and thegns. For the rest, the monarchy was omnipotent; it was what the king for the time being liked to make it.

Asser at the close of his book describes Alfred's masterful treatment of those whom he calls the *judices*, in words which show that the author was too much of a Welshman to understand thoroughly Saxon institutions. He says that there were constant quarrels in the moots, both among the thegn class and the freemen,* because men questioned the justice of *comites* and *praepositi*, that is, presumably, the ealdormen and the reeves. Hence there were frequent appeals to Alfred for justice. Alfred himself also thought it necessary to keep a close watch on the conduct of his 'judges'.

'For he enquired in a wise way into the judgments given in his absence throughout almost the whole kingdom.' He investigated the motives of those who had been unjust, making his inquiry either in person or by his *fideles*. If he found that the mistake was due to ignorance he told the 'judges' that they must either study the 'Saxon Books' and acquire a better knowledge of the law, or

* *nobiles et ignobiles.*

else give up their office. Asser's account misrepresents the working of Saxon institutions on certain points. He calls the presiding officers *judices*. Germanic usage was different; it accorded with the maxim 'the suitors are the judges'. The suitors were the thegns or freemen who attended the court. He also writes as if there was a regular appeal from the local courts to a king's court, whereas in reality the king had no regular court of his own, and whatever part he took in justice was in the nature of arbitration.

It has been inferred[4] that Alfred's investigations through his *fideles* into the judgements given in the local courts amounted 'to a system of special envoys analogous to the *missi Dominici* of Charlemagne': if the words really justify such an inference, the practice was no more than a short experiment which failed to become a recognized institution.

Such close supervision of local authorities by the monarchy was certainly unusual; but English institutions have always been elastic, and the demoralization produced by the wars may well have justified both the officials in taking a strong line in the local courts and the king in interfering with the officials. There is a petition addressed to Alfred's successor which forms an interesting commentary on Asser's rhetorical passage.[5] It gives us a picture of a suitor coming to Alfred for justice. 'And the king stood (and) washed his hands within the chamber at Wardour. When he had done washing' he investigated the case and decided that the accused, a biggish landowner and a king's man, though a thievish fellow, must 'take the oath if he could', on an appointed day in the folk-moot.

This is the kind of informal way in which the king, like a Tudor Council or Star Chamber, dealt with the disputes which were sure to abound after a period of war, and a sentence in the petition suggests that such interventions on the part of King Alfred were famous: 'Sire! If every judgment which king Alfred gave is to be upset, when shall we be done with negotiating?'

Asser's words are of high value in the passage where he lays

stress on the activity of the king in constantly controlling his
bishops, ealdormen, thegns, and reeves—'who next to the king
had all power in the kingdom'. He kept them up to the mark,
it is said, by continual instructions, sometimes praising their
efforts, sometimes severely censuring their folly, their obstinacy,
their slackness, or their corruption. Finally, if need were, he
ordered them to give up their offices.

If we try to translate Asser's account into the language of the
twentieth century, shall we be wrong in saying that Alfred
transformed the monarchy into something like a dictatorship?
Kemble, an early Victorian,[6] saw in Alfred's treason law the
'despotic tendencies of a great prince, nurtured probably by his
exaggerated love for foreign literature'; and it is indeed conceivable that the influence of Grimbald the Frank and of
Roman history studied in *Orosius*, may have turned his mind
into channels of political thought, unwonted for an Anglo-
Saxon. A sentence of his which seems to come from himself
rather than from the Latin he was translating[7] says: 'Wise
men say they can the more easily carry out and maintain
their wisdom if their power be absolute over the people subject
to them.' But any talk of despotism or dictatorship with reference
to the Anglo-Saxons is, of course, as much an anachronism as
the Victorian obsession about their democracy; and it would be
grotesque to regard a chance observation such as that just quoted
as representing fairly the cast of Alfred's mind. His head was
not turned by his Roman studies. No king could have been
more tactful in acknowledging that the witan were the reposi-
tories of national law.[8]

Alfred's views about kingship in general and about a king's
duties, towards both his poorer and richer subjects, are not
in doubt. His sympathies with the very poor are shown in the
provision in his Will which says:[9]

'I pray in the name of God and of His saints that none of my kinsmen
or legatees oppress any of the dependants* for whom I have paid. Now

* *cyrelif.*

the West-Saxon witan have duly declared to me that I may leave them bond or free, whichever I will. But I desire for the love of God and for the good of my soul, that they may be entitled to their freedom and their choice. And I enjoin . . . that no man put pressure upon them . . . so as to prevent them from choosing whatsoever man [? as a lord] they will.'

If then we sum up the changes produced in Saxon society in the Alfredian period, we may say that it was the king and the lords who were strengthened. The treason law, in which we find the spirit of the age clearly expressed, was little more than a symptom of this change. The aristocracy advanced in prestige because it was a fighting aristocracy. Similarly, the monarchy increased in authority because the king himself was the only man who could prevent the shires from drifting into separatism and torpor. The king alone could supply the driving power required for the efficient working of the State; Alfred's success and the tradition of devotion to the community which he bequeathed to his family, helped to give the monarchy a lasting claim to the gratitude of the English people.

ENCOURAGEMENT OF RELIGION AND LEARNING

No one perceived more clearly than Alfred the contrast between the England of Bede and the England which emerged from the Danish wars. He discussed the subject in the preface to his translation of Pope Gregory's *Cura Pastoralis*, the *Pastoral Care*, and his words give us the key to the situation:[10]

'Alfred king commandeth to greet Werferth, bishop, with his words in loving and friendly wise: and I would have you informed that it has often come into my remembrance what wise men there formerly were among the English race, both of the sacred orders and the secular; and what happy times those were throughout the English race, and how the kings who had the government of the folk in those days obeyed God and His ministers; and they on the one hand maintained their peace and morality and their authority within their borders, while at the same time they enlarged their territory abroad; and how they prospered both in war and in wisdom; and also the sacred orders, how zealous they were both in teaching and in learning and in all the services which they owed to God: and how foreigners came to this land for wisdom and instruction; and how we now should have to get them from abroad if we were to have them. So clean was it fallen away in the English race that there were very few on this side Humber who could understand their mass-books in English, or translate a letter from Latin into English; and I ween that there were not many beyond the Humber. So few of them were there that I cannot think of so much as a single one south of the Thames when I came to the throne. . . .

'When I considered all this I remembered also how I saw, before it had all been ravaged and burnt, how the churches throughout all England stood filled with treasures and books, and there was also a great multitude of God's servants, but they had very little knowledge of the books, for they could not understand anything of them because they were not written in their language. As if they had said: "Our fore-fathers, who formerly held these places, loved wisdom, and through it they obtained wealth and bequeathed it to us. In this we can still see their tracks, but we cannot follow them, and therefore we have lost both the wealth and the wisdom, because we would not incline our hearts after their example".'

Such was the problem as Alfred apprehended it. The whole nation had relapsed into ignorance and materialism. Many of the monasteries were utterly destroyed. Others had a struggle to obtain the bare necessities of life. The old ideals were almost extinguished. The culture which had flowed with so strong a stream after the Conversion had now become stagnant. In the middle decades of the ninth century, when the Danish ravages began to be systematic, the clergy had been rapidly barbar-ized. Decay suddenly became general.

Our knowledge of the evils of the age does not depend on the words of Alfred alone. Supporting evidence comes to us in five letters written to Alfred or his advisers from the Continent. Each letter either openly criticizes the condition of the English Church, or by its admonitions implies criticism.

The first, addressed by Pope John VIII to Ethelred, arch-bishop of Canterbury, in 877, exhorted the archbishop to see

† ÐEOS BOC SCEAL TO WIOGORA CEASTRE

Ælfred kyning hateð gretan Wærferð biscep his wordum luf-
lice & freondlice; & ðe cyðan hate ðæt me com swiðe oft ón ge-
mynd, hwelce wiotan iu wæron giond Angelcynn, ægðer ge godcundra
hada ge woruldcundra; & hu gesæliglica tida ða wæron giond Angelcynn; & hu ða kyningas ðe ðone ónwald hæfdon ðæs folces [on ðam dagum] Gode & his
ærendwreccum hyrsumedon; & hie ægðer ge hiora sibbe ge hiora
siodo ge hiora ónweald innanbordes gehioldon, & eac út hiora
eðel gerymdon; & hu him ða speow ægðer ge mid wige ge mid wisdome;
& eac ða godcundan hadas hu giorne hie wæron ægðer ge ymb lare
ge ymb liornunga, ge ymb ealle ða ðiowotdomas ðe hie Gode [don] scol-
don; & hu man utanbordes wisdom & lare hieder ón lond sohte, &
hu we hy nu sceoldon ute begietan, gif we hie habban sceoldon. Swa
clæne hio wæs oðfeallenu ón Angelcynne ðæt swiðe feawa wæron . . .

THIS BOOK IS FOR WORCESTER

'Alfred king commandeth to greet Werferth, bishop, with his words in loving and friendly wise: and
I would have you informed that it has often come into my remembrance what wise men there formerly
were among the English race, both of the sacred orders and the secular; and what happy times those
were throughout the English race, and how the kings who had the government of the folk in those days
obeyed God and His ministers; and they on the one hand maintained their peace and morality and
their authority within their borders, while at the same time they enlarged their territory abroad; and
how they prospered both in war and in wisdom; and also the sacred orders, how zealous they were
both in teaching and in learning and in all the services which they owed to God: and how foreigners
came to this land for wisdom and instruction; and how we now should have to get them from abroad
if we are to have them. So clean was it fallen away in the English race that there were very few (on
this side Humber who could understand their mass-books in English, or translate a letter from Latin
into English; and I ween that there were not many beyond the Humber).'

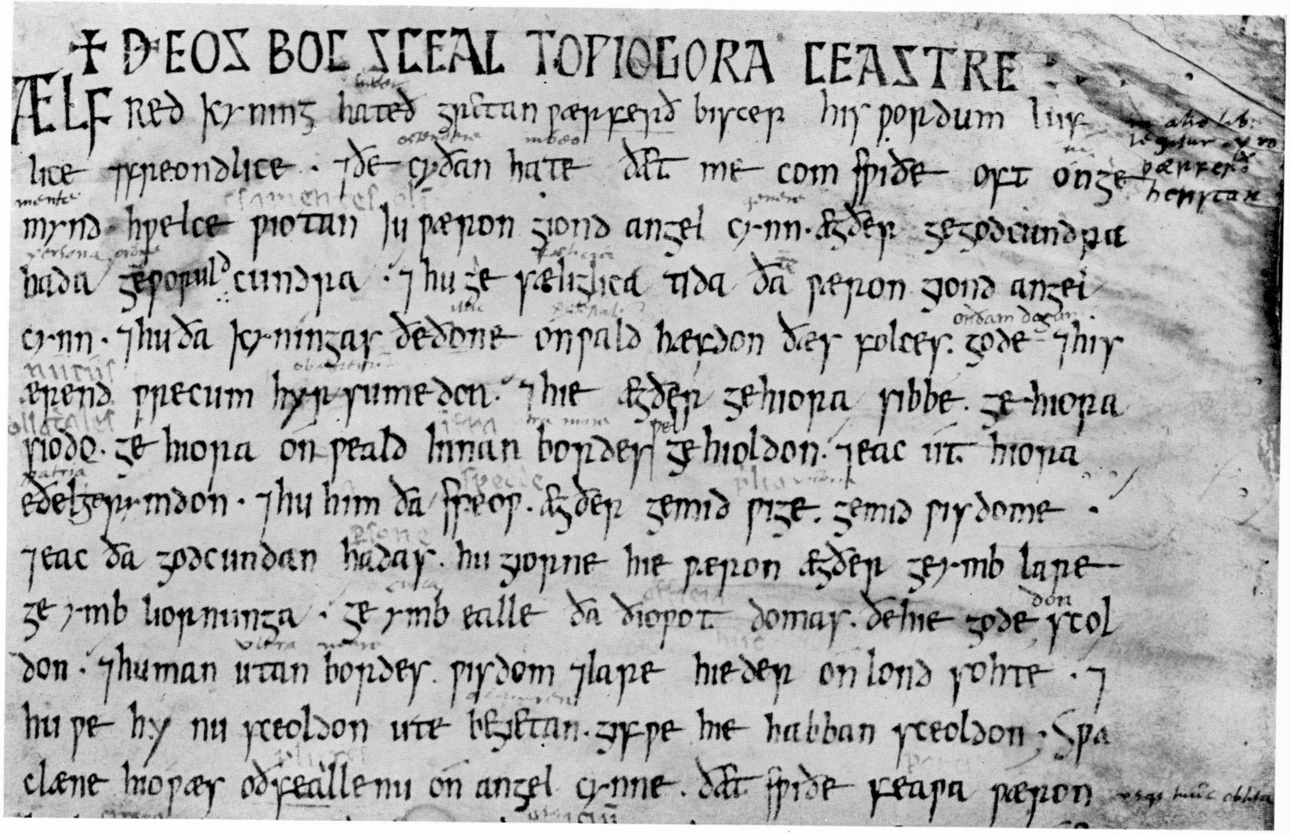

Beginning of the copy of the 'Pastoral Care' which Alfred sent to Worcester. (MS. Hatton 20, reduced)

ÐEOS BOC SCEAL TO WIOGORA CEASTRE

PLATE 75

PLATE 76

A NINTH-CENTURY PICTURE OF LAW-GIVING

Above, Moses climbing Sinai receives a roll. Below, Moses, in a Carolingian Palace, expounds the Law to a group of his chief men. (From the Grandval Bible. Brit. Mus. Add. 10546.) School of Tours. Towards the middle of the ninth century. Less than $\frac{1}{2}$

that the clergy of his province kept their Rule. Three of the
letters were written by Fulk, archbishop of Rheims. They denounced the evils of the English Church; the marriage of its
clergy, their ignorance and riotous living. The last official re-
proof came from Pope Formosus. His complaint was that
'abominable pagan rites were rampant' in England, and that
the English bishops kept silence, 'like dumb dogs that cannot
bark'.[11]

Yet another witness to the deterioration of the English Church
can be found in Asser. His statement[12] is as follows:

'For many years the desire for the monastic life had utterly died out
among that nation, as indeed it had done among many other nations;
and though very many monasteries still remain in existence in that land,
yet none keep the rule of that life rightly. I do not know whether this is
the result of the invasions of the foreign men which are so frequent both
by land and sea; or whether it is the result of the excessive wealth of
every kind of that nation; and I think that the latter is much more the
cause for the contempt in which the monastic life is held.'

We see then that while Asser and the foreign ecclesiastics are
as outspoken in their criticisms as was Alfred himself, their
charges differ from those of the king. Alfred in his preface to the
Pastoral Care complained chiefly that true learning was extinct
south of the Thames. The foreign critics denounced the neglect
of discipline and of the monastic ideal. They spoke of riotous
living and, in spite of the wars, of excessive wealth. The
charges are not identical, but they are sufficiently akin to corro-
borate one another. It was natural that when the attempts to
enforce a rule weakened in the stress of the Viking wars, learning should disappear along with discipline. The one depended
on the other.

We may think that Alfred—'Truth Teller' though he was
according to Asser—exaggerated, and that the ignorance of
Latin cannot have been quite as black as it was painted. But
even if there were some exaggeration in Alfred's complaint, the
situation was bad enough. The real problem went deeper than

the external damage done by the Vikings. It was the fact that the clergy, who should have rescued the nation from a relapse into half-heathen barbarism, were themselves too ignorant and too lacking in ideals to fulfil their proper functions. The salvation both of Church and State must therefore be initiated by the king and the king alone. Hence came the thought which long weighed on Alfred's mind, that he, the king, owing to his imperfect education, was not equipped to lead his clergy and people back to the learning which had once been theirs.

In the latter half of his reign Alfred, with the confidence of a ruler who had already saved his country in war, attacked the evils which were its sequel.

In the rest of this chapter we shall examine the remedies which he applied. We shall take first his efforts to reform his subjects by direct governmental action, that is, by punishing immorality and by establishing new monasteries. Later, we shall come to his more characteristic measures for educating himself and his subjects.

Reference has already been made to the laws in which Alfred utilized the power of the State to uphold morality. To illustrate the point further, these are the words in which he legislated against the abduction of nuns.[13]

'If anyone takes a nun from a convent without the king's or the bishop's leave, he shall pay 120 shillings, half to the king, and half to the bishop and the lord of the church under whose charge the nun is. If she lives longer than he who abducted her, she shall inherit nothing of his property. If she bears a child, it shall inherit no more of the property than its mother.'

This side of Alfred's work, the state enforcement of morality, is exemplified most strikingly in a charter[14] which tells how the king had confiscated the estate of a thegn, adulterous and therefore unworthy of thegnship. In so doing Alfred had disregarded the fact that the lands in question had been held by the thegn under the bishop of Winchester. The complaint raised in the charter suggests that the aggrieved bishop in comparison with

Alfred was half-hearted in his warfare against the sins of the flesh.

If he had lived some centuries earlier or some centuries later than he did, Alfred would without doubt have distinguished himself by founding or reforming monasteries. Something of the kind was indeed attempted by him, but on a small scale; and his foundations were not altogether successful. According to Asser:[15]

FIG. 72. Probable plan of Alfred's Church at Athelney.

(Cf. A. W. Clapham, *English Romanesque Architecture*, i. 147–8.)

'When he thought about the need of his soul, as was his wont . . . he ordered that two monasteries should be built . . . [Then, owing to the decay of monasticism] he was eager to collect monks of a different race in this monastery [Athelney]. First he placed there as abbot John, a priest and monk, an Old Saxon by birth; then he brought over certain priests and deacons from abroad. When he found that he had still not as many inmates as he wished, he collected very many of the same Gallic race. And some children he ordered to be instructed in the same monastery; and later to be raised to the monastic habit.'

The experiment at Athelney was not a success. The inmates were an ill-assorted community. Monks of diverse races and from every quarter, converted pagans, old men and children, regulars and seculars, very many of them 'Gauls'; and at the head of all, in spite of the already declared hostility between the two races, a German.

Asser tells with some relish the story of the attempt made by two of the Gallic brethren to murder their German abbot. It was the great scandal of the time. With such a bad beginning, the monastery never became a centre of illumination for the kingdom. The only other House which had been founded by Alfred when Asser wrote was a nunnery at Shaftesbury, placed near the east gate of the burh on the top of the hill, a site far better than Athelney in its amenities and not much inferior to it in point of safety, since it was well removed from the dangers of the sea-coast, and was not far from the shelter of Selwood. Alfred committed the rule of this foundation to one of his daughters. It seems that in his later years he also planned two new monasteries at Winchester, which were completed by his son. In one of them long known as the New Minster, then as Hyde Abbey, his own body was entombed and honoured until the Reformation. To the other, the 'Nunna-minster', his widow retired.[16]

We see then that Alfred's monastic programme was not an ambitious one. His foundations were few. He did not demand precise observance of the Benedictine Rule. He was content that secular clergy should be admitted to Athelney; and he subsidized, so Asser tells us, the older unreformed communities both in Wessex and Mercia. In his disregard of the strict monastic rule he was, of course, simply a man of his times; and even if he had been in this respect, as he was in so many others, ahead of his contemporaries, it would have been of little avail.

How wellnigh hopeless was a restoration of the monastic ideal in the ninth century is shown by every fact recorded of the experiment—the impossibility of finding Englishmen ready to give up the pleasures of the world, and the unruliness of the foreigners imported to make good the deficiency of natives. The scandal at Athelney was ill calculated to exhibit to the English the merits of the stricter monasticism of the continental type.

After noting the comparative lack of enthusiasm shown by Alfred in the restoration of the monasteries, we must not altogether pass over the charge brought against him by an Abingdon monk,[17] one who wrote, it is true, so late as the twelfth century, but who must be heard, since he at times used earlier materials. The charge is that Alfred confiscated land belonging to Abingdon in order to bestow it upon one of his thegns. If this is true—and it is not impossible that confiscations of the kind occurred—Alfred was only doing what Charles Martel and other good rulers of the Franks had done on a very much greater scale. He was cutting away rotten parts in order to build more securely.

A vindication of Alfred from the charge of being a general despoiler of monastic property can be found in the passage of Asser[18] which explains how he set aside a part of his revenue to be 'distributed among the monasteries which were near, in all the lands of the Saxons and in Mercia'. Alfred was not an upholder of rigorous monasticism because he wanted quick results. His aim was a practical one. What he needed was educated clergy—clergy of any kind—who were to be 'his tools' in reviving Christianity and learning. Having learnt his lesson at Athelney he developed his plans on other lines.

He determined to make his court circle a centre of education. He would attract foreigners to teach—teach every one: himself, his children, his nobles, their children, the clergy. The thing had been done by Charlemagne; it could therefore be repeated in England. Alfred himself must be the first to go to school. He must make good the years of his youth wasted over such things as wars and hunting.

Asser's account of the way he was drawn into Alfred's net gives a good idea of the king's methods. We see this Welsh priest, whose fame had spread to the Saxons, summoned, probably about 884–5, from his home in western Wales (Pl. 78) and escorted across Wessex until Alfred was found in the village of Dene in Sussex.[19] 'I was kindly received by him, and then, among other conversation, he begged me earnestly to devote myself to his service, and to become one of his household, and to leave for his sake all that I had to the west of the Severn.' The negotiations were long drawn out, and it was only the insistence of Alfred which, in the end, overcame the scruples of the Welshman. Asser gives us another picture of his intercourse with the king later on after he had settled down at the king's court for half

a year. We see them 'sitting together in the king's chamber, talking of all kinds of subjects, as usual'. They are reading together,
explaining, discussing, taking notes. The king draws from his
bosom a small book of Hours, psalms and prayers, which he has
carried about with him since his youth. He tells Asser to make
a note in it quickly. 'No,' says Asser, 'I had better write it on a
separate parchment. We are certain to find other passages which
you will wish to have added to it.' 'That is a good idea,' the king
agrees; and so a new commonplace book is begun, which the
king calls his '*Enchiridion*', and keeps at hand day and night.[20]

This was the king's way with his foreign helpers, and it was
thus that he slowly educated himself and prepared for the work
of translating into English the books which earlier generations
had been able to read in the original Latin.

The learned men whom Alfred collected round him were
drawn from diverse nations. Four of the earliest were Mercians.
Of these, two were men of note: Plegmund, raised to the see of
Canterbury in 890; and Werferth, who had become bishop of
Worcester in 873, 'a man well-versed in scripture', but a keen
man of business;[21] persistent, worldly-wise, one of the able rulers
who guided western Mercia and his own Worcester successfully
through the years when kingdoms and bishoprics were crashing
around him. Then there were men brought from the Continent:
John, the Old Saxon, recommended no doubt by his ability to
make himself understood in his own native tongue, one who
could tell Alfred about the conquest of the continental Saxons
by Charlemagne and the vigorous Christian civilization which
had sprung up since that conquest; last, and most notable of
all, Grimbald—some seventy years old when he arrived at
Alfred's court (about the same time as Asser, that is, probably
884–5), a man who must have been a storehouse of interesting reminiscences for a king who clearly never tired of asking
questions. For fifty years Grimbald had, it seems, been an inmate
of St. Bertin's Abbey, near what is now the town of St. Omer,
in the Pas de Calais. He could tell of days when a bastard son

of Charlemagne had been his abbot (no doubt enjoying the revenues rather than discharging the duties of that office); and when a paladin of the great Emperor had renounced a countship to enter the community as a simple brother. While Grimbald was an inmate, repercussions from the main storms had broken the peace of the countryside round his monastery; he had seen fugitives fleeing from the early Viking raids, and armies of fratricidal Carolings. In 861 a Viking band had appeared near St. Bertin's, and at its approach all the monks except four had fled to the woods—fled and later returned to find that the four of the brethren who had remained at their post had been tortured or martyred by the barbarians. Later, he had seen his monastery fortified in the hope of obtaining security from such brutalities in the future. It seems that Fulk (archbishop of Rheims 883–900), in the years when he was abbot of St. Bertin's, learnt to know the worth of Grimbald. At any rate, when Alfred wrote and asked that Grimbald might be sent to England to help him in his work, Fulk stipulated that his countryman should be received with fitting dignity.*

After Grimbald's arrival in England, the story fails. It must be left to imagination to fill in the picture of Alfred questioning his latest recruit with the eagerness of a child, just as he questioned Ohthere the sailor, about the manifold experiences of his long life. There is some evidence which indicates that Grimbald was allowed, like Asser, to return on occasions to his own people.[22] After Alfred's death he was given the Headship of the New Minster at Winchester, and he became so venerated in his adopted country that he soon won a place in the calendar of English Saints.

THE BEGINNINGS OF ENGLISH PROSE LITERATURE

The educational policy which Alfred set before himself and his leading churchmen is explained in his own words in the letter sent to Werferth, bishop of Worcester, together with a copy

* Below, p. 633.

of the *Pastoral Care*—the letter of which the beginning was quoted above.* He says:

'I command thee to do as I believe thou art willing, to disengage thyself from worldly matters as often as thou canst, that thou mayest apply the wisdom which God has given thee wherever thou canst. Consider what punishments came upon us in this world, when we neither loved wisdom ourselves nor suffered other men to obtain it: we loved the name only of Christian, and very few of the virtues.'

Then after the passage in which he describes how before the wars the churches had been filled with treasures and books, and how little knowledge the clergy then had of the books, because they were not written in English, he goes on to say:

'When I remembered all this, I wondered greatly that the good and wise men who were formerly all over England, and had perfectly learnt all the books, had not wished to translate them into their own language. But again I soon answered myself and said: "They did not think that men would ever be so careless, and that learning would so decay; they deliberately abstained from it, since they wished that the wisdom in this land might increase with our knowledge of languages." Then I remembered how the law was first known in Hebrew, and again, when the Greeks had learned it, they translated the whole of it into their own language, and all other books besides. And again the Romans, when they had learned them, translated the whole of them by learned interpreters into their own language. And also all other Christian nations translated a part of them into their own language. Therefore it seems better to me, if it so seems to you, for us also to translate some books which are most needful for all men to know into the language which we can all understand, and so we can very easily bring it about, if we have tranquillity enough, that is, that all the youth now in England of free men, who are rich enough to be able to devote themselves to it, be set to learn as long as they are not fit for any other occupation, until they are able to read English writing well: and let those be afterwards taught more in the Latin language who are to continue in learning, and be promoted to a higher rank.'†

* P. 608.

† A facsimile of the last sentence, taken from the book actually sent to Werferth (Hatton MS. 20 in the Bodleian), is given at the head of this chapter.

The sequel to this programme may be gathered from Asser. The king[23] 'with great care collected many nobles of his own nation and boys of humbler birth and formed them into a school'. It was a school attached to the royal household—a 'School of the Palace', as it would have been called by the Franks —and for its support a certain proportion of Alfred's revenue was earmarked. There the youngest of the king's sons was educated, 'in company with almost all the children of noble birth in the whole country, and even many of humbler birth. In the school, books in both languages, that is, in Latin and Saxon, were diligently read, and there was time also for writing. Accordingly, before they had the strength for manly pursuits such as hunting, and the other pursuits which befit noblemen, they with good study became skilled in the liberal arts.'

This description recalls in more than one way the Palace School of Charlemagne, over which Alcuin of York had for long presided. Alfred wished like Charlemagne to disseminate education as widely as the circumstances of the time permitted. It was not to be, as some clergy had desired, a monopoly of their order. Even grown-up men, the officials of the king, were compelled to make some effort to educate themselves. Whereupon, says Asser,[24] 'almost all the ealdormen, reeves, and thegns who had been illiterate from childhood took to their books, preferring to study laboriously the unaccustomed learning rather than to give up their posts'. And if any one was too old or too stupid to learn, he would order his son or his servant to read 'the Saxon Books' to him—more particularly, it has been supposed, the books of the laws.

By example, by command, by precept, the king gave sufficient impetus to the new studies for the movement to be continued after his death. But the school in the king's household could scarcely touch the nation as a whole, or to an appreciable extent expel the ignorance of the clergy which had been the main ground of Alfred's complaint. He had therefore a further scheme, that which we have heard him announce to Bishop

Werferth, for the education of 'all the youth now in England of free men . . . until they are able to read English writing well'.

It is not clear whether Alfred contemplated a general revival of the cathedral schools of the country. The bishop was to see to it that somehow or other the young sons of the well-to-do free men should be set to study.[24a]

And what were these Englishmen to study, these who were to be taught to read English but not Latin?

This also is outlined in the letter.

'It seems better to me if it so seems to you, for us also to translate some books which are most needful for all men to know, into the language which we can all understand. . . . When I remembered how the knowledge of Latin had formerly decayed throughout England, and yet many could read English writing, I began among other various and manifold troubles of this kingdom to translate into English the book which is called in Latin *Pastoralis*, and in English *Shepherd's Book*, sometimes word by word, and sometimes according to the sense, as I had learnt it from Plegmund, my archbishop, and Asser, my bishop, and Grimbald, my mass-priest, and John, my mass-priest.'

In dealing with the Old English prose literature produced in the latter half of his reign by Alfred and those who co-operated with him, it is well to differentiate two groups of writings. One group, the later in point of time, comprises those writings in which the king's own mind can be seen at work in the additions made to his Latin author—that is, the translations from Orosius, Boethius, and St. Augustine. In the other and the earlier group we have the works in which the translator kept close to his original. In these the king was feeling his way. He tried the plan of commissioning a bishop to do the translation for him. Then he tried to translate himself, in the way he has described to us in the *Pastoral Care*, with a helper at his elbow to guide him. Analysis of these earlier writings indicates that their final form came from one or other of the king's helpers rather than from the king himself.[25]

In this general history we are less concerned with the finer shades of Alfred's participation than with his scheme as a whole. To understand this let us try to arrange the series in the order in which the books were probably composed, realizing that this word 'probably' must be specially underlined, since the internal evidence on which for the most part we must depend is confused, owing to the joint authorship of most of the treatises coming from the king's scriptorium.

The *Dialogues* of Pope Gregory have the first place, since they are mentioned by Asser. They were a collection of stories about the wonders worked by saints and relics in the warfare between mankind and the demons. The fact that Alfred encouraged bishop Werferth to undertake the translation, that he had it circulated[26] and that he recommended his subjects to contemplate these fables in the midst of their earthly troubles, well illustrates the gulf which separates Alfred from ordinary Englishmen of the present day.

The *Pastoral Care* of Pope Gregory was pretty certainly the first book in which Alfred himself took a part in the actual work of translation. It was a handbook for the instruction of bishops and clergy, and it told these 'Shepherds' how to admonish their flocks, and how to save them from the Devil. The general use of the book had been recommended by Bede and Alcuin, it had been ordered by Charlemagne, and was still enjoined by Frankish metropolitans. Alfred therefore showed sound strategy but no originality in opening his educational campaign with the *Pastoral Care*. He saw that its instructions were well suited for the conditions of his own England. For example, the first maxim of the book, 'That the unlearned are not to presume to undertake the office of teacher,'[27] had an obvious bearing on the ignorance of the clergy as described in Alfred's letter to Werferth.

This 'Shepherd's Book' was more than a literary effort. It was the instructions of a commander-in-chief issued to his brigadiers, the bishops; and these on their part were expected to pass on their orders to their officers, the diocesan clergy. The versified proem, probably composed by Alfred himself, makes the book

Þis ærendgewrit Agustinus ofer sealtne sæ suðan brohte
iegbuendum, swa hit ær fore adihtode dryhtnes cempa, Rome
papa. Ryhtspell monig Gregorius gleawmod gindwód ðurh
sefan snyttro, searoðonca hord. Forðæm he monncynnes mæst
gestriende rodra wearde, Romwara betest, monna modwelegost, mær-
ðum gefrægost. Siððan min on Englisc Ælfred kyning awende
worda gehwelc, & me his writerum sende suð & norð; heht him . . .

[This message Augustine over the salt sea brought from the south to the islanders, as the Lord's
champion had formerly decreed it, Rome's Pope. The wise Gregory was versed in many true doctrines
through the wisdom of his mind, the treasury of his thoughts. So most of mankind he gained over
to the Guardian of heaven, best of Romans, wisest of men, most gloriously famous. Afterwards King
Alfred translated into English every word of me, and sent me to his scribes south and north; ordered
(more such to be brought to him after the pattern-book, that he might send them to his bishops, for
some of them needed it, who knew but little Latin).]

PLATE 77

FROM ALFRED'S TRANSLATION OF THE 'CURA PASTORALIS'. (MS. Hatton 20)

Above, Prefatory poem, written as prose (reduced). Below, Headings of the chapters about *b*, women; *c*, the young; *d*, the proud (same size)

PLATE 78

Castell, near St. Davids. Probably an early stronghold of the bishops of St. Davids

By permission of the Controller of H.M. Stationery Office

St. Luke from the Gospels 'of St. Chad'

Welsh, eighth century. Many of the illuminations resemble those of the Lindisfarne Gospels.
This stylized portrait is like renderings of the human figure in Irish MSS. and helps to
illustrate the contrast between the Celtic peoples and the Anglo-Saxons

say: 'King Alfred translated every word of me into English and sent me to his scribes, south and north, and ordered more such to be brought to him that he might send them to his bishops, for some of them needed it who knew but little Latin.' A facsimile of the beginning of the copy actually sent by Alfred to Bishop Werferth of Worcester is given on Pl. 75. The command of its opening words ('This book is for Worcester') is written in bold capitals. On Pl. 77 (*a*) is reproduced the beginning of the verse proem of the same book. The initial letter and the other small initial pictures (Pl. 77 (*b*), (*c*), and (*d*)) give some idea of the phase in the art of illumination reached at Alfred's court; also of some lighter moments in an Alfredian scriptorium. When the translation comes to its chapter xxiv, saying that women are to be admonished differently from men, 'more lightly' and 'with flattery', a woman's face is depicted, but it is given a yellow beard. When the admonition of 'the young' is mentioned, we are shown what looks like a squalling child holding a toy pig. The last face is the headpiece to the chapter about 'the proud'.

The evidence that the circulation of the new books was ordered by Alfred is stronger for the *Pastoral Care* than it is for the *Dialogues* or for the Chronicle; but the facts are cumulative and taken together they show that he did not leave the dissemination of the new learning to chance.

The translation of Bede's *Ecclesiastical History* may reasonably be assigned to an early phase of Alfred's literary campaign, since it has been shown to have strong resemblances to Werferth's *Dialogues*. Both translate word by word; they keep close to their originals—for example, rendering the ablative absolutes of the Latin by dative absolutes in Old English; their vocabulary and dialect are similar; they both have a habit of translating one Latin word by a pair of English ones. The only respect in which they differ, that in which the mind of Alfred may perhaps be best recognized, is in the bold excision in the *Bede* of much superfluous matter, such as long letters, epitaphs, and references to

4014.2   R

the Pelagian and Easter controversies. About one-quarter of Bede's long book was wisely omitted.

The Alfredian treatise which most nearly concerns students of history, that is the Chronicle, is the hardest of all to place; indeed, the part played by Alfred in its composition is questioned by modern scholars whose opinion cannot be lightly disregarded. Many of these believe that the Chronicle was first edited under Ethelwulf or even earlier, and one holds that the annals from 750 to 891 were written 'under the patronage of a great Somerset noble'. Some reasons for rejecting these views of the Chronicle will be found below (pp. 706-8).[28] Here the reader is asked to believe that the work was substantially a product of Alfred's reign, inspired by Alfred and at times loosely supervised by him, though like other Alfredian works not actually written at his dictation.

There is no saying exactly when or how the idea of the Chronicle found its way into Alfred's brain. It may have come from Queen Judith or from one of her Frankish attendants. The crude character of much of its writing, the changes in style, the absence of information about continental affairs until 880, suggest that the scheme was well under way before Grimbald and the other foreigners settled down at Alfred's court.

The Chronicle was certainly a work in which many co-operated. There may have been from quite early in the reign a succession of historiographers royal, clerics commissioned by Alfred to collect what information they could about the history of his dynasty and its relation to the history of the island.

These efforts did not produce the early Chronicle in the form in which it has come down till shortly before 892, when Alfred seems, as his custom was, to have circulated copies of the archetype to different places, and it is an early tenth century transcript of one of these copies which is the oldest extant manuscript of the work. It is known as the Parker MS. because it was given in the time of Elizabeth by Archbishop Parker to Corpus Christi College, Cambridge, and is commonly designated by the letter A. It is written in one hand down to the annal for 891 (cf. Pl. 25). The only way to understand how it came into existence is to distinguish the various sections of the work hidden beneath the uniformity of the handwriting.

(1) The section, containing annals from the birth of Christ to the conquest of Hengist and Horsa, was evidently composed about the same time as Alfred's *Orosius*. The two seem to have been on the stocks together. Much of the Chronicle is taken from Orosius. On the other hand, the sentence which the Alfredian circle found in another of their sources—namely, that 'Titus . . . said that he considered the day lost in which he did no good'—was incorporated both in the Chronicle and in the translation of the *Orosius*. This sentence more than any other connects the early Chronicle with Alfred or his circle.

(2) From A.D. 449 to the Conversion the Chronicle is in the main a primary authority. The annals about the Conquest and Ceawlin have been quoted and discussed so fully in earlier chapters that it is only necessary here to recall the fact that the source and value of these short sentences about the Conquest are still highly disputable. Statements taken from Bede and from regnal tables, perhaps from heroic sagas and from primitive annals, and antiquarian guesses about the Conquest based on place-names—all are mingled; but whether the fusing of these elements was effected in the reign of Alfred or in some earlier period is a question about which there is no occasion to dogmatize. One thing, however, cannot be denied: that the kingdoms whose origins are successively mentioned—those of Kent, Sussex, and Wessex—are just the kingdoms well known to Alfred, those whose traditions or records he or his helpers could tap through the clergy at Canterbury, or through discussions while he was on progress from one royal hall to another.

(3) When the story of the Conversion was reached the compilers of the Chronicle naturally came to depend on Bede—on his convenient epitome rather than on his detailed history. But mixed with Bede are entries from earlier local annals, from Canterbury, Winchester, and perhaps Mercia.[29]

The chroniclers were hard put to it to find anything which could be served up as history for the middle and end of the eighth century. They laid their hands on their lists of kings and bishops and other meagre chronologies: then when it was seen how unsatisfying was this trickle of information, was it not at Alfred's suggestion that the splendid though unclerical story about the death of Cynewulf was added? Other touches of the Alfredian editors, such as the retrospective record of the first coming of the Danes are sufficiently obvious.

(4) From the year 823 or thereabouts, that is, from the beginning of the story of Egbert's great victories, a more definite change comes over the Chronicle. The jottings of earlier annalists fade away. Entries which seem to be based on the tradition of the elders or the editor's own remembrances become more frequent. From this point, therefore, it is increasingly evident that the editors—or editor—had some well-defined points of view. They were interested in the Viking raids, in their beginnings as well as in their wearisome repetitions. They recalled clearly enough the places raided, but the precise numbers of the attackers had become blurred with time. When they wanted to say that a raiding party was (for those days) a big one, their habit was to say that it contained 'thirty-five ships'. They were interested in the wars which gave Egbert his imperial position and in the nature of that imperialism. They knew Bede's *History* well, and made use of that knowledge to exalt Egbert's position, incorporating his passage about the seven imperial kings.

Even more significant are the subjects which they omit; their blindness to the greatness of Offa and of other Mercian kings is easily intelligible. Their neglect of the early history of Egbert, however, is strange. They are more discreet than the garrulous Asser, and avoid any mention of incidents which were discreditable to the dynasty, such as the scandalous plots and poisonings of Queen Eadburh, the daughter of Offa, and the conspiracy of Ethelbald and Bishop Ealhstan to depose Ethelwulf. Another subject on which the editors are curiously silent is the doings of Alfred's brothers. Ethelred's campaigns against the Great Army in 868–71 are indeed noticed with unwonted detail, but whenever he is mentioned his brother Alfred is mentioned alongside of him. Ethelred as king could not be ignored, but Alfred remains the hero of the Year of Battles.

Against those who believe that an important part in the making of the Chronicle was played by a 'First Editor' who brought the record down to the genealogy of Ethelwulf in 855 and who did his work under that king, our contention is that the whole section from 823 to Alfred's Year of Battles (871) is all of a piece, that it must have been composed by a dependant of Alfred and not of Ethelwulf or any other, and that the whole Chronicle from start to finish except in those entries which simply reproduce earlier annals has value in bringing us into contact with the ideas of Alfred's circle, and therefore indirectly with those of Alfred himself. Let us sum up the more noteworthy of these ideas.

First, pride in the hard fighting of the West Saxons. The chroniclers felt that great things had been done, and that the memory of them should be perpetuated. There was pride also in the blood royal of the House of Egbert and in its descent from Cerdic (good propaganda for all Anglo-Saxons); also in its descent from Woden (this probably had some propaganda value in conversation with heathen Danes). The emphasis on the Bretwaldaship was also as likely as not something more than a piece of antiquarianism. This magniloquent theory is the counterpart to the imperialism of Charlemagne; the Chronicle staked out for Egbert's dynasty a rather academic claim to empire within Britain, and it laid some stress on the help which the West Saxons had given the Mercians. A political motive may perhaps be once more detected in the emphasis laid by the Chronicle on the doings of Alfred in contrast with the almost blank record of his brothers: this might have weight when the question of the succession to the crown should come before the nation.

If these conjectures are near the truth, they may help to explain the last development of the Alfredian Chronicle.

(5) This last stage was begun about 891, when at least two copies were made of the archetype—one, it seems, being deposited at Winchester, and another being carried to a Northumbrian monastery, probably Ripon. From these two and perhaps from others sent later to Worcester, Canterbury, and elsewhere, a number of other versions were made in later times. It is conceivable that the sending out of the transcripts had political significance. A record like this might help to spread, if only among the Northumbrian clergy, some knowledge of Wessex—of the antiquity of its dynasty, of the claims of its kings to be successors to the Northumbrian Bretwaldas, of its record as the champion of Christianity against Viking heathendom.

If we accept the view that an element of propaganda went to the making of the Old English Chronicle, it is natural to read a somewhat similar explanation into Asser's Life of Alfred, written in 893–4. For what did Asser do? He omitted (except for a passing reference) the early sections of the Chronicle which, with their record of victories over the Britons, would have infuriated his fellow Welshmen. He translated those entries which brought out the dangers of the Viking wars and the victories of Alfred, the one Christian king who had organized successful resistance. Asser's book served up in Latin for Welsh or Cornish readers information about a local king who was laying the foundations of a new British imperialism. It is a counterpart to the version of the Chronicle sent to the north for the Northumbrians.

It would of course be ridiculous to argue that this was the only motive of Asser in writing. His motives were mixed: he had a story worth telling in itself, he wished to praise a really great man, to show gratitude to a patron, to emulate Einhard's Life of Charlemagne, probably also he wished to defend himself in the eyes of his countrymen against the charge of deserting his own people in order to serve an alien.[30]

Let us next consider the History of the World by Orosius, originally called the *Seven Books of Histories against the Pagans.** The two titles between them correctly describe the contents. It was indeed a universal history of the then known world, the first of its kind, beginning with the Creation and coming down to 407, the age of Orosius himself; but its purpose was frankly apologetic—to prove from history that in spite of the recent sack of Rome by the Goths in 410, the calamities of mankind were worse before the coming of Christ than any sufferings that had befallen them after that event. The theme was obviously appropriate for men who were exposed to a new plague of northern barbarians.

The place to be assigned to Alfred's translation of Orosius in the cycle of his works has been long debated. If, however, the view expressed above (p. 625) is correct, that it was being produced about the same time as the archetype of the Chronicle, it cannot be much later than 891, the date at which the archetype ends, but both it and the Chronicle may have been for many years in the hands of their editors.

According to this view, while the *Orosius* was produced when Alfred was somewhere about forty, it represents a comparatively early stage in his process of self-education. In it he translates freely, according to the method of 'sense for sense' begun in the *Pastoral Care*; he cuts about his Latin original with a bold hand as in the *Bede*; and for the first time, when the spirit moves him, he occasionally throws down his Latin book and adds long passages of his own. Sections of the geographical introduction are completely re-written, stories of the adventurous voyages of seamen, as narrated by them to Alfred, are inserted.† On almost every page of the history Alfred launches out into comments, moralizings, and attempted explanations; and the generally fluent and natural language displays a marked advance on the clumsy faithfulness of the *Pastoral Care*.

Alfred shows great independence, but his numerous faults, his

---

* i.e. *Historiarum adversum Paganos Libri* vii.   † See below, pp. 642–7.

mistranslations, his tiresome repetitions, indicate that he was still new to the business of literature, and that he was much interrupted in his work.

*The Consolation of Philosophy** by Boethius, and the *Soliloquies* of St. Augustine, are the further translations of Alfred which deserve attention. It is now commonly believed that they were last in point of time: they deal with the problems of life and death, the subject to which his active brain might be expected to devote itself as his end drew near.

In these books Alfred is clearly translating to satisfy himself and his own questionings rather than to educate his subjects. He is less than ever content merely to translate or even to render sense by sense. As in the geographical section of the *Orosius*, he becomes himself an author. His additions, whencesoever derived, are substantial. They have the stamp of his virile personality. Philosophy appearing in the guise of a venerable woman brought her Consolation to Boethius, the Roman patrician, when imprisoned in 523 by Theodoric the Ostrogoth. This Consolation was a summary of much ancient, and especially Platonic, thought about such subjects as true happiness, the existence of evil, and the nature of the highest good. Later we shall see how far Alfred was able to assimilate the abstract ideas of this religious philosophy.

In the present chapter enough has been said to give the reader an impression of the intelligible and consistent scheme which seems to underlie the literature produced by Alfred and those who co-operated with him. The *Pastoral Care* of Pope Gregory was to educate the clergy in the art of shepherding their flocks, the *Dialogues* to confirm their faith with stories about miracles. The works of Orosius and of Bede were to teach Englishmen what was known about the history of the world in general, and of the golden age of Christian England in particular; and finally, as a stimulant for the national spirit of his countrymen, the Chronicle was compiled to paint the past glories of the

* *Philosophiae Consolatio.*

West Saxons and to tell how the kingdom had been delivered through the hard fighting of Alfred and his followers.

This may have been the scheme; but what was the reality? The sequel in the tenth century will show that some of the seed sown by Alfred fell on stony ground. The *Soliloquies*, for example, only survives in a single copy. The school of the king's household did not give rise to a tradition of learning comparable with that which emanated from the palace of Charlemagne. It could boast no patron of learning like Charlemagne's grandson, Charles the Bald. Ethelweard, an ealdorman descended from one of Alfred's brothers, wrote, a century after Alfred's death, an almost untranslatable Latin Chronicle. This is the only evidence of the survival of any kind of learning within the West Saxon royal family.

Some of Alfred's ideas were many hundreds of years before their time. Others were more fruitful. His Chronicle brought forth in time a crop of smaller Chronicles. His Laws were the first of a long-continued series. Throughout the tenth century much of the interest of English history will centre round the results of Alfred's labours.

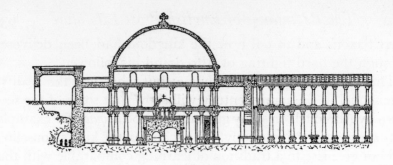

XVIII

ALFRED'S FOREIGN POLICY

RELATIONS WITH THE CONTINENT

UP to this point it has been possible to follow the history of the Anglo-Saxons with only an occasional reference to any political relations with the Continent. The short-lived quarrel between Offa and Charlemagne, the marriage of Ethelbert with the Frankish Bertha and that of Ethelwulf with the Frankish Judith, these have been the only outstanding incidents. With the reign of Alfred, however, the foreign policy of the king of Wessex becomes more interesting. This is not due, as might be expected, to the fact that the break-up of the Carolingian Empire left behind it a new rivalry between French and Germans. Its significance lies in the points of contrast with modern diplomacy rather than in any similarities. We shall hear of letters and embassies between Alfred and some of his neighbours—an archbishop of Rheims, a count of Flanders, and Popes Formosus and Marinus. We shall find Alfred showing an interest in the remote parts of the known world, in the churches of Jerusalem and 'India', and in the peoples of northern Europe, especially those living within the Arctic circle and round the shores of the Baltic. Lastly, we shall take stock of his relations with the other kingdoms within this island, a subject which brings us nearer to his foreign policy in the modern sense.

HEADPIECE.—Part of the church of the Holy Sepulchre, one of the churches for which Elias, the Patriarch of Jerusalem, sent begging letters.

1. The archbishops of Rheims had been throughout the ninth century foremost among the great churchmen of Gaul. Their desire was to arrogate to themselves metropolitan authority of the widest possible extent. Hincmar, the archbishop of Rheims who had helped to entertain Ethelwulf and the boy Alfred during their visit to the Frankish court in 856, had played a great part as the right-hand man of Charles the Bald and afterwards as the controller of the weaker kings who followed him. Fulk, the successor of Hincmar (883–900), was a lesser man, but he was equally active and ambitious. As a loyalist to the House of Charlemagne after 888—the year when the Western Franks discarded that House and took for their king Odo, count of Paris, the heroic defender of Neustria and of Paris—Fulk was led into a network of political intrigues. With maxims about the need for unity on his lips, he kept the kingdom of the West Franks divided, impeding Odo instead of supporting him against the Northmen. It was this potentate of the Church—so much more powerful than many of the shadow kings who pass across the later years of the ninth century—to whom Alfred, probably about 884–5, sent messengers with gifts of well-bred wolf-hounds and the request that Grimbald, priest and monk, might be sent to help him in his work. The letter in which Fulk replied is the only letter addressed to Alfred of which we know the full contents.[1] He makes it fairly clear that in his eyes the English were what they had been in the time of St. Augustine, 'a rude and barbarous race'. He had scruples in exposing Grimbald to the 'barbaric rudeness' of Alfred's subjects. But he took pity on their ignorance; and so he extended to Alfred his 'counsel and protection'. He stipulated that the deputation of Englishmen, presumably those who were to be the electors of Grimbald to a bishopric, should come in person to declare in the presence of the whole Church of Rheims that they would keep the rules of the Church as they should learn them from Fulk and from Grimbald. Fulk's letter was not a model of tact.

Alfred, remembering it may be the failure of an earlier

Frankish bishop of Wessex, evaded the demand that Grimbald should be promoted to a bishopric. Fulk's talk of 'protection'* could also be ignored. What counted were his kindly intention to help the Saxon Church, and the principles which he professed: 'if one member suffers, all members suffer with it' and 'the Catholic and Apostolic Church is one, whether it be of Rome or beyond the seas'.† However hackneyed or ambiguous, these words were clearly no empty phrases, even from Fulk, the spreader of dissensions in his own land; and we may believe that they were received with a deeper meaning by Alfred, to whom they were addressed.

Fulk sent other friendly letters[2] to Alfred, one to congratulate, one to exhort. But apart from words, their relations amounted simply to this: the export of English wolf-hounds to the Frankish archbishop, and the import of Grimbald, the learned monk, to the court of Alfred.

2. Alfred's relations with Baldwin II, count of Flanders, so far as they are known, may also be dismissed in a few words. Ælfthryth, the third daughter of the English king, was married, some time between 893 and 897, to Baldwin. The event is significant from many points of view. Hitherto the kingly families of the English had with very few exceptions found their wives and husbands within the island. The union of Ælfthryth to the Count of Flanders was a turning-point. It showed that Alfred realized the need for solidarity among the Christian rulers who bordered the English Channel; it was thus the beginning of a new policy which was for a time followed by his descendants. The choice of young Baldwin is also interesting owing to the fact that he was the son of Judith, Alfred's own step-mother and sister-in-law; for Judith, after scandalizing the English by marrying her eldest stepson, King Ethelbald, had returned to France and scandalized her father and countrymen by a runaway match with Baldwin I 'of the Iron Arm', the Count of Flanders who by his valour had built up the fortunes of his family in the Low Countries.

---

* *patrocinium.*   † *sive Romana sive transmarina.*

The Flemish alliance was, no doubt, sound policy for a king of England in the ninth as in later centuries; but it brought the House of Alfred into contact with a great crime. The story is this. After 892 Baldwin and Archbishop Fulk quarrelled over the appointment of a new abbot to the important abbey of St. Bertin. Fulk supported the monks who wished to elect one of their number named Grimbald (possibly though not certainly the same monk who had been sent to help Alfred in England). Baldwin was aggressive and violent; and in June 900 the quarrel ended in the murder of the Archbishop and his devoted followers at the hands of Baldwin's retainers. The Gallic bishops discharged their battery of curses against Alfred's son-in-law and his abettors. They were cursed in the city and cursed in the field; cursed in the fruit of their body, and cursed in the fruit of their lands; in their herds and in their flocks. They were cursed indoors and cursed out of doors. Baldwin, however, survived the anathemas, ruling in apparent prosperity for another nineteen years.

3. Alfred's attitude to the Papacy is well explained by the words in which Archbishop Fulk asserted the unity of the Church: 'una est Ecclesia sive Romana sive transmarina.' It was a unity of sentiment and not of mere theory, and at no time was the devotion of the English to the Papacy more in evidence than in this age. Thus, in 864 certain Englishmen came to Rome and set up in the chapel dedicated to St. Gregory in St. Peter's a silver tablet.[3] In this manner the English nation expressed gratitude for its conversion, to Gregory the Great, whom Alfred in the proem to his *Pastoral Care* called 'the best of the Romans, the wisest of men'. In the same year the piety of the English people was again signalized when some pilgrims rescued the *lignum Domini*, that is, a fragment of the Holy Rood. On this occasion the precious relic which had been preserved at Rome for more than five hundred years, ever since it had been brought thither by the Empress Helena, was thrown into the mud during a riot, and the splendid cross containing it was

broken. It was fitting that Englishmen, fellow countrymen of the poet who had told in verse the story of Helena (the *Elene*) should have collected the fragments and restored them to the clergy in charge of the Cross.[4] Whether or not there was any direct connexion between this incident and the interchange of gifts between Alfred and the Pope, it is remarkable that the entry in the Saxon Chronicle which gives the first mention of their intercourse should record the presentation of a piece of the Rood to Alfred.

'A.D. 882. Marinus the Pope sent the *lignum Domini* to king Alfred. And in the same year Sighelm and Athelstan took the alms which king Alfred promised [to send] thither, and also to St. Thomas in India, and to St. Bartholomew, at the time when they [i.e. Alfred, Sighelm, and Athelstan] besieged the Army at London; and they were very successful, thanks be to God, according to the promises.'[5]

In four of the following years, down to '890', the sending of the alms to Rome—generally called the 'alms of the West Saxons and of King Alfred'—appears as a chief entry of the annal. The money was sent in the charge of an ealdorman or an abbot. The regularity of the gift at this time is evident from the annal of 889, which says that 'in this year there was no journey to Rome, except that king Alfred sent two couriers with letters'.

The annual gift was clearly a resumption of the payment (called in later times Hearth Money or Peter's Pence) promised by Offa and by Ethelwulf,* and no doubt interrupted by the Viking wars. Like the silver tablet of 864, it was the expression of the filial devotion felt to the successors of St. Gregory.

Alfred obtained in return for his alms the *lignum Domini*, a relic valued above all gold and silver, preserved in later centuries at Canterbury, along with part of the seamless garment of Our Lord, part of the clothing of St. Mary, and five boxfulls of other holy relics.[6] Nor was this all; Alfred persuaded 'the good Pope Marinus' (882–4) to 'free' the School of the English at Rome—free it, no doubt, from papal taxation. This, too, was a conces-

* See above, pp. 390, 512.

sion not without its value. For think what in previous times must have been the disillusionment of the pious English pilgrims who, endured all the hardships of the long journey, buoyed up with the thought that when they reached the Shrines of the Apostles all would be well in this world and the next, only to find that at Rome there were tax-collectors waiting for them with demands heavier and more pressing than any they had known in their lonely English villages.

Alfred's early embassies to Rome were acts of devotion, not acts of policy. But there may have been an element of worldly wisdom in his encouragement of pilgrimage to the centre of Western Christendom. Rome might impress and influence the ealdormen carrying the alms of the West Saxons, as it had impressed Alfred himself. What better education could there be for the ruler of an English shire than to journey through the towns of Gaul and Italy and across the Alps to the City whose massive buildings and whose living traditions proclaimed the civilization of the ancient world? These things might cause some ferment even in the brain of an unimaginative Saxon countryman.

The existence of an English colony at Rome, comprising both clergy and distinguished laymen, is well attested. For example, Burhred, the deposed king of Mercia, died at Rome in 874, and his widow, Alfred's sister, died on her way to the Holy City fourteen years later. A papal ordinance of the period[7] requires the English clergy in Rome to wear the long Roman tunic reaching to the heels instead of their former fashion, the short tunic like that worn by the laity.

Rome, like Rheims, was inclined to over-criticize the English and not to appreciate sufficiently the difficulties which faced their rulers. 'When we heard', wrote Pope Formosus (891–6) to the Archbishop of Canterbury, 'that the abominable rites of the pagans had revived in your country, and that like dumb dogs you kept silent, we were minded to cut you off from the body of the Church.'[8] If the Papacy did not fully understand the situation in England with its new-made Danelaw, it was as well that the English on their part were far removed from the happenings in Rome which made these later years of the ninth century one of the deplorable periods in the history of the Roman Church. Round Formosus (the Pope whose letter we have just quoted) there was gathered a gang of licentious Romans. It was said that one of them embezzled the treasure of the Roman Church and that, after poisoning his brother, for the sake of his mistress, and murdering his wife, the niece of a former pope, he in the end escaped condemnation by bribery. Punishment came only after Pope Formosus had been buried; his mummied corpse was taken from its grave. It was clad in pontifical vestments and was arraigned in a 'synod of horror'. When the corpse returned no answer to its accusers, the vestments were torn from it, the fingers which had given the blessing were cut off, and the mummy was carried with wild shouts through the streets of Rome and cast into the Tiber. The Pope who in this synod condemned the corpse of Formosus was himself strangled; his successors were the creatures of a day. The papacy failed to raise itself from the mud into which it had sunk.

Whether Alfred continued to send alms and embassies we do not know. His chronicler certainly turned his attention to other interests.

Thus the letters of the period as a whole make it clear that Alfred was almost isolated. He had to steer his course through the storms of the Viking age with little or no support from continental kingdoms. 'Good Pope Marinus' had sent him the *lignum Domini*; Archbishop Fulk had lent him the learned Grimbald; and that was all.

4. It is characteristic of Alfred that his interests did not stop short at Rome. He looked yet further, to the East. Asser's statement[9] that Elias, Patriarch of Jerusalem (*c.* 879–907), sent Alfred gifts and letters which Asser had himself seen and read is confirmed by other documents. The actual letters of the Patriarch have not been preserved. But we can guess their contents,

since we have a begging letter of his to the Emperor Charles the
Fat, and he was too good a beggar to contradict himself. Here
then is the gist of what the Patriarch told the Frank. He said
that he had to write because his tribulations were many and
great, and the one which tortured him above all others was the
sight of his churches daily falling into ruins. He implored God's
mercy, that they might be restored in his time. He asserted (no
doubt the Frank would not examine too closely into his statements) that the Prince of his part of the world having become
a Christian (!) had decreed that the churches should be restored
by the Christians. It was impossible for the Patriarch and his
flock to do this themselves; and he therefore appealed for the
help of other nations. He explained further that poverty had
forced him to pledge his olive-groves and vine-yards and even
the sacred vessels of his churches. Accordingly the oil for the
lamps of his shrines was failing. The poor were pining from
hunger. Many captives were unransomed. The Patriarch was
unable to collect the money required for the redemption of his
property from pawn. 'Show to us your bowels of kindness . . .
for you know "if one member suffers, all the members suffer
with it".'

Unhappy indeed was the lot of Elias. For two hundred years
and more his Jerusalem had been in the hands of the infidels.
Christians remained in the Holy City but only on sufferance; the
church of the Holy Sepulchre was overtopped by the mosque of
Omar. His appeal doubtless met with a better response from
Alfred than from the Frank; for Alfred's generosity to foreign
churches was specially extolled by Asser.

It may be presumed that Alfred in his reply sent a message to
the Patriarch asking him to impart to him some of the wisdom
of the East. He may have asked specially for medical wisdom.
That, at any rate, is what he received. The remedies recommended by Elias to Alfred were copied by later Anglo-Saxons
into their medical books,[10] and by comparison with the more
magical Anglo-Saxon prescriptions, some of which have been

quoted in an earlier chapter, these of Elias were worth keeping. The Patriarch says that balsam is

'very good for cough and carbuncle. . . . Smear with balsam against fever and against abrasions and against all pollutions. Petroleum also is good to drink and to smear outwardly on a winter's day, since it hath very much heat. . . . And if anyone's speech faileth, then let him take it and make the mark of Christ under his tongue. . . . Triacle is a good drink for all inward tendernesses, and the man who so behaveth himself as is here set down, he may much help himself. On the day on which he shall drink triacle he shall fast until midday, and not let wind blow on him that day; then let him go to the bath, let him sit there till he sweat; then let him take a cup and put a little warm water in it, then let him take a little bit of the triacle and mingle with the water and drain through some thin raiment, then drink it, and let him go to his bed and wrap himself up warm, and so lie till he sweat well.'

Simple remedies! 'Go to bed and sweat and keep out of draughts.' That was the wisdom of the East sent to the king of Wessex.

There can be no doubt about the fact of Alfred's intercourse with the Holy Land, but are we to believe the late and ambiguous annal quoted above which says that he either sent or intended to send a mission to 'St. Thomas in India and to St. Bartholomew'? It must be granted that the story, which is not found in the Alfredian Chronicle but only in later versions, is not well authenticated. Moreover, 'India' was in those days a wide term which might mean little more than 'Asia'; and the body of St. Thomas, whatever its original resting-place, was commonly reputed in the Dark Ages to be enshrined at Edessa in Syria. Thus there are in the story difficulties at every turn; and though we may argue that it was just like Alfred to stretch out hands to the uttermost parts of the known world and to go one better than Charlemagne in intercourse with the Orient, we cannot be certain that his messengers penetrated even as far as Edessa.

Enough has now been told to illustrate the general character of Alfred's relations with the outside world. We have seen no

statecraft, no political alliance (except perhaps with Baldwin of *e*
France), no diplomacy in the ordinary sense of the word. Instead,
we have heard of friendly interchanges of letters and gifts: wolf-
hounds and alms offered by Alfred; a learned cleric, a relic, a
medical prescription received by him. It is right that we should
note this exchange of courtesies since it is typical of the Age of
Faith, when, in spite of the disintegration of the Carolingian
Empire and the consequent engendering of an implacable feud
between Frenchmen and Germans, Christian potentates from
Asia to Britain still paid something more than lip-service to
the principle that 'if one member suffers all the members suffer
with it'.

Alfred's own observance of the principle is mentioned in a
sentence of Asser[11] which tells how the king directed that from
the share of his revenue 'dedicated to God' some of a one-fourth
part should be given to the churches in Wales, Cornwall, Gaul,
Brittany, Northumbria, 'and sometimes too in Ireland', as well
as to the monasteries in Wessex and Mercia.

The mention of Ireland is interesting since we do not hear of
Alfred drawing any of his literary helpers from that island in
spite of its reputation for learning. What the Chronicle does tell
us is that in 891 'three Scots [Irishmen] came to king Alfred in
a boat without any oars from Hibernia, whence they stole away
because they would go on a foreign pilgrimage for the love of
God, they recked not where. The boat in which they came was
made of two hides and a half; and they took with them food for
seven days. And within seven days they came to land in Cornwall, and soon afterwards went to King Alfred. They were thus
named: Dubslane, and Macbeth, and Mælinmun. And Swifneh
[i.e. Sweeney], the best teacher that there was among the Scots,
departed this life.' The surprising thing in this entry is that the
arrival of the three Irishmen should have made so great an
impression on the mind of the Chronicler. Irishmen had mani-
fested their sanctity by wandering in this way from their native
island ever since the fifth century. In addition to the saints who

had committed themselves to the sea to go 'for the love of God, they recked not where', there had been flocks of other Irish clergy who emigrated to seek a living where they could.[12] In 816 an English Synod, resenting the presence of Irish intruders and their competition for baptismal and other church fees, had adopted a policy of ecclesiastical nationalism, and had excluded Irishmen 'summarily in a body and individually, without benefit of clergy'.[13] During the rest of the ninth century the stream of Irishmen, many of them refugees whose monasteries had been destroyed by the Vikings, flowed strongly, but flowed to the Continent. There these wanderers, tramping the dusty paths of France and Germany, recognizable by their long hair, their sombre clothing, their tall walking-sticks, their wallets and water-bottles, were as characteristic a feature of the ninth century as the more terrifying Vikings with their gaily coloured cloaks, their gold and silver armlets, and their burnished spears and swords. But in England the Irish, at any rate those of the type of Macbeth, were a rarity. Accordingly by the time of Alfred the anti-Irish sentiment of 816 had died down; and after Alfred in the tenth century Irish scholars at Glastonbury became an important influence in the revival of learning.

ALFRED'S INTEREST IN NORTHERN EUROPE

To understand Alfred's relations with the world outside Britain we must see his world as he saw it. This we are able to do because he has described it for us at the beginning of his translation of Orosius.

Asia, Europe, and Africa, the three parts of this 'Mid-earth' are surrounded by the ocean 'which is called [in English] *garsecg*'. Britain is in the ocean, opposite *Gallia Belgica*. West of Britain is Ireland,* surrounded on every side by the ocean. 'On the north-west of Ireland is that outmost land called Thule [Iceland]; and it is known to few because of its great distance.' Except for Ireland and Thule, Britain was on the outskirts of the world.

* 'Ibernia which we call Scotland.'

PLATE 79

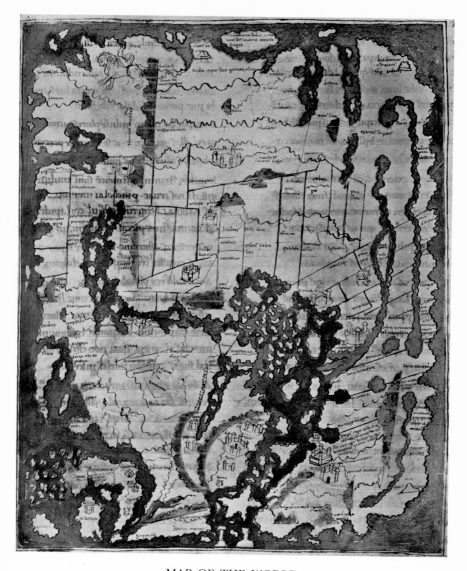

MAP OF THE WORLD
(from MS. Cott. Tib. B. V, f. 58 v.) *c.* 11th century
Brittannia, Hibernia, and Thule are in the left bottom corner. The peninsula opposite
the top of Brittannia is 'Norweci'

PLATE 80

Air-photograph showing semicircle of the old ramparts within which
was crowded a network of small houses

The ramparts
HEDEBY (formerly called *Haithabu*, and by Alfred æt Hæthum)

It faced in two directions. One side was to Gaul; through Gaul it looked to Rome and the Mediterranean Sea; through the Mediterranean Sea to the world of civilization and history;

ultimately to India 'where Mount Caucasus is on the north and the River Indes on the west and the Red Sea on the south and the ocean on the east'.

But Britain also faced the ocean which had on its other side the Northmanna-land. From that part of the ocean led the Ost Sæ (the Baltic) and the Cwen Sæ (? the Gulf of Bothnia). Now between the Don (Danai) and the Rhine and the Cwen Sæ 'are many nations; but they call it all Germania'.

What we have now to study is this northern half of Alfred's world and his attitude to it.[14]

To begin with, why did he so strangely extend 'Germania'? Excuses for his mistake may be found: the fact that the Goths had wandered into Scythian lands before they burst into the Roman Empire; also, in Alfred's own times, the eastward migration of the Scandinavians along the southern coasts of the Baltic and, under Rorik, into Russia. But no doubt the mistake was chiefly due to carelessness and misunderstanding. After all, Alfred was a pioneer tackling a new subject. If he had any map, it was necessarily erroneous (cf. Pl. 79). The wonder is that he did not make much worse mistakes. Alfred realized that the account of northern Europe given by Orosius was altogether inadequate. His own attempt to better the book was beset by difficulties: he could not fix the positions of countries by latitude and longitude; he could only describe their relative positions by the points of the compass. He therefore took certain peoples who specially interested him—the East Franks, in touch with Britain; the 'Old' Saxons, distant kinsmen of his own Anglo-Saxons; the Moravians, who in the ninth century had built up a flourishing kingdom; the South Danes and the North Danes, stocks from which had sprung the mass of his enemies. These and others he made his central points and described the neighbours round each of them. It was a cumbrous method, involving much repetition as well as error. But it tells us more about northern Europe than can be learnt from any previous writer.

Why did Alfred take such pains to explain the geography of 'Germania' to his English subjects? One suggestion[15] is that there was 'a practical, a commercial, a political' side to his geography. It is certainly noteworthy that five of Alfred's 'middle points' lay round the Baltic, and it is conceivable that he was considering the possibility of bringing pressure to bear on the Vikings in their home-lands. But these are conjectures which cannot be pressed. There is better ground for thinking that even if Alfred's knowledge of Germania had no commercial aim of its own it was collected from travelling merchants. We can see how men of that type were entertained by him, in the accounts which he gives of the voyages of Ohthere and Wulfstan. He suddenly breaks off from his description of 'Germania' to tell about the voyages of these sea-captains with much of the freshness of their own yarns.

The first expedition of Ohthere round the North Cape to the White Sea was a daring undertaking, a voyage of discovery.

'Ohthere told his lord, king Alfred, that he dwelt farthest north of all Northmen. . . . He said that at a certain time he wished to find out how far the land extended due north; or whether any man dwelt to the north of the waste. Then he went due north along the coast: he left, all the way, the waste land on his starboard and the open sea on his larboard, for three days. Then was he as far as whale-hunters ever go. He then went yet due north as far as he could sail in the next three days.' Having thus reached the North Cape he found that 'the land bent due east'. He then tells how he sailed to the land of the 'Beormas' on the White Sea. He found it well-peopled in contrast to what he had passed on the voyage, the waste lands not inhabited by any but fishermen, fowlers, and hunters, all of them 'Finns', that is Lapps.

'The Beormas told him many stories both about their own country and about the countries which were around them, but he knew not what was true because he did not see it for himself. . . . He chiefly went thither, in addition to the seeing of the country, on account of the horse-whales [walruses] because they have very good bone in their teeth; of these teeth, they brought some to the King; and their hides are very good for ship-ropes.'

Alfred then gives Ohthere's account of himself and of the way men lived in his country, 'Halgoland' (now Helgeland). 'He [Ohthere] was a very wealthy man in those possessions in which their wealth consists, that is, in the wilder [animals]. When he came to the King, he had six hundred tame deer unsold. They call these reindeer; of these, six were decoy-deer, which are very valuable among Finns, because with them they take the wild-deer. He was among the first men in the land, though he had not more than twenty horned cattle, twenty sheep, and twenty swine; and the little that he ploughed, he ploughed with horses.'

Ohthere in referring to his second voyage said it took him more than a month to sail from Halgoland to Sciringesheal, the chief port of southern Norway—a useful reminder for us of the remoteness of one province of the Northmen from another. What most interested Alfred in Ohthere's third voyage—from Sciringesheal to Hedeby (Hæthum)—was the fact that Jutland and certain islands which he passed were 'lands in which the Angles lived before they came to this country'.

The other sea-captain, Wulfstan, was probably an Englishman. The tale which he told was of a voyage from Hedeby to the mouth of the Vistula, and the part of the tale which took the king's fancy was that about the curious customs of the Esti—their diet, their horse-racing, their methods of cremation, and so on.

From Alfred's relations with these two sea-faring friends of his we can judge better than from his meagre notes on the geography of 'Germania' what was his attitude to the northern countries. The fact that he tells us so little about the Norwegians or the Danes is itself significant. It was the outlandish, the abnormal, peoples—the Finns, the Beormas, and the Esti—who interested him. The chief lesson to be learned from his description of northern Europe is the absence of bitterness in his attitude to the Danes. They and the Angles and the Saxons had once been neighbours in 'Germania'. They were not outside the pale like the Finns and the Esti. They were so much like the English in their manner of life that it was unnecessary to dilate upon minor differences.

These geographical sections of Alfred's book unfortunately ignore political questions, and they therefore make no reference to the achievements of Harold, Alfred's greatest contemporary in the north. But the voyages described cover all the seas of the Northmen, and the stories wipe out any idea that Scandinavians and English were glaring at one another in hatred across the North Sea. Alfred was as ready to learn about the Northmen's method of doing things—about their boat-building, their rope-making, their secrets of fishing—as to teach them the mysteries of his own Faith.

RELATIONS WITH OTHER STATES IN BRITAIN

The history of the Danish wars has already given us clues to Alfred's position within Britain. We have seen how he, as the successful organizer of war against the Vikings, became the natural leader and lord of the neighbouring Christian States in the island; and how his readiness to make friends with law-abiding Scandinavians, especially with those who like Guthrum accepted Christian baptism, prepared the way for the union of the Danelaw with Wessex.

Circumstances had thus dictated that Alfred should have one policy for his neighbours in the east of the island, and another one for the Mercians and Welsh.

His eastern policy is illustrated by his treaty with Guthrum (? 886) and by the unsuccessful attempts which he made in the war of 892–6 to bind the Danish immigrants and invaders with oaths.

His Mercian policy is illustrated by his control of the western Midlands through Ethelred. The control was effective, and was to bear good fruit in the successful military co-operation of Mercians and West Saxons in the years 893–5. But a wise ambiguity, we have seen, was allowed to surround the superiority of the West Saxon king over his Midland neighbours. The superiority was a complex growth; in it were mingled traditions of the overlordship won by the armies of Egbert, memories of the many occasions on which West Saxon troops had come to the help of the Mercians, the influence of intermarriages now most happily reinforced by the marriage of Ethelred of Mercia to the eldest daughter of Alfred, and above all the moral ascendancy of Alfred's own personality, and the sense that he alone could save what was left of Anglo-Saxon England and of Anglo-Saxon civilization.

It remains to note the results of Alfred's western and eastern policies in the later years of his reign.

Alfred's position as the champion of all Christian peoples against the heathen was in time recognized by the Welsh, as it had been by the Mercians. Thus Asser, in dedicating his biography to Alfred, addresses him as 'the ruler* of all the Christians of the island of Britain', and in his text he describes how one Welsh kinglet after another sought or accepted the lordship† or empire‡ of his patron. The sense of Christian solidarity was not, it is true, the only influence which led to the opening of this new chapter in the relations between Briton and Saxon. The kings of Dyfed and of Brycheinoig seem to have feared chiefly the violence of the sons of Rhodri Mawr (Roderick the Great), the king who had for a short spell

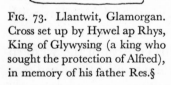

FIG. 73. Llantwit, Glamorgan. Cross set up by Hywel ap Rhys, King of Glywysing (a king who sought the protection of Alfred), in memory of his father Res.§

(844–78) united north and middle Wales. Asser, journeying between Dyfed and the court of Alfred, helped to persuade the southern Welsh that the once-hated Saxons had become their natural protectors against the aggressive war-bands of the House

---

* *rector.*   † *dominium.*   ‡ *imperium.*

§ The inscription reads: in nomine dī patris et
(s)peretus santdi anc
(cr)ucem houelt prope
(ra)bit pro anima res pa
(tr)es eus

of Rhodri. The kings of Glywysing* and of Gwent experienced
an argument of another kind in the forceful compulsion of ealdorman Ethelred and his Mercians. The sons of Rhodri who had
divided up the kingdom of their father, for a time after 881 placed
politics before Christianity, and allied themselves with the Danes
of York. However, when Asser wrote, about 893, they had found
that they got more harm than good out of their alliance with the
heathen; and their leader, Anarawd of Gwynedd, had come to
the court of Alfred, 'the first visit of the kind on record paid by a
Welsh to an English king'.[16] He had been received with great
honour by Alfred, and been well gifted. And on his part he had
undertaken that he and his would be 'obedient in all things to the
king's will in the same way as Ethelred and the Mercians'. It
was 'the Dominion status' of the day.

To the north of Wales were the Cymri of Cumbria. These,
freed from Anglian dominion by the downfall of Northumbria,
now re-established a kingdom of their own reaching to the Clyde;
but the history of this kingdom is a blank, and it does not enter
into the picture of Alfred's influence.

Turning to the eastern side of the island, we must seek to discover Alfred's relations with the regions which had come under
the power of the Danes. Here we have no word from Asser to
help us. From Ethelweard's Chronicle[17] it may be gathered that
'foul bands of Northumbrians' troubled the English down to
the year of Alfred's death. But this is not the whole story. There
was something else besides raids of the heathen and retaliation
by the Christians.

For the reconstruction of the history of Northumbria in the
age of Alfred we have various but unsatisfactory evidence. From
a Durham book of the tenth or eleventh century[18] we have a
story which tells how, after an interregnum of six years (877–83)
following the death of Halfdene, an abbot of Carlisle had a
vision of St. Cuthbert, who bid him cross the Tyne and seek out
a boy named Guthred of royal birth.[19] The boy, who had been

* Glamorgan.

sold to a Christian, was to be redeemed and presented to the Danes as their future king. It is claimed that the abbot fulfilled his mission, and that Guthred reigned with all piety from 883 to 894; that he endowed the monks of St. Cuthbert with the lands between the Tyne and the Wear; and that the grant was confirmed by Alfred. Impudent and unscrupulous hagiography? No doubt; but with some core of truth. There is much to be said for the view that this Guthred was also called Cnut; and coins exist which have on one side 'Cnut Rex' and on the other 'Elfred Rex'[20] (cf. Pl. 81, 10). To this story Simeon of Durham adds a statement that on the death of Guthred in 894 'king Alfred had the disposal of the kingdom of the Northumbrians'.* The tale told by the coins seems to be that after Cnut came a King Siegfred. This Siegfred no longer has Alfred acknowledged as *rex* on the reverse side of his coins, a fact which tallies with the last war of Alfred. He may be identified with the 'pirate Sigeferth', who made raids from Northumbria in 894.[22]

The strangest part of this bit of Northumbrian history does not come till the death of Alfred. Then the Army of the Northumbrians (i.e. the Danes) accept as their king a nephew of Alfred who had unsuccessfully claimed the succession in Wessex in opposition to Edward, the son of Alfred.

On the whole the literary and the numismatic evidence sufficiently confirm one another to justify the view that Alfred was in a vague and occasional way recognized in the north as what we may call Head King in England—the foremost of all by virtue of his descent, his legitimacy, and his military strength. It must be remembered that Christianity, though under a cloud, was still strong in the Danish districts. Christians of the Anglian stock must have formed the greater proportion of the inhabitants. They may well have agreed with the Welsh in regarding Alfred as the 'ruler of all the Christians of the island'. At the same time the statement in the Chronicle that Alfred was king over 'all England except the part that was under the power of the Danes'

* *Mortuo Guthredo, rex Elfredus Northanhumbrorum regnum suscepit disponendum.*[21]

PLATE 81

1. GOLD DINAR OF OFFA
Copy of a caliph's coin

2. OFFA

3. CYNETHRITH, WIFE
OF OFFA

4. EADBEARHT PRAEN
KING OF KENT

5. EGBERT (HECBEARHT REX)

6. HALFDENE (ALFDENE RX)
with a winged Victory
Reverse. Monogram of London

7. ALFRED
(AELFRED REX ANGLORUM)
Reverse. Winged Victory

8. ST. EDMUND
(SC. EADMUND REX)
Memorial coinage (*c.* 870–905)

9. Bust of ALFRED
Reverse. LINCOLLA in
monogram

10. CNUT (? GUTHRED
King of York, *c.* 878–94)
Reverse. DNS DS REX

SILVER PENNIES (except 1) OF THE EIGHTH AND NINTH
CENTURIES

gives the substantial truth. The Christian Church in North-umbria had not altogether lost its organization. Many bishoprics and monasteries had been completely wiped out; but some remained. The archbishop of York, after a temporary flight to Wharfedale during the storm of 867, had been able to return to his city. The great stone church at York, built by Wilfrid, still stood towering above the wooden houses of the Angles and Danes and above the Roman walls which enclosed them. The church still had its services. The archbishop was still in touch with the south, and when it became necessary to consecrate a new arch-bishop, the ceremony was performed at London.[23] With Wil-frid's monastery surviving at Ripon (and it may be others of which we have less information), and with the monks of St. Cuthbert re-endowed with lands north of the Wear, the Church was still a rallying point for the old order, a potential ally of the West Saxon dynasty.

No doubt the situation was somewhat similar in East Anglia. Here also the official attitude of the Danish ruler changed from reign to reign. Christianity was so far accepted under Guthrum-Athelstan that the moneyers thought it fitting that the king's name should be inscribed in its Christian form. They also issued memorial pennies of 'Saint' Edmund in great numbers: 1,800 of them have been found in one horde (Pl. 81, 8). Though the suc-cession of the bishops at Elmham and at Dunwich was broken, though the see of Leicester was removed to Dorchester-on-Thames, Christianity survived in the east Midlands as in the north, and re-emerged with some vigour in the second quarter of the tenth century.

On the whole it is safe to say that the reign of Alfred was a turning-point in the relations between Wessex and the east and north of England. Wessex could improve its position without any formal recognition of superiority. There was relative advance because, while its older rivals had been destroyed, the Danish kingdoms which had taken their place were weak. They failed at any rate for the time being to produce any great ruler, able to establish a well-rooted dynasty. Wessex gained in prestige by comparison with the chaotic condition of the conquered lands of the Danelaw. The Danes in the first generation of their rule in eastern England failed to produce a great leader or organizer. Neither the confused monarchy of Northumbria nor Guthrum and his successor in East Anglia managed to keep much control over the 'armies' of the settlers. Already, it may be, the 'armies' of the eastern Midlands were drifting apart from the Danish kingdoms, and those to the north of the Welland may already have been forming their group of the 'Five Burghs'.

If then we bring our ideas about Alfred's relations with the English north of the Thames, with the Danes, and with the inhabitants of the Danelaw, to a conclusion, we shall refrain from stressing[24] the fact that Alfred 'exercised no real sovereignty north of the Thames'. The union of Britain was inevitably a gradual process. But a change of sentiment may be a step both more difficult and more decisive than a change in legal title. Alfred did, as a matter of fact, establish over western Mercia a superiority sufficiently definite to be expressed in legal language. In addition to this he led his dynasty towards the empire of Britain, and it was a fact of no small significance that he should be regarded as the 'ruler of all Christians in Britain', the one table element in a chaotic and shifting world.

DOMINO MEO VENERABILI PIISSIMOQVE·
OMNIVM BRITTANNIE INSVLAE XPIANO
RVM · RECTORI · ÆLFRED · ANGLORVM SAXO
NVM · REGI·

ælfred angul faxonum rex

[Extracts from the facsimile of the beginning of Asser, i.e. of the unique MS. burnt in 1731. Early 11th century.]

XIX

ALFRED'S LAST WAR

IN the late autumn of the year 892[1] there might have been descried off the shores of southern Kent an armada of 250 ships. They had come from the port of Boulogne, and bearing straight across the Channel, they put into the estuary of the Limen, now a part of Romney Marsh (Map, p. 657). Formidable as was this fleet transporting the Great Army, it was not the only force of the Vikings that was planning to invade the kingdom of Alfred. For soon after, and presumably in alliance with the Great Army, another fleet of 80 vessels sailed into the Thames mouth, and established itself on the northern coast of Kent. The twofold attack was clearly no casual raid; it was an invasion deliberate and well-planned, heralding years of warfare.

If we are to understand what these Northmen were aiming at we must have some knowledge of what they had been doing on the Continent. About this we are unusually well informed. It is clear that a nucleus of the Army had been the body which wintered at Fulham in 879 and then sailed to France. For many years they and their allied bands raided the Low Countries and the Rhineland. In 885 they coalesced and made their supreme effort in the great siege of Paris. It was said, no doubt with much exaggeration, that they collected for the siege 40,000 men, and that they had 700 ships excluding transport vessels. They brought up battering-rams, catapults, and other siege engines, and their storming parties attacked the weak places in the defences with unwonted recklessness. The Christians, on their part, realized that for them the crisis in the Viking struggle had arrived. For instance, Fulk, archbishop of Rheims, wrote a letter to Charles the Fat, the descendant of Charlemagne to whom had fallen almost all the territories once ruled by his great ancestor, and pointed out to him that if Paris was captured, the Franks would suffer the loss of the whole kingdom. Nothing, he said, would be safe from Paris to Rheims. No house would be secure unless its owner became a pervert from Christianity. Already, he asserted, many men were forsaking Christianity, and were putting themselves under the protection of the pagans.[2] The unhappy Emperor, diseased and inefficient, at last mustered a polyglot army from his vast dominions, and marched to the neighbourhood of Paris. But that was all. He 'did nothing worthy of the imperial majesty'.[3] He negotiated an ignominious treaty with the heathen and surrendered the interior of France to their marauding bands.

This siege of Paris in 885–6 was in more ways than one a turning-point in the history of western Europe. It taught the Northmen the limits of their strength. They discovered that the greatest and best-equipped army which they could collect was unable to capture a well-fortified town. And the Christians also learnt their lesson from the siege. The bankruptcy of the House of Charlemagne was now patent to all. The time had come to replace the incompetent Carolings with local leaders who had proved by hard fighting their ability to save and direct the people. Count Odo had been the hero of the defence, and it was he who was crowned king, the ancestor of monarchs who were to rule France for nine centuries.

In the six years between the siege of Paris and the descent on England, the Northmen penetrated farther than ever into the heart of France. None the less they had many checks. They were baffled both by fortified monasteries and by fortified towns, and some of them suffered a famous defeat at the battle of the Dyle (891). There Arnulf, a Caroling bastard, who had climbed to power in the German kingdom, stormed a camp, filled the river with corpses of Northmen, and captured sixteen royal standards. We see then that the army which crossed from Boulogne came to England because things were no longer going well on the Continent. Continuous devastation had produced its natural consequence, a grievous famine. It was a hungry monster which turned once more to England, hungry for food as well as for plunder.

The leader of the second of the two armies, that which landed in the north of Kent, was Hæsten.[4] Twenty-five years before this Hæsten had made a name for himself by killing in one skirmish two of the most capable leaders of the Franks, one of them being Count Robert the Strong, the father of Odo, now king of France. Tradition afterwards said that Hæsten had taken part in the great Mediterranean voyage of 859–61. Subsequently he had raided in Brittany and the Somme lands. Little is known of him in these years: enough, however, to show that he had on at least one occasion co-operated with the Great Army—a fact which confirms the suspicion that the two armies in 892 were again in league.

Let us now hear the Chronicle's account of the invasion:

'In this year the Great Army about which we formerly spoke came again from the east kingdom [i.e. the kingdom of Arnulf] westward to Boulogne, and was there shipped so that they crossed over in one voyage with horses and all. And they came up into the mouth of the Limen with two hundred and fifty ships. That mouth is in East Kent at the east end of the great wood which we call Andred. The wood is in length from east to west one hundred and twenty miles long, or longer, and thirty miles broad. The river of which we before spoke flows from the forest.* On the river they towed up their ships as far as the forest, four miles from the sea, and there they stormed a fort. Within the fort were

* OE. *weald.*

a few ceorls, and it was only half-constructed. Then soon after that came Hæsten, with eighty ships, into the Thames mouth, and made him a fort at Milton [near Sittingbourne] and the other Army [did the like] at Appledore.'

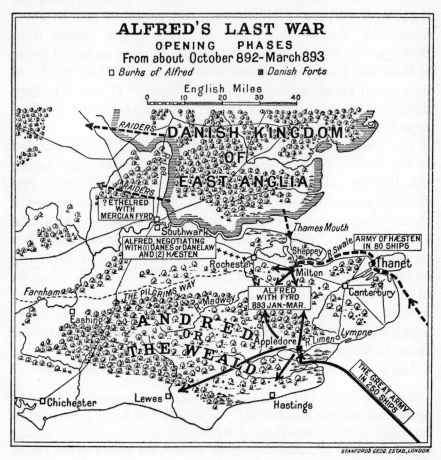

As usual, the Viking armies had an immediate and an ultimate aim. Immediately, they were hunting food and plunder. Ultimately, at the back of their minds a political idea may be read into their plan of campaign. It was surely not by accident that the leaders of the Army and Hæsten had directed their ships to the neck of Kent, where the estuary of the Limen stretched inland to within twenty miles of the marshes of the Swale in the north. The camps of Appledore and at Milton were doubtless intended to produce a stranglehold on the eastern half of Kent. If the scheme had succeeded, the whole of the east coast of England from the Channel to the Tees would have been in the

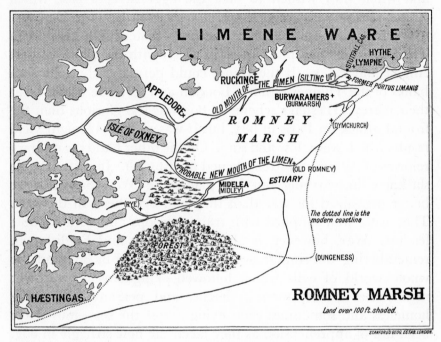

ROMNEY MARSH

Land over 100 ft. shaded.

hands of the Northmen. The metropolitan city of the English Church would have been lost, and the main road of communication between England and the Continent would have been cut. With Kent in the hands of the Danes, the balance of power within the island might have been weighted against the English. Kent might once more have brought with it Supremacy.

In 892 there was one very threatening feature in the situation. There was the Danelaw;* and in the Danelaw were veterans from the old armies of invasion, still mostly heathen, still restless and predatory. Their hostility was all the more dangerous for

---

* *Denalagu.* For its restricted early sense cf. Laws of Edward and Guthrum, c. 7.

being covert and opportunist. Alfred was not definitely at war with the Danish settlers, but Guthrum-Athelstan, his convert, had died in 890–1. Alfred had now no kind of hold over the southern Danelaw, and it was to become a recruiting-ground for the new invaders—a good refuge for them when hard pressed; and when they wished to take the aggressive, a base which stretched slantwise across the Midlands from Essex to Derby.

We may suppose that from the first Hæsten with his fleet in Thames waters had put himself in touch with the Danes of East Anglia and Essex. If the Danes could permanently hold both banks of the Thames estuary, London and its trade would be at their mercy. Hæsten's scheme of 892 was less glorious than the frontal attack on Paris in 885, but it was clever. It might yield results which were slow and sure. On the other hand the military reforms of Alfred had strengthened the English. In spite of some slackness in carrying out his plans, the West Saxons were better organized for war than they had ever been in the past. They were well supplied with trained troops and with capable leaders. War, however, is always a lottery; and Englishmen, remembering the similar descent of the Danes in 865 and the whole world of evils which followed—kingdoms overthrown; monasteries burnt; monks, thegns, and peasants wandering homeless and sometimes even flying across the sea—must have been full of apprehension as they faced the new struggle in 892.

Alfred at the outset of the war met the danger with diplomacy rather than with force. Remembering the good results which had followed from the baptism of Guthrum and the personal relations then established with his convert, Alfred tried to win over Hæsten in a similar way. He persuaded the Viking leader to have his two sons baptized. Alfred himself stood godfather to one, and Ealdorman Ethelred of Mercia to the other. There was evidently a meeting like the meeting with Guthrum. Alfred gave Hæsten 'much money', and Hæsten in return 'bound himself with oaths'. The date of this agreement is not clear. We only know that it was 'ere Hæsten came to Benfleet', therefore before April, 893. This is one example of the uncertain chronology which mars the glowing story of Alfred's last war.

The campaigns of this last war are narrated in the contemporary Chronicle with unusual detail. The glowing patriotism of the story does not, however, altogether compensate for its great defect, confusion in the sequence of events. Thus we are not clearly told, but have to infer, that for some months after the Danish landing Alfred tried to dispel the danger by diplomacy. It is evident that one of his opening moves was to negotiate not only with Hæsten but also with the Danes of the Danelaw. He induced both the Northumbrian and the East Anglian Danes to 'give oaths' to him; and the latter handed over hostages. But it was to no purpose. Many of the new settlers were still Vikings at heart. They could not be restrained either by compacts or by kindness. Plundering a countryside was better than farm labour. Alfred's diplomacy failed to avert the war; and the dreaded coalition, in spite of oaths and hostages, proceeded to do its worst against Christian England. Thus the opening phase of the war saw no military operation of any importance. The Danes were busy raiding. Alfred was busy negotiating and preparing.

Early in the year 893 the war passed into a second phase.

'The Northumbrians and East Angles' [a phrase which seems to cover all the Danes of the Danelaw] 'broke their agreements and as often as the other plundering armies went out in full force, they also went out, either with them or on their behalf. Then King Alfred gathered his fyrd and marched so that he encamped between the two Armies, at a point as nearly as possible equidistant from each, in so far as the natural obstacles of wood and water would allow, so that he might get at either of them if they should seek any open country. Then, after that, they [that is, it seems, the men of the Appledore army] went through the forest in bands and companies, wherever the countryside was most clear of the fyrd, and almost every day other [English] companies both from the [king's] army and also from the burhs were seeking out the Danes both by day and by night. The king had divided his fyrd into two, so that they were continually half at home and half in the field, except those men whose duty it was to hold the burhs. The whole Army did not come out of their camp oftener than twice; one time when they first

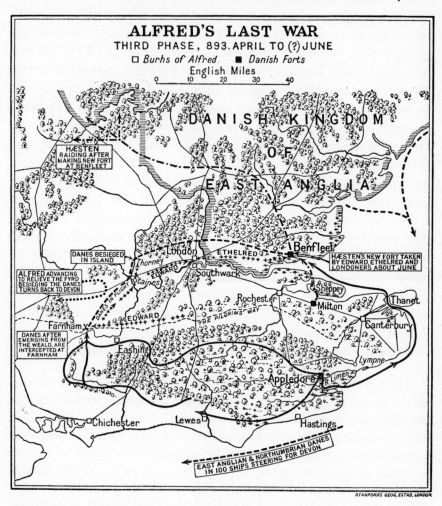

landed, before the fyrd was mustered; the other time when they wished to go from their camp.'

This was the military situation during the first months of 893. The passage gives a clear idea of the guerrilla warfare that was carried on round the outskirts of the great forest. It is our

best account of Alfred's military organization, of the part taken
by the new burhs as centres for attack as well as for defence, and
of the new method of dividing the fyrd. It shows us Alfred at the
head of his troops adopting a Fabian strategy (a lesson taught
him perhaps by his recent study of Orosius), his main object
being not only to worry the bands of plunderers whenever they
appeared in the open, but also to prevent the Danes from uniting
their armies. A sentence of the tenth-century chronicle of Ethelweard,[5] though it refers to the obscure campaign of 885, gives
a good idea of what the Danes were doubtless planning to do in
892–3. He says that 'twice in the year the Danes counted the
spoil which they had obtained by fraud in the densely wooded
land that lay to the south of the Thames'. These words help us
to picture what a Viking war now meant—straggling bands
of the heathen carrying in their spoil of crosses, chalices,
brooches and bracelets, and driving captured cattle along
forest paths to a camp or rendezvous where the plunder was
stored; then, at intervals, a general gathering of the army at
which the dividend was declared and paid over. 'Business first'
probably had become more than ever the password of the
Danes.

Soon after Easter (April 1) the war took on a new phase—
phase 3—and the raiding of the opening months gave place to
more considerable operations. The Danes began to draw together in the way which Alfred had doubtless feared. Three
things happened. First, Hæsten demonstrated his ill-faith by
constructing the new fort at Benfleet on the Essex shore of the
Thames, thus bridging the estuary with his fleet and making
open declaration of alliance between the invaders and the East
Anglian Danes. Secondly, the army in the Andredsweald broke
cover and attempted to make a dash across the Thames to join
their allies in Essex. Thirdly, the Danes of Northumbria and of
East Anglia caused a diversion by a double attack on Western
Wessex. They sent out two expeditions. One, with the crews
of a hundred ships, laid siege to Exeter. The other, forty

ships strong, attacked a fort in North Devon. This was yet another threat of the Viking-Cornish combination.

The crisis had come, but Alfred's dispositions proved sound, and all sections of his army acquitted themselves well. The Danes who broke northwards from the shelter of the Andredsweald were overtaken at Farnham by a mounted division of the fyrd. (Ethelweard says it was commanded by Alfred's eldest son, Edward.) They were defeated so thoroughly that they left their booty and fled—a headlong flight, twenty miles over the Surrey heaths—carrying their wounded commander with them. They crossed the Thames, though it was broad and unfordable, and finally took shelter six miles up the Colne on an island near Thorney.[6] After that they only escaped because the division of the fyrd which had defeated and pursued them, having consumed its food as well as served its appointed time, withdrew before its reliefs had got into position: an incident which shows that the chronic weakness of the fyrd was not cured by Alfred's reform and was, indeed, incurable.

The journey of this detachment of the Appledore army to Essex was, it seems, more or less according to plan. They made their way to Hæsten's new 'work' at Benfleet—a fort on a low spit of land by the Thames, with earthworks still traceable a thousand years later.[7] On their arrival they found that Hæsten and his men had gone out to plunder, leaving their women and children in the fort.

This was the moment which Edward and Ethelred of Mercia* chose to retrieve the recent failure on the Colne. They determined to attack the Army which had escaped from the Colne island, as it lay behind the works of the Benfleet fort. Their attack was the boldest stroke which had been attempted since Alfred, at about Edward's age, had led his troops against the camp at Reading. Since that repulse Saxons had at times beleaguered but had never tried to storm an encampment of the heathen. Strong detachments of the fyrd were now collected at

* They are named as the leaders in Ethelweard, and not in the Chronicle.

London under Alfred's son and son-in-law. These, with the
trained garrison of the burh, marched out to Benfleet, 'and put
the Army to flight and stormed the fort and took all that there
was within, as well goods as women and children, and brought
all to London. And all the ships they either broke in pieces* or
burnt or brought to London or to Rochester. And Hæsten's
wife and his two sons were brought to the king, and he restored
them to him, because the one of them was his godson, the other
the ealdorman Ethelred's.'

This success, then without precedent in England since the first
coming of the Danes, marks the end of the third phase of the war.
In the weeks which had elapsed since the Appledore army had
marched from the Weald to transport its plunder to the Danelaw, it had twice suffered signal defeat. True, the remnant of
the force was still at large; it was still in touch with Hæsten,
and Hæsten himself was still unbeaten. But the worst danger was
past. The English troops had shown that they could still hold
their own against the Danes. They had shown that they could
even drive the Danes from their entrenchments; and that their
success was no longer dependent on the presence of Alfred himself. Edward and Ethelred had demonstrated their general-
ship and power of co-operation—the characteristics which,
after Alfred's death, were to achieve the re-conquest of the
whole Danelaw.

If any one had been at fault, it was Alfred himself. His
lieutenants had captured valuable hostages from the enemy,
and Alfred had surrendered them. It may be argued that the
return of Hæsten's wife and sons is a testimony to Alfred's sense
of chivalry or to his religious scruples or to nothing more than
the simplicity of his character. Hæsten had already shown that
he was not to be trusted, and in this case generosity was scarcely
the best policy. A doubt, however, remains: the story is not
complete, and the name of Hæsten does not enter into the

---

* Their charred fragments together with quantities of human bones were found at
Benfleet by railway navvies in the nineteenth century.

narrative of the later campaigns. The king's generosity may not have been unrewarded.

Alfred's conduct of the war in Devon is barely mentioned in the Chronicle. The writer of these annals was in closer touch with the fighting in the east than with that in Devon. He says

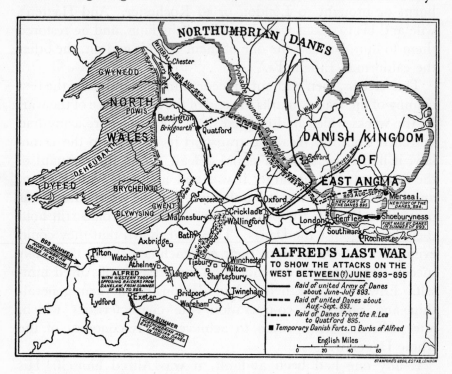

that Alfred was successful in raising the siege of Exeter, but the rest is obscure and we are left to infer that he took more than a year to clear the Danes from the west country.

The remaining operations of the war may be grouped together as a fourth and last phase. Since these later events are of less importance than those of the earlier stages, and their sequence is complicated, it is enough to understand their general character and to note one or two of the most interesting incidents which stand out in the Chronicler's animated but tangled story. The chief feature of this last phase is the repeated attacks of the Danes

on western Mercia. In the summer months of 893, when the
Appledore army had joined forces with the army of Hæsten and
established yet a new camp at Shoebury in Essex, 'then both
armies went together up along the Thames and large reinforcements joined them, both from the East Angles and from the
Northumbrians. They then went up along the Thames until
they reached the Severn. Then up along the Severn.' Meanwhile
Ethelred of Mercia and the ealdormen of Wilts and Somerset
'and the king's thegns who were then at home in the works [i.e.
the burhs] gathered together from every town east of the Parret,
as well west as east of Selwood, and also north of the Thames and
west of the Severn, and some part of the North Welsh race'. The
Danes, finding the pursuit too hot, took cover in a fort which
they made at Buttington, on the Severn.[8] After being besieged
for many weeks till most of their horses had been eaten and the
others had died, they sallied out, were defeated with great
slaughter, and those of them who escaped were saved only by
flight. The first dash to west Mercia is memorable in that it was
the most complete trial of strength in the war between the Grand
Army of the Danes (comprising the army of Hæsten, the Appledore army, and contingents from the Danelaw) and a Grand
Army of the Christians (including Mercians, West Saxons, and
Welsh). The Danes with all available forces had done their worst
and had failed miserably. Henceforth their one remaining hope
could be to wear down Alfred's defences by the frequency of their
assaults, to tire out the English fyrd as they had tired them in 871,
or to throw everything into confusion by a surprise attack, as in 878.

Later in this same year, 893, at harvest time, a second and
somewhat similar expedition down the Watling Street to the
deserted Roman walls of Chester was circumvented by Fabian
tactics. The English commanders adopted the heroic measure,
as wise as it was successful, of wasting the surrounding country
in order to starve out the enemy. The Danes then broke out of
Chester, for a time ravaged in North Wales, and returned to
Essex through Northumbria and East Anglia.[9]

A third and last sally of the Danes from Essex to Quatford near Bridgenorth on the Severn was made towards the end of 895, and there they spent the winter in a fort.

Now if we consider this thrice repeated movement we may feel sure that it cannot have been mere chance which led the Danes right across the midland shires to Buttington-on-Severn, to Chester, and finally to Quatford. What then is the reason for it? The explanation may perhaps be found in the fact that the boundary of the Danelaw, running diagonally across the Midlands (in part along the Watling Street), made it easy for the invaders to attack western Mercia and gave them their good assurance that in case of need they had an escape into the Danelaw (an escape which they did, in fact, use in 893 and 896). But we should also remember that north-west Mercia was the exposed point of the political promontory of Christian England. On one side of it were the Welsh, who had till recently been friends of the Danes of Northumbria and who may still have hesitated between their dislike of the Saxons and their dislike of the heathen. And on the other side were the Danes, occupying Derby, Nottingham, Leicester, and their other Midland burhs. May we not then conjecture that though food and plunder were as much as ever the immediate objects of these expeditions, a political aim also lurked in the minds of the more statesman-like of the Danish leaders, namely, the hope that the renewal of their alliance with the House of Rhodri Mawr might assist them to add western Mercia to the Danelaw; and that in this manner their previous failures—first, to establish themselves in eastern Kent and then in western Dumnonia—might be redeemed, and that territorial conquests might still be made, sufficient to give the Danish race the upper hand in the island?

So much for the general character of the concluding years of the war. It remains to notice two memorable incidents. The first of these illustrates the successful working of Alfred's new arrangements for coastal defence. When the ships of the Northumbrians and East Angles were returning in 894 from their long

campaign in the south-west, as they coasted along the shore of
Sussex on their way home to the Danelaw, 'they harried inland
in Sussex near Chichester and the *burhware* put them to flight,
and slew many hundreds of them, and took some of their ships'.
The success of the troops of the Chichester burh in punishing the
raiders as well as checking the raid, is good evidence for the
value of the new burh organization.

The other incident was the bottling up of the Danish ships in
the River Lea. It is best told in the words of the Chronicle:

'Before winter [the winter of 894–5] the Danes who abode in Mersea
[a new island camp off the Essex coast which replaced the Shoebury
camp] towed their ships up the Thames and then up the Lea'. After the
turn of the year, 'the aforesaid Army made a fort by the Lea twenty
miles above Lunden burh. Then, in the summer (895), a large contingent of the *burhware* and also of other folk went and encamped close to
the fort of the Danes, but they were there repulsed and some four of the
king's thegns were slain. Then, in the autumn, the king camped close
to the burh whilst they reaped their corn, so that the Danes might not
deprive them of the crop. Then one day the king rode up by the
river, and looked at a place where the river might be obstructed so that
they could not bring their ships out. And they then did so. They made
two forts on the two sides of the river, and when they had just begun
that fort and had encamped there, then the Army perceived that they
could not bring their ships out. Thereupon they left them and went
across country till they came to Quatford [the expedition already mentioned above] . . . and the men of Lunden burh fetched the ships, and
all that they could not take away they broke up, and all that were worth
taking they brought into Lunden burh.'

The credit given to Alfred in this story for his quickness in
recognizing the right place in which to block the Lea, is notable;
for in the rest of the chronicler's narrative of this last war little
else is put down to Alfred's credit. He had been slow at the first
in collecting the fyrd. He had allowed himself to be fooled by
Hæsten once and again. Otherwise his name has been scarcely
mentioned; and if Ethelweard's additions to the story can be

trusted, the honours of the campaign lay rather with Edward and the ealdormen. The victory at Farnham, the assault on the camp at Benfleet, the success at Buttington, these had been the great deeds of the war, and none of them are attributed to Alfred, who as a young man at the battle of Ashdown had charged uphill 'like a wild boar', and in the stress of the Athelney campaign had been a leader of guerrilla warfare. In this, his last war, being worn with ill health and, it may be, prematurely old, he seems to have become the organizer of victory, the commander-in-chief, whose brain co-ordinated the efforts of a dozen or more ealdormen and some forty garrison burhs.

It was almost a year after the success at the River Lea and the descent of the Danes on Quatford before the war petered out. At last, in the summer of 896, came proof that they had realized that their game was up. 'The Army dispersed, some to East Anglia, some to Northumbria; and those who were money-less got themselves ships and went south oversea to the Seine. Thanks be to God, the Army had not too much afflicted the English people.' Henceforth the Danes would have their work cut out to defend the territories which they had appropriated. The invaders departed for France, or settled down by the side of the veterans of Halfdene and Guthrum as colonists of the Danelaw.

After this there is for some years no mention of regular warfare in the Chronicle. But it seems that Alfred until his death (probably to be placed in 899)[10] was never entirely free from hostilities: there is an obscure reference to a civil war (*discordia*) among Englishmen and Northumbrians even in the months preceding his death;[11] there is also, in the Chronicle under 896, a long account of the chequered fortunes of his new long-ships, sent out to deal with raiding Danes who came from East Anglia and Northumbria. These disturbances end the long chapter of ninth-century raiding and they also mark the beginning of a fresh chapter in English history, that of the struggle between Wessex and the Danelaw. Since the raiders had set out from English homes, they raise a new question. How are the Danish settlers to be controlled? The obvious answer, the re-conquest of the Danelaw, is left over for the tenth century.

 næfde þe hſie godſ·
þon cᵹ· un ʒæl cᵹn eallſ· þoᵹ·ſſiðe ʒebᵹocoð

['Thanks be to God, the Army had not too much afflicted the
English people.' Chronicle (Parker MS.), *sub anno* 897.]

XX

ALFRED THE MAN AND HIS MESSAGE

ALFRED'S ABILITY

THE cult of Alfred, 'the Great', 'the Truth Teller', reached its height in the Victorian age. At the present day it is less popular. His virtues perhaps seem conventional, ready-made; to some there may seem to be a certain smugness about his rectitude. In any case repeated praise becomes tedious. None the less, there are good reasons for pursuing the subject of Alfred's character. The greatest of English historians, neither a Christian nor a Victorian, has described Alfred as 'the greatest of English kings';[1] and it is well that a nation should be brought back time and again to study and check its impressions of its really great men. Alfred is the one English layman before the Norman Conquest whose intimate thoughts are revealed to us in his writings. In him best of all we can see the mental workings of our primitive fighting Christian ancestors.

There is much in the character of Alfred which is not open to dispute; but there are other points about which there may well be differences of opinion. One of these is the character and extent of his ability. That he was exceptionally versatile is self-evident. The story of his reign has shown him as both a fighting soldier and an organizer of war; as both Admiral and Admiralty; and much more than this—as his own Minister of

HEADPIECE.—Head of Alfred from a silver penny.

IV. GOLD JEWELLERY, MAINLY OF THE NINTH CENTURY

Above, rings of Alfred's father, King Ethelwulf, and of his sister Ethelswith.
Centre, brooch from Dowgate Hill, City of London. Below, the Alfred
Jewel. $\frac{1}{1}$

Home and Foreign Affairs, his own legislator, architect, master-craftsman, the effective head of his Church, the educator of himself and the educator of his people. In every kind of activity, both in war and in peace, Alfred is found taking the lead.

In whatever he attempted, so far as our knowledge goes, his goodness, his perfect devotion to duty, his impetuosity, his capacity for rapid decision, his good sense, are unquestionable. But what is not so clear is whether in any or all of his activities he showed ability of the highest order. Was his work of such a kind that it would have placed him in the front rank if he had not worn a crown?

Now in the only direction in which we can check Alfred's work in detail—that is, in his Laws and in his writings—we have seen much that is defective. In his Laws there is confusion—moral applications juxtaposed with legal; Biblical precepts with Saxon 'dooms'; all thrown together with little order or sequence. In his translations his mistakes are equally glaring. His schoolboy howlers are more easy to forgive than his clumsy omissions and expansions which impede the argument of the author whom he is translating. His repetitions become wearisome. His simplicity and similes are at times puerile.

These defects, however, like his elementary mistakes, are explicable by the circumstances in which he wrote his translations. What could be expected of a man who had to educate himself but could not begin his task seriously—could not grapple with Latin—till he was about 40 years old? At any rate he had this to his credit: that he was able to make more progress than Charlemagne, who never advanced far enough in his studies to write with his own hand, much less to become an author such as Alfred. Then too his repetitions, his long digressions, his hurried endings, are the natural faults of one who had to depend on the help of a changing body of learned men, and who could only write, as he himself complains, in the times snatched from the more pressing business of State.

All this may be readily admitted, but there is room for differ-

ence of opinion on the question whether he possessed any
originality of the kind which is commonly described as genius.
It has been said[2] that Alfred was 'an adaptor rather than an
originator', that 'his mind was constructive rather than creative'.
This means little more than that we can often recognize influences which fructified in his brain. We see that he borrowed
ideas from the Danes in his ship-building and in his fortified
burhs; that he followed Charlemagne in his love of foreigners,
his 'school', and perhaps also in his national Chronicle. It is
possible that some words of Orosius may have suggested to him
the plan of dividing his army so that the divisions could take
turns in service. But no statesman operates *in vacuo*. His ideas
must come to him from his contemporaries or from the books
he reads. He must be judged by the use he makes of these ideas,
the developments and applications which he gives them. If the
inventions of Alfred seem obvious enough to-day, we must
remember that this is the way with inventions. To appreciate
his originality it is necessary to think ourselves back into the
thoughts of the ninth century, and this is not easy. What could
be simpler than to see that the only effective reply to the
Viking raids was to build ships, and better ships? Yet so far as
we know, the only Christian rulers in the ninth century able
to perceive this obvious point were Charlemagne and Alfred.

It seems equally simple to realize that the best hope of re-
kindling culture in a barbarized kingdom was to translate books
from the dead languages into the living. The reader will remember the process of reasoning by which Alfred arrived at this idea:
his wonder 'that the wise men who were formerly all over England
and had learnt all the books fully did not wish to translate them
into their own language', and his argument that as the Greeks
had translated the Hebrew scriptures into Greek and the Romans
had translated them into Latin, the obvious thing for Englishmen was 'to translate the most needful books . . . into the
language which we can all understand'.

Simple reasoning! Yes, but revolutionary. Centuries will pass before Frenchmen, Germans, or Italians will do what Alfred is doing. All learned and educational treatises had been written in Latin for so many centuries that to translate them into the vernacular seemed to be as much out of the question as to translate a modern book from literary English into, say, the Yorkshire dialect. Old English prose had indeed been used for some legal documents, for passages from Scripture and for Saints' Lives; but to render books on clerical discipline or philosophy into the vernacular was altogether unheard of. Alfred is one of the men of genius who discovered the obvious, and so changed the fate of mankind.

There is no denying that he was a plodder and too often a dull one. But sooner or later his inquisitiveness and power of reasoning things out for himself brought him to discoveries. Some of his inventions, like the famous candle lanterns for measuring time, were ingenious trifles. But others were notable advances towards modernity. And even if they were not always fruitful in their results, this failure was the fault of the English rather than of Alfred. Alfred, then, in seeing the obvious which was hidden from almost all his contemporaries, displayed the faculty which we call genius. This was exhibited in four ways: in the building of a fleet to deal with the Vikings; in the organizing of a network of fortified burhs; in the development of English literary prose; and in his pioneering interest in the geography of northern Europe. Any one of these new departures is enough in itself to place Alfred in the front rank of the men who contributed to the progress of the age; taken together they show that he possessed something which can be better described as genius than capacity.

HIS SCIENTIFIC AND RELIGIOUS THOUGHTS

At this point some description of Alfred himself, that is, of his outward appearance, should be given. This, however, is impossible, since there is no information on the subject. Asser only says that he was better looking than his brothers. The silver pennies of Alfred give plenty of portraits of him, but they are obviously untrustworthy. All that we can do is to study his character and the workings of his mind.

Let us begin with his views about the phenomena of nature. They will illustrate how all subjects in the Dark Ages led to religion, and were swallowed up in religion. His thoughts must be gathered from the passages in his translations where he changed or added to his Latin author. We shall put these together so as to let him give his ideas as he doubtless expounded them to the men around him.

First let us hear what he has to say about the world in which he found himself, that which Bede called the Nature of Things (*De Natura Rerum*). Alfred is profoundly interested in the mysteries of the heavenly bodies and of this earth. His interest, however, is mostly expressed in praises of the Almighty.

God, he says, has made the earth fast very wonderfully. It is firm so that it leans to no side nor stands on any earthly thing. Wonderful too are the motions of the heavenly firmament, for every day it turns round about the earth with exceeding swiftness. Observe how strangely varied are the movements of the stars. They are full of interest. Look for instance at icy Saturn, roaming beyond other stars high above any other heavenly body. Look at the Evening Star and note its remarkable course. It appears in the west and betokens eventide. Then it passes with the sun into the earth's shadow until it overtakes the sun from behind and rises in front of him. Then, says Alfred, we call it the Morning Star, for it rises in the east and heralds the sun's coming.[3]

Now one may lay it down as a general principle that 'Almighty God has so constrained all his creatures that each of them is in conflict with the other, so that they may not break away but are brought round to the old course and start afresh'. One of the most interesting examples of this phenomenon (it is a subject to which Alfred often recurs) is the dispensation ruling the waters of the earth. No brook is too small to seek the sea; afterwards it passes from the sea into the earth, and so it goes winding through the earth till it comes again to the same (!) spring from which it flowed at first, and so again to the sea.

Subjects such as these were constantly churning in Alfred's mind. He puzzled over the causes of the tides and thunder, and the growth of seeds in the earth.[4] His views about such things give the background of his mind. They illustrate the manifold problems which occupied his active brain. What he tells us is not simply taken, as has been suggested, from some commentary. Commentaries indeed there were on Boethius, and it is only natural that their notes should bear a certain resemblance to Alfred's additions. In all probability he picked up his ideas in conversation with Grimbald and his other helpers. These of course had obtained their knowledge from the standard books of the age, and also, no doubt, from commentators; but whatever came to Alfred received the impress of his own brain. We may give him credit for avoiding some of the crudest notions which appear in popular works such as the medical books. He is enlightened enough not to speculate about the activities of elves and witches, and the like. But either owing to faults of his own or to those of his helpers, he did not always succeed in assimilating the most reasonable opinions of his age. His confusion of Lucifer with Vesper, his notion about the water returning from the sea to its source, can be paralleled in Capella or other treatises of the Dark Ages; but Bede had known better, and Alfred is definitely less scientific than Bede. On the other hand he has in him the spirit which has given birth to modern science, the wish to understand the cause of everything. It was the wondering and questioning of men like Alfred which was in time to lead mankind through the accumulated rubbish of unscientific ages to knowledge.

Alfred's scientific ideas, so quickly passing into psalms of praise, are a good introduction to the subject of his religion; and religion is the master-key to the man. He was 'our most religious king' in a sense other than that of the *Book of Common Prayer*. His religious fervour is as plain in Asser's biography as in his own writings.

Asser's statements are reminiscent of the common-places of hagiography. He tells of Alfred's frequent attendance at Mass and at psalm-singing, of his zeal in prayer and reverence for relics, of his anxiety to receive from heaven in return for his gifts tenfold reward.

Asser's Alfred is almost a crowned monk, worthy of a niche by the side of St. Louis of France. Thus, the king turns aside from hunting in Cornwall in order to pray before the relics of St. Gueriir; he visits churches at night-time or at cock-crow to pray in solitude; he vows to give one half of his energies as well as one half of his wealth to God's service—a vow which leads to the candle inventions in order that the time devoted to God may be accurately measured. The man who made that vow surely felt drawn to the cloister by his instincts, though held to his throne by a sense of duty.

Asser also helps us to obtain an insight into the experiences which gave the mind of Alfred such a strong religious bent. There was his upbringing, the influence of his mother, 'an extremely religious woman', and of Ethelwulf, who even more than most of his contemporaries was convinced that the Viking scourge was a punishment for sin. Every raid of the heathen no doubt plunged Ethelwulf himself and all his family into heart-searchings and serious thoughts about the dispensations of God. And more disturbing still to Alfred's peace of mind were the moral troubles of adolescence and the physical complaints which afflicted him almost all his life.*

Though the tone of Asser is that of all hagiography and is therefore misleading, there is no irreconcilable discrepancy between what he tells us and the habit of mind which Alfred reveals in his books and in his actions. In these also everything is centred round religion. Religion came first and last: battles

* See above, p. 538.

were begun with a Mass; wars were ended with a baptism; Alfred's Laws were prefaced with the Decalogue and the Golden Rule of Christ. His thegns were liable to forfeit their estates for a breach of the Divine Law; one half of the revenue was dedicated to God—that did not seem much to give when it was to God that he owed his own salvation and that of his kingdom.

Asser observes that Alfred 'from his cradle was filled with the love of Wisdom above all things'. The truth of Asser's words is demonstrated in his writings; but the Wisdom which he sought was, as with the Jews of the Dispensation, synonymous with Divinity. 'Wisdom', says Alfred,[5] 'is of such kind that no man of this world can conceive her as she really is, but each strives according to the measure of his wit to understand her if he may, . . . for Wisdom is of God.'

Here we have touched the last phase of Alfred's thought. Let us turn back to the beginning.

It is legitimate to think that the first stage of his mental growth is represented by the *Dialogues* of St. Gregory. The translation is, it is true, the work of Werferth; but it was undertaken at the king's request. This collection of tales about demons and wonders—a clerical substitute for secular fairy-stories—is redolent of the child-mind, and typifies the ideas which nourished Alfred's brain in his youth and early manhood, when he was most burdened with ill health and fear of the Danes.

The religious notions discernible in Alfred's *Orosius* are only a shade less primitive. He here attacks the devil-worship of the pagans and the magic and craft of the devils,[6] but he could scarcely show his readers the more positive side of Christianity. Very different, however, is the train of thought in the additions made by him in his last two translations, that is in the *Consolation* of Boethius and in the *Soliloquies* of St. Augustine. The change is in part, but only in part, explicable by the change of subject. The writings which he now translates have guided him to new heights of vision. He moves, it is true, with the awkwardness of a barbarian among the philosophical conceptions through which he has to make his way. He strains to master the abstract concepts of his authors by the help of their metaphors. These he elaborates into long-drawn-out similes. He tries to grasp the general idea by visualizing the metaphor. Thus, Boethius speaks of the *summum bonum*, the highest good, and shows that it is God Himself. In his discussion a passing reference to the *summam rerum verticem* seems to give Alfred the idea of comparing this Highest Good or God to 'the highest roof'. And time after time he returns to his unhappy simile. God is 'the highest roof', he says, because 'there is naught above Him nor beneath Him nor round Him, but all things are within Him and in His power'. Let us take another example. Boethius in a difficult passage about Providence and Fate throws out a comparison of Providence to the hinge (*cardo*) round which all things are turned or wheeled. Alfred seizes on the comparison. He realizes that this at any rate he can understand. He works out the simile *ad nauseam*. He drags it into other sections. 'The wheels of a wagon turn upon its axle while the axle stands still and yet bears all the wagon and guides all its movement. The wheel turns round, and the nave next the wheel moves more firmly and securely than the felly does. Now the axle is as it were the Highest Good we call God and the best men move next unto God just as the nave moves nearest to the axle. The middle sort of men are like the spokes . . .' and so on for a page or more.[7]

Thus it was that the mind of the self-educated Saxon layman operated. He pondered and puzzled over the deeper problems of existence. He would not be beaten. He tried to storm the heights of knowledge as he had stormed the shield-walls of the Danes. He was obstructed by the tangles of an unexplored country and by the inadequacy of his native language to express the terms of philosophy. But with the help of Grimbald and the others he fought his way through.

When Alfred came to translate the *Soliloquies* of St. Augustine he felt more keenly than ever the longing to understand the relationship of man to God. 'I can understand very little of

Him, or nothing at all, and yet at times, when I think carefully of Him, [an] inspiration comes to me about the eternal life.'[8]

The *Consolation* of Boethius had ended with the question: What is Eternity? Alfred finding the answer of Boethius too abstruse had put the book aside and added for his conclusion a psalm of his own, composed round themes like the following: 'To God all is present'; 'He knoweth all'; 'He is ever watching, never sleeping'; 'He is ever free and not compelled to do any work'; 'God seeth it all and all He requiteth'. That is Alfred's end of the *Consolation of Philosophy*. But we may say, if we accept the usual view of the relation of the Old English *Soliloquies* to the Old English *Boethius*,[9] Alfred was not satisfied. He felt that he must return to this question of Eternity and Immortality. His advisers therefore guided him to the *Soliloquia* of St. Augustine. Alfred describes it as the book 'concerning the meditation and doubts in his (Augustine's) mind—how his reason answered his mind when the mind doubted about anything or wished to know anything that it could not before clearly understand'. The first two books of Alfred's translation professed to follow Augustine. But Alfred is here in his most inventive mood. 'I would have such knowledge about God, in my reason and in my understanding, that nothing could disturb me nor bring me into any doubt.' This is his motive and it leads him to many of his most characteristic similitudes. He compares the relation between man and God to a ship's cable. 'Though the ship be out among the billows it will remain sound and unbroken if the cable holdeth.' He compares the ways by which men find God to the many roads by which a king's subjects find their way to his court. 'I can teach thee other parables about Wisdom. Consider now whether any man seeketh there the king's home where he is in town, or his court, or his army, or whether it seemeth to thee that they all must come thither by the same road; on the contrary, I suppose they would come by very many roads: some would come from afar, and would have a road very long and very bad and very difficult; some would have a very long and very direct and very good road; some would have a very short and yet hard and strait and foul one; some would have a short and smooth and good one; and yet they all would come to one and the same lord. . . . So is it likewise with Wisdom. Each one who wisheth it and who anxiously prayeth for it, he can come to it and abide in its household and live near it; yet some are nearer it, others farther from it; just so is every king's court: some dwell in cottages, some in halls, some on the threshing-floor, some in prison; and yet they all live by the favour of one lord, just as all men live under one sun, and by its light see what they see.' Alfred has ceased to lament the miserable want of education of his youth. He now takes the measure of his understanding with more resignation. 'Enjoy the wisdom which thou hast,' he says, 'and have joy in the part which thou canst.' But his thirst for knowledge is as intense as ever. 'I would know whether after the parting of the body and the soul I shall ever know more than I now know of all that which I have long wished to know; for I cannot find anything better in man than that he know, and nothing worse than that he be ignorant.'[10]

As Alfred translated the *Soliloquia* he found that this treatise did not satisfy him. He put it aside and turned to a letter of Augustine which was known in the king's circle by the title *De Videndo Deo*. This surely should give him an answer to the question to which above all others he was now trying to find an answer—the ever-insistent question, What is the nature of immortality: 'Whether after the parting of body and soul it would wax or wane, or whether it would do both as it before did.' But Augustine was still too subtle for him. Once more he broke loose from his Latin authority; and talking from his heart he discoursed of Faith. It was by Faith, he says, that he knew who built the city of Rome. 'Must I not needs do one of two things—either believe some men or none? I know not who built the city of Rome for the reason that I myself saw it—but because it was told me.' What a man can do is this: '. . . Increase his intelligence while he is in this world, and also wish and desire that he may come to the eternal life, where nothing is hid from us.'[11] Here then is his last answer to his questionings about Eternity: Have Faith; increase your intelligence; and wish for the Eternal Life where nothing is hid. This was his *De Videndo Deo*. It was probably his final message to his subjects. It is for us the end of his story.

In following the religious thought of Alfred we have not wandered outside the true course of English history. No one can read his writings without perceiving that his mind returned whenever it was free into the channels which we have indicated. And in this he is a true, though it may be an extreme, representative of the Anglo-Saxon people. We have now followed the wanderings and conflicts of this people, both of their bodies and of their minds, for five hundred years. When we first encountered them in the region of the Elbe and the Weser, we found the best trace of them in those black earthen pots in which they were accustomed to place the charred fragments of their dead. In Britain we tracked them by the graves in which they furnished their dead kinsfolk with the food and weapons and brooches which the dead might possibly require in the next world. When we came to their Conversion it appeared that the chief argument for their acceptance of Christianity was the hope of solving doubts about the Whence and the Whither of man. Christianity then solved those doubts; but by making the Anglo-Saxons conscious of their sins it increased their disquietude. Those who had minds enough to rise above the level of animal existence were haunted by the sense that their lives contradicted the creed they now professed. Christianity, in giving them new hopes, stimulated their fears—the fears of hell which we have seen in their poetry—fears which could not be wholly allayed even by the proximity of holy relics, by meritorious donations to the clergy, nor even by the old magic, fortified with tags from Christianity. Alfred then put into words the faith and the longings of the Anglo-Saxon laity at their best. In his writings we

see the efforts made by a thoughtful Saxon layman to understand the teaching of the Church; and more than that, to apprehend, to perceive, the Godhead. *De Videndo Deo* is the note on
which Alfred's writings seem to end. This surely had been the
recurrent thought of the Anglo-Saxon race since the days when
they burnt their dead on the pyre. *De Videndo Deo!* To perceive,
to approach, Divinity—this had been one, though not the only
quest; and the approach had been, as in Alfred's simile, 'by very
many roads'.*

Again, merely as a factor in the political history of the age, the
religion of Alfred must be taken into account. What saved
Wessex in the stress of the Viking wars was clearly first and foremost the steadfastness of its king, and this as clearly was supported by religious Faith—a Faith which was not, as with some
earlier kings, simply imposed on him by the Church's authority,
but was at least in part compounded of his own experience and
thought.

A chief ingredient of his religious thought can be found in
the Psalms. Alfred, we know, carried about with him a book in
which psalms had been copied out by his own hand. It is said
that he himself translated a part of the Psalms into Old English.[12]
It was thus natural that they should colour his views of life
and that humanity should be divided into simple categories: on
the one hand the good, and on the other 'the wicked man', 'the
fool', 'the covetous man', 'the unrighteous and intemperate'.
Such as these seemed 'like beasts of the field'.[13]

This clear-cut dichotomy was made easy by the circumstances
of Alfred's life. From the first there had been a direct conflict
between Christian and heathen, between the law-abiding and
the lawless. It needs no argument to prove that he and those
who fought behind him derived much of their success from the
conviction that the angels were on their side, and only the devils
on that of their enemies. For the more part, however, Alfred
owed his success to those other qualities which differentiate him

---

* *hi cumen on swiðe manige wegas.*

from his contemporaries and even assimilate him to the modern type of civilized humanity—his spirit of inquiry, his readiness ever to learn, by questioning or by experiments. We have seen his military measures adapted from the Danes and his educational schemes adapted from the Franks. We have seen

Fig. 74. 'Wicked men', of the Psalms.

his inquiring spirit reaching out in endeavour to apprehend the mysteries of this world and those of the next; in interrogation of an explorer about his discoveries; in missions to Jerusalem, and possibly to India.

The results which he obtained are proof that in all his questionings he was actuated by something more than curiosity. In practical matters and to some extent even in the sphere of thought he could criticize and reason. As there was something which faintly anticipates the spirit of the modern scientist in his keenness to inquire, to discover, to criticize, and to reason, so there was also something modern in his appreciation of order. His sense that both private and public affairs should be organized according to what we should call 'business principles', seen, for example, in the division of his revenue, in his division of the fyrd, in his plans for a rota of duty among his followers, in the systematic collection of learned men, in his clear agreements with Asser, in the self-imposed regulation of his working day. These glimmerings of modernity cannot be ignored, but they must not be exaggerated.

When we come to consider the development of West Saxon institutions in the tenth century we may infer that Alfred's love of mathematical calculation bore fruit in certain well-known reforms; but his chief message to his subjects, that for which he may better be remembered at the present day, is very different. From the many additions or changes which he made in the original texts of Orosius, Boethius, and Augustine, we may extract four characteristic passages containing four doctrines for everyday life. These may be regarded as his testament.

First is his doctrine of Friendship. 'Every other thing in this world man desireth either because it will help him to power, or to get some pleasure, save only a true friend; him we love for love's sake and for our trust in him, though we can hope for no other return from him.'[14]

The second is the rule of one good deed a day, attributed by Alfred to Titus, and, wherever Alfred found it, we may claim that he made the principle his own by inserting it in the Old English Chronicle as well as in his *Orosius*. 'Titus was of so good a disposition that he said he lost a day on which he did not do any good.'

The third is the doctrine that good work cannot fail.[15] 'Perhaps thou wilt say the good at times begin what they cannot bring to an issue; but I say they always accomplish it. Though they may not be able to bring to pass the deed, yet they have the full purpose; and the unwavering purpose is to be accounted an act performed, for it never fails of its reward, here or in the next world.' 'Thou oughtest not to despair because thou canst not come at once to that which thou desirest for thyself.'

The fourth is the sum of all, and is rightly hackneyed, since it is the epitome of Alfred.[16] 'Without wisdom no faculty can be fully brought out, for whatsoever is done unwisely can never be accounted as skill. To be brief, I may say that it has ever been my desire to live worthily while I was alive and after my death to leave to them that should come after me my memory in good works.'

This is the fourfold message of Alfred: friendly co-operation; hard work; good intentions, kept up day by day; and above all, Wisdom, and the true aim of Wisdom, to leave good works as one's memorial. The translations of Alfred are stuffed with dozens of similar maxims which he makes his own even when there is about them some suggestion of the Latin original. If these sermonizings are little to the taste of a sophisticated generation, it must be remembered that the goodness of Alfred, of which they are the outward expression, had not been acquired without a struggle; it was not effortless. In the four rules of conduct just mentioned may be found the secret of Alfred's victories—over himself (in what he calls the 'soul's tempest'),[17] over the Danes, and over the ignorance and indifference of his subjects.

There is another aspect of Alfred's character about which something should be said—the mingling of barbarian and Roman strains in his mind; it is a subject which may throw further light on his success. The combination of the two strains form such different patterns in all the great historical characters of the Dark Ages that it is well to consider which of them was dominant in Alfred. Test him by his writings: in his *Orosius* he accepts almost fully the Roman standpoint of the author whom he is translating. His sympathies seem to lie perhaps more with the race from whom he derived culture and religion than with his ancestors by blood. But when he comes in the book to the period of the barbarian invasions, some sense of loyalty to his race by birth can be traced. He refrains from speaking of the Germanic invaders of the Empire as barbarians (he calls them either Danes or Huns), and he omits the reference of Orosius to the plundering raids of the Saxons. The fact seems to be that the Anglo-Saxons, thanks to their Roman Church, felt themselves to be within the pale of the Roman world. The sense of antagonism had long since vanished. To Alfred, the Romans 'are yet reigning'; 'reigning as well in their Christianity and in their Empire as by their Emperors'. The barbarian and the Romano-Christian could be easily reconciled. Alfred had no qualms in accepting the genealogy which carried his descent back to Woden. He could even speak of Weland, the Germanic demi-god, with a certain amount of affectionate admiration— admiration for his skill as a goldsmith.[18]

In previous chapters, in the lives of eminent churchmen like Wilfrid, we have been able to study the intermingling of the Romano-Christian culture with Germanic traditions. Here in Alfred the two strains are easily recognizable; but at first sight they do not seem to be well blended. We almost see in him two different men. Look at him heading the attack at Ashdown or riding from one timbered hall to another; outwardly he has the appearance of a barbarian, with his long hair, his large gaudy brooch, his legs wrapped in linen and cross-gartered. See him on one of his war-ships; he might almost be a Saxon pirate of old: or see him at the chase, the keenest of hunters, talking with the falconers, hawkers, and dog-keepers. He is insistent that his sons should be taught his favourite art of hunting. In these ways he must be just like his barbarian ancestors, living much the same life which they had lived for hundreds of years before him; ruthless to his enemies on occasions, as when in one of his last years[19] he has a whole band of lawless Danes put to death. But then there is the other picture—Alfred when the day of work, of administration, and of hunting, is over, sitting by the side of Grimbald or Asser or whatever other learned man is in attendance. Here he is assimilating the thoughts of the

Romans—Romans, it is true, of the fifth and sixth centuries; he is discovering everything he can about the story of the Mediterranean; he himself is learning to think like a Roman —at any rate up to the point when he tumbles into some child-like simile, or strikes some Germanic survival such as the thought of Woden or Weland buried deep in the memory of his race. Out in the open also, when he is campaigning against the heathen, he is something more than a leader of the old heroic type. He is fighting with his brain as well as with brute force—reasoning out how to counter the attacks of the enemy, and pondering over past stratagems narrated by Orosius.

This mingling of the Roman and Germanic strains in the greatest of English kings is a note on which we well might end. Yet though Alfred and his followers succeeded in checking the Danes by sheer, hard, hand-to-hand fighting of the old heroic kind, the word 'heroic' must be discarded. It was not an English word; and in so far as the English recognized any heroes, they were men who had fought and died in other lands than England. Alfred's personality and exploits did not become tinged with romance like those of his counterpart, Charlemagne. He remained sufficiently well known to be used for the purpose of advertisement, his fame being exploited by clever monks to push the claims of this or that Saint, and after the coming of the Normans the English learnt to look back to him with growing affection as 'the Englishmen's shepherd, the Englishmen's darling'.*

END OF THE NINTH CENTURY—SCANDINAVIA AND ENGLAND

The last year or two of Alfred's life are blank in the Chronicle. In those years he was no doubt engaged in his last translations. He was dictating his additions, giving salutary advice to his subjects. For the rest, tradition tells of him beginning to build a new

---

* *Engle hirde, Engle derling. Proverbs of Alfred* (ed. H. P. South (1931), p. 102).

minster at Winchester, and girding his small grandson Athelstan with a sword.

When his death came, it was entered in the Chronicle in the usual formal phrase, but marked with a cross in the margin. Even Asser the Welshman, who seemed to realize the greatness of this Saxon king better than did his own subjects, was apparently too much occupied with the affairs of his diocese in the Cornish peninsula to have time to re-edit his life of Alfred and write up the story of his last years.

The death of Alfred roughly coincides with the end of the first Viking movement. Throughout the ninth century the long undecked ships of the Scandinavians had been passing to and fro across the North Sea. The immediate results of that intercourse on the Anglo-Saxon kingdoms have been told, and its further results will be unfolded in the course of the tenth century. But Fate, in spinning this bit of the world's history, had entangled the fortunes of the Anglo-Saxons so closely with those of the Scandinavians that to complete our story we must once more glance at the homelands of the Vikings. We must see what wealth and prosperity had come to the Northmen from their century of plunder in Western Christendom. Wealth? Yes. The Viking age is in Scandinavia an age of gold and silver. Its profusion of precious neck-rings, arm-rings, brooches, can be seen in the Northern museums. The chalices and other treasures stolen from our islands are not plentiful—no doubt they were soon hammered into personal ornaments; but they exist. Finds of English currency are also less plentiful than one might suppose. But the story told by Ohthere to Alfred has shown that towards the end of the ninth century the Scandinavians were prospering by lawful trade as well as by Viking plunder. Coins minted, either at Hedeby, or at Birka in Sweden, after English models, are good illustrations of the way the raiders, or their kinsmen, were now imitating the customs of the raided.

As far as the Danes are concerned, the social and political

repercussions of the Viking movement are still hidden from us. The rumours of Danish civil wars which found their way into the Frankish annals earlier in the ninth century—when the Franks took an interest in the doings of their neighbours—are enough to show that the Vikings at times used what we have called their 'southern route' for other purposes than the transport of plunder. They could return to Denmark to take part in their own civil wars. Whole dynasties might be wiped out. Among others, the family of Ragnar vanishes from the scene. When Alfred speaks of the Danes he simply says that they are divided into North Danes and South Danes. It will be in the tenth century that we shall begin to hear of a new dynasty, that of Gorm, which will unite all the Danes and produce the imperially-minded Sweyn and his son, Canute.

By 900 men of Norwegian stock are becoming prolific poets, and their skilful 'Eddic' poems put to shame Alfred's amateur attempts to versify parts of his *Boethius*. From the Danes—this race which has thrust itself into so much of the best land of Northumbria, Mercia, and East Anglia—we have little more than a few snatches of a song, the *Biarkamal*, extant only in Latin and Icelandic versions.[20] This song does but hark, nobly enough, on the perennial theme of the North—the glory of loyalty to a lord and the baseness of treason; loyalty, even when the odds are hopeless, and the gods are adverse. From Sweden there come to us messages in runes, some inscribed, it seems, by Vikings or their kinsmen returned from the wars. There is, for example, the Rök runic stone.[21] 'In memory of Wæmoth stand these runes, but Warin fashioned them, a father in memory of his dead son. Let us tell to the youth what were the two war-booties that were taken twelve times, the two war-booties, each of them from different men. . . . Let us say to the youth: be bold.'

In Norway around Harold Fairhair, the first king to unite the whole land from north to south, there are poets who give us more realistic pictures of this younger contemporary of Alfred. One poet[22] describes the famous sea-fight at Hafursfirth* in which Harold, after sweeping into one great kingdom the petty States between Westfold and Trondhjem, had to meet a big combination of the western folks, those which had contributed the main stream of migrants by way of the Shetlands to the British Isles. The tide of sea-farers for the moment turned, and the Vikings sailed back to help their kinsmen against the king who was trying to reduce the North to order.[23] The poet says, 'Ships came from the east, ready for war, with grinning heads and carven beaks, impelled with desire for battle. They were laden with warriors, with white shields, with Western spears and swords from France. . . . The berserks were howling, the wolf-coats [i.e. champions dressed in wolf-coats] were yelling, and swords were clashing.' This well-contested fight which firmly established Harold's power over all Norway has been called[24] 'the most important battle in the history of Norway'.

Equally memorable is the description of Harold's court and of the magnificence and fiery energy of the war-band which followed him and enabled him to defeat all his enemies.[25]

'If he have his own desire the resolute-hearted prince will drink his Yule at sea and play the game of Freyr [? fighting]. Even in his youth he showed no liking for the fireside and indoor life, the warm bower and pillows stuffed with down. . . .

'Very magnificent is the life enjoyed by the glorious champions who play chess in Harold's court. They are enriched with money and with splendid swords, with the metal of Hunaland [? gold] and with girls from the East.

'Their spirits are high when they know that there is a prospect of battle. Eager are they to leap up and bend their oars, to break the oar loops and split the tholes, to churn up the waters with mighty strokes.'

The poem goes on to praise the magnificence of the poets who dwelt with Harold—their red cloaks with gay borders, their swords bound with silver, their coats of mail, their gilded

* *Hafrsfjorð.*

baldricks, graven helmets and bracelets; all of them gifts of the king. It is a court where men laugh and enjoy life. Besides the poets, it has professional jesters and jugglers, and (it sounds like a Victorian music-hall) an earless dog which plays the fool.

Through all the noise is heard the old heroic theme—the glorification of war, of the generous war-lord and of the brave war-band: the old theme with new variations, for Harold's court is a sophisticated place, and here is luxury in many new forms. The East and the West have been ransacked to make the existence of the warriors enviable and brilliant. Fashions have been copied from the courts of the Franks and of the English. Silks have been imported from the Orient, weapons and armour from the Rhinelands. Everything is gay with the bright colours and the gilt of the Viking age. The fighting men are not allowed to marry, but their generous lord has organized prostitution as he has organized amusements. Hence it was[26] that 'those only became guardsmen to King Harold who were foremost in strength or courage or most skilled; with such only was his ship manned, for he had now good choice of men to pick out for his body-guard from every folk'.

Harold's court was assuredly either the model or the copy of the Northman's Valhalla. As in the days of Tacitus, perfect idleness alternated with frenzies of energy, blood-lust, battle. The delights of the court were those of the senses. But the ideal of hardihood—this ideal which we have recognized as one main product of the Viking age—was expressed with a new deliberation. The king's poets encouraged the king's warriors to despise the allurements of peace, the indolence and luxury of life indoors. The man who was indeed a man sought adventure on the sea even in the storms of winter.

The Northmen, we have seen,* agreed with Alfred: 'One thing will never die, the reputation we all leave behind on our death.' Where they differed was about the kind of reputation desired.

* Above, p. 501.

The ideal of Fairhair's court set against the ideal of Alfred brings out the contrast between the heathenism of the northern lands and the Romano-German blend of Christianity of the ninth-century Englishman—the contrast which has been perceptible in the history of the English ever since the Viking ships sailed into our seas and sacked the monastery of Lindisfarne. But there is another reason why Fairhair's court deserves our attention: it shows better than anything else the kind of civilization to which the Angles and Saxons might have been guided if the Conversion to Christianity had not turned them into other courses. Even as things had fallen out there was much in common between the way men thought in the court of the Norwegian king and the way they were encouraged to think by Alfred in the court of Wessex. In either men's fighting qualities had to be encouraged and loyalty to the death upheld. Without this, defeat or anarchy would quickly overtake a State. There was enough in common to make the intermingling of English and Scandinavians an easy process in Britain.

The differences between the two are obvious: the difference between the creed of Woden and the creed of Christ. And the results will be obvious in the sequel: Alfred's work was perfected by his family; Harold's was almost, but not quite, undone by his sons—a score or so of sons by some half-score of wives, 'riotous men' who drive out the king's officials and slay one another, breaking up the unity and the good order created by Harold. The son of Harold who will do most for Norway will be one educated at the court of Wessex under a grandson of Alfred, namely Hakon, 'Athelstan's foster son'; but after him the Everlasting Battle of the Northmen[26a] will be resumed, and it will be many generations before a well-founded order is established in Norway. The contrast between the court of Harold Fairhair and the court of Alfred cannot be ignored, but once more the records scarcely bring us to the essential truth of what was happening in this primitive world. Its changes were being made, as usual, by the peoples rather than by the courts. What counted for much more than the 'good works' of Alfred and the war-bands of Harold were the everyday activities of their peoples in the farms and villages. In particular the migration of the Danes went on silently and without a record, transplanting to the east of England some of those characteristics which we saw existing among the Scandinavians at the opening of the Viking period—their independence, their energy, their fierceness, their worldly wisdom.

The death of Alfred ends some five hundred years of the history of our Anglo-Saxon forefathers—five hundred years which had not only changed their place of residence but also their religion and therewith their character. J. R. Green called this section of his story the 'Making of England'. With equal, perhaps with greater truth, the result might have been summed up as the 'Making of the English character'. It is impossible to look back on the period which lies between the pirates who manned ships of the Nydam type (reputed to be the fiercest of all the barbarians) and the Saxons for whom Alfred translated the *Consolation of Philosophy*, without concluding that this was the formative age of our race, that in which it found itself and grew from youth to manhood. The two outstanding events which had completely altered the circumstances of these Germanic tribes—the migration to Britain and the Conversion to Christianity—had established a new variety of Nordic character. If, placing ourselves at the close of the ninth century, we compare the Anglo-Saxons who acknowledged Alfred as their king with the so-called 'Old Saxons' of the Continent who followed King Arnulf (the last of the German Carolingians) in expeditions across the Alps into Italy, we see that the island Saxons and their cousins in the Elbe lands are both of them a fighting race, both have given a lesson to plundering Danes. But the Saxons who are the subjects of Alfred have lost that fever of the continental Germans which urged them to turn southwards with a dream of improving their fortunes; they have, for the time being at any rate, become content with insularity. Some may say that they have developed a certain softness or sluggishness: certainly they are not exposed to the charges of brutality which a Lombardic chronicler brings against the Germans of Arnulf.[27]

How exactly the interplay of the new insular environment, of cross-breeding with Celts and acceptance of a half-Roman, half-Scottish Christianity, wrought the change, it is in vain to speculate. What matters is that the change had somehow come. And the best way to illustrate the fact that, a type of man had been produced which was different from all others, is to point to those Anglo-Saxons whose thoughts we have been able to follow most intimately, such as Bede and Alfred: these we feel to be unlike the men of other nations but like the best among ourselves. Both in Bede and in Alfred, though one was a monk and scarcely left his cloister, and the other the most active of our kings, are to be found one common trait: a certain humanity or practical sense which makes it possible to see good in an opponent, even when his actions or his beliefs are to be condemned, and as an accompaniment to this, a readiness to bear and forbear.

That which in the common run of the race may become sluggishness or heavy seriousness may in these finest specimens, without losing its strength, flower into an unrivalled graciousness and serenity of spirit. Even among more ordinary Anglo-Saxons, that is, among the clergy and the kings who figure in Bede's *History* or in the Chronicle, the standard of character reaches a high average. With a few exceptions the racial type seems to have avoided the violence and vice which branded the Merovingian Franks, and the extravagances of asceticism which made many of the Celtic saints ridiculous. Moderation, compromise, respect for authority, and devotion to their kings— these seem already to stand out as characteristic features of the race.

After the reign of Alfred the study of Anglo-Saxon character will be complicated by the infusion of a new strain. The existence of Scandinavians in the East and North will give a new turn to the story of England; it will necessarily have its effects on the breed and on the character of the English people.

TAILPIECE.—*Left*, silver chalice of Alfred's reign, from Cornwall. $\frac{2}{5}$. *Right*, wooden idol, probably Danish, from Dagenham, Essex. Scale *c*. $\frac{1}{9}$.

NOTES

[*For the abbreviations used in the Notes see vol. ii, pp. 712–17.*]

X. THE STRUGGLE FOR SUPREMACY

[1] *Ep. Bon.*, 340–7.

[2] See F. M. Stenton in *E.H.R.* xxxiii (1918), 439 ff.

[3] *A.S.C.*, s.a. 752. Commonly identified with Burford in Oxfordshire.

[4] F. M. Stenton, op. cit., 443.

[5] Ibid., 444–50. For an earlier informal use of the style *rex Anglorum* see P. Gonser, *Das angelsächsische Prosa-Leben des hl. Guthlac*, pp. 16–17, 104. Compare also its use on East Anglian coins (Brooke, 31).

[6] F. M. Stenton, op. cit., 448–50.

[7] *Ep. Alc.*, 128, 131, 145–6.

[8] H. and S. iii. 447.

[9] See *Arch. Camb.* lxxxi–vi (1926–31).

[10] J. Allan, in *Num. Chron.* xiv (1914), 77 ff.; R. C. Lockett in ibid. xx (1920), 57 ff.

[11] Sir C. Oman, in *Num. Chron.* ser. 5, ix (1929), 170.

[12] *Ep. Alc.*, 107.   [13] Ibid., 179.

[14] *A.S.C.*, s.a. 755. Cf. Plummer, ii. 47. The translation is based on that of R. W. Chambers in *England before the Norman Conquest*, 176–7.

[15] Bede, iii, c. 14.

[16] See references in Freeman, i. 542, 556; Stubbs, i. 180–1.

[17] Birch, ii, no. 706; cf. 705.   [18] Eddius, c. 20.

[19] Maitland, 506–15; W. J. Corbett, *T.R.H.S.* (N.S.), xiv (1900), 187–230; Chadwick, *Institutions*, 263–8; Brownbill, in *E.H.R.* xxvii (1912), 625–48, and xl (1925), 497–503.

[19a] Harvey, *Corolla*, xvi ff. Cf. ibid., *The History of King Eadmund the Martyr* (1929), 11–12.

[19b] See note [17a] to c. xi about the bishopric of Whitern in the 9th century.

[20] This is questioned by Skene, *Celtic Scotland*, i. 310.

[21] See W. G. Searle, *Anglo-Saxon Bishops*, &c., 302–15, and references there given.

[22] *Ep. Bon.*, 343–4.

[23] Ine's Laws, cc. 23, 24, 33; *A.S.C.*, s.a. 865.

[23a] Some data bearing on this obscure subject will be found collected by Miss H. M. Cam in *Essays . . . J. Tait*, 13–21.

[24] Cf. *Antiquity*, vii (1933), 297–310 and 473–5.

[25] Birch, i. 334.

[26] F. M. Stenton in *Ency. Brit.*, 14th ed., viii. 482.

[27] Bede, ii, c. 3. Cf. P. Kletler, *Nordwest-Europas Verkehr, Handel und Gewerbe*

(1924), 75, 91; Vogel, *Gesch. d. deutschen Seeschiffahrt* (1915), 74–8; Hoops, iii. 21; Birch, i, nos. 149–152.

[28] Cf. Birch, i, no. 189.

[29] The last sentence is found only in 'F', a post-Conquest version of the Chronicle, written at Canterbury, and in S.D. i. 94–5. W.M., *G.R.*, i, § 95, has a different story.

[30] Birch, i, no. 384; Hunt, 249.

XI. THE CHURCH IN THE CENTURY AFTER BEDE

[1] Plummer, *Bede*, i. 403–23.

[2] cc. 3 and 5, H. and S. iii. 363 ff.

[3] c. 4, H. and S. iii. 450.

[4] e.g. Hunt, c. xii.

[5] *Ep. Bon.*, 342; Kylie, 165–6.   [6] Ibid., 349 ff.; Kylie, 176 ff.

[7] *Ep. Alc.*, nos. 16 and 230.

[8] Ibid., pp. 191–2 (Letter to the people of Kent).

[9] *Ep. Bon.*, 343.   [10] Ibid., 356.

[11] Liebermann, ii. 383 (*Eigenkirche*) and 539 (*Kirchenherr*); H. Boehmer, in *Texte und Forschungen* . . ., 301 ff.; E. W. Watson in *C.M.H.* vi. 528 ff.

[12] Alfred, c. 21; cf. Theodore's *Penitential*, Book ii, c. 1 and c. 9, 2; H. and S. iii. 190 and 197.

[13] M. Deanesley in *Essays to Tout*, 6–8.

[14] J. A. Robinson in *J.T.S.* xxvii. 233 ff.

[15] Birch, i, no. 342.

[16] Ibid., i, no. 283. From J. A. Robinson, *St. Oswald and the Church of Worcester* (Brit. Acad. Suppl. Papers, V), p. 8.

[17] H. and S. iii. 364, c. 5; 450, cc. 4 and 5; 545–7; 580, c. 4.

[17a] K. Sisam in *P.B.A.*, xviii (1932), 326, shows that there was at least one bishop at Whitern after 805.

[18] e.g. the *Dialogue of Egbert*, H. and S. iii. 403–13.

[19] See M. Deanesley in *E.H.R.* xlii (1927), 1–11.

[20] xiii, § 11 in H. and S. 429.

[21] E. W. Watson, *C.M.H.* vi. 534.

[22] *De laudibus virginitatis*, quoted by J. Lingard, *History and Antiquities of the Anglo-Saxon Church*, i. 229.

[23] H. and S. iii. 368–74, cc. 19, 20, 28.

[24] cc. 21, 20; H. and S. iii. 369.

[25] This is only reported in the twelfth-century *Vita S. Oswaldi*, c. 21 (printed in S.D., i. 361).

[26] *Ep. Bon.*, 377.

[27] c. 7, H. and S. iii. 365.   [28] Ibid. iii. 510.

[29] *Carmen de Pontificibus* in Raine, 349 ff., esp. 391–6.

[30] For a better idea see the beautifully illustrated monograph of W. G. Collingwood, *Northumbrian Crosses*. His theories about the chronology of the crosses rest on two questionable assumptions: (1) that the failure of Bede to mention stone crosses means that they are all post-Bedan; and (2) that a considerable lapse of time is needed for the development of the best work.

[31] So Clapham, p. 65.

[32] A. W. Clapham in *Arch.* lxxvii. 219 ff.; R. A. Smith in ibid. lxxiv. 235 ff.; C. R. Peers in *P.B.A.* xii (1926), 45–59. For the sculptured stone at Castor see *Ant. Journ.* iv (1924), 421.

[33] For Cynewulf see C. W. Kennedy, *Poems of Cynewulf* (1910); and K. Sisam in *P.B.A.* xviii. 303–31. For bibliography see Hensinkveld and Bashe, 68 ff.

XII. THE RESULTS OF CHRISTIANITY

[1] Eddius, cc. 30, 50, 58.   [2] v, c. 7. Cf. also c. 19.

[2a] See also an interesting papal grant of privileges to the monasteries of Bermondsey and Woking in *Essays . . . James Tait*, 320–1. F. M. Stenton is inclined to accept its claim to emanate from the period 708–15.

[3] Liebermann, ii. 608 ff.; O. Jensen, in *T.R.H.S.* (N.S.), xv (1901), 171 ff. and xix (1905), 229 ff.

[4] H. and S. iii. 559.

[5] L. Gougaud, *Gaelic Pioneers of Christianity*, 33–4.

[6] J. Braude, *Die Familiengemeinschaften der Angelsachsen*, 1932. Cf. G. J. Turner in *Essays . . . James Tait*, 357–86—an attempt to controvert Vinogradoff's explanation given above. Turner argues that 'folkland' meant, as Stubbs and others believed, the land of the folk, that is of the State. Since the word only occurs in three documents, and these are not explicit, doubts may well exist. But if Turner is right, a new word is wanted to represent 'folkland' in the sense which Vinogradoff gave it. Turner's contention that there was bookland before there were landbooks is scarcely satisfactory. A criticism of Turner by J. E. A. Jolliffe is in *E.H.R.* (1935).

[6a] See an English Coronation Order of the ninth century in L. G. Wickham Legg, *English Coronation Records* (1901), 3–13.

[7] *Genesis*, ll. 80 and 284, ed. by G. P. Krapp in *The Junius Manuscript*.

[8] *Exodus*, ll. 154–65; Gordon, p. 126.

[9] *Elene*, ll. 1236 ff., ed. by G. P. Krapp in *The Vercelli Book* (1932); translation of K. Sisam in *P.B.A.* xviii (1932), p. 319.

[10] G. P. Krapp, *The Vercelli Book*, 61–2; Gordon, 261–2.

[11] See references in A. S. Cook, *Connecticut Academy of Arts and Sciences*, vol. xxvii (1925), 248 ff.

[12] *Christ*, ll. 659 ff. in Grein-Wülker, iii. 22.

[13] C. H. Krapp, *Andreas*, xxxiii ff.

[14] *Andreas*, ll. 231 ff.; S. Brook, ii. 251.

[15] Ibid., ll. 371–7; Gordon, 207.

[16] Ibid., ll. 1145–8; Gordon, 221.

[17] I, c. 15, in H. and S. iii. 189–90.

[18] Council of 747, c. 3; Council of 787, cc. 3 and 19—in H. and S. iii. 364, 449, 458. Cf. also *Dialogue of Archbishop Egbert*, xv, in H. and S. iii. 410.

[19] For Anglo-Saxon ideas about disease and medicine see O. Cockayne, *Saxon Leechdoms* (R.S.), 3 vols. (1864–6); Singer, c. iv; Hastings, *E.R.* iv. 760, &c. for bibliographies; Chadwick, *G. of L.*, 446 f.; J. F. Payne, *English Medicine in the Anglo-Saxon Times* (1904).

[20] Cockayne, ii. 136–9.   [21] Singer, 149–52.

[22] Gordon, 94–5; Cockayne, iii. 52–5.

[23] Cockayne, i. 403–5; Gordon, 99.

[24] e.g. Grein-Wülker, ii. 250–72, and 92–107; Gordon, 307 and 310.

XIII. THE VIKINGS

[1] Bibliographies for the Vikings will be found in T. D. Kendrick, *History of the Vikings* (1930), 389–92, and in *C.M.H.* iii (1922), 618–24. The best books are: in English (in addition to Kendrick), C. F. Keary, *The Vikings in Western Christendom* (1891); W. G. Collingwood, *Scandinavian Britain* (1908); A. Mawer, *The Vikings* (1913); E. V. Gordon, *Introduction to Old Norse* (1927); B. S. Phillpotts, *Edda and Saga* (1932); *Saga Book of the Viking Club*, i–x (1896–1930): in German, Vogel, *Die Normannen und das fränkische Reich* (1906); in Danish and Norse, the works of Steenstrup, A. Bugge, and Arup (for titles, see List of Abbreviations). A summary of recent work on the culture of the Vikings is given by P. Paulsen in *R.G.K.* xxii (1932), 182–254.

[2] From the 'Worcester' Chronicle, usually referred to as D.

[3] *M.H.B.*, 509.

[4] *Ep. Alc.*, 42–3.

[5] Ibid., 57, 43, 192.

[6] B. Nerman in *Saga Book*, x (1928), 113–31 (a summary from the author's greater work, *Det svenska rikets uppkomst*).

[7] Adam of Bremen, iv, c. 1.

[8] See R. W. Chambers, *Beowulf* (1932), 408–19.

[9] *Ynglinga Saga*, c. vi.

[10] *Chron.* i. 9; *M.G.H.* (ed. Pertz), *S.S.* iii. 739–40.

[11] Cf. M. Ashdown in *Saga Book*, x (1928), 75 ff.

[12] Olric, *H.L.*, 308–9; Hermann, 252.

[13] H. Shetelig, *Préhistoire*, 215–16; and in *Saga Book*, iv (1906), 336–7.

[14] H. Shetelig, *Préhistoire*, 216.

[15] Brøgger, 20.

[15a] Paulsen in *R.G.K.* xxii (1932), 211.

[16] See facing map and cf. Kendrick, 96–7; Wadstein, *Norden*, c. vii. See also P. Kletler, *Nordwest-Europas Verkehr*, &c. (1924), 31, 41 ff.

[17] *Saxo* (ed. Holder), p. 4.

[18] See Brøgger, c. 1–4; M. Olsen, *Farms and Fanes of Ancient Norway* (1928), *passim*; Shetelig, *Préhistoire*, c. viii.

[19] W. Vogel, 58–61, 75–7, 85–6. Cf. N. T. Belaiew in *Saga Book*, x. 280; and in *J.B.A.A.* xxxvii (1932), 194 ff.

[20] *Ann. Xantenses*, s.a. 873. *Fel*, or *felo*, in Late Latin means a malefactor, felon, traitor.

[21] *Ann. Bertin.*, p. 28.

[22] Harmer, no. vi.

[23] The name, appearing in various modern forms, is a common one and no identification can be certain. The *C.M.H.* (iii. 349) selects Oakleigh by Gravesend. An old favourite Ockley, on the Stane Street, is opposed by Stevenson, 178, and in *E.P.N.S.* xi. 276. Ockley in Merstham parish is a possibility (*Surrey Archaeological Coll.* xxv (1912), 136–8).

[24] *Oseberg fundet*, vol. i, *passim*; also H. Shetelig in *Saga Book*, x (1928), 12–56.

[25] Identified with Godfred, opponent of Charlemagne, in *C.M.H.* iii. 313, and elsewhere; but cf. Kendrick, 90, note with references.

[26] A. Bugge, in *Saga Book*, vii (1912), 175.

[27] Brøgger, 15.

[28] Ibid., 19.

[29] Edited by D. E. Martin-Clark (1923); also in *C.P.B.* i. 2 ff. For other editions and bibliographies see B. S. Phillpotts, *Edda and Saga* (1931), 250.

[30] For recent discussions about Ragnar, see Vogel, 409–12; A. Mawer, in *Saga Book*, vi (1908), 68 ff.; Herrmann, 613 ff.

[31] For references see F. Lot and L. Halphen, *Charles le Chauve*, 130 ff.

[32] Cf. F. Lot in *Bibl. de l'École des Chartes*, lxx (1909), 443–4. He undervalues the Danish traditions of the eleventh century.

[33] Heimskringla, *Hacon the Good*, c. 17; ibid., *Ynglinga Saga*, c. 30.

[34] Cf. Brøgger, 14.

[35] N. Nicolaysen, *The Viking Ship discovered at Gokstad*; H. Shetelig in *Saga Book*, iv (1906), 326 ff., &c.

[36] That of Vogel, 38–9.

[37] There are two methods of estimating the numbers carried in the Viking ships. One is that of calculating from the size of the ships and the number of the rowing benches. The flaw here is that we really do not know what the ordinary ships were like in the middle of the ninth century (the Vikings used trading ships as well as fighting ships), nor exactly how far the fighting ships fell short of the later Gokstad ship. The other method is to draw inferences

from statements in the Chronicles, but this is unsatisfactory because medieval chroniclers are notoriously unreliable in their statistics. Hence historians have differed widely in their estimates. Steenstrup (*Normannerne*, i. 352–3) suggests crews of about fifty. Keary (p. 140) thinks that the Gokstad ship would have 'not less than 120 men', but admits that 'the great majority of the craft in early times were quite small boats, with nothing like the 32 oars of the Gokstad ship'.

[38] From J. Stefansson, in *Saga Book*, vi (1909), 31 ff., quoting Ibn-al-Kutia, who died in 977.

XIV. THE COMING OF THE GREAT ARMY

[1] *Ann. Bertin.*, s.a. 839, pp. 18–19.

[2] Stevenson, 186–91. Cf. A. Schultze, *Augustin und der Seelteil*, in *Abhand. d. philol.-histor. Klasse d. Sächsischen Akad.* xxxviii, Nr. 14 (1928).

[3] Cf. Liebermann, ii. 609.

[4] c. 42.

[5] From Harmer, no. xi.

[6] *M.G.H.* (ed. Pertz), *S.S.* xix. 506.

[7] e.g. F. Lot, in *Bibl. de l'École des Chartes*, lxix (1908), 5 ff.

[8] *Ann. Xantenses*, s.a. 865.

[9] It should be noted that, in this and the following chapter, I follow the chronology worked out by M. R. L. Beaven, in *E.H.R.* xxxiii (1918), 328–42, and interpret the year-numbers of the Chronicle to represent years beginning at the September indiction. Thus '866' of the Chronicle is taken to mean according to our reckoning the twelve months from September 24, 865 to September 23, 866. I have some doubt whether the Great Army arrived in East Anglia about October 865 or (say) August 866. To avoid confusion I have accepted the earlier date, since it is Beaven's.

[10] Cf. Brooke, 30–1. He infers from the coin evidence that Edmund's reign only began *c.* 865. The coin evidence is also discussed by Sir H. Howorth in *Num. Chron.* 4th S., xxiv (1908), 222–65. While it throws no certain light on Edmund himself, it shows that East Anglia was ruled after 825 by Athelstan (the son of Egbert), and that Edmund's predecessor was Ethelweard, whose name sufficiently indicates some connexion with the House of Egbert. Lord F. Hervey examines the written evidence—partly drawn from the tenth century, but for the most part legendary and post-Conquest—in his *Corolla Sancti Eadmundi* (1907), pp. vii–xlix, and in his *History of King Eadmund the Martyr* (1929), 11–14. The sources are so unsatisfactory that it is impossible to put much faith in his conclusions.

[11] ed. Arnold, i. 55.

[12] For the evidence see the works quoted above in note 30 of cap. xiii.

The leadership of Inguar rests (1) on inference from Asser, c. 54, who says that the raid on Devon in 878 was led by a 'brother of Inwar and Halfdene'; (2) on the late tenth-century authorities, Ethelweard, p. 512; Abbo, *P.S.E.* i. 8; and *V.S.O.* i. 404; (3) on inferences from the verses attributed to Sighvat when he visited Canute, 1027 (*C.P.B.* ii. 135); and (4) on the twelfth-century Scandinavian traditions in Saxo, 314–15.

13 See *Ann. Ulst.* for the years 856, 858, 862 (corresponding to 857, 859, and 863).

14 *Ann. Fuld.*, s.a. 873.

15 *C.P.B.* ii. 339, 352. The *A.S.C.*, s.a. 1137, asserts that there were snake-pits in England in the twelfth century.

16 e.g. Herrmann, 617–18.

17 *C.P.B.* ii. 135.

18 We have referred above (p. 700) to the difficulty of estimating the average crew of a Viking ship. It follows that any estimate for the total number of a Viking army must be even more speculative. We may notice the number of ships which is sometimes recorded. The expeditions of 810, 815, and 861 (Weland's) were all said to have 200 ships. The only figures about the Great Army of 865 come to us from Saxo (ed. Holder, 315), who says that two of Ivar's brothers sailed to England with reinforcements in 400 ships. There is always a chance that Saxo may have some old poem behind a statement of his. There is general agreement that the 30,000 or 40,000, credited to the Viking army which attacked Paris in 885, is a gross exaggeration. It is a check on such figures to remember that the numbers of William's army of invasion in 1066 are, with a better basis for calculation, put at about 7,000, perhaps less. (Delbrück, ii. 156.)

19 *Ann. Bertin.*, s.a. 861.

20 Chron. E., s.a. 870.

21 Abbo, c. 5, from Lord F. Hervey, *Corolla*, 19–21.

22 *Ann Ulst.*, s.a. 870.

23 e.g. *Vita Anskarii*, c. 38; *Vita Rimberti*, cc. 16, 18; *Ann. Xantenses*, s.a. 845.

24 *Const. Hist.* i. 217.

XV. THE DANISH WARS, 871–8

1 *Boethius*, ed. W. J. Sedgefield, p. 73, line 27.

2 The best general books about Alfred's reign are those by Plummer and Miss B. A. Lees. W. H. Stevenson, *Asser's Life of Alfred*, is a mine of information on all aspects of the period. For the campaign of 871 cf. W. H. Simcox in *E.H.R.* i. 218 ff.

3 *The Battle of Maldon*, ll. 50–3.

4 For weapons found on Ashdown see H. Peake, *Berkshire* (1931), 150.

See also Stevenson, 254; G. B. Grundy in *Arch. Journ.* lxxv (1918), 189. For the White Horse see *Antiquity*, v. 37–46.

⁵ Cf. Lees, 124.

⁶ Cf. E. Ekblom, *Place-Names of Wilts* (1917), 122–3; *V.C.H. Surrey*, i. 333–4; Grundy, *Arch. Journ.* lxxv (1918), 191–2.

⁷ Ethelweard, *M.H.B.* 514.

⁸ Asser, c. 43.

⁹ The length of this occupation is uncertain. A charter (Birch, ii. No. 533) speaks of one year. Brooke (p. 34) calculates three. On the other hand Alfred seems only to have recovered London in 883.

¹⁰ Birch, ii, no. 533.

¹¹ So H. Lindkvist, *Middle English Place-Names of Scandinavian Origin* (1912); A. H. Smith in *Saga Book*, x (1925), 190.

¹² The identity of Imhar and his brother Olaf is still in dispute. See (e.g.) *C.M.H.* iii. 317; D. W. H. Marshall, *Sudreys in Early Viking Times* (1929), 20–8; H. Shetelig, in *Antiq. Journ.* xii (1932), 181.

¹³ *Ann. Ulst.*, s.a. 870.

¹⁴ It is possible, though not provable, that Halfdene, the leader of the Danish army in England, is the same man as the Halfdan who, with a brother Siegfried (Sigfridus), succeeded Horic II in Denmark, or at any rate in a Danish kingdom north of the Eider, in 873. (*Ann. Fuld.*, s.a. 873; Vogel, 247, 410–12.)

¹⁵ S.D. i. 68.

¹⁶ Ibid., i. 56–70.

¹⁷ See A. H. Smith in *Saga Book*, x (1925), 188 ff., especially 208.

¹⁸ Asser, c. 49.

¹⁹ Chron., s.a. 876 and 877. The chronology is here confused.

²⁰ e.g. W. G. Collingwood, *Scandinavian Britain* (1908), p. 109.

²¹ Cf. F. M. Stenton, *The Danes in England* (1927), 1 ff.

²² Ethelweard, *M.B.H.*, p. 515.

²³ *Pastoral Care*, i, p. 4.

²⁴ Birch, ii, no. 595.

²⁵ *Vita Johannis Gorziensis*, *M.G.H.* (ed. Pertz), SS. iv. 343.

²⁶ Stevenson, pp. 44, 138, 265–7.   ²⁷ *Orosius*, 192.

²⁸ See Stevenson, 267–8. Stevenson suggests that the stone may have been one afterwards known as 'the boundstone'. G. B. Grundy, *Arch. Journ.* lxxv (1918), 178–81, arguing from the road system, places it at Willoughby Hedge, six miles to the east. Cf. J. E. Jackson, *Wilts. Arch. and Nat. Hist. Mag.* xiii. 107 ff.; also, for an unsatisfactory theory about the campaign, A. F. Major, *Early Wars of Wessex* (1913), 145–80.

²⁹ e.g. *Orosius*, 142, line 14; 230, line 15; 232, line 7; 240, lines 15 and 22; 278, line 12.

[30] *Ann. Fuld.*, s.a. 891.

[31] *Judith* (Grein-Wülker, ii. 306), ll. 200–36; from R. K. Gordon's *Old English Poetry.* Cf. A. Brandl in Paul's *Grundriss* (1909), ii. 1091.

[32] Mon. Sangall., *Gesta Karoli*, Bk. II, c. 19. (*M.G.H.* SS. ii. 762.)

[33] Hinkmar, *Ann.*, s.a. 873.

[34] Cf. Gregory of Tours, ii, c. 31.

XVI. WAR AND PEACE, 878–92

[1] Birch, ii, no. 537.

[2] This is inferred from Birch, ii, nos. 551 and 574. Cf. Chadwick, *Institutions*, 304–5; Stevenson, 147 and 300.

[3] By M. R. L. Beaven in *E.H.R.* xxxiii. 341–2.

[4] c. 83. See Stevenson, 324.

[5] F. M. Stenton in *Essays . . . to Tout*, 20.

[6] *Laws of Hlothere and Eadric*, c. 16; Liebermann, ii. 571 ff.; Chadwick, *Institutions*, 277–9; Birch in *J.A.A.* xliv. 334–5; *Num. Chron.* (1924), 239. It is open to question whether the mention of Lundenburh in the Chronicle, s.a. 851 and 872, implies that there was any military organization of the place before 886.

[7] Birch, ii, no. 561; cf. also no. 577.

[8] Supporters of the theory that the Anglo-Saxon ceorls were in fact a depressed class and that the treaty did no more than recognize the fact are: F. Seebohm, *Tribal Custom in Anglo-Saxon Law*, 351–76; Chadwick, *Institutions*, especially 50 and 392–405. Against them are ranged Vinogradoff, *G. of M.* 131–2; W. J. Corbett in *C.M.H.* iii. 359.

[9] Vinogradoff, op. cit. 298.

[10] Saxo, ed. Holder, 153.

[11] *Conquest of England*, i. 161.

[12] Birch, ii, nos. 537, 547, 551, 574, 577.

[13] Birch, ii, no. 561.

[14] On this see Lees, 245–7; W. Vogel in Hoops, iv. 121–2, and (for bibliography) 114.

[15] Cf. Oman, 424.

[16] Cf. Maitland, 502–6; Chadwick, *Institutions*, 204–12; Liebermann, ii. 330–1, 659 ff.; Oman, 468–70; C. Stephenson, *Borough and Town* (1933), 52 ff. If we may assume that there had been some preliminary defences constructed at Warwick before the more notable burh-building of 915, the document as a whole can be best assigned to the end of Alfred's reign.

[17] At the end of Alfred's reign Kent was apparently again under its own under-king, Edward, son of Alfred. (Birch, ii, no. 576; cf. Chadwick, *Institutions*, 297, 360–1.)

¹⁸ Cf. *V.C.H. Dorset*, ii. 127; and see note by Dr. Mawer, below, p. 711.

¹⁹ Cf. the repair of Towcester, *A.S.C.*, s.a. 921.

²⁰ See W. H. Stevenson, in *E.H.R.* xxix (1914), 689 ff.; Liebermann, iii. 688.

²¹ Cf. Birch, ii, no. 416.

²² c. 45.

^{22a} See *Oudheidkundige Mededeeling* (1926), cx ff., for a plan of a fort which seems to be a river fort of Charlemagne.

²³ Maitland, 172 ff.

²⁴ Asser, c. 91.

²⁵ Harmer, no. xiii.

²⁶ Chadwick in one place (*Institutions*, 311–18, see also 346 ff.) calculated from the charters that there were not more than twenty King's Thegns in the time of Ethelwulf. In his later book (*Origin*, 158–62), while admitting that the King's Thegns 'were a comparatively small class', he suspected 'that we ought to reckon [them] in scores rather than in hundreds'.

²⁷ *Boethius*, xxxvii, p. 111.

²⁸ Cf. *Song of Maldon*, line 24.

²⁹ Cf. Liebermann, iii. 58.

³⁰ Cf. *A.S.C.*, s.a. 905.

³¹ Chadwick, *Institutions*, 88–97, 378–81; Vinogradoff, *G. of M.* 125–6; *Laws of Ine*, c. 24.

³² Supporters of the theory of a popular fyrd are (besides the older historians, Stubbs, Freeman, and Green) Vinogradoff, *G. of M.* 129–30, 197–8, 216–20; cf. his *E.S.* 22–34; Lees, 44–8, 233–4; Oman, 471. For the other side see Chadwick, references as above; also *Origin of the English Nation*, 159–62.

³³ Boethius, xvii. 40.

³⁴ e.g. Green, *C.E.*, c. 4.

³⁵ Liebermann, ii. 419; Vinogradoff, *G. of M.* 127 ff. and 238 ff.; e.g. Birch, i, nos. 201 and 246.

³⁶ On swords see London Museum Catalogues, no. 1, *London and the Vikings* (1927), 29–37; *B.M. Guide*, 92–6; B.B. iii. 204–31; J. Petersen, *De Norske Vikingesverd* (1919), 4 ff., 54 ff.

XVII. THE RESTORATION OF ORDER AND OF LEARNING

¹ Laws of Alfred, cc. 26, 28; Ine, c. 13; Alfred, cc. 5, 42.

² I Ed. Prolog; II Ed. 5, § 2. Cf. Liebermann, iii. 39.

³ Liebermann, iii. 33.

⁴ Plummer, *Alfred*, 125.

⁵ Harmer, no. xviii.

⁶ *Saxons in England*, ii. 208, note 2.

⁷ *Boethius*, 124–5.

⁸ Cf. Alfred's Will, in Harmer, p. 50. It is true that the Will (A.D. 873–89) is probably prior to the *Orosius*.

⁹ Ibid., p. 52, and note on p. 102.

¹⁰ *Pastoral Care*, i. 2 ff.

¹¹ Migne, *P.L.*, Ep. 95; Birch, ii. nos. 555 and 573; Flodoard, *Hist. Eccles. Rem.*, in *M.G.H.* (ed. Pertz) SS. xiii. 566, 568.

¹² Asser, c. 93.

¹³ Alfred's Laws, c. 8.

¹⁴ Birch, ii, no. 623.

¹⁵ Asser, cc. 92–4.

¹⁶ *Liber monasterii de Hyda*, ed. J. Stevenson (1866), cc. xxvi–xxix.

¹⁷ *Chron. de Abingdon*, ed. J. Stevenson (1858), i. 50. Cf. F. M. Stenton, *Early History of the Abbey of Abingdon* (1913), 31.

¹⁸ Asser, c. 102.

¹⁹ c. 79.

²⁰ Asser, c. 79; and c. 88–9, freely rendered.

²¹ Cf. Birch, ii. nos. 540, 541, 547, 559, 560, 561, 570, 574.

²² See Stevenson, 307–11, and the authorities there cited. Stevenson confuses the sequence of events.

²³ Asser, cc. 102 and 75.

²⁴ Asser, c. 106.

²⁴ᵃ Alfred's schemes for wide-spread education should be compared with those of the Franks in the ninth century. See *Laistner*, 159 f.

²⁵ See S. Potter, *On the Relations of the Old English Bede to Werferth's Gregory and to Alfred's Translations* (Prague, 1931). The most convenient bibliographies of Alfredian literature will be found in the *Cambridge History of English Literature* (1908), i. c. 6, and in Heusinkveld and Bashe (1931), 103–8.

²⁶ K. Sisam in *M.L.R.* xviii (1923), 254–6.

²⁷ *Pastoral Care*, i. 25.

²⁸ The following comments on the theories about the Chronicle mentioned on p. 624 are a short defence of the line there taken:

A. Miss A. J. Thorogood (in *E.H.R.* xlviii (1933), 353–63) has urged 'that the history of the *A.S.C.* can be carried a stage behind the reign of Alfred to an earlier annalist who covered the period 802–842'. Her article brings out well variations in the method of reckoning the years in the annals 794–855. But (1) if she had paid attention to the contrast in the style and phraseology of the Chronicle before and after 823 she could scarcely have maintained that the annals for the reign of Egbert are a distinct entity and contemporary. (2) Her contention that the year was considered to begin on the 25th December throughout the annals of Egbert's reign rests partly on a charter (Birch, no.

389) which is both spurious and corrupt. (3) In any case her conclusion quoted above scarcely follows from the facts which she establishes.

B. The chief reasons for dissenting from the theory of F. M. Stenton (in *Essays to Tout*, 15–24) that the annals for 750–891 were written 'not far from the boundary between Somerset and Dorset' and 'under the patronage of a great Somerset noble' are (1) that the events in the east (e.g. the campaign of 871) are really as well known to the author as those in the west, and that the connexion with the king's court is the best explanation of his wide range; and (2) that Stenton's view does not explain the resemblances between the Chronicle and the *Orosius*.

C. The view that the Chronicle down to the genealogy s.a. 855 is the work of an editor writing under Ethelwulf is formidable because it rests on a microscopic analysis by Liebermann (in *Archiv für das Studium der neueren Sprachen*, civ (1900), 188–99), accepted and amplified by Brandl (in Paul's *Grundriss*, ii (1909), 1054 ff.), and is followed by most modern writers, e.g. G. H. Wheeler in *E.H.R.* xxxvi (1921), 167 ff.; and Lees, 336. Cf. also Chadwick, *Origin*, 25.

Their chief reasons are (1) the fact that the genealogy s.a. 855 is only carried down to Ethelwulf. Against this, one may imagine that Alfred told the Chronicler to trace his father's descent to Cerdic, Woden, and Adam. Every one knew that Alfred was the son of Ethelwulf. (2) An argument that the chronological dislocation running from 754 to 851 could only be the error of a copyist and that an interval of time is needed for this error to occur. Against this, I suggest that the wrong dates from 823 onwards (the section where the argument carries weight) may have been caused, at any rate in part, by mistakes of memory. They vary in extent from year to year. But even if they are 'purely mechanical', as Plummer asserted, the fact is not fatal to the view which I am advocating. A mechanical error in copying can be made soon after a book has been written.

In support of the 'Alfredian' authorship, note

I. That the language from 823 to 871 and beyond is on the whole Alfredian (cf. Brandl, 1060); e.g. the phrases and words,

> micel wæl geslægen (823, etc., to 871)
> micel wælsliht (839 and 871)
> gefægene wærun (855 and 878)
> geþuærnesse (827 and 860)
> micle (or lytle) werede (823, 878),

give this section a unity, and in varying degrees link it with other Alfredian writings.

II. The passage s.a. 853 about Alfred being hallowed as king at Rome shows that the section could not have been written before Alfred's accession. Brandl can only escape from this obvious conclusion by suggesting that the words are interpolated.

III. The retrospective entries s.a. 851 and 855 confirm this view.

IV. See Plummer, ii, cii. ff.; Plummer, *Alfred*, 146 ff.; and Stevenson, 153 and 181. And note S. Potter, 60. The differing characteristics of the changing groups of helpers employed by Alfred (as worked out by Potter, *passim*) make it easy to explain why the language of the Chronicle sometimes changes and is often crude, and why its outlook is more limited than that of Alfred himself.

[29] See analysis in Liebermann, op. cit.; G. H. Wheeler, op. cit. 162; Chadwick, *Origin*, 36.

[30] So L. C. Jane, Asser's *Life of King Alfred* (1908), xix–xxxv.

XVIII. ALFRED'S FOREIGN POLICY

[1] Birch, ii. no. 555. Cf. Stevenson, p. 308.

[2] Flodoard, *Hist. Eccles. Remensis* in *M.G.H.* (ed. Pertz), SS. xiii. 566.

[3] *Liber Pontificalis* (ed. Duchesne), ii. 161.

[4] Hincmari, *Ann.*, s.a. 864.

[5] In the Alfredian version of the Chronicle (the Parker MS. (A)) there is a short reference to the intercourse with Marinus, but none to that with India. We have quoted from the fuller though less authentic passage in MSS. D and E. Cf. Stevenson, 286–90.

[6] Thorpe, *Diplomatarium*, p. 402. A forged post-Conquest charter, attributed to King Edward the Confessor.

[7] Jaffé, *R.P.*, 2995; C. H. Thurston in *The Month*, 1901, Oct., p. 350.

[8] Letter of Formosus to Archbishop Plegmund. Birch, ii, p. 215.

[9] c. 91. Cf. Stevenson, p. 328, and references there given.

[10] Cockayne, ii. 289–90.

[11] c. 102.

[12] See Gougaud, c. 5; Kenney, i. c. 6, pp. 486–604.

[13] E. Bishop in *J.T.S.* viii (1906–7), 285 ff.

[14] For what follows see H. Geidel; G. Hübener, in *Englische Studien*, lx (1925), 37–57; K. Malone, *Speculum*, v (1930), 159–67, and viii (1933), 67–78; S. H. Cross in *Speculum*, vi (1931), 296–9.

[15] Hübener, 39. On the other hand K. Malone (in *M.L.R.* xxv. 78–81, 1930) argues, though not convincingly, that Ohthere told his story not later than 871.

[16] Lloyd, i. 328.

[17] *M.H.B.* 519, a corrupt passage; cf. Lees, 410.

[18] The *Historia de S. Cuthberto*, S.D., i. 203.

[19] *De Primo Saxonum Adventu*, ibid. ii. 377.

[20] See A. Mawer in *Saga Book*, vii (1911), 38–50; Steenstrup, *Normannerne*, ii. 90–103; A. Bugge, *Vikingerne*, ii. 252 ff.; F. M. Stenton in *E.H.R.* xxiv. 80; Brooke, 34–5.

[21] S.D. i. 71.

[22] Ethelweard in *M.H.B.* 518.

[23] Ibid., 519.

[24] Cf. W. J. Corbett in *C.M.H.* iii. 361.

XIX. ALFRED'S LAST WAR

[1] For the date and time see F. M. Stenton in *E.H.R.* xxiv (1909), 79; R. H. Hodgkin in *E.H.R.* xxxix (1924), 501–6.

[2] Flodoard, *Hist. Rem. Eccles.* iv, c. 5; *M.G.H.* SS. xiii. 563.

[3] Regino, s.a. 886.

[4] See W. C. Abbott in *E.H.R.* xiii (1898), 439 ff.

[5] *M.H.B.* 516.

[6] F. M. Stenton in *E.H.R.* xxvii (1912), 512.

[7] F. C. J. Spurrell in *Arch. Journ.* xlii (1885), 294.

[8] Probably, as shown on the map, Buttington in Montgomeryshire, but the site is disputed. See Lees, 403; Oman, 487; Birch in *J.A.A.* xliv. 337.

[9] See F. M. Stenton in *E.H.R.* xxiv. 81–2, for an expedition sent by Alfred to York and perhaps intended to intercept the returning army which was raiding in the Welland valley.

[10] For the uncertainty surrounding this date see Lees, 427–32, and the references there given; also M. L. R. Beaven in *E.H.R.* xxxii (1917), 526–31.

[11] See F. M. Stenton in *E.H.R.* xxiv (1929), 83–4.

XX. ALFRED THE MAN AND HIS MESSAGE

[1] Gibbon, quoted by F. York Powell, in O. Elton's *Life of F. York Powell*.

[2] Lees, 423–5.

[3] *Boethius*, xxxiii. 81, l. 10; xxxix. 125, l. 30; xxxvi. 105, l. 12; xxxix. 126, l. 9; xxxix. 135–6. These and the following references to *Boethius* refer to Sedgefield's edition of the OE. text. My quotations are taken from Sedgefield's translation in *King Alfred's Version of the Consolation of Boethius, turned into Modern English* (1900).

[4] Ibid. xxiv. 53 l. 5; xxxiv. 83, l. 3, and 86, l. 18; xxi. 49, l. 25; xxxix. 126, l. 18; 136, l. 18.

[5] Ibid. xli. 145, l. 7.

[6] *Orosius*, 102.

[7] *Boethius*, xxiv. 52, l. 25; xxxiv. 88, l. 11, &c.; xxxvi. 108, l. 19; xxxix. 129–30; xxv. 57, l. 32; xxxiii. 81, l. 27.

[8] H. L. Hargrove, *OE. Version of St. Augustine's Soliloquies*, 25, l. 15 (adapted). The following quotations are made from Hargrove's translation of the above in Yale Studies xxii (1904).

⁹ Hargrove, xxxiv–xxxvi; W. Endter, *König Alfred's Bearbeitung der Soliloquien des Augustinus* (1922), xi.

¹⁰ Hargrove, pp. 2, l. 20; 22, l. 7; 43–4; 47, l. 15; 56, l. 13.

¹¹ Ibid., pp. 65 and 69–70.

¹² W.M., *G.R.* ii, § 123. Cf. G. P. Krapp, *Paris Psalter*, &c. (1933), xix.

¹³ *Boethius*, xiv. 30, l. 5.

¹⁴ Ibid., xxiv. 54, l. 13; cf. also xxix. 67, l. 20 (though not marked as an addition by Sedgefield), also Hargrove, 25.

¹⁵ *Boethius*, xxxvi. 110, l. 32; and Hargrove, 30, l. 20.

¹⁶ *Boethius*, xvii. 40, l. 27.

¹⁷ *Pastoral Care*, i. 58.

¹⁸ *Orosius*, 278, l. 8; 58, l. 30; 62, l. 30; *Boethius*, 46, l. 16.

¹⁹ *A.S.C.*, s.a. 897.

²⁰ A. Olrik, *Heroic Legends*, passim.

²¹ E. V. Gordon, *Introduction to Old Norse* (1927), 168–70.

²² Either Thorbiorn Hornklofi or Thiodolf of Hvin. Kershaw, 88–91; *C.P.B.* i. 254–9 (changing *austan* into *vestan*, 'from the west').

²³ As has been already said, the date of the battle of Hafursfirth is doubtful. The researches of Ari in the twelfth century fixed it at *c.* 872. Vigfusson and York Powell argued (*C.P.B.* ii. 487–500) that Harold's reign was much later, i.e. 900–45. The *C.M.H.* in ii. 261, dates the battle 872, and in vi. 364, following H. Koht, *Innhogg og Utsyn* (1921), 34–49, dates it *c.* 900. Modern opinion (e.g. Hermansson, 3–4) inclines to an intermediate date, i.e. to about 884.

²⁴ Bugge, *Vikingerne*, ii. 217.

²⁵ Kershaw, 82–7.

²⁶ *Saga of Harold Fairhair*, c. 9.

²⁶ᵃ Cf. *C.P.B.* ii. 2–7. A scene from the story of the Everlasting Battle had been engraved on the shield of Ragnar Lothbrok.

²⁷ Liudprand, *Antapodosis*, quoted by A. Kleinclausz, *L'Empire Carolingien* (1902), 541.

ADDITIONAL NOTES

P. 442, *The Vespasian Psalter.*—My interpretation of this picture may be criticized on various grounds. First, it may be assumed that the dancing and playing figures are copied from earlier pictures (compare, for example, Bibliothèque Nationale, MS. lat. 1152, fol. 1). Secondly, Mr. K. Sisam has pointed out to me that its interlinear gloss is in the Mercian dialect and that it is very doubtful whether the Psalter was produced at Canterbury.

P. 586, *Burghal Hidage.*—Dr. A. Mawer, Provost of University College, London, replying to a question whether the *Brydian* of the 'Tribal Hidage' should be identified as Bridport or Bredy, wrote as follows:

'*Bridport* and *Bredy* (Long and Little). The forms in the Burghal Hidage and on the coins would, from the formal point of view, fit either Bredy or Bridport, the only difficulty being the absence of the second element *port* in these forms. That is no difficulty in the coin-forms, which are necessarily abbreviated, and should not be regarded as an insuperable difficulty in the Burghal Hidage list, for one can assume with some reason the addition of *port* to an earlier and shorter name, cf. *Huntendunport* side by side with *Huntandun*. Further, Bridport is an ancient borough, and as such might well appear in the Burghal Hidage. We have no knowledge, apart from the references under consideration, that either of the Bredys was ever a borough. The only difficulty in this identification is the coincidence of the element *Brydie, Brydye*, etc. appearing in the name of both Bredy and Bridport. It is easy to explain its presence in Bredy, for there is good evidence that *Brydie* is the old form for the River Bride on which the Bredys stand (Ekwall, *River-names*, 52). Ekwall would explain its presence in Bridport as due to Bridport's being the port of the Bredys, but it is on a different river and Bridport is not itself on the sea. Bridport itself is on a river *Brit*, but that is a late back-formation, the earlier name of the river being *Wooth* (Ekwall, loc. cit.). As that name is however of English origin, it may be that the river had a still earlier Celtic name *Brydie*. The only difficulty in that case would be the use of the same name for two different rivers closely adjacent to one another.'

ABBREVIATIONS

Åberg.	N. Åberg, *The Anglo-Saxons in England* (1926).
Abbo, P. S. E.	Abbo, 'Passio Sancti Eadmundi', in *Memorials of St. Edmund's Abbey*, ed. T. Arnold, R.S. (1890).
Adam of Bremen.	*Adami Gesta Hammaburgensis Ecclesiae Pontificum*, M.G.H., Scriptores in usum scholarum (1876).
Adamnan.	Adamnani, *Vita S. Columbae*, ed. J. T. Fowler (1920); also ed. with translation by W. Reeves in vol. vi of the *Historians of Scotland* (1874).
Alc. Ep.	'Alcuini Epistolae' in M.G.H., *Epistolae Karolini Aevi*, ii, ed. E. Dümmler (1895).
Anglia.	*Anglia*, Zeitschrift für englische Philologie (1877–).
Ann. Bertin.	*Annales Bertiniani*, M.G.H., Scriptores in usum scholarum, ed. G. Waitz (1883).
Annales Cambriae.	*Annales Cambriae*, ed. J. Williams ab Ithel, R.S. (1860). Also (a better edition) ed. E. Phillimore, in *Y Cymmrodor*, ix. 141 ff. (1888).
Ann. Fuld.	*Annales Fuldenses*, M.G.H., s.i.u.s., ed. F. Kurze (1891).
Ann. Ulst.	*Annals of Ulster*, ed. W. M. Hennessy and B. MacCarthy (1887–1901).
Ann. Xantenses.	*Annales Xantenses*, M.G.H., s.i.u.s., ed. B. de Simson (1909).
Anskarii Vita.	*Anskarii Vita*, M.G.H., s.i.u.s., ed. G. Waitz (1884).
Antiquity.	*Antiquity*, A Quarterly Review of Archaeology, ed. O. G. S. Crawford (1927–).
Arch.	*Archaeologia*, published by the Society of Antiquaries of London (1874–).
Arch. Camb.	*Archaeologia Cambrensis* (1846–).
Arch. Journ.	*Archaeological Journal* (1844–).
Arup.	E. Arup, *Danmark's Historie* (1925).
A.S.C.	C. Plummer, *Two of the Saxon Chronicles Parallel* (1892–9).
Asser.	W. H. Stevenson, *Asser's Life of King Alfred* (1904).
B.B.	G. Baldwin Brown, *Arts of Early England*, 6 vols. (1903–30) (2nd ed. of vol. ii).
Beddoe.	J. Beddoe, *The Races of Great Britain* (1885).
Bede.	Bede, *Historia ecclesiastica gentis Anglorum*, ed. C. Plummer, 2 vols. (1896).
Birch.	W. de Gray Birch, *Cartularium Saxonicum* (1885–93).
B.M. Guide.	British Museum, *A Guide to the Anglo-Saxon and Foreign Teutonic Antiquities* (1923).
Boeles.	P. C. J. A. Boeles, *Friesland tot de Elfde Eeuw* (1927).
Boethius.	*King Alfred's Old English Version of Boethius*, De Consolatione Philosophiae, ed. by W. J. Sedgefield (1899).
Bosworth-Toller.	J. Bosworth, *An Anglo-Saxon Dictionary*, ed. T. N. Toller (1882); and T. N. Toller, *An Anglo-Saxon Dictionary, Supplement* (1921).
Bright.	W. Bright, *Early Chapters in English Church History*, 3rd ed. (1897).
Brit. Num. Journ.	*The British Numismatic Journal* (1903–).

Brøgger.   A. W. Brøgger, *Ancient Emigrants* (1929).
Brooke.   G. C. Brooke, *English Coins* (1932).
Browne, *Boniface*.   G. F. Browne, *Boniface of Crediton and his Companions* (1910).
Brunner.   H. Brunner, *Deutsche Rechtsgeschichte*, 2nd ed. (1906, 1928).
Bugge, *N. H.*   A. Bugge, *Norges Historie*, vol. i (1912).
Bugge, *Vik.*   Id., *Vikingerne* (1904–6).
Bury, *Patrick.*   J. B. Bury, *The Life of St. Patrick and his Place in History* (1905).
Cabrol.   F. Cabrol, *Dictionnaire d'archéologie chrétienne et de liturgie* (1901–).
C.A.S.P.   *Cambridge Antiquarian Society Proceedings* (1851–).
Chadwick, *Institu-*   H. M. Chadwick, *Studies on Anglo-Saxon Institutions* (1905).
tions.
Chadwick, *G. of L.*   H. M. and N. K. Chadwick, *The Growth of Literature*, vol. i (1932).
Chadwick, *H. A.*   H. M. Chadwick, *The Heroic Age* (1912).
Chadwick, *Origin.*   Id., *The Origin of the English Nation* (1907).
Chambers, E. K.   E. K. Chambers, *Arthur of Britain* (1927).
Chambers, R. W.   R. W. Chambers, *England before the Norman Conquest* (1926).
C.M.H.   *Cambridge Medieval History* (1911–).
Cockayne.   T. O. Cockayne, *Leechdoms, Wort-Cunning, and Starcraft*, R.S. (1864–).
C.P.B.   G. Vigfusson and F. York Powell, *Corpus Poeticum Boreale* (1883).
Crawford   Char-   A. S. Napier and W. H. Stevenson, *The Crawford Collection of Early
ters.   Charters and Documents* (1895).
Cymmrodor.   *Y Cymmrodor* (Cymmrodorion Society, 1877–).
Delbruck.   H. Delbrück, *Geschichte der Kriegskunst*, 2nd ed. (1923).
D.N.B.   *Dictionary of National Biography* (1885–1900).
Eddius.   Eddius Stephanus, *The Life of Bishop Wilfrid*, ed. B. Colgrave (1927).
E.E.T.S.   *Early English Text Society* (1864, &c.).
E.H.R.   *English Historical Review* (1886–).
Ehwald.   M.G.H., *Auctores Antiquissimi XV*, ed. R. Ehwald (1919).
Ekwall, *E.P.N.I.*   E. Ekwall, *English Place-Names in -ing* (1923).
Engelhardt.   C. Engelhardt, *Denmark in the Early Iron Age* (1866).
Ep. Bon.   S. Bonifatii et Lulli Epistolae in M.G.H., *Epistolae Merowingici
                       et Karolini Aevi*, i, pp. 215–431, ed. E. Dümmler (1892).
E.P.N.S.   *English Place-Name Society Publications*, general editors A. Mawer
                       and F. M. Stenton (1925–).
Essays . . . James   *Historical Essays in Honour of James Tait*, ed. by J. G. Edwards (and
Tait.   others) (1933).
Essays . . . to Tout   *Essays in Medieval History presented to T. F. Tout*, ed. A. G. Little
                       and F. M. Powicke (1925).
Ethelweard.   Chronicon Aethelweardi in M.H.B., 499–531.
Faral.   É. Faral, *La Légende arthurienne*, Bibliothèque de l'École des
                       Hautes Études, fasc. 255 (1929).
Freeman.   E. A. Freeman, *History of the Norman Conquest*, 3rd ed. of vols. i–ii
                       (1877).
Geidel.   H. Geidel, *Alfred der Grosse als Geograph* (1904).
Gougaud.   L. Gougaud, *Christianity in Celtic Lands* (1932).
Green, *C. E.*   J. R. Green, *The Conquest of England*, Eversley edition, 2 vols.
                       (1899).

Grein-Wülker.	C. W. M. Grein, *Bibliothek der angelsächsischen Poesie*, ed. R. P. Wülker (1883–98).
Hargrove.	H. L. Hargrove, *King Alfred's Old English Version of St. Augustine's Soliloquies* (Yale Studies in English, 1902).
Harmer.	F. E. Harmer, *Select English Historical Documents of the Ninth and Tenth Centuries* (1914).
Harvey, *Corolla*.	Lord Francis Harvey, *Corolla Sancti Eadmundi* (1907).
Hastings, *E.R.E.*	*Encyclopaedia of Religion and Ethics*, ed. J. Hastings (1908–20).
Hauck.	A. Hauck, *Kirchengeschichte Deutschlands* (1904–20).
Haverfield, *Roman Occupation*.	F. Haverfield and Sir G. MacDonald, *Roman Occupation of Britain* (1924).
Hefele-Leclercq.	C. J. Hefele, *Conciliengeschichte*, ed. M. Leclercq (1907).
Heimskringla.	*Heimskringla*, by Snorri Sturluson, ed. Finnur Jónsson (1911). Translations: (1) E. Monsen, *Heimskringla* (1932); (2) W. Morris and E. Magnusson, *The Stories of the Kings of Norway* (1893–1905). (Note—the numbers of the chapters are sometimes different in the edition of Morris.)
Hermannsson.	H. Hermannsson, *The Book of the Icelanders* (1930).
Herrmann.	P. H. Herrmann, *Die Heldensagen des Saxo Grammaticus* (1922).
Heusinkveld and Bashe.	*A Bibliographical Guide to Old English*, compiled by A. Heusinkveld and E. J. Bashe, in *University of Iowa Studies*, Humanistic Studies, vol. iv, no. 5 (1931).
Hincmar.	*Annales Bertiniani*, auctore Hincmaro, in M.G.H., s.i.u.s. (1883).
History.	*History*, The Journal of the Historical Association (1916–).
Hollingworth and O'Reilly, *Girton*.	E. J. Hollingworth and M. M. O'Reilly, *The Anglo-Saxon Cemetery at Girton College, Cambridge* (1925).
Hoops, *Waldbäume*.	J. Hoops, *Waldbäume und Kulturpflanzen im germanischen Altertum* (1905).
Hoops.	Id., *Reallexikon der germanischen Altertumskunde* (1911–19).
H. and S.	A. W. Haddan and W. Stubbs, *Councils and Ecclesiastical Documents* (1869–78).
Hunt.	William Hunt, *A History of the English Church from its foundation to the Norman Conquest* (1899).
Jaffé.	P. Jaffé, *Regesta Pontificum*, ed. W. Wattenbach (1885–8).
J.B.A.A.	*Journal of the British Archaeological Association* (1846–).
Jolliffe.	J. E. A. Jolliffe, *Pre-Feudal England, The Jutes* (1933).
J.R.A.I.	*Journal of the Royal Anthropological Institute* (1871–).
J.R.S.	*Journal of Roman Studies* (1911–).
J.T.S.	*Journal of Theological Studies* (1899–).
Karlström.	S. Karlström, *Old English Compound Place-Names in -ing* (1927).
Keary.	C. F. Keary, *The Vikings in Western Christendom* (1891).
Kemble.	J. M. Kemble, *The Saxons in England* (1876).
Kendrick.	T. D. Kendrick, *History of the Vikings* (1930).
Kendrick and Hawkes.	T. D. Kendrick and C. F. Hawkes, *Archaeology in England and Wales, 1914–1931* (1932).
Kenney.	J. F. Kenney, *The Sources for the Early History of Ireland*, i (1920).
Kershaw.	N. Kershaw, *Anglo-Saxon and Norse Poems* (1922).
Kylie.	E. Kylie, *The English Correspondence of Saint Boniface* (1911).
Lacour.	V. Lacour, *Sønderjyllands Historie* (1931).

Laistner.	M. L. W. Laistner, *Thought and Letters in Western Europe, A.D. 500–900* (1931).
Leeds.	E. T. Leeds, *Archaeology of the Anglo-Saxon Settlements* (1913).
Lethbridge.	T. C. Lethbridge, *Recent Excavations in Anglo-Saxon Cemeteries in Cambridgeshire and Suffolk* (1931).
Liebermann.	F. Liebermann, *Die Gesetze der Angelsachsen* (1898–1916).
Lindqvist.	S. Lindqvist, *Vendelkulturens Alder och Ursprung* (1926).
Lloyd.	J. E. Lloyd, *A History of Wales from the Earliest Times to the Edwardian Conquest* (1912).
Macdonald, *Roman Britain, 1914–1928.*	Sir G. MacDonald, *Roman Britain, 1914–1928* (British Academy Supplemental Papers, No. VI).
Mager, *Entwicklungsgeschichte Schleswig.*	F. Mager, *Entwicklungsgeschichte der Kulturlandschaft des Herzogtums Schleswig in historischer Zeit*, i (1930).
Maitland.	F. W. Maitland, *Doomsday Book and Beyond* (1897).
Manitius.	M. Manitius, *Geschichte der lateinischen Literatur des Mittelalters* (1911–31).
Mawer, *Problems.*	A. Mawer, *Problems of Place-Name Study* (1929).
Mélanges, Bémont.	*Mélanges d'histoire offerts à M. Charles Bémont* (1913).
M.G.H., auct. ant.	*Monumenta Germaniae Historica, Auctores antiquissimi*, ed. T. Mommsen (1877–).
M.G.H. (ed. Pertz), SS.	*Monumenta Germaniae Historica, Scriptores*, ed. G. H. Pertz and others (1826–96).
M.G.H., s.i.u.s.	*Monumenta Germaniae Historica, Scriptores in usum scholarum.*
M.H.B.	*Monumenta Historica Britannica*, ed. H. Petrie and T. Sharpe (1848).
Migne, *P.L.*	J. P. Migne, *Patrologia latina* (1844–).
M.L.R.	*Modern Language Review* (1905–).
Nennius.	Nennius, *Historia Brittonum*, ed. T. Mommsen, in *M.G.H. auct. ant.* xiii. 111–219 (1898); also in new and handier edition, *Nennius et L'Historia Brittonum*, ed. F. Lot (Bibliothèque de l'École des Hautes Études, 1934).
N.E.D.	Sir J. Murray, *New English Dictionary.*
Num. Chron.	*The Numismatic Chronicle* (1838–).
Olrik.	A. Olrik, *Heroic Legends of Denmark* (1919).
Oman.	Sir Charles Oman, *England before the Norman Conquest* (1910, &c.).
Orosius.	H. Sweet, *King Alfred's Orosius*, Part 1 (E.E.T.S.) (1883).
Osebergfundet.	*Osebergfundet*, ed. A. W. Brøgger, H. Falk, H. Schetelig (1917–1928).
Pastoral Care.	*King Alfred's West Saxon Version of Gregory's Pastoral Care*, ed. H. Sweet (1871).
Pauly-Wissowa.	A. F. von Pauly, *Real-Encyklopädie der klassischen Altertumswissenschaft*, ed. G. Wissowa (1904–).
P.B.A.	*Proceedings of the British Academy* (1903–).
Pertz, *M.G.H.*	*Monumenta Germaniae Historica, Scriptores*, ed. G. H. Pertz (1826–).
Philippson.	A. E. Philippson, *Germanisches Heidentum bei den Angelsachsen* (1929).
Phillpotts, *Kindred.*	B. S. Phillpotts, *Kindred and Clan in the Middle Ages and After* (1913).
Plettke.	A. Plettke, *Ursprung und Ausbreitung der Angeln und Sachsen* (Band III of C. Schuchhardt's *Die Urnenfriedhöfe in Niedersachsen*) (1921).
Plummer, *Alfred.*	C. Plummer, *Life and Times of Alfred* (1902).

Plummer, *Bede.*	C. Plummer, *Historia Ecclesiastica gentis Anglorum* (1896).
Plummer, *Chron.*	Id., *Two of the Saxon Chronicles Parallel* (1892–9).
P.M.L.A.	*Publications of the Modern Language Association of America* (1884–).
Pollock and Maitland.	F. Pollock and F. W. Maitland, *The History of English Law*, 2nd ed. (1898).
P.R.I.A.	*Proceedings of the Royal Irish Academy* (1836–).
P.S.A.	*Proceedings of the Society of Antiquaries of London* (1853–).
P.S.A. Scot.	*Proceedings of the Society of Antiquaries of Scotland* (1832–).
Raine.	*Historians of the Church of York*, ed. J. Raine, Rolls Series (1879–94).
Ramsay, *Foundations.*	Sir J. M. Ramsay, *The Foundations of England* (1898).
R.C.H.M., *Roman London.*	Royal Commission on Historical Monuments, . . . London, vol. iii, *Roman London* (1928).
Regino.	*Regino Prumiensis Abbas Chronicon*, M.G.H., ed. F. Kurze (1890).
Rev. Celt.	*Revue Celtique* (1870–).
Rev. Hist.	*Revue Historique* (1876–).
R.G.K.	*Römisch-germanische Kommission des Kaiserlichen Archäologischen Instituts* (1905–).
Ripley.	W. Z. Ripley, *The Races of Europe* (1899).
Roeder, *Neue Funde.*	F. Roeder, *Neue Funde auf kontinental-sächsischen Friedhöfen der Völkerwanderungszeit* (1933).
Roeder, *Sächsische Schalenfibel.*	Id., *Die sächsische Schalenfibel der Völkerwanderungszeit* (1927).
Roeder, *Typol.-chronol. Stud.*	Id., *Typologisch-chronologische Studien zu Metallsachen der Völkerwanderungszeit* (1930).
Sagabook.	*Sagabook of the Viking Club* (1895–).
Saxo, ed. Holder.	A. Holder, *Saxonis Grammatici Gesta Danorum* (1886).
Scheletig or Shetelig.	H. Shetelig, *Préhistoire de la Norvège* (1926).
Schetelig or Shetelig, *Cruciform Brooches.*	Id., *The Cruciform Brooches of Norway*, Bergens Museums Aarbog (1906).
Schmidt.	L. Schmidt, *Geschichte der deutschen Stämme bis zum Ausgange der Völkerwanderung* (1911).
Schubert.	H. von Schubert, *Geschichte der christlichen Kirche im Frühmittelalter* (1921).
Schütte.	G. Schütte, *Our Forefathers the Gothonic Nations* (1929–33).
S.D.	*Symeon of Durham*, ed. T. Arnold, Rolls Series (1882).
Searle.	W. G. Searle, *Anglo-Saxon Bishops, Kings, and Nobles* (1899).
Sedgefield.	W. J. Sedgefield, *King Alfred's Version of the Consolations of Boethius* (1900).
Seebohm, *T.C.*	F. Seebohm, *Tribal Custom in Anglo-Saxon Law* (1902).
Siebs.	T. Siebs, 'Die Friesen und die nächstverwandten Stämme', in *Mitteilungen der Schlesischen Gesellschaft für Volkskunde*, xxxi–xxxii (1931), 44–84.
Singer.	C. Singer, *From Magic to Science* (1928).
Skene.	W. F. Skene, *Celtic Scotland* (1876).
Social England.	*Social England*, ed. H. D. Traill and J. S. Mann, illustrated edition, vol. i (1901).

Steenstrup, *D.R.H.*	J. I. H. R. Steenstrup, *Danmark's Riges Historie*, vol. i (1904).
Steenstrup, *Normannerne.*	Id., *Normannerne* (1876–82).
Stevenson.	W. H. Stevenson, *Asser's Life of King Alfred* (1904).
Stubbs, *C.H.*	William Stubbs, *The Constitutional History of England* (1895–7).
Stubbs, *Charters.*	Id., *Select Charters*, ed. H. W. C. Davis (1921).
Texte und Forschungen.	H. Boehmer and others, *Texte und Forschungen zur englischen Kulturgeschichte*, Festgabe für F. Liebermann (1921).
Thorpe.	B. Thorpe, *Diplomatarium Anglicum Ævi Saxonici* (1865).
Trans. Soc. Cymmrod.	*The Transactions of the Honourable Society of Cymmrodorion* (1893–).
T.R.H.S.	*Transactions of the Royal Historical Society of Great Britain* (1871–).
V.C.H.	*Victoria County History.*
Vinogradoff, *E.S.*	P. Vinogradoff, *English Society in the Eleventh Century* (1908).
Vinogradoff, *G.M.*	Id., *The Growth of the Manor* (1905).
Vit. Cuthb. Anon.	*Vita S. Cuthberti* auctore anonymo, in Bede's *Opera*, ed. J. Stevenson (1838), 259–84.
Vita Rimberti.	*Vita Anskarii* (containing *Vita Rimberti*), M.G.H., ed. G. Waitz (1884).
Vogel.	W. Vogel, *Die Normannen und das fränkische Reich* (1906).
Wadstein, *Origin.*	E. Wadstein, *On the Origin of the English* (1907).
Wadstein, *Norden.*	Id., *Norden och Väst-Europa i Gammal Tid* (1925).
Watson.	W. J. Watson, *History of the Celtic Place-Names of Scotland* (1926).
W.M., *G.P.*	William of Malmesbury, *De Gestis Pontificum Anglorum*, ed. N. E. S. A. Hamilton, Rolls Series (1870).
W.M., *G.R.*	William of Malmesbury, *De Gestis Regum*, ed. W. Stubbs, Rolls Series (1887–9).
Wheeler, *Wales.*	R. E. M. Wheeler, *Prehistoric and Roman Wales* (1925).
Wilts. Arch. and Nat. Hist. Mag.	*Wiltshire Archaeological and Natural History Magazine* (1854–).
Ynglingasaga.	*See* Heimskringla.
Zachrisson.	R. E. Zachrisson, *Romans, Kelts and Saxons in Ancient Britain* (1927).
Zimmermann.	E. H. Zimmermann, *Vorkarolingische Miniaturen* (1916).

GENEALOGICAL AND CHRONOLOGICAL TABLES

The following symbols and abbreviations are used in the Tables:

†	= died	M^{ia}	= Mercia
⚔	= battle of	N.	= North
×	= somewhere *between* two dates	NN.	= No Name
b.	= born	N^{ia}	= Northumbria
c.	= circa	P.	= Pope
d.	= daughter	R.	= River
def.	= defeat	S.	= South
def^d	= defeated	s.	= son
E.	= East	S^y	= Supremacy
Emp.	= Emperor	W.	= West
fl.	= floruit	w.	= with
K.	= King	W^x	= Wessex
K^{dom}	= Kingdom		

In the Chronological Table—a name with only a date implies that the man was a king or ruler. Kings who are said or thought to have exercised Supremacy are printed in black type.

GENEALOGICAL TABLES

TABLE I

MERCIAN KINGS

To save space, the descent from WODEN *is placed horizontally.*

WODEN — WATHOLGEOT — WAGA — WIHTLÆG — WERMUND — OFFA[1] — ANGENGEOT — EOMER — ICEL[2] — CNEBBA— CYNEWALD — CRIODA —

PYBBA

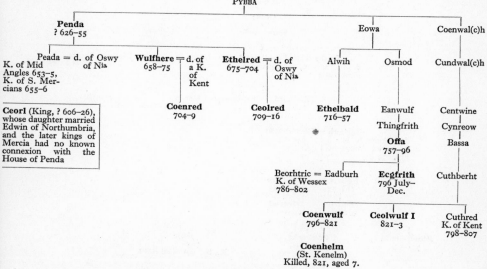

Penda
? 626–55

Peada = d. of Oswy
K. of Mid   of Nia
Angles 653–5,
K. of S. Mer-
cians 655–6

Ceorl (King, ? 606–26), whose daughter married Edwin of Northumbria, and the later kings of Mercia had no known connexion with the House of Penda

Wulfhere ⊤ d. of
658–75   a K.
          of
          Kent

Coenred
704–9

Ethelred ⊤ d. of
675–704   Oswy
           of Nia

Ceolred
709–16

Eowa

Alwih   Osmod

Ethelbald   Eanwulf
716–57   Thingfrith
               Offa
               757–96

Coenwal(c)h

Cundwal(c)h

Centwine
Cynreow
Bassa

Beorhtric = Eadburh
K. of Wessex
786–802

Ecgfrith
796 July–
Dec.

Cuthberht

Coenwulf
796–821

Ceolwulf I
821–3

Cuthred
K. of Kent
798–807

Coenhelm
(St. Kenelm)
Killed, 821, aged 7.

[1 'The Offa of Angel' of *Widsith*.]
[2 Hence members of the kingly family were called Iclingas.]

4014.2

TABLE II

KINGS OF KENT

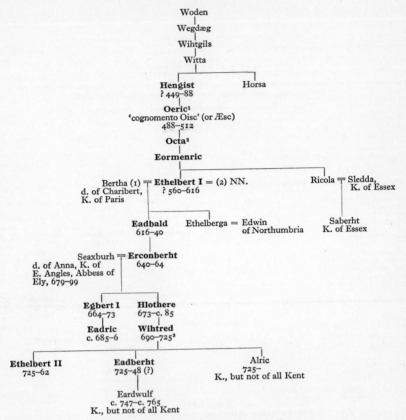

Woden
|
Wegdæg
|
Wihtgils
|
Witta
|
Hengist — Horsa
? 449–88

Oeric[1]
'cognomento Oisc' (or Æsc)
488–512

Octa[2]

Eormenric

Bertha (1) = **Ethelbert I** = (2) NN.   Ricola = Sledda,
d. of Charibert,   ? 560–616   K. of Essex
K. of Paris

Eadbald   Ethelberga = Edwin   Saberht
616–40   of Northumbria   K. of Essex

Seaxburh = **Erconberht**
d. of Anna, K. of   640–64
E. Angles, Abbess of
Ely, 679–99

Egbert I   **Hlothere**
664–73   673–c. 85

Eadric   **Wihtred**
c. 685–6   690–725[3]

Ethelbert II   **Eadberht**   **Alric**
725–62   725–48 (?)   725–
                                        K., but not of all Kent

Eardwulf
c. 747–c. 765
K., but not of all Kent

[1] 'From him the kings of Kent are commonly called Oiscingas,' Bede, ii, c. 5.
[2] Son of Hengist, according to Nennius.
[3] 686–90, Kent was under *reges dubii vel externi*. For these and other later kings see H. M. Chadwick, *Anglo-Saxon Institutions*, 271–4, and W. G. Searle, *Anglo-Saxon Bishops, Kings, and Nobles*, 262 f.

TABLE III

WEST SAXON KINGS

To save space, the descent from WODEN *is placed horizontally.*

WODEN—BÆLDÆG—BRAND—FRITHUGAR—FREAWINE [= FROWINUS SLESWICENSIUM PREFECTUS, of SAXO]—WIG [= VIGO, of SAXO]—GEWIS [hence, perhaps, the name GEWISSE of the WEST SAXONS]—ESLA—ELESA—

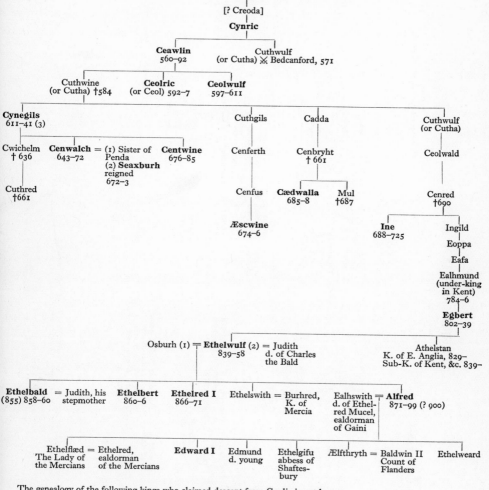

The genealogy of the following kings who claimed descent from Cerdic is not known:

Ethelheard	725–40
Cuthred	740–56
Sigebryht	756–7
Cynewulf	757–86
Beorhtric	786–802.

NOTE. There are many discrepancies in the early versions of Cerdic's descendants. The above seems to be the most probable reconstruction, but it does not tally with other recent conjectures. Cf. G. H. Wheeler in *E.H.R.*, xxxvi (1921), 161–71, and H. M. Chadwick in Palgrave's *Collected Works*, v, Table i; ibid., *Origin of the English Nation*, cap. 2.

TABLE IV

NORTHUMBRIAN KINGS

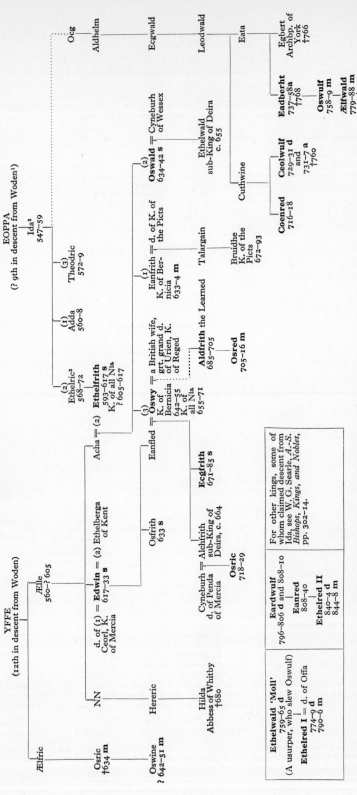

[1] Eoppa's descent from Woden was traced, like that of the W. Saxon kings, through Bældæg.

[2] Early kings of Bernicia, (?) not descended from Ida—Glappa, 559–60; Frithuwald, 579–85(6); Hussa, 585(6)–92(3).

[3] According to Nennius, cap. 63, Ethelric was the son of Adda, not of Ida.

NOTE. In this Table the kings who ruled over *both* kingdoms are in heavy type.

The following abbreviations are used: **a** = abdicated; **d** = deposed; **m** = murdered; **s** = slain in battle.

CHRONOLOGICAL TABLE

THE EMPIRE	THE CHURCH
360–3 Julian, last Emp. of House of Constantine	360–3 Julian tries to revive paganism
364–75 Valentinian I, Emp. in W.	
366 Alamanni raid E. Gaul	
	373 Death of Athanasius
375–83 Gratian, Emp. in W.	
378 ✗Adrianople, Valens, Emp. in E. defeated by Goths	
379–95 Theodosius, Emp. in E. and 392–5 also Emp. in W.	
	381 General Council condemns Arians
383–92 Valentinian II	
	c. 385 Papal decretals begin
388 The usurper Maximus def^d by Theodosius	
	392 Paganism proscribed
395 Empire again divided—Arcadius Emp. in E.	
395–425 Honorius, Emp. in W. Stilicho regent	395–430 St. Augustine, Bp. of Hippo
	399 Death of St. Martin of Tours
402 Visigoths under Alaric invade Italy	
407 Vandals, &c., invade Gaul	
408 Stilicho executed	
410 Alaric takes Rome	410–31 Pelagius of Britain, heretic
411–35 Burgundian K^{dom} of Worms	
c. 416 Visigothic K^{doms} in Gaul and Spain	
	c. 417 Orosius writes his History
	420 Death of St. Jerome
425–55 Valentinian III, Emp. in W.	
429 Vandals invade Africa	429 Council condemns Pelagianism
433–53 Aëtius, chief minister	
434–53 Attila and Huns threaten W.	
443–534 Burgundian K^{dom} in S.E. Gaul	
450–1 Attila invades Gaul	
	451 Council of Chalcedon

TABLE

BRITAIN	CELTIC LANDS	NORTHERN EUROPE
360–7 Invasion of Picts, Irish, and Saxons; villas destroyed.		? c. 360 Wermund, K. of Angel
368–9 Count Theodosius reconquers Britain		
388 Maximus leads troops from Britain to Gaul. ? Roman Wall denuded		
389 St. Patrick b.		? c. 390 Offa, K. of Angel
	c. 400 Cunedda from N. expels Irish from N. Wales	
c. 400 St. Patrick carried captive to Ireland	c. 400 Niall, of Tara, raids in Britain	? c. 400 Nydam boat
	c. 400–40 St. Ninnian in N. Britain	
402 Troops withdrawn by Stilicho		
407 Constantine, usurper, leads troops to Gaul. Saxon raid		
410 Rescript of Honorius to the cities		
428 ? *Adventus Saxonum* (Nennius)		
429 1st visit of St. Germanus	432–61 Mission of St. Patrick to Ireland	
442 Britain 'under dominion of Saxons'		
446 Britons appeal to Aëtius		
c. 447 2nd visit of St. Germanus		
c. 449 Hengist and Horsa (Bede)	c. 450 St. Patrick writes to Coroticus	

EUROPE	S.E. BRITAIN	WESSEX
	c. 449 Hengist and Horsa land	
455 Vandals sack Rome	? 455–75 Conquest of Kent	
455–76 'Shadow' Emperors in W.	? 457 Britons flee to London	
476 END OF EMPERORS IN W. RISE OF MEROVINGS	? 477 Ælle and S. Saxons land	
481–511 Clovis, K. of Franks, conquers all Gaul and W. Germany	? 488–512 Oeric (or Oesc), K. of Kent	
	? 491 Fall of Anderida	
493–526 Theodoric the Ostrogoth K. of Italy		? 495 Landing of Cerdic
496 Clovis adopts Catholicism	? c. 500 Wehha, 1st K. of E. Angles (?)	? c. 500 Settlements in Thames valley
		? 508 Fight at Cerdicesford
511 Partition of Frankish K^dom		? 519 Cerdic King
524 Boethius executed		
527–65 Justinian Emp. in E.	? 527 Æscwine, ? 1st K. of E. Saxons	
	? c. 530 Wuffa, K. of E. Angles	
531 Franks with Saxons conquer Thuringia		
533 E. Empire reconquers Africa and Italy		? 534 Cynric King
540 Saxones Eutii yield to Franks		
543 Death of St. Benedict		
		552 ⚔ Searoburh
553 Procopius says Britain is abode of the dead		556 ⚔ Beranburh
	? 560–616 Ethelbert, K. of Kent	560–92 Ceawlin
568 Lombards conquer N. Italy	568 ⚔ Wibbandun	
	? c. 570 Tyttla, K. of E. Angles	571 ⚔ Bedcanford
573 Lombards besiege Rome Gregory founds St. Andrew's		577 ⚔ Deorham
c. 588 Gregory sees Anglian slaves		**S͞y of Ceawlin**
590–604 Gregory I, Pope	? 593–c. 627 Raedwald, K. of E. Angles	592–7 Ceolric
594 Gregory of Tours†	**? S͞y of Ethelbert**	
596 P. Gregory sends St. Augustine		
	597 St. Augustine converts Ethelbert	

MERCIA, ETC.	NORTHUMBRIA	CELTIC LANDS	SCANDINAVIA
? From c. 450, settlements in E. Midlands		c. 450 Age of Vortigern	c. 450–500 Danes occupy Denmark
		(?) General ruin (*Gildas*)	
		463 Death of St. Patrick	
	(?) Octa of Kent in N. Britain (*Nennius*)		
		(?) Age of Ambrosius Aurelianus	
		(?) Age of Arthur	Youth of Beowulf
		? 493 × 516 (8) ⚹ Mt. Badon	
		520 St. Columba b.	c. 520 Raid of Hygelac in Frisia
		c. 520 St. David b.	
			c. 525 Hrolf Kraki
			Beowulf, King of Geats
		c. 545 Gildas writes	
		c. 545 Columba founds Derry	
	547–59 Ida, K. of Bernicia	547 (9) Death of Maelgwn of N. Wales	
	560–? 605 Ælle, K. of Deira		
	560–8 Adda, K. of Bernicia	563 St. Columba on Iona	
	568–72 Ethelric, K. of Bernicia	Urien and Riderch fight against Bernicians	
	572–9 Theodric, K. of Bernicia		
? Crioda		580 St. David†	
		527–612 St. Kentigern fl.	
	593–617 Ethelfrith, K. of Bernicia 'exterminates' Britons and plants English		
? Pybba		597 St. Columba†	

EUROPE, ETC.	S.E. ENGLAND	WESSEX
	597 BEGINNING OF CONVERSION	597–611 Ceolwulf
c. 602 Theodore of Tarsus b.		
	604(5) Death of St. Augustine	
	c. 616 Sy of Raedwald, K.	
610–42 Heraclius, Emp. in E.	**of E. Angles**	611–41(3) Cynegils
	616–40 Eadbald, K. of Kent	
	616 Heathen reaction	
622 Flight of Mahomet		626 Edwin slays 5 Ks. of
622–80 Monothelite contro-		Wessex
versy	c. 627 Eorpwald, K. of E.	c. 628 Hwicce lost
	Angles	
	631–4 Sigbert, K. of E. Angles	
	c. 631 Mission of Felix to E.	
634 Arabs conquer Syria, &c.	Angles	
Theodore and others		
migrate to W.		
c. 635 P. Honorius sends		c. 635 St. Birinus converts
Birinus	c. 636 Mission of Fursey to E.	Cynegils
	Angles	
	640–64 Erconberht, K. of	
	Kent, forbids heathen	
643–56 Grimoald, Mayor of	rites	643–72 Cenwal(c)h drives
Palace		back Britons
		652 ⚔ Bradford-on-Avon
	653 Mission of Cedd to E.	
	Saxons	
656–81 Ebroin, Mayor of		658 ⚔ Penselwood
Palace in Neustria		Plague
	664 Plague	
668 P. Vitalian consecrates		
Theodore		
669–96 Arabs conquer N.	669–70 Theodore at Canter-	
Africa	bury	
	672 Council of Hertford	
	673–85 Hlothere, K. of Kent	
		674–84 Rule of *Subreguli*
		676–85 Centwine
679–80 Wilfrid at Rome	679 Council of Hatfield	
	681–6 Wilfrid converts S.	
	Saxons	682 Britons driven to sea
RISE OF CAROLINGS	END OF THE CONVERSION	685(6)–8 Cædwalla revives
687–714 Pepin, Mayor of		Wessex, ravages
Palace, restores K^{dom}		Kent
of Franks		
688 Cædwalla of Wessex at		688–725 Ine
Rome	690–725 Wihtred, K. of Kent	
692 and 704 Wilfrid's appeals		
to P.		
	705 New See of Selsey	705–9 Aldhelm, 1st Bp. of
		Sherborne
711 Arabs invade Spain		
716–54 Missions of Boniface		
to Frisia, Germany, &c.		
717–41 Charles Martel,		
Mayor	725 Rule of 3 joint Ks. in Kent	725–40 Ethelheard
		726 Ine dies at Rome

MERCIA	NORTHUMBRIA	CELTIC LANDS
		Scots and N. Britons def[d]
	603 ⚔ Degsastane	603 Conferences of St. Au-
	? 605 Ethelfrith unites Deira	gustine with British
? 606 Ceorl, ? 1st K. of M[ia]	and Bernicia	bishops
	c. 616 ⚔ Chester	N. Welsh def[d]
	617 ⚔ of R. Idle	
	617–33 S[y] of Edwin	Oswald at Iona
	625 Mission of St. Paulinus	
? 626–55 Penda		
	627 Conversion of Edwin	
633 Penda allies w. Cad-	633 ⚔ Heathfield	633–4 Welsh overrun N[ia]
wallon	634 ⚔ Heavenfield	634 Cadwallon slain
	634–42 S[y] of Oswald	
	635 Mission of St. Aidan	
642–55 S[y] of Penda	642 ⚔ Maserfield	
	642–71 Oswy, K. of Bernicia	
645 S[y] over Wessex		
650 S[y] over E. Angles	651 Death of St. Aidan	
653 Cedd converts Mid-		
Angles		
655 Penda def[d] and killed	655 ⚔ of R. Winwæd	
c. 656 Diuma, Bp. of Mercia	**655–8 S[y] of Oswy**	
658–75 S[y] of Wulfhere		
Plague	Plague	
	664 Synod of Whitby	
	664–87 St. Cuthbert fl.	
	666–709 St. Wilfrid Bp.	
	671–85 Ecgfrith	
		672–93 Bruidhe, K. of the
		Picts, wars on Strath-
	674–82 Wearmouth–Jarrow	clyde, &c.
675–704 Ethelred	founded	
	678–80 Wilfrid's 1st exile	
		684 Raids of N[ia] on Ireland
Equilibrium between King-	685 Ecgfrith def[d] and killed	685 Picts win ⚔ Nectansmere
doms	685–705 Aldfrith the	Decline of Northumbrian
	Learned	power
	691–735 Bede fl.	
	692–702 Wilfrid's 3rd exile	692–7 Adamnan's *Life of*
c. 697–714 St. Guthlac at		*Columba*
Crowland		
704–9 Cenred	705–16 Osred	
709–16 Ceolred		710 Picts adopt Roman
		Easter
716–57 Ethelbald	716–29 Osric	716 Iona adopts Roman
		Easter
	729–37 Ceolwulf	
c. 730–57 S[y] of Ethelbald	731 Bede's *Historia Ecclesiastica*	

W. EUROPE	S.E. ENGLAND	WESSEX
717–41 Charles Martel		
		725–40 Ethelheard
732 ✗ Poitiers. Arabs def[d]		
		733 ✗ Somerton
END OF MEROVINGS		740–56 Cuthred
	747 Synod of Clovesho	750 ✗ Beorhford, M[ia] def[d]
752–68 Pepin, King of the Franks		751–786 Cynewulf
754 Pepin made Patricius by P.		
768–814 CHARLEMAGNE, K. of the Franks		
772–804 Charlemagne conquers Saxons		
774 Charlemagne K. in Italy, Patricius	775 ✗ Otford, victory of Offa in Kent	
782 Charlemagne receives Alcuin		779 ✗ Bensington—W[x] def[d]
	c. 784–6 Ealhmund, father of Egbert under-king in Kent	786 Death of K. Cynewulf
		786–802 Beorhtric
		1ST VIKING RAID
795–816 P. Leo III		
	796 Eadbert Præn revolt in Kent	? 796–9 Egbert exiled
800 WESTERN EMPIRE revived		
		802–39 **Egbert**
	805–32 Archbp. Wulfred, reformer	
810 Godfred's fleet raids Frisia		
814–40 Lewis the Pious, Emp.	817–25 Archbp. Wulfred quarrels with Ks. of M[ia]	
	825 S.E[n] K[doms] accept W. Saxon S[y]	825 } Sy of Egbert 829 }
826 Baptism of Harold the Dane —grant of Frisian lands to Danes		
	829 E. Anglia accepts W. Saxon S[y]	
833 Empire weakened by civil strife. Renewal of Viking raids on Dorestad and Frisia	Ethelwulf under-king	
	835 Renewal of Viking raids	Viking raids
		839–56 Ethelwulf

MERCIA	NORTHUMBRIA	CELTIC LANDS	SCANDINAVIA
716–57 **Ethelbald** wins supremacy			
	732–56 Egbert, abp. of York	730–after 805 Anglian see at Whitern	
	737–58 Eadberht Mians raid Nia		
740 60 yrs. peace with Nia ends		Aengus, K. of Picts, allies with Nia agst. N. Britons	?c.750 ✕ Bravalla
	756 Sy over Strathclyde recovered		
757 Beornred **757–96 Offa**	759–65 Ethelwald Moll Feuds over Kship	768 Welsh adopt Roman Easter	
774 Offa styled *Rex Anglorum*		(?) Offa's Dyke	
	776–82 Alcuin head of York school		
786–7 Papal Legates in England	786 Council of Finchale		
787 Council of Celchythe			
787–803 Lichfield archbishopric	More feuds		
793 Offa has Ethelbert, K. of E. Angles, beheaded	793 1st Viking raids on Nia	795 Vikings in Irish Sea	Godfred, K. of Danes (? Gudröd) War agst. Franks
796 Ecgferth			
796–821 Coenwulf			
		802 Vikings raid Iona 802–25 Vikings dominate Ireland	
	806 Charlemagne persuades Nians to take back K. Eardwulf		
	810–40 Eanred		810 Godfred sends out 200 ships Civil war in Denk
817–25 Quarrel with Archbp.			813–54 Horic I
821–3 Ceolwulf		825 Cornish defd	
823–5 Beornwulf, defd at ✕ Ellendun		825–44 Merfyn founds new dynasty in Gwynedd	
		c. 826 Nennius fl.	
829 Wiglaf deposed by Egbert		c. 834–45 Turgeis, Viking ruler of N. Ireland	830 Anscar's mission to Sweden
830–9 Wiglaf restored by Egbert		838 ✕ Hinxton Down Cornish and Danes defd	
839–52 Beorhtwulf			

W. EUROPE	S.E. ENGLAND	WESSEX
	Athelstan under-king	839–56 Ethelwulf
840 Emp. Lewis the Pious dies —strife betw. his sons— ⚔ Fontenoy	841 Raid on Thanet	
843 EMPIRE DIVIDED, Treaty of Verdun Middle K^{dom} to Lothair, Emp. Eⁿ K^{dom} to Lewis the German Wⁿ K^{dom} to Charles the Bald		849 Birth of Alfred
843 Raids on Hamburg and Paris	850–1 DANES 1ST WINTER in ENGLAND—in Thanet	851 ⚔ Aclea—Danes def^d 852–62 St. Swithin, bp. of Winchester 853 1st Journey to Rome
854–66 Vikings on Somme, Seine, &c. 855–69 Lothair II, K. in Lorraine	854–5 Danes in Sheppey	855–6 2nd Journey to Rome Ethelwulf m. Judith in France
	Ethelwulf keeps Kent, &c.	856 Ethelbald usurps throne —compromise
858–67 P. Nicholas I enhances Papacy 859–62 Viking raid to Mediterranean	858 Ethelbert under-king 860 End of under-kingdom 865 Raid on Kent	858–60 Ethelbald K. of all Wessex 865–71 Ethelred: Alfred his *Secundarius*
866 Vikings leave France		867 Expedition to Nottingham
870 Partition of Lorraine at Meersen		871 Danes at Reading. ⚔ Ashdown
872–82 P. John viii 875–7 Wars within Empire, and increasing disintegration 877 Death of Charles the Bald	879 A Danish army at Fulham 882 and 885 Alfred's ships fight Danes	**871–99 Alfred** 876 2nd invasion, to Wareham 877 Exeter 878 Athelney, ⚔ Ethandun, baptism of Danes at Wedmore
883–900 Fulk, archbp. of Rheims 884–7 Reunion under Charles the Fat 885 Decline of Papacy 885–6 Vikings besiege Paris 887 Final disruption of the Empire 888–98 Odo, K. of France 887–99 Arnulf, K. of Germany 891 Arnulf defeats Vikings, ⚔ Dyle 891–6 P. Formosus 896 Arnulf crowned Emp.	890–914 Plegmund, archbishop 892–3 Invasion of Hæsten and Great Army 897 Alfred's bigger ships	Alfred sends alms to Pope c. 884–5 Grimbald and Asser join Alfred Period of literary activity and education begins c. 891 Copies of Chronicle sent out 892–6 Alfred's last war c. 893 Asser writes Life of Alfred c. 895 Marriage alliance with Flanders 899 (? 900) Death of Alfred

MERCIA AND E. ANGLIA	NORTHUMBRIA	CELTIC LANDS	SCANDINAVIA
			813–54 Horic I, K. of Denmark
839–52 Beorhtwulf			
842 Raid on London			
	848–67 Osberht		
		844–78 Rhodri Mawr unites N. and Mid-Wales	
851 Mercians def^d by Danes			
852–74 Burhred			
			854 Feuds in Denmark. Horic II and Roric Ks.
	861–7 Feuds—Ælle, a rival K. (?) Kills Ragnar		
865 COMING OF GREAT ARMY			862–932 Harold Fairhair (Ari's dates)
865 To E. Anglia	866 END OF ANGLIAN YORK		
867 To Nottingham			
869 To E. Anglia Martyrdom of St. Edmund	Anglian Bernicia survives under Kings & ealdormen		c. 870 (? likelier date, Harold's accession)
871–2 To London			873 Sigfred and Halfdan Ks. in Denmark
872–3 To Torksey			
873–4 To Repton, Army divides			
874–5 To Cambridge	876 DANES SETTLE under Halfdene (876–7)		874 Settlers in Iceland
877 ? DANES SETTLE in E. Mercia and E. Anglia	877–83 Interregnum	878 Rhodri's K^{dom} divided between 6 sons	
878–90 Guthrum (Athelstan), K.	883–94 Guthred-Cnut	S͞y of Alfred	
c. 886 Ethelred m. Ethelflæd and rules W. Mercia		c. 885 Asser joins Alfred	
885–6 Alfred restores London		(?) Anarawd of Anglesey turns from Danes to W^x	
? Treaty of Alfred and Guthrum			? c. 890. ✗ Hafursfirth. Vikings def^d by K. Harold, now K. of all Norway
890–902 Eric, K. of E. Anglia	893–6 Siegfred		
893–6 Danish attacks on W. Mercia			

INDEX

PRINTED IN
GREAT BRITAIN
AT THE
UNIVERSITY PRESS
OXFORD
BY
JOHN JOHNSON
PRINTER
TO THE
UNIVERSITY